AF513044

Second Edition

OBJECTIVE INDIAN POLITY

For Civil Services Preliminary Examination

About the Author

M Laxmikanth obtained his postgraduate degree in Political Science from Osmania University in 1989. He is the former founder and director of an erstwhile coaching institute called Laxmikanth's IAS Academy, Hyderabad. Other books authored by him include ***Indian Polity, Governance in India, Public Administration*** and ***Constitution of India***.

Second Edition

OBJECTIVE INDIAN POLITY

For Civil Services Preliminary Examination

M Laxmikanth

Former Founder-Director
Laxmikanth's IAS Academy (Closed)
Hyderabad

McGraw Hill Education (India) Private Limited

Published by McGraw Hill Education (India) Private Limited
Registered Office: Anjana Complex No: 5/90 A, Butt Road, St. Thomas Mount, Chennai – 600016

Objective Indian Polity, 2e

Twelfth reprint 2026

Print Edition:
ISBN-13: 978-93-5460-144-6
ISBN-10: 93-5460-144-8

E-Book Edition:
ISBN-13: 978-93-5460-145-3
ISBN-10: 93-5460-145-6

13 14 15 16 17 RAJ 30 29 28 27 26

Typeset at CoKrator Content Solutions Private Limited and printed and bound in India at
Rajkamal Electric Press, Kundli, Haryana-131028.

Cover Design: Creative Designer

Visit us at: www.mheducation.co.in
Write to us at: support.india@mheducation.com
CIN: U80302TN2010PTC111532
Toll Free Number: 1800 103 5875

Dedicated
to
My Family Elders
Late Mamadgi Hashappa
Late Mamadgi Janamma
Late Mamadgi Paramma
and
My Native Place
Dhanasiri (Zaheerabad – Telangana)

Preface to the Second Edition

I am pleased to place before the civil services aspirants this revised, updated and enlarged edition. This question bank is structured and patterns on the lines of the latest edition of Indian Polity book.

During the revision of this question bank, the various new developments like Constitutional Amendments, Parliamentary Legislations, Executive Decisions and Supreme Court Judgements have been taken into account.

Changes in this Edition:

1. Addition of 13 new chapters
2. Replacement of Assertion & Reason and Matching questions
3. Out-dated questions have been replaced with new questions
4. Inclusion of new questions in various chapters
5. Shifting, merger and deletion of some chapters

New Chapters:

1. Parliamentary Group
2. Judicial Review
3. Judicial Activism
4. Public Interest Litigation
5. Goods and Services Tax Council
6. National Commission for BCs
7. NITI Aayog
8. National Investigation Agency
9. National Disaster Management Authority
10. Role of Regional Parties
11. Election Laws
12. Voting Behaviour
13. Coalition Government

Therefore, it is hoped that this comprehensive question bank will be more useful and relevant for the civil services, state services and other competitive examinations.

I invite suggestions and comments from the readers of this book. They will be incorporated in the next edition of the book.

M LAXMIKANTH

Preface to the Second Edition

Preface to the First Edition

I am pleased to place before the aspirants of civil services this comprehensive question bank on the subject of **Indian Polity**.

This book has been modelled on the popular *Indian Polity* book, with questions of each chapter and appendix aligned to the text of each chapter and appendix in the original.

This book contains high-quality, objective-type questions on the Indian Constitution and political system. These questions are of two categories viz., those questions which are freshly framed and those questions which have been sourced and edited. The framed questions are in accordance with the latest trends in the examinations and the sourced and edited questions are from the test papers of various competitive examinations.

During the course of preparation of this question bank, various **new developments** related to the Indian Constitution and political system, like recent constitutional amendments, parliamentary legislations, executive decisions and Supreme Court judgements have come in. These have also been **taken into account**.

This book has the following three segments:

1. Chapter-wise question bank
2. Appendix-wise question bank
3. Ten Model Test Papers

The chapter-wise/appendix-wise question bank is designed to help the candidates test their understanding of the different dimensions of the subject of Indian Polity. The Model Test Papers will help candidates in assessing their preparation for the examination as well as in managing time judiciously and productively.

I invite suggestions and comments from the readers. They will be incorporated in the next edition of the book.

I am grateful to the editorial team at McGraw Hill Education (India) for their cooperation in bringing out this book in time.

M Laxmikanth

Preface to the First Edition

Acknowledgements

During the course of preparation of this question bank, I have received the help, encouragement and assistance from my teachers, students, family members, colleagues, friends, library staff and others. I am thankful to all of them.

I am particularly grateful to my wife, Smt. Mamadgi Vidya, for her encouragement and support that she provided during the preparation of this question bank.

I am deeply indebted to the eminent writers, experts and research scholars whose valuable works have been highly useful in preparing this detailed and comprehensive question bank.

I also used the test paper of the Union Public Service Commission (UPSC), the State Public Service Commissions (SPSCs), the Staff Selection Commission (SSC), the University Grants Commission (UGC) and other recruitment bodies.

In the end, my thanks are also due to Mr. Tanweer Ahmad, Mr. Srivatsan, Ms. Shreya Soni and Ms. Anjali Chakravarty of McGraw Hill India Private Limited for their cooperation in bringing out this revised edition on time.

M LAXMIKANTH

Contents

Part-XI
Working of the Constitution

Part-XII
Appendices-1

Part-XIII
Appendices-2

Part-XIV
Model Test Papers

TOTAL NUMBER OF MCQs IN THE BOOK

Part No.	Part Title	Chapters Covered	No. of Questions
I	Constitutional Framework	1-11	256
II	System of Government	12-16	110
III	Central Government	17-29	335
IV	State Government	30-37	121
V	Local Government	38-39	109
VI	Union Territories and Special Areas	40-41	24
VII	Constitutional Bodies	42-53	142
VIII	Non-Constitutional Bodies	54-63	93
IX	Other Constitutional Dimensions	64-68	42
X	Political Dynamics	69-79	89
XI	Working of the Constitution	80	5
XII	Appendices-1	I-V	54
XIII	Appendices-2	VI-X	27
XIV	Model Test Papers	1-10	250
Total			**1657**

PART-I CONSTITUTIONAL FRAMEWORK

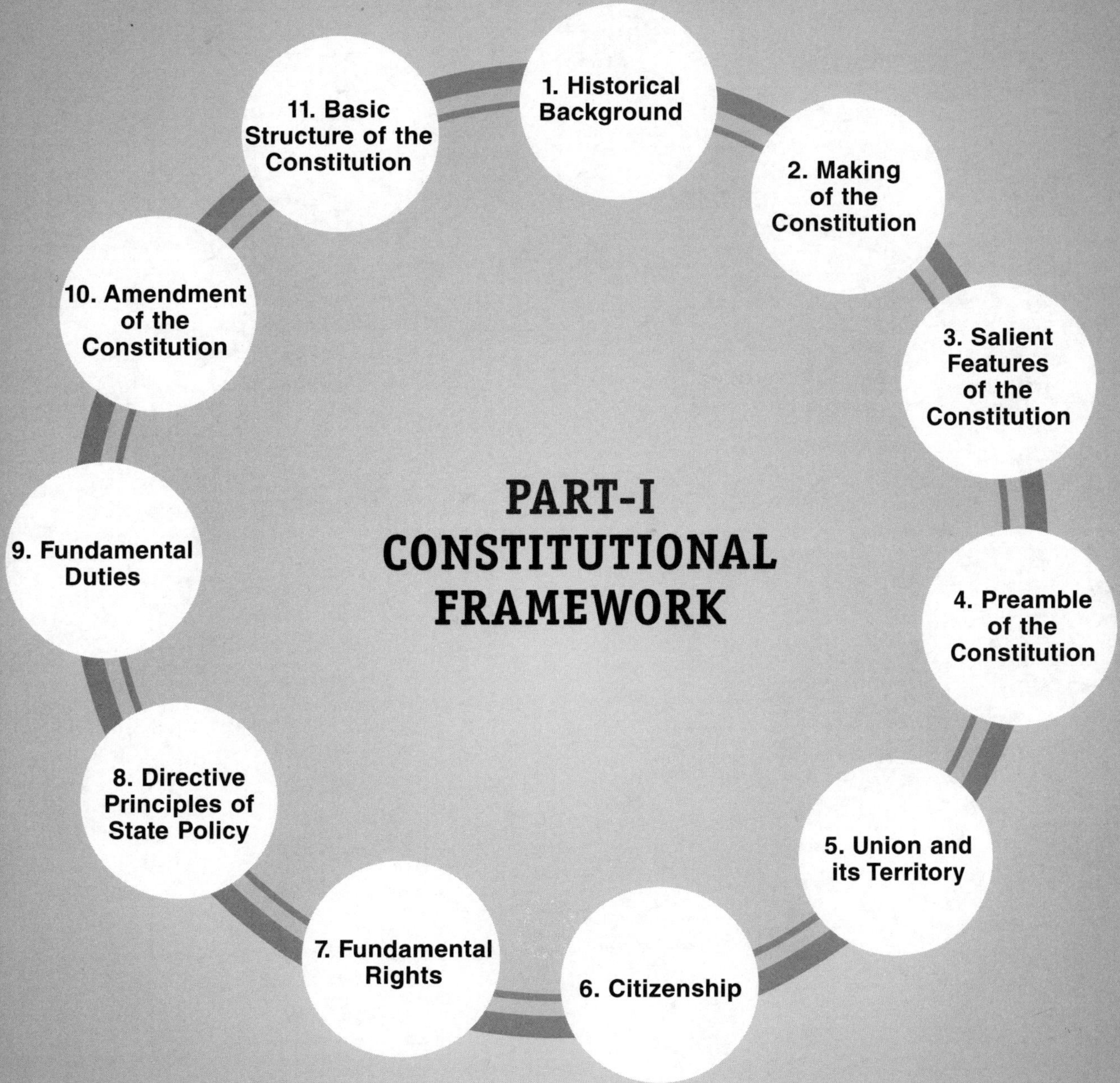

1 Historical Background

1. Consider the following statements:
   1. Under the Government of India Act, 1919, the Indian Legislature was made more representative and for the first time bicameral.
   2. The Government of India Act, 1935, prescribed a federation taking the Provinces and the Indian States as units.

   Which of the statements given above is/are correct?

   (*a*) 1 only (*b*) 2 only
   (*c*) Both 1 and 2 (*d*) Neither 1 nor 2

2. Which of the following are the principal features of the Government of India Act, 1919?
   1. Introduction of dyarchy in the executive government of the Provinces.
   2. Introduction of separate communal electorates for Muslims.
   3. Devolution of legislative authority by the Centre to the Provinces.
   4. Expansion and reconstitution of Central and Provincial Legislatures.

   Select the correct answer from the codes given below:

   (*a*) 1, 2 and 3 (*b*) 2, 3 and 4
   (*c*) 1, 2 and 4 (*d*) 1, 3 and 4

3. Consider the following statements:
   1. The first Public Service Commission in India was set up in the year 1926, on the recommendation of the Lee Commission on the Superior Civil Services in India.
   2. The Government of India Act, 1935, provided for setting up of public service commissions at both the federal and provincial levels.

   Which of the statements given above is/are correct?

   (*a*) 1 only (*b*) 2 only
   (*c*) Both 1 and 2 (*d*) Neither 1 nor 2

4. Which one of the following Acts provided the setting up of the Board of Control in Britain, through which the British Government could fully control the British East India Company's civil, military and revenue affairs in India?

   (*a*) Regulating Act, 1773
   (*b*) Pitt's India Act, 1784
   (*c*) Charter Act, 1833
   (*d*) Government of India Act, 1858

5. Which one of the following Acts made a provision for the transfer of power from the East India Company to the British Crown?
   (*a*) The Government of India Act, 1935 (*b*) The Indian Councils Act, 1909
   (*c*) The Government of India Act, 1919 (*d*) The Government of India Act, 1858

6. Partially, the responsible governments in the Provinces were established under which one of the following Acts?
   (*a*) The Government of India Act, 1919 (*b*) The Government of India Act, 1935
   (*c*) The Indian Councils Act, 1909 (*d*) The Indian Councils Act, 1892

7. The initial idea of recruitment on merit principle can be traced to the:
   (*a*) Lee Commission (*b*) Macaulay Committee
   (*c*) Islington Commission (*d*) Maxwell Committee

8. Which of the following Acts separated, for the first time, provincial budgets from the central budget?
   (*a*) Government of India Act, 1919 (*b*) Indian Councils Act, 1909
   (*c*) Indian Councils Act, 1892 (*d*) Government of India Act, 1935

9. Which one of the following pairs is correctly matched?
   (*a*) Indian Councils Act, 1892 : Principle of Election
   (*b*) Indian Councils Act, 1909 : Responsible Government
   (*c*) Government of India Act, 1919 : Provincial Autonomy
   (*d*) Government of India Act, 1935 : Dyarchy in States

10. Consider the following statements:
    1. The Charter Act, 1793, extended the trade monopoly of the company in India for another period of twenty years.
    2. The Charter Act, 1813, abolished the trade monopoly of the company in India.

    Which of the statements given above is/are correct?
    (*a*) 1 only (*b*) 2 only
    (*c*) Both 1 and 2 (*d*) Neither 1 nor 2

11. In the Federation established by the Act, 1935, residuary powers were given to the:
    (*a*) Federal Legislature (*b*) Provincial Legislature
    (*c*) Governor-General (*d*) Provincial Governor

12. Which of the following Acts is also known as Morley-Minto Reforms?
    (*a*) Government of India Act, 1858
    (*b*) Indian Councils Act, 1861
    (*c*) Indian Councils Act, 1909
    (*d*) Government of India Act, 1919

13. The Government of India Act, 1919, was based upon:
    (*a*) Morley-Minto Reforms (*b*) Montague-Chelmsford Report
    (*c*) Ramsay McDonald Award (*d*) Nehru Report

14. Under which one of the following Acts, was the Communal Electorate System introduced by the British in India for the first time?
    (*a*) Government of India Act, 1909
    (*b*) Government of India Act, 1919
    (*c*) Indian Councils Act, 1861
    (*d*) Indian Councils Act, 1892

15. What were the salient features of the Government of India Act, 1935?
    1. Abolition of Council of India
    2. Dyarchy at the Centre
    3. Abolition of Dyarchy in the States
    4. Establishment of Federal Court

    Select the correct answer using the codes given below:
    (*a*) 2 and 3 only (*b*) 1, 2 and 3
    (*c*) 1, 3 and 4 (*d*) 1, 2, 3 and 4

16. Which of the following was a feature of the Indian Councils Act, 1861?
    (*a*) Federal Scheme of Government
    (*b*) Dyarchy in Provincial Government
    (*c*) Communal Representation
    (*d*) Rigid Centralisation

17. Who among the following was the Finance Minister of India in the Interim Government during 1946-1947?
    (*a*) R.K. Shanmukham Chetty
    (*b*) John Mathai
    (*c*) Liaquat Ali Khan
    (*d*) Chintamanrao Deshmukh

18. Which one of the following Acts laid the foundation of the British Administration in India?
    (*a*) Regulating Act, 1773 (*b*) Pitt's India Act, 1784
    (*c*) Indian Councils Act, 1861 (*d*) Indian Councils Act, 1892

19. Which of the following was a provision of the Charter Act, 1833?
    (*a*) Designation of the Governor-General of Bengal as the Governor-General of India
    (*b*) Dyarchy introduced in Indian Government
    (*c*) All-India Federation and Provincial Autonomy
    (*d*) Control of the Government of India transferred from the East India Company to the British Crown

20. Who among the following was the first Law Minister of India?
    (*a*) Jawaharlal Nehru
    (*b*) Maulana Abul Kalam Azad
    (*c*) Dr. B.R. Ambedkar
    (*d*) T.T. Krishnamachari

21. With reference to the period of the British Rule in India, Indian Statutory Commission is popularly known as the:
(*a*) Cabinet Mission
(*b*) Hunter Commission
(*c*) Sadlar Commission
(*d*) Simon Commission

22. During the British Rule in India, who was the first Indian to be appointed as Law Member of the Governor General's Council?
(*a*) Raja Kishori Lal Goswami
(*b*) Motilal Nehru
(*c*) Satyendra Sinha
(*d*) Tej Bahadur Sapru

23. In which of the following years, the system of budget was introduced in British India?
(*a*) 1780
(*b*) 1860
(*c*) 1890
(*d*) 1920

24. Which of the following Acts made a provision for the appointment of the Secretary of State for India?
(*a*) Regulating Act, 1773
(*b*) Government of India Act, 1858
(*c*) Pitt's India Act, 1784
(*d*) Charter Act, 1833

Answers

1. (*c*)	2. (*d*)	3. (*c*)	4. (*b*)	5. (*d*)
6. (*a*)	7. (*b*)	8. (*a*)	9. (*a*)	10. (*c*)
11. (*c*)	12. (*c*)	13. (*b*)	14. (*a*)	15. (*d*)
16. (*d*)	17. (*c*)	18. (*a*)	19. (*a*)	20. (*c*)
21. (*d*)	22. (*c*)	23. (*b*)	24. (*b*)	

2

Making of the Constitution

1. Consider the following statements regarding the composition of the Constituent Assembly:
   1. The representatives were to be elected from the four constituents–Hindu, Muslim, Sikh and Christian.
   2. The chairman of the Union Constitution Committee was Sardar Vallabhbhai Patel.
   3. The total strength of the Constituent Assembly was 389.
   4. The Drafting Committee under the chairmanship of Dr. B.R. Ambedkar consisted of eight members.

   Which of the statements given above is/are correct?

   (*a*) 1, 2, 3 and 4 (*b*) 1, 2 and 4
   (*c*) 3 only (*d*) 1 only

2. Which of the following provisions of the Constitution of India was/were given immediate effect from November 26, 1949?
   1. Citizenship
   2. Emergency Provisions
   3. Elections
   4. Federal System

   Select the correct answer from the codes given below:

   (*a*) 1 only (*b*) 2 and 3 only
   (*c*) 1 and 4 only (*d*) 1 and 3 only

3. What was the procedure followed for the adoption of the Constitution of India?

   (*a*) It was submitted to the people of India for ratification.
   (*b*) It was submitted to the Governor-General for his assent.
   (*c*) It was adopted when the Interim Government approved it.
   (*d*) It was adopted when it received the signature of the President and the Members of the Constituent Assembly.

4. Who among the following was the Chairman of the States Committee of the Constituent Assembly?

   (*a*) Dr. B.R. Ambedkar (*b*) Jawaharlal Nehru
   (*c*) Dr. Rajendra Prasad (*d*) Sardar Patel

5. The Constitution of India as framed by the Constituent Assembly was finally adopted and enacted on:

   (*a*) 15th August, 1947 (*b*) 30th January, 1948
   (*c*) 26th November, 1949 (*d*) 26th January, 1950

6. Which one of the following committees of the Constituent Assembly was chaired by J.B. Kripalani?
   (*a*) Steering Committee
   (*b*) Fundamental Rights Sub-Committee
   (*c*) Union Constitution Committee
   (*d*) Provincial Constitution Committee

7. The members of the Constituent Assembly were:
   (*a*) Directly elected by the people.
   (*b*) Nominated by the Governor-General.
   (*c*) Elected by the Legislatures of various Provinces and nominated by the rulers of the princely states.
   (*d*) Nominated by the Congress and the Muslim League.

8. Who among the following was the Constitutional Advisor to the Constituent Assembly?
   (*a*) Dr. B.R. Ambedkar (*b*) K.M. Munshi
   (*c*) Sir B.N. Rau (*d*) T.T. Krishnamachari

9. Consider the following statements:
   1. Tiger was adopted as the symbol (seal) of the Constituent Assembly.
   2. Prem Behari Narain Raizada was the calligrapher of the Indian Constitution.

   Which of the statements given above is/are correct?
   (*a*) 1 only (*b*) 2 only
   (*c*) Both 1 and 2 (*d*) Neither 1 nor 2

10. Who among the following moved the "Objectives Resolution" in the Constituent Assembly?
    (*a*) Sir B.N. Rau (*b*) Dr. B.R. Ambedkar
    (*c*) Jawaharlal Nehru (*d*) Rajendra Prasad

11. Consider the following statements:
    1. Dr. Sachchidanand Sinha was elected as the Provisional President of the Constituent Assembly.
    2. H.C. Mukherjee was elected as the Vice-President of the Constituent Assembly.

    Which of the statements given above is/are correct?
    (*a*) 1 only (*b*) 2 only
    (*c*) Both 1 and 2 (*d*) Neither 1 nor 2

12. Consider the following statements:
    1. Originally, the Constitution of India did not make any provision with respect to an authoritative text of the Constitution in the Hindi language.
    2. Later, a provision in this regard was made in 1978.

    Which of the statements given above is / are correct?
    (*a*) 1 only (*b*) 2 only
    (*c*) Both 1 and 2 (*d*) Neither 1 nor 2

13. Consider the following statements:
    1. The President shall cause to be published under his authority the translation of the Constitution in Hindi language.
    2. The President shall cause to be published under his authority the translation in Hindi of every amendment of the Constitution made in English.

    Which of the statements given above is / are correct?

    (*a*) 1 only (*b*) 2 only
    (*c*) Both 1 and 2 (*d*) Neither 1 nor 2

14. In pursuance of which of the following Articles of the Constitution of India, the President published an authoritative text of the Constitution in the Hindi language?

    (*a*) Article 393 (*b*) Article 394
    (*c*) Article 394A (*d*) Article 395

15. Which of the following Parts of the Constitution of India deals with the authoritative text of the Constitution in the Hindi language?

    (*a*) Part XXI (*b*) Part XIX
    (*c*) Part XVII (*d*) Part XXII

16. Which of the following Constitutional Amendment Acts made a provision with respect to an authoritative text of the Constitution of India in the Hindi language?

    (*a*) 56th Amendment Act
    (*b*) 58th Amendment Act
    (*c*) 54th Amendment Act
    (*d*) 55th Amendment Act

17. Consider the following statements:
    1. The translation of the constitution and its every amendment published shall be construed to have the same meaning as the original text in English.
    2. The translation of the constitution and its every amendment published shall be deemed to be, for all purposes, its authoritative text in Hindi.

    Which of the statements given above is/are correct?

    (*a*) 1 only (*b*) 2 only
    (*c*) Both 1 and 2 (*d*) Neither 1 nor 2

Answers

1. (*c*)	2. (*d*)	3. (*d*)	4. (*b*)	5. (*c*)
6. (*b*)	7. (*c*)	8. (*c*)	9. (*b*)	10. (*c*)
11. (*c*)	12. (*a*)	13. (*c*)	14. (*c*)	15. (*d*)
16. (*b*)	17. (*c*)			

3 Salient Features of the Constitution

1. Which of the following statements about the Constitution of India is/are correct?
   1. Popular sovereignty and adult franchise are the basic features of the Constitution.
   2. The Constitution, in so far as the division of powers between the Centre and the States is concerned, is rigid.
   3. The Constitution recognises the interdependence of civil and economic rights.
   4. The Constitution mentions direct control by the people such as referendum, initiative and recall.

   Select the correct answer from the codes given below:

   (*a*) 1 only (*b*) 1, 2 and 4
   (*c*) 2, 3 and 4 (*d*) 1, 2 and 3

2. Consider the following statements related to secularism in India:
   1. It entails strict separation of religion from politics.
   2. It bans parties with religious affiliations from contesting elections.
   3. It grants religious liberty to all communities.
   4. It accepts community personal laws.

   Which of the statements given above are correct?

   (*a*) 3 and 4 only (*b*) 1 and 2 only
   (*c*) 1, 3 and 4 (*d*) 1, 2, 3 and 4

3. Which one of the following schedules of the Constitution of India incorporates salaries and allowances of the Chairman and the Deputy Chairman of the Rajya Sabha, and the Speaker and the Deputy Speaker of the Lok Sabha?

   (*a*) Fifth Schedule (*b*) Second Schedule
   (*c*) Ninth Schedule (*d*) Tenth Schedule

4. Which of the following is the subject of Part VI of the Constitution of India?

   (*a*) Finance, Property, Contracts and Suits (*b*) The Union Judiciary
   (*c*) The Executive of States (*d*) Relations between the Union and the States

5. Which one of the following is not a salient feature of the Constitution of India?

   (*a*) Written Constitution and supremacy of the Constitution
   (*b*) Quasi-federal structure
   (*c*) Committed Judiciary
   (*d*) Distribution of Powers

6. Consider the following statements:

   The Indian Constitution is:

   1. an unwritten constitution.
   2. a written constitution.
   3. largely based on the Government of India Act, 1935.
   4. a gift of British Parliament.

   Which of the statements given above are correct?

   (*a*) 2 and 4 only (*b*) 2 and 3 only
   (*c*) 1 and 4 only (*d*) 1 and 3 only

7. The Second Schedule of the Constitution of India does not contain the provisions as to who among the following?

   (*a*) The President
   (*b*) The Speaker of the House of People
   (*c*) The Comptroller and Auditor-General of India
   (*d*) The Chairman, Union Public Service Commission

8. Which of the following provisions in the Constitution of India has been adopted from USA?

   (*a*) Emergency Provisions (*b*) Fundamental Rights
   (*c*) Parliamentary System (*d*) Directive Principles of State Policy

9. Which one of the following pairs is not correctly matched?

(*a*) Languages	:	Eighth Schedule
(*b*) The forms of oaths or affirmations	:	Second Schedule
(*c*) Allocation of seats in the Council of States	:	Fourth Schedule
(*d*) Provisions as to disqualification on the ground of defection	:	Tenth Schedule

10. Consider the following statements with reference to Secularism in India:

    1. Secularism means that the State has no recognised religion of the State.
    2. Secularism means that the State treats all the religions equally.
    3. Secularism means that the State regulates the relation of man with God.

    Which of the statements given above are correct?

    (*a*) 1, 2 and 3 (*b*) 1 and 2 only
    (*c*) 2 and 3 only (*d*) 1 and 3 only

11. Consider the following statements:

    1. According to the critics, the Indian Constitution is "un-Indian" or "anti-Indian" because it does not reflect the political traditions and the spirit of India.
    2. According to the critics, the Indian Constitution is un-Gandhian because it does not contain the philosophy and ideas of Mahatma Gandhi.

    Which of these statements given above is/are correct?

    (*a*) 1 only (*b*) 2 only
    (*c*) Both 1 and 2 (*d*) Neither 1 nor 2

12. Which one of the following statements correctly describes the Seventh Schedule of the Constitution of India?
    (*a*) It contains the languages recognised in the Constitution.
    (*b*) It contains the provisions regarding the administration of tribal areas.
    (*c*) It lists distribution of powers between the Union and the States.
    (*d*) It deals with the salaries and emoluments of the constitutional functionaries.

13. Consider the following statements:
    The salient features of the Indian Constitution provide for:
    1. Single citizenship for the whole of India.
    2. Strictly federal form of government.
    3. Unique blend of rigidity and flexibility.

    Which of the statements given above are correct?
    (*a*) 1, 2 and 3 (*b*) 1 and 2 only
    (*c*) 2 and 3 only (*d*) 1 and 3 only

14. Which of the following schedules of the Constitution of India contains provisions regarding land reforms legislations?
    (*a*) Ninth Schedule (*b*) Tenth Schedule
    (*c*) Eleventh Schedule (*d*) Sixth Schedule

15. Who of the following has called the Indian Constitution as a "lawyer's paradise"?
    (*a*) H.K. Maheshwari (*b*) Sir Ivor Jennings
    (*c*) N. Srinivasan (*d*) Lokanath Misra

16. Which one of the following members of the Constituent Assembly made the following comment on the foreign nature of the Indian Constitution?
    "We wanted the music of veena or sitar, but here we have the music of the English band."
    (*a*) Lakshminarayan Sahu (*b*) P.R. Deshmukh
    (*c*) H.V. Kamath (*d*) K. Hanumanthaiya

Answers

1. (*d*)	2. (*c*)	3. (*b*)	4. (*c*)	5. (*c*)
6. (*b*)	7. (*d*)	8. (*b*)	9. (*b*)	10. (*b*)
11. (*c*)	12. (*c*)	13. (*d*)	14. (*a*)	15. (*b*)
16. (*d*)				

4 Preamble of the Constitution

1. The following are enshrined in the Preamble of the Constitution of India:
   1. Equality of status and opportunity.
   2. Liberty of thought, expression, belief, faith and worship.
   3. Justice—social, economic and political.
   4. Fraternity assuring the dignity of the individual.
   5. Unity and integrity of the nation.

   Which one of the following is the correct order in which they appear in the Preamble?

   (*a*) 5, 1, 2, 4, 3
   (*b*) 3, 2, 1, 4, 5
   (*c*) 3, 1, 2, 5, 4
   (*d*) 1, 2, 4, 3, 5

2. The philosophical postulates of the Constitution of India are based on:

   (*a*) Nehru Report, 1928.
   (*b*) Objectives Resolution of Pandit Nehru, 1947.
   (*c*) Mahatma Gandhi's Article "Independence in Young India", 1922.
   (*d*) Indian National Congress's Resolution for Complete Independence, 1929.

3. The Preamble of the Indian Constitution is:

   (*a*) Not a part of the Constitution.
   (*b*) A part of the Constitution but it neither confers any powers nor imposes any duties nor can it be of any use in interpreting other provisions of the Constitution.
   (*c*) A part of the Constitution and can be of use in interpreting other provisions of the Constitution in cases of ambiguity.
   (*d*) A part of the Constitution and it confers powers and imposes duties as any other provisions of the Constitution.

4. Which one of the following statements is correct?

   The Preamble of the Indian Constitution declares the resolve of the people of India to secure to all its citizens:

   (*a*) Freedom of residence anywhere in the country.
   (*b*) Right to establish and administer educational institutions of choice.
   (*c*) Liberty of belief, faith and worship.
   (*d*) Right to education at primary level.

5. The term "economic justice" in the Preamble of the Constitution of India, is a resolution for:
   (*a*) equal distribution of wealth.
   (*b*) economy in the administration of justice.
   (*c*) socio-economic revolution.
   (*d*) cheap justice to the poor.

6. Which of the following terms mentioned in the Preamble to the Indian Constitution implies that the head of state is not a hereditary monarch?
   (*a*) Republic (*b*) Secular
   (*c*) Democratic (*d*) Sovereign

7. The text of the Preamble of the Constitution of India aims to secure:
   (*a*) Fundamental Rights to all individuals.
   (*b*) Fundamental Duties to citizens of India.
   (*c*) Dignity of the individual and unity and integrity of the nation.
   (*d*) Security of service to Government servants.

8. Which of the following terms was not included in a "Union of Trinity" by Dr. B.R. Ambedkar in his concluding speech in the Constituent Assembly?
   (*a*) Liberty (*b*) Flexibility
   (*c*) Equality (*d*) Fraternity

9. The words "Socialist" and "Secular" were inserted in the Preamble by the:
   (*a*) Fifteenth Amendment
   (*b*) Thirty-ninth Amendment
   (*c*) Forty-second Amendment
   (*d*) Forty-fourth Amendment

10. The sequence in which the given terms are mentioned in the Preamble to the Constitution of India is:
    (*a*) Sovereign, Socialist, Secular, Democratic, Republic
    (*b*) Socialist, Secular, Sovereign, Democratic, Republic
    (*c*) Secular, Sovereign, Democratic, Socialist, Republic
    (*d*) Sovereign, Democratic, Secular, Socialist, Republic

11. The Preamble to the Constitution of India:
    (*a*) Is not a part of the Constitution.
    (*b*) Indicates the objectives to be achieved.
    (*c*) Cannot be amended by the Parliament.
    (*d*) Is a source of authority of the Constitution of India.

12. Consider the following statements:
    1. In the Berubari Union case (1960), the Supreme Court opined that Preamble is not a port of the Constitution.
    2. The question as to whether the Preamble can be amended under the Article 368 of the Constitution arose for the first time in the Kesavananda Bharati case (1973).

Which of the statements given above is/are correct?

(*a*) 1 only (*b*) 2 only

(*c*) Both 1 and 2 (*d*) Neither 1 nor 2

Answers

1. (*b*)	2. (*b*)	3. (*c*)	4. (*c*)	5. (*a*)
6. (*a*)	7. (*c*)	8. (*b*)	9. (*c*)	10. (*a*)
11. (*b*)	12. (*c*)			

5 Union and its Territory

1. Consider the following statements:
   1. The Parliament is empowered to alter the boundaries of any existing State of India.
   2. A Bill pertaining to the alteration of the boundaries of any existing State of India can be introduced only in the Rajya Sabha and only on the recommendation of the President of India.

   Which of the statements given above is/are correct?

   (*a*) 1 only (*b*) 2 only
   (*c*) Both 1 and 2 (*d*) Neither 1 nor 2

2. Consider the following with respect to the Union of India:
   1. Formation of the State of Nagaland.
   2. States Reorganisation Act.
   3. Formation of the State of Haryana.
   4. Formation of the State of Gujarat.

   Which one of the following is the correct chronological order of the above?

   (*a*) 4, 2, 3, 1 (*b*) 2, 4, 3, 1
   (*c*) 4, 2, 1, 3 (*d*) 2, 4, 1, 3

3. The boundary of a State in India can be altered through the procedure laid down in:

   (*a*) Article 368 (*b*) Article 130
   (*c*) Article 70 (*d*) Article 3

4. In 1953, Prime Minister Jawaharlal Nehru announced the formation of a commission to study the reorganisation of states on a linguistic basis under the chairmanship of:

   (*a*) T.T. Krishnamachari
   (*b*) Vallabhbhai Patel
   (*c*) Fazl Ali
   (*d*) G.B. Pant

5. The Parliament of India passed the States Reorganisation Act in 1956 to create:

   (*a*) 16 States and 3 Union Territories
   (*b*) 15 States and 5 Union Territories
   (*c*) 14 States and 6 Union Territories
   (*d*) 24 States and 9 Union Territories

6. The States of the Indian Union can be reorganised or their boundaries altered by:
   (*a*) The Union Parliament by a simple majority in the ordinary process of legislation.
   (*b*) Two-thirds majority of both the Houses of the Parliament.
   (*c*) Two-thirds majority of both the Houses of the Parliament and the consent of the Legislatures of the concerned States.
   (*d*) An executive order of the Union Government with the consent of the concerned State Governments.

7. The Constitution of India divided the states of India in categories A, B and C in the year 1950. In this context, which of the following statements is correct?
   (*a*) The Chief Commissioner was the executive head of category A states. The Rajpramukh was the executive head of category B states. The Governor was the executive head of category C states.
   (*b*) The Rajpramukh was the executive head of category A states. The Chief Commissioner was the executive head of category B states. The Governor was the executive head of the category C states.
   (*c*) The Governor was the executive head of category A states. The Rajpramukh was the executive head of category B states. The Chief Commissioner was the executive head of category C states.
   (*d*) The Governor was the executive head of category A states. The Chief Commissioner was the executive head of category B states. The Rajpramukh was the executive head of category C states.

8. Who among the following was the head of the Linguistic Provinces Commission appointed in the year 1948 to enquire into the desirability of linguistic Provinces?
   (*a*) Jawaharlal Nehru (*b*) Justice S.K. Dhar
   (*c*) Justice Fazl Ali (*d*) Pattabhi Sitaramayya

9. What is the correct chronological order in which the following States of the Indian Union were created or granted full statehood?
   1. Andhra Pradesh 2. Nagaland
   3. Maharashtra 4. Haryana

   Select the correct answer using the codes given below:
   (*a*) 1, 3, 4, 2 (*b*) 3, 1, 2, 4
   (*c*) 1, 3, 2, 4 (*d*) 3, 1, 4, 2

10. Who, among the following, was not a member of the States Reorganisation Commission (SRC) appointed by Pandit Jawaharlal Nehru?
    (*a*) Justice Fazl Ali (*b*) Potti Sriramulu
    (*c*) K.M. Panikkar (*d*) Hridayanath Kunzru

11. Consider the following statements with reference to the linguistic reorganisation of states in independent India:
    1. The separate state of Andhra for the Telugu people came into existence in 1953.
    2. Jawaharlal Nehru was particularly in favour of the movement for linguistic reorganisation of states that came in the wake of the success of the Andhra movement.

Which of the statements given above is/are correct?

(*a*) 1 only (*b*) 2 only

(*c*) Both 1 and 2 (*d*) Neither 1 nor 2

12. Which of the following was granted full statehood in 1972?

(*a*) Goa (*b*) Haryana

(*c*) Meghalaya (*d*) Sikkim

13. Consider the following statements:

1. The 100th Constitutional Amendment Act, 2015 was enacted to give effect to the acquiring of certain territories by India and transfer of certain other territories to Bangladesh.
2. Under this amendment, India transferred 121 enclaves to Bangladesh, while Bangladesh transferred 61 enclaves to India.

Which of the statements given above is/are correct?

(*a*) 1 only (*b*) 2 only

(*c*) Both 1 and 2 (*d*) Neither 1 nor 2

Answers

1. (*a*)	2. (*d*)	3. (*d*)	4. (*c*)	5. (*c*)
6. (*a*)	7. (*c*)	8. (*b*)	9. (*c*)	10. (*b*)
11. (*a*)	12. (*c*)	13. (*a*)		

6

Citizenship

1. Consider the following statements:
   1. A person, born on 26th January 1951 in Rangoon, whose father was a citizen of India by birth at the time of his birth, is deemed to be an Indian citizen by descent.
   2. A person, born on 1st July 1988 in Itanagar, whose mother is a citizen of India at the time of his birth but the father is not, is deemed to be a citizen of India by birth.

   Which of the statements given above is/are correct?

   (*a*) 1 only (*b*) 2 only
   (*c*) Both 1 and 2 (*d*) Neither 1 nor 2

2. Under the Citizenship Act, 1955, by which of the following ways can a person become a citizen of India?
   1. By birth
   2. By descent
   3. By registration
   4. By nationalisation
   5. By incorporation of territory

   Select the correct answer using the codes given below:

   (*a*) 1, 2, 3, 4 and 5 (*b*) 1 and 2 only
   (*c*) 1, 2, 3 and 5 (*d*) 3, 4 and 5

3. Which of the following Articles of the Indian Constitution deal with citizenship in India?

   (*a*) Articles 333 to 337 (*b*) Articles 17 to 20
   (*c*) Articles 5 to 11 (*d*) Articles 1 to 4

4. In which of the following years, the Citizenship Act, 1955 was amended?
   1. 1986
   2. 1992
   3. 2003
   4. 2005

   Select the correct answer using the codes given below:

   (*a*) 2, 3 and 4 (*b*) 1, 2 and 4
   (*c*) 1, 2, 3 and 4 (*d*) 1, 2 and 3

5. Which Article of the Constitution of India deals with the rights of citizenship of certain persons of Indian origin residing outside India?

   (*a*) Article 7 (*b*) Article 10
   (*c*) Article 8 (*d*) Article 9

6. Which one among the following has the power to regulate the right of citizenship in India?

   (*a*) The Union Cabinet (*b*) The Parliament
   (*c*) The Supreme Court (*d*) The Law Commission

7. In which Part of the Constitution, details of citizenship are mentioned?
(*a*) Part I
(*b*) Part II
(*c*) Part III
(*d*) Part IV

8. Which of the following provisions pertaining to citizenship is contained in Article 9 of the Constitution?
(*a*) Rights of citizenship of certain persons who have migrated to India from Pakistan
(*b*) Persons voluntarily acquiring citizenship of a foreign state not to be citizens
(*c*) Citizenship at the commencement of the Constitution
(*d*) Rights of citizenship of certain migrants to Pakistan

9. According to the Citizenship Act, 1955, by which of the following ways can a person lose citizenship of India?
1. By Renunciation
2. By Termination
3. By Deprivation

Select the correct answer using the codes given below:
(*a*) 1 and 2 only
(*b*) 2 and 3 only
(*c*) 1, 2 and 3
(*d*) 1 and 3 only

10. Consider the following statements:
1. Originally, the Citizenship Act,1955, also provided for the Commonwealth Citizenship.
2. The provision for Commonwealth Citizenship was repealed by the Citizenship (Amendment) Act, 2005.

Which of the statements given above is/are correct?
(*a*) 1 only
(*b*) 2 only
(*c*) Both 1 and 2
(*d*) Neither 1 nor 2

11. Who of the following was the chairman of the Committee on the Indian Diaspora setup by the Government of India in 2000?
(*a*) J.S. Verma
(*b*) M.M. Punchhi
(*c*) L.M. Singhvi
(*d*) L.M. Sharma

12. Which one of the following amendments to the Citizenship Act 1955 replaced the nomenclature of "Overseas Citizen of India" with that of "Overseas Citizen of India Cardholder"?
(*a*) Citizenship (Amendment) Act, 1992
(*b*) Citizenship (Amendment) Act, 2003
(*c*) Citizenship (Amendment) Act, 2005
(*d*) Citizenship (Amendment) Act, 2015

Answers

1. (*c*)	2. (*c*)	3. (*c*)	4. (*c*)	5. (*c*)
6. (*b*)	7. (*b*)	8. (*b*)	9. (*c*)	10. (*a*)
11. (*c*)	12. (*d*)			

7

Fundamental Rights

1. Consider the following statements:
   In view of Article 20 of the Constitution of India, no person accused of an offence can be compelled to:
   1. Give his signature or thumb impression for identification.
   2. Give oral testimony either in or out of the court.

   Which of the statements given above is/are correct?
   (*a*) 1 only (*b*) 2 only
   (*c*) Both 1 and 2 (*d*) Neither 1 nor 2

2. Consider the following statements:
   1. The writ of mandamus is available not only against judicial authorities but also against administrative authorities.
   2. The writ of prohibition is issued only against judicial or quasi-judicial authorities.

   Which of the statements given above is/are correct?
   (*a*) 1 only (*b*) 2 only
   (*c*) Both 1 and 2 (*d*) Neither 1 nor 2

3. Consider the following statements:
   1. There is no provision in the Constitution of India for reservation in the matters of promotion in the services under the state in favour of the scheduled castes and the scheduled tribes.
   2. As per provisions of the Constitution of India, for getting reservation for appointments and posts under the state, a class must be backward and should not be adequately represented in the services under the state.

   Which of the statements given above is/are correct?
   (*a*) 1 only
   (*b*) 2 only
   (*c*) Both 1 and 2
   (*d*) Neither 1 nor 2

4. Consider the following statements:
   1. A constitutional amendment inserting a regulation in the Ninth Schedule can be challenged on the ground of violation of basic structure of the Constitution.
   2. Any legislation enacted by the Parliament cannot be successfully challenged for affecting the basic structure of the Constitution.

Which of the statements given above is/are correct?

(*a*) 1 only (*b*) 2 only

(*c*) Both 1 and 2 (*d*) Neither 1 nor 2

5. Which one of the following pairs is not correctly matched?

(*a*) Freedom of speech and expression : Include the freedom of press

(*b*) Freedom of conscience : Include the right to wear and carry kirpans by Sikhs

(*c*) Right to personal liberty : Include the right to carry on any trade or business

(*d*) Right to equality : Include the principle of natural justice

6. Consider the following statements:

1. All the Fundamental Rights are available against the arbitrary action of the state.
2. Some of the Fundamental Rights are also available against the action of private individuals.

Which of the statements given above is/are correct?

(*a*) 1 only (*b*) 2 only

(*c*) Both 1 and 2 (*d*) Neither 1 nor 2

7. Which of the following are envisaged by the Right Against Exploitation in the Constitution of India?

1. Prohibition of traffic in human beings and forced labour
2. Abolition of untouchability
3. Protection of the interests of minorities
4. Prohibition of employment of children in factories and mines

Select the correct answer using the codes given below:

(*a*) 1 and 2 only (*b*) 1 and 3 only

(*c*) 2, 3 and 4 (*d*) 1 and 4 only

8. Which of the following writs is related to the correctional directions to subordinate courts?

(*a*) Habeas Corpus (*b*) Mandamus

(*c*) Quo-Warranto (*d*) Certiorari

9. As far as the Armed Forces are concerned, the Fundamental Rights granted under Articles 14 and 19 of Constitution are:

(*a*) Not available at all

(*b*) Available to the Armed Forces but not to other forces

(*c*) Available only at the discretion of the Chief of the Army staff

(*d*) Available only according to law made by the Parliament

10. In Indian Constitution, the power to issue a writ of "Habeas Corpus" is vested only in:

(*a*) The Supreme Court

(*b*) The High Courts

(*c*) The Subordinate Courts

(*d*) The Supreme Court and the High Courts

11. Which of the following rights is not explicitly mentioned in the Fundamental Rights but has been upheld to be so by several pronouncements of the Supreme Court?
    (*a*) Equity before law
    (*b*) Right to non-discrimination in public employment
    (*c*) Right to form associations or unions
    (*d*) Right to freedom of press

12. Which of the following statements are true with regard to the Fundamental Rights of the minorities in educational matters?
    1. The minority has only the right to administer the educational institutions.
    2. The minority has the right to establish and administer educational institutions.
    3. The right is absolute and not subject to any restriction.
    4. Reasonable restrictions may be imposed to promote efficiency and prevent maladministration.

    Select the correct answer using the codes given below:
    (*a*) 1, 2 and 3 (*b*) 2 and 4 only
    (*c*) 2, 3 and 4 (*d*) 1 and 3 only

13. Which one of the following pairs is not correctly matched?

(*a*) Article 15	:	Special provisions for socially and educationally backward classes
(*b*) Article 22	:	Safeguards under Preventive Detention
(*c*) Article 20	:	Immunity from double punishment
(*d*) Article 16	:	Discrimination in favour of women in service under the State

14. Which of the following statements is/are correct of the writ of prohibition?
    1. It is an order issued by a higher court commanding a lower court to cease from proceeding in some matters not within its jurisdiction.
    2. It can be claimed by an aggrieved party as a matter of right.

    Select the correct answer using the codes given below:
    (*a*) 1 only (*b*) 2 only
    (*c*) Both 1 and 2 (*d*) Neither 1 nor 2

15. Which of the following provisions is contained in the cultural and education rights?
    (*a*) Liberty of thought and expression
    (*b*) Freedom of speech and expression
    (*c*) Making special provision for women and children
    (*d*) Protection of interests of minorities

16. Under the Indian Constitution, which one of the following is not a specific ground on which the State can place restrictions on the freedom of religion?
    (*a*) Public order (*b*) Morality
    (*c*) Social Justice (*d*) Health

17. The scope of "life and personal liberty", as envisaged in Article 21 of the Constitution of India, has expanded considerably over the years. Which one of the following can still not be subject of this protection?
(*a*) The Right to good health
(*b*) The Right of a bonded labour to rehabilitation after release
(*c*) The Right, under a settlement, to claim bonus or dearness allowance
(*d*) The Right to livelihood by means which are not illegal, immoral or opposed to public policy

18. Consider the following statements:
1. The Supreme Court has declared the right to road in hilly areas as the part of Article 21 of the Constitution.
2. The right to appropriate life insurance policy was not declared as the part of Article 21 of the Constitution by the Supreme Court.

Which of the statements given above is/are correct?
(*a*) 1 only (*b*) 2 only
(*c*) Both 1 and 2 (*d*) Neither 1 nor 2

19. Which of the following is not included in Article 19 of the Constitution of India, pertaining to the Right to Freedom?
(*a*) Right to reside and settle in any part of the territory of India
(*b*) Right of minorities to establish and administer educational institutions
(*c*) Right to form associations or unions
(*d*) Right to assemble peaceably and without arms

20. Consider the following statements:

The "State" under Article 12 of the Indian Constitution includes:
1. the Government and the Parliament of India.
2. the governments and the Legislatures of the states.
3. local authorities or other authorities within the territories of India or under the control of Government of India.

Which of the statements given above are correct?
(*a*) 1, 2 and 3 (*b*) 1 and 2 only
(*c*) 2 and 3 only (*d*) 1 and 3 only

21. Which one of the following rights was described by Dr. Ambedkar as "the heart and soul" of the Constitution?
(*a*) Right to equality (*b*) Right against exploitation
(*c*) Right to constitutional remedies (*d*) Right to freedom of religion

22. Which one of the following freedoms is not guaranteed by the Constitution of India?
(*a*) Freedom to own, acquire and dispose of property
(*b*) Freedom to move freely throughout the country
(*c*) Freedom to assemble peaceably and without arms
(*d*) Freedom to practice any trade or profession

23. Consider the following statements:
    1. In 2019, the Central Government issued an order providing 20 per cent reservation to the Economically Weaker Sections (EWSs) in admission to educational institutions.
    2. The benefit of the above reservation can be availed by the persons belonging to EWSs who are not covered under any of the existing schemes of reservation for SCs, STs and OBCs.

    Which of the statements given above is/are correct?

    (*a*) 1 only (*b*) 2 only
    (*c*) Both 1 and 2 (*d*) Neither 1 nor 2

24. Which of the following cases is related to the procedure established by law?

    (*a*) Indra Sawhney Case (*b*) Minerva Mills Case
    (*c*) Gopalan Case (*d*) Shankari Prasad Case

25. Which one of the following is the correct statement?

    Right to privacy as a Fundamental Right is implicit in:

    (*a*) The Right to Freedom (*b*) The Right to Personal Liberty
    (*c*) The Right to Equality (*d*) The Right Against Exploitation

26. Which of the following amendment is related to the reservation for Economically Weaker Sections in public employment?

    (*a*) Ninety-Third Amendment Act, 2005
    (*b*) Ninety-Fifth Amendment Act, 2009
    (*c*) One Hundred and Second Amendment Act, 2018
    (*d*) One Hundred and Third Amendment Act, 2019

27. Right to Education is a Fundamental Rights emanating from the right to:

    (*a*) Freedom of speech and expression under Article 19
    (*b*) Culture and education under Articles 29 and 30
    (*c*) Life and personal liberty under Article 21
    (*d*) Equality before law and equal protection of the laws under Article 14

28. The State shall not make any law which takes away or abridges the Fundamental Rights. Which one of the following shall not be construed as law for this purpose?

    (*a*) Ordinance (*b*) Bye-law
    (*c*) Rule (*d*) Constitutional amendment

29. On which one of the following freedoms, can reasonable restrictions be imposed on the ground of the security of the state?

    (*a*) Speech and expression (*b*) Peaceful assembly
    (*c*) Association or union (*d*) Movement

30. Which of the following are mentioned under separate Articles in Part III of the Constitution of India pertaining to the Fundamental Rights?
    1. Abolition of untouchability
    2. Abolition of titles

3. Freedom as to payment of taxes for promotion of any particular religion
4. Protection of interests of minorities

Select the correct answer by using the codes given below:

(*a*) 1 and 2 only (*b*) 2, 3 and 4
(*c*) 3 and 4 only (*d*) 1, 2, 3 and 4

31. Fundamental Rights guaranteed in the Indian Constitution can be suspended only by:
(*a*) A proclamation of national emergency
(*b*) An Act passed by the Parliament
(*c*) An amendment of the Constitution
(*d*) The judicial decisions of the Supreme Court

32. The Right to Property was converted into a legal right from a Fundamental Right, because it:
(*a*) Tied the hands of the government to prevent corruption
(*b*) Gave rise to litigations that made judiciary overburden
(*c*) Led to severe conflict between judiciary and the Parliament
(*d*) Increased public resentment

33. Which of the following writs is related to the trial of the right to a title or elective office?
(*a*) Writ of mandamus (*b*) Writ of injunction
(*c*) Writ of certiorari (*d*) Writ of quo-warranto

34. Under Article 22 of the Constitution of India, with the exception of certain provisions stated therein, what is the maximum period for detention of a person under preventive detention?
(*a*) 2 months (*b*) 3 months
(*c*) 4 months (*d*) 6 months

35. Which one of the following Fundamental Rights is guaranteed only to the citizens of India and not to the foreigners living in India?
(*a*) Equality before law and equal protection of laws
(*b*) Freedom of speech and expression
(*c*) Right to life and liberty
(*d*) Right to the freedom of religion

36. To include which of the following has the Supreme Court increased the ambit of the Right to Life (Article 21)?
1. Right to life includes the right to live with dignity
2. Right to life includes the right to livelihood
3. Right to life includes the right to receive minimum wages
4. Right to life includes the right to guaranteed employment for 100 days in a year

Select the correct answer using the codes given below:

(*a*) 4 only (*b*) 1 and 2 only
(*c*) 1, 2 and 3 (*d*) 1, 2, 3 and 4

37. In accordance with the text of the Constitution, a reasonable restriction in the interest of "sovereignty and integrity" of India can be imposed on the right to:
    (*a*) Freedom of speech and expression
    (*b*) Move freely throughout the territory of India
    (*c*) Reside and settle in any part of the territory of India
    (*d*) Carry on any occupation, trade or business

38. Which one of the following is the best justification for the affirmative action policies in India?
    (*a*) The principle of non-discrimination
    (*b*) The principle of equal opportunity
    (*c*) The principle of group disadvantage
    (*d*) The principle of radical redistribution

39. Which of the following rights were declared by the Supreme Court as the Part of Article 21 of the Constitution?
    1. Right to sustainable development
    2. Right to sleep
    3. Right to opportunity
    4. Right to freedom from noise pollution

    Select the correct answer using the codes given below:
    (*a*) 1 and 2 only (*b*) 3 and 4 only
    (*c*) 2 and 3 only (*d*) 1, 2, 3 and 4

40. Under the term "Double Jeopardy" implied in Article 20 of the Constitution of India, a person:
    (*a*) Convicted by a court of law cannot be punished under departmental proceedings for the same offence.
    (*b*) Punished departmentally cannot be prosecuted in a court of law for the same offence.
    (*c*) Shall not be prosecuted and punished for the same offence more than once.
    (*d*) Cannot be subjected to proceedings in civil courts for disobedience of an injunction along with criminal proceedings.

41. Reservation of seats in educational institutions in favour of Scheduled Castes and Scheduled Tribes is governed by:
    (*a*) Article 15 of the Constitution (*b*) Article 16 of the Constitution
    (*c*) Article 29 of the Constitution (*d*) Article 14 of the Constitution

42. What is the correct sequence of the following?
    1. Scheduled Castes Order
    2. Untouchability Offences Act
    3. Protection of Civil Rights Act
    4. Scheduled Castes and Scheduled Tribes (Prevention of Atrocities) Act

    Select the correct answer using the codes given below:
    (*a*) 3, 4, 1, 2 (*b*) 4, 1, 2, 3
    (*c*) 1, 2, 3, 4 (*d*) 2, 3, 4, 1

43. Which one of the following pairs is not correctly matched?

(*a*) Right to equality	: Includes the principle of natural justice
(*b*) Right to personal liberty	: Includes right to livelihood
(*c*) Protections available to an accused person	: Includes protection against ex-post facto laws in civil matters
(*d*) Protections against arrest and detention	: Includes right to consult and to be defended by a legal practitioner of one's choice

44. Which of the following Fundamental Rights cannot be suspended during emergency?
   (*a*) Freedoms under Article 19
   (*b*) Right to constitutional remedies under Articles 32 and 226
   (*c*) Rights under Articles 21 and 22
   (*d*) Rights under Articles 20 and 21

45. Consider the following statements:
   1. The Child Labour (Prohibition and Regulation) Amendment Act, 2016, amended the Child Labour (Prohibition and Regulation) Act, 1986.
   2. The above amendment has renamed the Principal Act as the Child and Adolescent Labour (Prohibition and Regulation) Act, 1986.

   Which of the statements given above is/are correct?
   (*a*) 1 only (*b*) 2 only
   (*c*) Both 1 and 2 (*d*) Neither 1 nor 2

46. Which of the following statements about the right to freedom of religion is not correct?
   (*a*) The State can regulate the economic, financial, political or other secular activities which may be associated with religious practices.
   (*b*) Restrictions can be imposed on the right to freedom of religion on grounds of maintenance of public order, morality or health.
   (*c*) Every religious denomination has the right to establish and maintain institutions for religious and charitable purposes.
   (*d*) Funds appropriated by a religious denomination for promoting and maintaining a particular religion are taxable.

47. Through which provisions does the Constitution of India explicitly prohibits racial discrimination in India?
   (*a*) Articles 14 and 17 (*b*) Articles 17 and 23
   (*c*) Articles 15 and 16 (*d*) Article 17 only

48. Which one of the following rights cannot be inferred from Article 21 of the Constitution?
   (*a*) Right against inhuman treatment (*b*) Right against delayed execution
   (*c*) Right against solitary confinement (*d*) Right to form association

49. Which one of the following pairs is correctly matched?

(*a*) Writ of Habeas Corpus	: Available against private individuals as well
(*b*) Writ of Quo-Warranto	: Available against subordinate courts only
(*c*) Writ of Certiorari	: Available against autonomous bodies only
(*d*) Writ of Prohibition	: Available against public servants only

50. Consider the following statements:
   1. The concept of "equality before law" is an element of the concept of "Rule of Law", propounded by A.V. Dicey.
   2. The Supreme Court held that the "Rule of Law" as embodied in Article 14 is a "basic feature" of the constitution.

   Which of the statements given above is/are correct?
   (*a*) 1 only (*b*) 2 only
   (*c*) Both 1 and 2 (*d*) Neither 1 nor 2

51. Which one of the following Fundamental Rights is available to both the citizens and aliens?
   (*a*) The right to equality of opportunity in public employment
   (*b*) The right to freedoms under Article 19
   (*c*) Cultural and educational rights
   (*d*) The right to equality before law

52. Which of the following are not included in the right to freedom of religion in the Constitution of India?
   1. Freedom of conscience and the right to practise and propagate religion
   2. Levying of taxes or use of funds of the Government for the promotion or maintenance of any religion
   3. Establishment and maintenance of religious and charitable institutions
   4. Imparting of religious instructions in any government maintained institution

   Select the correct answer using the codes given below:
   (*a*) 1 and 2 only (*b*) 1, 2 and 3
   (*c*) 1, 3 and 4 (*d*) 2 and 4 only

53. Which one of the under mentioned rights is guaranteed to citizens as right to freedom under Article 19?
   (*a*) The right to vote
   (*b*) The right to citizenship
   (*c*) The right to contest an election
   (*d*) The right to assemble peaceably and without arms

54. Which of the following is related to the 103rd Amendment Act, 2019?
   (*a*) Reservation of seats for women in local bodies
   (*b*) Reservation for other Backward Classes in educational institutions
   (*c*) Provision of free education for children
   (*d*) Reservation for Economically Weaker Sections in educational institutions

55. Which of the following are the grounds on which discrimination of citizens for admission into educational institutions is constitutionally prohibited?
   1. Religion and Race
   2. Sex and Place of Birth
   3. Nationality and Colour
   4. Age and Nativity

Choose the correct answer from the codes given below:

(a) 1, 2, 3 and 4
(b) 1 and 2 only
(c) 1, 2 and 3
(d) 1, 2 and 4

56. Which one of the following is the correct association?

(a) Indra Sawhney Case : Basic structure of the Constitution
(b) Minerva Mills Case : Invocation of Article 356
(c) Menaka Gandhi Case : Just, fair and reasonable procedure of law
(d) Gopalan Case : Financial Emergency

57. Consider the following statements:

1. Article 31C is an exception to Article 14.
2. The Supreme Court held that "where Article 31C comes in, Article 14 goes out."

Which of the statements given above is/are correct?

(a) 1 only
(b) 2 only
(c) Both 1 and 2
(d) Neither 1 nor 2

58. Which of the following writs is related to a dispute with respect to the appointment of a university teachers?

(a) Habeas Corpus
(b) Mandamus
(c) Quo-Warranto
(d) Certiorari

59. Which of the following amendment is related with the reservation for Other Backward Classes in educational institutions?

(a) 103rd Amendment Act, 2019
(b) 93rd Amendment Act, 2005
(c) 81st Amendment Act, 2000
(d) 85th Amendment Act, 2001

60. Which of the following Article (s) of the Constitution of India is/are exceptions to the Fundamental Rights enumerated in Article 14 or Article 19?

(a) Article 31A only
(b) Article 31C only
(c) Article 31A and Article 31C both
(d) Neither Article 31A nor Article 31C

61. Consider the following statements:

1. The right to family pension was not declared as the part of Article 21 of the Constitution by the Supreme Court.
2. The Supreme Court has declared the right to social and economic justice and empowerment as the part of Article 21 of the Constitution.

Which of the statements given above is/are correct?

(a) 1 only
(b) 2 only
(c) Both 1 and 2
(d) Neither 1 nor 2

62. For which of the following can special provisions be made under Article 15 of the Constitution of India?

1. Women and children
2. Scheduled tribes
3. Economically backward classes
4. Socially backward classes

Select the correct answer using the codes given below:

(*a*) 1, 2 and 4 (*b*) 1 and 3 only
(*c*) 2, 3 and 4 (*d*) 1, 2, 3 and 4

63. Consider the following statements:

1. Quo-warranto is a very powerful instrument for safeguarding against the usurpation of public offices.
2. High Court can issue a mandamus to compel a court or judicial tribunal to exercise its jurisdiction when it has refused to exercise it.

Which of the statements given above is/are correct?

(*a*) 1 only (*b*) 2 only
(*c*) Both 1 and 2 (*d*) Neither 1 nor 2

64. Which of the following writs is related to the transferring of a case from an inferior court to a court of higher jurisdiction?

(*a*) Mandamus
(*b*) Habeas Corpus
(*c*) Certiorari
(*d*) Quo-warranto

65. Freedom of the press in India is:

(*a*) Available to the people under the law of the Parliament
(*b*) Specifically provided in the Constitution
(*c*) Implied in the right to freedom of expression
(*d*) Available to the people of India under executive order

66. The right to freedom of religion guaranteed in Article 25 of the Constitution of India is subject to which of the following?

(*a*) Public order, morality and to the other provisions of Part III of the Constitution of India
(*b*) Public order, morality and health
(*c*) Reasonable restrictions in the interests of the security of the State
(*d*) Public order, morality and health and to the other provisions of Part III of the Constitution of India.

67. Which one of the following writs examines the procedures of inferior Courts or Tribunals?

(*a*) Quo-warranto (*b*) Mandamus
(*c*) Prohibition (*d*) Certiorari

68. The 86th Constitutional Amendment deals with which of the following?

(*a*) Allocation of more number of parliamentary seats for recently created states.
(*b*) Reservation of 30% posts for women in Panchayati Raj Institutions.
(*c*) Insertion of Article 21A related with free and compulsory education for all children between the age of 6 and 14 years.
(*d*) Continuation of reservation for backward classes in government employment.

69. The Article of the Constitution which automatically becomes suspended on proclamation of emergency is:
    (*a*) Article 14
    (*b*) Article 19
    (*c*) Article 21
    (*d*) Article 32

70. Which one of the following rights conferred by the Constitution of India is also available to non-citizens?
    (*a*) Freedom of speech, assembly and form association
    (*b*) Freedom to move, reside and settle in any part of the territory of India
    (*c*) Freedom to carry on any occupation, trade or business
    (*d*) Equality before law and equal protection of laws

71. Which one of the following writs is issued by an appropriate judicial authority/body to free a person who has been illegally detained?
    (*a*) Quo-warranto
    (*b*) Mandamus
    (*c*) Certiorari
    (*d*) Habeas Corpus

72. Untouchability has been abolished by the Constitution of India under:
    (*a*) Article 14
    (*b*) Article 15
    (*c*) Article 16
    (*d*) Article 17

73. Which of the following constitutional amendments have added Article 15(5) in the Constitution of India providing for reservation in educational institutions in the private sector also?
    (*a*) 81st Amendment
    (*b*) 86th Amendment
    (*c*) 91st Amendment
    (*d*) 93rd Amendment

74. The writ of certiorari is issued by a superior court to:
    (*a*) An inferior court to stop further proceedings in a particular case
    (*b*) An inferior court to transfer the record of proceedings in a case for review
    (*c*) An officer to show his right to hold a particular office
    (*d*) A public authority to produce a person detained by it before the court within 24 hours

75. Which one of the following statements is not correct?
    (*a*) Right to livelihood is an integral facet of the Right to life
    (*b*) Natural justice is implicit in Article 21
    (*c*) The Right to life includes the Right to health
    (*d*) Right to go abroad is not a Fundamental Right under Article 21

76. Which one of the following is the correct statement?

    The writ of Mandamus can be issued:
    (*a*) against the Legislature for making law.
    (*b*) for performance of a public duty.
    (*c*) for exercise of discretionary powers.
    (*d*) for deciding legality of an arrest.

77. According to the Constitution of India, which one of the following rights cannot be taken away during emergency?
(*a*) Right to speak
(*b*) Right to freedom of movement
(*c*) Right to life
(*d*) Right to organise

78. The right to property was removed from the list of the Fundamental Rights enlisted in the Constitution through which one of the following amendments?
(*a*) 73rd Amendment
(*b*) 23rd Amendment
(*c*) 44th Amendment
(*d*) 76th Amendment

79. Which of the following writs implies the command to perform public duty?
(*a*) Habeas Corpus
(*b*) Mandamus
(*c*) Certiorari
(*d*) Quo-Warranto

80. Under the provisions of the Indian Constitution, a community can be declared a minority community on the basis of:
(*a*) Religion only
(*b*) Either religion or language
(*c*) Either language or caste
(*d*) Either religion or race

81. Article 30 of the Indian Constitution deals with the:
(*a*) Freedom of conscience
(*b*) Right to propagate religion
(*c*) Right of minorities to establish and manage educational institutions
(*d*) Cultural and educational rights of the majority community

82. The 93rd Amendment to the Constitution of India deals with:
(*a*) Right to education
(*b*) Rights in respect of physically handicapped persons for appointments in the services under the state
(*c*) Reservation for admission in educational institutions
(*d*) Reservation in the matters of promotion in the services under the State in favour of the Other Backward Classes.

83. The Supreme Court of India declared by issuing a writ that "the respondent was not entitled to an office he was holding or a privilege he was exercising". Which writ is that?
(*a*) Habeas Corpus
(*b*) Prohibition
(*c*) Quo-Warranto
(*d*) Certiorari

84. When an emergency under Article 352 of the Constitution is proclaimed, the President of India has no power to suspend the Fundamental Rights contained in which of the following Articles?
(*a*) 20 and 21
(*b*) 19 and 20
(*c*) 21 and 22
(*d*) 19 and 21

85. Which one of the following is not covered under Article 20 of the Constitution of India?
(*a*) Ex post facto laws
(*b*) Preventive detention
(*c*) Double jeopardy
(*d*) Self-incrimination

Answers

1. (*b*)	2. (*c*)	3. (*b*)	4. (*a*)	5. (*c*)
6. (*c*)	7. (*d*)	8. (*d*)	9. (*d*)	10. (*d*)
11. (*d*)	12. (*b*)	13. (*d*)	14. (*c*)	15. (*d*)
16. (*c*)	17. (*c*)	18. (*a*)	19. (*b*)	20. (*a*)
21. (*c*)	22. (*a*)	23. (*b*)	24. (*c*)	25. (*b*)
26. (*d*)	27. (*c*)	28. (*d*)	29. (*a*)	30. (*d*)
31. (*a*)	32. (*c*)	33. (*d*)	34. (*b*)	35. (*b*)
36. (*b*)	37. (*a*)	38. (*b*)	39. (*d*)	40. (*c*)
41. (*a*)	42. (*c*)	43. (*c*)	44. (*d*)	45. (*c*)
46. (*d*)	47. (*c*)	48. (*d*)	49. (*a*)	50. (*c*)
51. (*d*)	52. (*d*)	53. (*d*)	54. (*d*)	55. (*b*)
56. (*c*)	57. (*c*)	58. (*c*)	59. (*b*)	60. (*c*)
61. (*b*)	62. (*a*)	63. (*c*)	64. (*c*)	65. (*c*)
66. (*d*)	67. (*d*)	68. (*c*)	69. (*b*)	70. (*d*)
71. (*d*)	72. (*d*)	73. (*d*)	74. (*b*)	75. (*d*)
76. (*b*)	77. (*c*)	78. (*c*)	79. (*b*)	80. (*b*)
81. (*c*)	82. (*c*)	83. (*c*)	84. (*a*)	85. (*b*)

8

Directive Principles of State Policy

1. Which of the following statements about a uniform civil code is/are correct?
   1. It is binding on the State that a uniform civil code must be made applicable to all.
   2. The provision regarding a uniform civil code is contained in Part III of the Constitution.

   Select the correct answer using the codes given below:

   (*a*) 1 only (*b*) 2 only
   (*c*) Both 1 and 2 (*d*) Neither 1 nor 2

2. Directive Principles of State Policy direct the State for which of the following?
   1. To secure a social order for the promotion of welfare of the people
   2. To separate judiciary from executive
   3. To improve public health

   Select the correct answer using the codes given below:

   (*a*) 1 and 2 only (*b*) 2 and 3 only
   (*c*) 1 and 3 only (*d*) 1, 2 and 3

3. Consider the following statements:

   Directive Principles of State Policy are:
   1. Directives in the nature of ideals of the state
   2. Directives influencing and shaping the policy of State
   3. Non-justiciable rights of the citizens

   Which of the statements given above is/are correct?

   (*a*) 1 only (*b*) 2 and 3 only
   (*c*) 3 only (*d*) 1, 2 and 3

4. Which of the following statements about the changes made by the 42nd Amendment to the Constitution relating to the Directive Principles of State Policy are correct?
   1. It enabled State to provide free legal aid to its citizens.
   2. It provided for the State to secure the participation of workers in the management of undertakings.
   3. It required the state to minimise inequalities in income and status.

   Select the correct answer using the codes given below:

   (*a*) 1 and 2 only (*b*) 1 and 3 only
   (*c*) 2 and 3 only (*d*) 1, 2 and 3

5. Which one of the following is the real guiding factor for the State to meet social needs and for the establishment of new social order?
   (*a*) Fundamental Rights
   (*b*) Preamble of the Constitution
   (*c*) Directive Principles of State Policy
   (*d*) Distribution of Powers

6. Which one of the following is not stated as a Directive Principle of State Policy in the Constitution of India?
   (*a*) Organisation of village panchayats
   (*b*) Uniform civil code for the citizens
   (*c*) Separation of Judiciary from Executive
   (*d*) Right of minorities to establish and administer educational institutions

7. Which of the following Directive Principles of State Policy are socialistic principles?
   1. To secure equal pay for equal work for men and women.
   2. To provide equal justice and to provide free legal aid to the poor.
   3. To organise agriculture and animal husbandry on modern and scientific lines.

   Select the correct answer using the codes given below:

   (*a*) 1 and 2 only (*b*) 2 and 3 only
   (*c*) 1 and 3 only (*d*) 1, 2 and 3

8. Though the Directive Principles of State Policy contained in the Constitution are not enforceable by any court, yet they are:
   (*a*) Fundamental in the governance of the country
   (*b*) Binding on the State
   (*c*) Enforceable at the instance of the President of India
   (*d*) Superior to Fundamental Rights

9. Which of the following are included in the Directive Principles of State Policy in the Constitution of India?
   1. Uniform civil code for the citizens
   2. Separation of judiciary from executive
   3. Protection of monuments of national importance

   Select the correct answer by using the codes given below:

   (*a*) 1 and 2 only (*b*) 2 and 3 only
   (*c*) 1 and 3 only (*d*) 1, 2 and 3

10. With respect to the Directive Principles of State Policy, which one of the following pairs is not correctly matched?
    (*a*) To secure just and humane conditions of work and maternity relief : Article 42
    (*b*) To organise village Panchayats as units of self-government : Article 40
    (*c*) To secure the improvement of public health and the prohibition of intoxicating drinks and of drugs which are injurious to health : Article 47
    (*d*) To protect all monuments of historic interest and national importance : Article 50

11. Which one of the following is not a Directive Principle of State Policy?
    (*a*) The State shall endeavour to secure for the citizens a uniform civil code.
    (*b*) The State shall promote with special care the educational and economic interest of the weaker sections.
    (*c*) The State shall endeavour to promote adult education to eliminate illiteracy.
    (*d*) The State shall endeavour to protect every monument, place or object of artistic or historic interest.

12. Which one of the following is not the objective of the Directive Principles of State Policy?
    (*a*) To establish a welfare state
    (*b*) To ensure socio-economic justice
    (*c*) To establish a religious state
    (*d*) To establish a secular state

13. Which of the following Directive Principles of State Policy are Liberal-Intellectual principles?
    1. To separate the judiciary from the executive in the public services of the state.
    2. To make provision for just and humane conditions of work and maternity relief.
    3. To secure for all citizens a uniform civil code throughout the country.

    Select the correct answer by using the codes given below:
    (*a*) 1 and 2 only
    (*b*) 2 and 3 only
    (*c*) 1 and 3 only
    (*d*) 1, 2 and 3

14. Which one of the following is a correct statement?
    (*a*) Primacy is given to all the Directive Principles contained in Part IV of the Constitution over Fundamental Rights.
    (*b*) Primacy is given to all the Fundamental Rights conferred by Article 14-32 of the Constitution over Directive Principles.
    (*c*) Primacy is given to all the Fundamental Rights conferred by the Part III of the Constitution over Directive Principles.
    (*d*) Primacy is given only to Directive Principles in the clauses (*b*) and (c) of Article 39 over Fundamental Rights conferred by Articles 14 and 19 of the Constitution.

15. Which one of the following Directive Principles was not originally provided for in the Constitution of India?
    (*a*) Citizen's right to an adequate means of livelihood
    (*b*) Free legal aid
    (*c*) Uniform civil code for the citizens
    (*d*) Prohibition of the slaughter of cows and calves

16. The term "equal pay for equal work" is a:
    (*a*) Directive Principle of State Policy
    (*b*) Fundamental Right
    (*c*) Fundamental Duty
    (*d*) Constitutional Right

17. From which of the following constitutions, the framers of the Indian Constitution have borrowed the Directive Principles of State Policy?
    (*a*) Spanish Constitution
    (*b*) American Constitution
    (*c*) Irish Constitution
    (*d*) French Constitution

18. Which one of the following is not a Directive Principle of State Policy?
    (*a*) Organisation of Village Panchayats
    (*b*) Uniform Civil Code for citizens as well as non-citizens
    (*c*) Right to work, to education and to public assistance in certain cases
    (*d*) Participation of workers in management of industries

19. "Directive Principles of State Policy are the conscience of the Constitution which embody the social philosophy of the Constitution" was described by:
    (*a*) Granville Austin (*b*) A.V. Dicey
    (*c*) Dr. B.R. Ambedkar (*d*) K.C. Wheare

20. Which part of the Constitution of India refers to the responsibility of the state towards international peace and security?
    (*a*) Fundamental Rights (*b*) Directive Principles of State Policy
    (*c*) Emergency Provisions (*d*) Preamble to the Constitution

21. Which of the following statements is/are correct?
    1. 42nd Amendment to the Constitution of India gave primacy to Directive Principles over Fundamental Rights.
    2. Minerva Mills case ruled that there has to be a balance between Part III and Part IV of the Constitution.
    3. National Commission for Review of the Working of the Constitution has recommended that Directive Principles be made justiciable.

    Select the correct answer using the codes given below:
    (*a*) 1 and 2 only (*b*) 2 and 3 only
    (*c*) 1 and 3 only (*d*) 2 only

22. Which of the following Directive Principles of State Policy was added by the 44th Amendment Act, 1978?
    (*a*) To protect and improve the environment and to safeguard forests and wildlife.
    (*b*) To minimise inequalities in income, studies, facilities and opportunities.
    (*c*) To secure opportunities for healthy development of children.
    (*d*) To provide early childhood care and education for all children until they complete the age of six years.

23. Which of the following is/are among Directive Principles of State Policy?
    1. The State shall strive to promote science and technology for development.
    2. The State shall endeavour to secure for citizens a Uniform Civil Code throughout India.
    3. The State shall try to develop population policy and family planning programmes.
    4. The State shall take steps to promote tourism.

    Select the correct answer using the codes given below:
    (*a*) 1 and 3 only (*b*) 2 and 4 only
    (*c*) 2 only (*d*) 1, 2, 3 and 4

24. The Directive Principles of State Policy are fundamental for the:
(*a*) Upliftment of backward classes
(*b*) Protection of individual rights
(*c*) Administration of justice
(*d*) Governance of state

25. Who of the following contended that the Directive Principles are "no better than the new year's resolutions, which are broken on the second of January"?
(*a*) K.C. Wheare
(*b*) Nasiruddin
(*c*) K.T. Shah
(*d*) T.T. Krishnamachari

26. Which one of the following statements regarding the current status of the relationship between Fundamental Rights and Directive Principles is correct?
(*a*) Directive Principles cannot get priority over Fundamental Rights in any case.
(*b*) Directive Principles always get priority over Fundamental Rights.
(*c*) Fundamental Rights always get priority over Directives Principles.
(*d*) In some cases, Directive Principles may get priority over Fundamental Rights.

27. Right to work in India is a:
(*a*) Fundamental right
(*b*) Directive principle
(*c*) Constitutional right
(*d*) Constitutional duty

28. Which of the following Directive Principles of State Policy are Gandhian Principles?
1. To protect and improve the environment and to safeguard forests and wildlife.
2. To promote cottage industries on an individual or co-operation basis in rural areas.
3. To promote the educational and economic interests of SCs, STs and Other Weaker Sections.

Select the correct answer by using the codes given below:
(*a*) 1 and 2 only
(*b*) 2 and 3 only
(*c*) 1 and 3 only
(*d*) 1, 2 and 3

29. Consider the following statements:
Directive Principles of State Policy are:
1. Not amendable
2. Not enforceable by any court
3. Fundamental in the governance of the country

Which of the statements given above are correct?
(*a*) 1 and 2 only
(*b*) 1 and 3 only
(*c*) 2 and 3 only
(*d*) 1, 2 and 3

30. The "Instrument of Instructions" contained in the Government of India Act, 1935, has been incorporated in the Constitution of India in the year 1950 as:
(*a*) Fundamental Rights
(*b*) Directive Principles of State Policy
(*c*) Fundamental Duties
(*d*) Emergency Provisions

31. Which one of the following is not a correct description of the Directive Principles of State Policy?
    (*a*) Directive Principles are not enforceable by the courts.
    (*b*) Directive Principles have a political sanction.
    (*c*) Directive Principles are declaration of objectives for State Legislation.
    (*d*) Directive Principles promise equal income and free healthcare for all Indians.

32. Consider the following statements:
    1. Article 46 of the Constitution of India provides for free legal aid to Scheduled Castes and Scheduled Tribes.
    2. Article 44 of the Constitution of India provides for promotion of cottage industries.

    Which of the statements given above is/are correct?
    (*a*) 1 only (*b*) 2 only
    (*c*) Both 1 and 2 (*d*) Neither 1 nor 2

Answers

1. (*d*)	2. (*d*)	3. (*d*)	4. (*a*)	5. (*c*)
6. (*d*)	7. (*a*)	8. (*a*)	9. (*d*)	10. (*d*)
11. (*c*)	12. (*c*)	13. (*c*)	14. (*d*)	15. (*b*)
16. (*a*)	17. (*c*)	18. (*b*)	19. (*a*)	20. (*b*)
21. (*a*)	22. (*b*)	23. (*c*)	24. (*d*)	25. (*b*)
26. (*d*)	27. (*b*)	28. (*b*)	29. (*c*)	30. (*b*)
31. (*d*)	32. (*d*)			

9

Fundamental Duties

1. Which of the following are Fundamental Duties of an Indian citizen according to Article 51A of the Constitution?
   1. To believe in socialism, secularism and democracy
   2. To abide by the Constitution and respect the National Flag and the National Anthem
   3. To protect the sovereignty, unity and integrity of India
   4. To preserve the rich heritage of the country's composite culture
   5. To help the poor and weaker sections of the society

   Select the correct answer using the codes given below:

   (*a*) 1, 2 and 3 (*b*) 2, 3 and 4
   (*c*) 3, 4 and 5 (*d*) 1, 4 and 5

2. Which of the following statements regarding the Fundamental Duties contained in the Indian Constitution are correct?
   1. Fundamental Duties can be enforced through writ jurisdiction.
   2. Fundamental Duties have formed a part of the Indian Constitution since its adoption.
   3. Fundamental Duties became a part of the Constitution in accordance with the recommendations of the Swaran Singh Committee.
   4. Fundamental Duties are applicable only to the citizens of India.

   Select the correct answer using the codes given below:

   (*a*) 1, 2 and 3
   (*b*) 1, 2 and 4
   (*c*) 2 and 3 only
   (*d*) 3 and 4 only

3. Which of the following duties have been prescribed by the Indian Constitution as the Fundamental Duties?
   1. To defend the country
   2. To pay income tax
   3. To preserve the rich heritage of our composite culture
   4. To safeguard public property

   Select the correct answer using the codes given below:

   (*a*) 1 and 2 only (*b*) 2 and 4 only
   (*c*) 1, 2 and 4 (*d*) 1, 3 and 4

4. Which of the following is a fundamental duty of every citizen of India?
   (*a*) To be truthful to one's duties
   (*b*) To renounce practices derogatory to the dignity of children
   (*c*) To renounce practices derogatory to the dignity of human beings
   (*d*) To renounce practices derogatory to the dignity of women

5. The Fundamental Duties are intended to serve as a reminder to:
   (*a*) The State to perform duties conferred by the Constitution
   (*b*) The judiciary to administer justice properly
   (*c*) Every citizen to observe basic norms of democratic conduct
   (*d*) The Legislature to make laws for the welfare of the people

6. Which of the following are included in the list of Fundamental Duties in the Constitution?
   1. To abide by the Constitution and respect its ideals and institutions
   2. To safeguard public property and to abjure violence
   3. To uphold and protect the sovereignty, unity and integrity of India
   4. To uphold and protect secularism

   Select the correct answer using the codes given below:

   (*a*) 1, 3 and 4 (*b*) 1, 2 and 4
   (*c*) 2, 3 and 4 (*d*) 1, 2 and 3

7. Respect for the National Flag and the National Anthem is:
   (*a*) A Fundamental Right of every citizen
   (*b*) A Fundamental Duty of every citizen
   (*c*) A Directive Principle of state policy
   (*d*) An ordinary duty of every citizen

8. Consider the following statements:

   The Fundamental Duties provided in the constitution are:
   1. To protect the sovereignty, unity and integrity of India
   2. To safeguard private property
   3. To protect and improve the natural environment including forests, lakes, rivers and wildlife

   Which of the statements given above are correct?

   (*a*) 1, 2 and 3 (*b*) 1 and 2 only
   (*c*) 2 and 3 only (*d*) 1 and 3 only

9. Fundamental Duties have been added in the Constitution by 42nd Amendment Act, 1976, in accordance with the recommendations of:
   (*a*) Santhannam Committee
   (*b*) Sarkaria Committee
   (*c*) Swaran Singh Committee
   (*d*) Indira Gandhi-Nehru Committee

10. Which one of the following has not been enumerated in the Constitution of India as being amongst the Fundamental Duties of the citizens?
    (*a*) To value and preserve the rich heritage of our composite culture
    (*b*) To safeguard public property and to abjure violence
    (*c*) To develop the scientific temper, humanism and the spirit of inquiry and reform
    (*d*) To secure a social order for the promotion of welfare of the people

11. Which one of the following is not a fundamental duty?
    (*a*) To respect the National Anthem
    (*b*) To safeguard public property
    (*c*) To protect monuments and places of national importance
    (*d*) To protect and improve the natural environment

12. Consider the following statements:

    Fundamental Duties:
    1. Have always been a part of the Constitution of India
    2. Have been added through an amendment
    3. Are mandatory on all citizens of India

    Which of the statements given above is/are correct?
    (*a*) 1 and 3 only (*b*) 1 only
    (*c*) 2 only (*d*) 2 and 3 only

13. Which one of the following is not a fundamental duty under Article 51A of the Constitution of India?
    (*a*) To render national service when called upon to do so
    (*b*) To cast vote in the elections
    (*c*) To strive for excellence
    (*d*) To develop scientific temper

14. Following duties have been prescribed for the State and the citizens:
    1. To develop scientific temper
    2. To promote common brotherhood
    3. To organise village panchayats
    4. To minimise the inequalities in income
    5. To secure a uniform civil code
    6. To defend the country

    Among these, the Fundamental Duties of the citizens would include:
    (*a*) 1, 3 and 4 (*b*) 3, 4 and 5
    (*c*) 1, 2 and 6 (*d*) 2, 5 and 6

15. Which one of the following is not included as a Fundamental Duty in the Constitution of India?
    (*a*) To cherish and follow the noble ideals which inspired our national struggle
    (*b*) To develop the scientific temper, humanism and the spirit of inquiry and reform
    (*c*) To protect the minorities
    (*d*) To safeguard public property and to abjure violence

16. Protection of lakes is an objective expressly stated in which one of the following?
    (*a*) Fundamental Duties (*b*) Directive Principles of State Policy
    (*c*) Fundamental Rights (*d*) Eleventh Schedule to the Constitution

17. In which of the following years, the Fundamental Duties have been added in the Constitution of India?
    (*a*) 1965 (*b*) 1976
    (*c*) 1979 (*d*) 1982

18. Which of the following Articles of the Constitution of India relate to the protection and improvement of environment?
    (*a*) Article 48A only (*b*) Article 51A only
    (*c*) Both Article 48A and Article 51A (*d*) Neither Article 48A nor Article 51A

19. Consider the following statements:
    1. The 86th Amendment Act, 2002 has included the duty of every citizen of India to provide opportunities for education to his child or ward between the age of six and fourteen years.
    2. The Verma Committee on Fundamental Duties of the Citizen, 1999, has not identified the existence of legal provisions for the implementation of some of the Fundamental Duties.

    Which of the statements given below is/are correct?
    (*a*) 1 only (*b*) 2 only
    (*c*) Both 1 and 2 (*d*) Neither 1 nor 2

20. The Fundamental Duties in the India Constitution are inspired by the Constitution of:
    (*a*) Japan (*b*) Australia
    (*c*) Erstwhile USSR (*d*) Canada

Answers

1. (*b*)	2. (*d*)	3. (*d*)	4. (*d*)	5. (*c*)
6. (*d*)	7. (*b*)	8. (*d*)	9. (*c*)	10. (*d*)
11. (*c*)	12. (*c*)	13. (*b*)	14. (*c*)	15. (*c*)
16. (*a*)	17. (*b*)	18. (*c*)	19. (*a*)	20. (*c*)

10

Amendment of the Constitution

1. Consider the following statements:
   1. An amendment of the Constitution of India can be initiated by the introduction of a Bill only in the Lok Sabha.
   2. The Bill for amendment of the Constitution of India has to be passed in each House by a majority of the total membership of that House and by a majority of not less than two-thirds of the members of that House present and voting.

   Which of the statements given above is/are correct?

   (*a*) 1 only (*b*) 2 only
   (*c*) Both 1 and 2 (*d*) Neither 1 nor 2

2. If an amendment of the Constitution of India seeks to make any change in certain items, the amendment requires to be ratified by the Legislatures of not less than one-half of the States before the Bill making provision for such amendment is presented to the President for assent. Which of the following are those items?
   1. Representation of States in the Parliament
   2. Any of the Lists in the Seventh Schedule
   3. Manner of election of the President of India

   Select the correct answer using the codes given below:

   (*a*) 1 and 2 only
   (*b*) 2 and 3 only
   (*c*) 1 and 3 only
   (*d*) 1, 2 and 3

3. Restriction of the writ jurisdiction of the High Courts under Article 226 of the Constitution is possible through:

   (*a*) An amendment of the Constitution passed by two-thirds majority of members present and voting and a majority of the total membership of each House of the Parliament.
   (*b*) An amendment of the Constitution passed by a simple majority of members present and voting in both Houses of the Parliament.
   (*c*) An amendment of the Constitution passed by two-thirds majority of members present and voting and a majority of the total membership of each House of the Parliament together with the ratification of half of the State Legislatures.
   (*d*) An amendment of the Constitution passed by two-thirds majority of members present and voting and a majority of the total membership of each House of the Parliament together with the ratification of three quarters of the State Legislatures.

4. On receipt of a constitutional amendment bill, after passing by each House of Parliament, the President:
   (*a*) Shall give his assent
   (*b*) May give his assent
   (*c*) May withhold his assent
   (*d*) May return the bill for reconsideration

5. Which of the following are matters on which the Parliament has the power to modify provisions of the constitution by a simple majority?
   1. Alternation of names, boundaries and areas of States
   2. Appointment of additional judges
   3. Abolition of the second chamber of a State Legislature
   4. Administration of Scheduled Areas

   Select the correct answer using the codes given below:
   (*a*) 1, 2 and 3 (*b*) 1, 2 and 4
   (*c*) 1, 3 and 4 (*d*) 2, 3 and 4

6. The constituent power of the Parliament to amend the Constitution:
   (*a*) Includes power to amend by way of addition, variation or repeal of the provision of the Constitution
   (*b*) Is unrestricted by any inherent and implied limitations
   (*c*) Is not procedurally limited and restricted
   (*d*) Is extra-constituent

7. A change in which of the following does not require ratification by the Legislatures of not less than one-half of the states by resolutions to that effect passed by those Legislatures before the Bill making provisions for an amendment in the Constitution of India is presented to the President for assent?
   (*a*) Any of the lists in the Seventh Schedule
   (*b*) The provisions of Article 368
   (*c*) Article 73 about extent of executive power of the Union
   (*d*) Article 161 about power of Governor to grant pardon

8. Which of the following features are present in the Indian Constitution?
   1. Multiple procedures for amendment
   2. States are not empowered to initiate amendment
   3. Joint-sittings of the Parliament to resolve disputes regarding constitutional amendments.

   Select the correct answer from the codes given below:
   (*a*) 1 and 3 only (*b*) 1 and 2 only
   (*c*) 2 and 3 only (*d*) 1, 2 and 3

9. A constitutional amendment shall also be ratified by Legislatures of not less than one-half of the States by a resolution if it is meant to make any change in:
   (*a*) Fundamental Rights (*b*) Directive Principles
   (*c*) Fundamental Duties (*d*) High Court Provisions

10. An amendment of the Constitution of India for the purpose of creating a new state must be passed by:
   (*a*) Simple majority in the Parliament
   (*b*) A simple majority in the Parliament and ratification by not less than half of the states
   (*c*) Two-thirds majority in the Parliament and ratification by not less than two-thirds of the states
   (*d*) Two-thirds of the members of both Houses of the Parliament present and voting

11. The provision of Article 368 of the Constitution of India deals with:
   (*a*) Power of the Parliament to amend the Constitution
   (*b*) Procedure for amendment of the Constitution to be followed by the Parliament
   (*c*) Power as well as procedure for amendment of the Constitution
   (*d*) Passing and ratification of amendment Bills by State Legislatures

12. How can an amendment in a list in the Seventh Schedule of the Constitution of India be initiated?

   If the Bill seeking amendment is passed in either House of the Parliament by:
   (*a*) A majority of the total membership of that House.
   (*b*) A majority of the total membership of that House and by a majority of not less than two-thirds of the members of that House present and voting.
   (*c*) A majority of the total membership of that House and by a majority of not less than two-thirds of the members of that House present and voting and the amendment shall also require to be ratified by the Legislatures of not less than one-half of the States.
   (*d*) A majority of the total membership of that House and by a majority of not less than two-thirds of the members of that House present and voting and the amendment shall also require to be ratified by the Legislatures of not less than two-thirds of the States.

13. Amendment of which one of the following provisions of the Constitution requires ratification by the Legislatures of the States?
   (*a*) Article 157 relating to the qualifications for appointment as Governor of the State.
   (*b*) Article 123 relating to the powers of the President to promulgate ordinances on a subject mentioned in Concurrent List during the recess of the Parliament.
   (*c*) Article 56 relating to the term of the office of the President.
   (*d*) Article 54 relating to the election of the President.

14. Consider the following statements related to Article 368 of the Constitution:
   1. A constitutional amendment bill can be passed at a joint session of the Parliament in case of deadlock between the two Houses.
   2. It is obligatory for the President of India to give his assent to a constitutional amendment bill passed under Article 368.
   3. To amend 7th Schedule of the Constitution, ratification of more than half of the State Legislatures is essential.
   4. A proposal to amend the Constitution can only be introduced in the House of the People.

   Which of the statements given above are correct?

   (*a*) 1 and 2 only (*b*) 1 and 3 only
   (*c*) 2 and 3 only (*d*) 1, 2 and 3

15. Consider the following statements:
    1. The provisions of the Constitution relating to the Goods and Services Tax Council can be amended by a special majority of the Parliament.
    2. The Part XXI of the Constitution deals with the powers of the Parliament to amend the Constitution and its procedure.

    Which of the statements given above is/are correct?

    (*a*) 1 only (*b*) 2 only
    (*c*) Both 1 and 2 (*d*) Neither 1 nor 2

Answers

1. (*b*)	2. (*d*)	3. (*c*)	4. (*a*)	5. (*c*)
6. (*a*)	7. (*d*)	8. (*b*)	9. (*d*)	10. (*a*)
11. (*c*)	12. (*c*)	13. (*d*)	14. (*c*)	15. (*d*)

11 Basic Structure of the Constitution

1. Which of the following are considered as the parts of the basic structure of the Indian Constitution?
   1. Republication and democratic form of Government
   2. Secular character of the Constitution
   3. Division between Fundamental Rights and Directive Principles of State Policy
   4. Federal character of the Constitution

   Select the correct answer using the codes given below:

   (*a*) 1, 2 and 3 (*b*) 2, 3 and 4
   (*c*) 1, 3 and 4 (*d*) 1, 2 and 4

2. Consider the following statements:
   1. The doctrine of basic structure of the Constitution was reaffirmed and applied by the Supreme Court in the Indira Nehru Gandhi case (1975).
   2. In this case, the Supreme Court invalidated a provision of the 39th Amendment Act (1975) which kept the election disputes involving the Prime Minister and the Speaker of Lok Sabha outside the jurisdiction of all courts.

   Which of the statements given above is/are correct?

   (*a*) 1 only (*b*) 2 only
   (*c*) Both 1 and 2 (*d*) Neither 1 nor 2

3. Which one of the following is the correct statement?

   The power of the Parliament to amend the Constitution of India as a constitutional power was laid down under Article 368 by:

   (*a*) The Constitution (First Amendment) Act, 1951
   (*b*) The Constitution (Twenty-fourth Amendment) Act, 1971
   (*c*) The Constitution (Twenty-sixth Amendment) Act, 1971
   (*d*) The Constitution (Forty-second Amendment) Act, 1976

4. In which case did the Supreme Court pronounce the judgement for the first time that the "basic structure" of the Constitution cannot be amended by the Parliament?

   (*a*) Shankari Prasad case
   (*b*) Golaknath case

(*c*) Kesavananda Bharati case
(*d*) Minerva Mills case

5. Which one of the following statements is correct?
(*a*) The Constitution clearly lays down what its basic structure is
(*b*) The Supreme Court has elaborately defined the basic structure of the Constitution
(*c*) The Law Commission of India with the help of Attorney-General of India has defined the basic structure of the Constitution
(*d*) Neither the Supreme Court nor the Parliament have defined the basic structure of the Constitution

6. Which one of the following amendments inserted provision saying that "Nothing in Article 13 shall apply to any amendments made under Article 368?"
(*a*) Forty-second Amendment Act
(*b*) Forty-fourth Amendment Act
(*c*) Twenty-fourth Amendment Act
(*d*) Twenty-second Amendment Act

7. Under Article 368, the Parliament has no power to repeal Fundamental Rights because these are:
(*a*) Enshrined in Part III of the Constitution
(*b*) Human Rights
(*c*) Transcendental Rights
(*d*) Part of basic structure of the Constitution

8. Which one of the following cases prompted the Parliament to enact 24th Constitutional Amendment Act?
(*a*) Golaknath case
(*b*) Shankari Prasad case
(*c*) Kesavananda Bharati case
(*d*) Minerva Mills case

9. Which of the following are regarded as "basic features" of the Constitution?
1. Powers of the High Courts under Articles 226 and 227
2. Powers of the Supreme Court under Articles 32, 136, 141 and 142
3. Principles (or essence) underlying the Fundamental Rights
4. Effective access to justice

Select the correct answer using the codes given below:
(*a*) 1 and 2 only
(*b*) 3 and 4 only
(*c*) 2 and 3 only
(*d*) 1, 2, 3 and 4

10. The Supreme Court invalidated a provision of the 42nd Amendment Act, which enlarged the scope of Article 368 to amend the Fundamental Rights on the ground that the:
    (*a*) Requisite number of States had not ratified the amendment
    (*b*) Amendment has been enacted during the emergency
    (*c*) Amendment abrogated a basic feature of the Constitution
    (*d*) Rajya Sabha had not passed the amendment with the prescribed majority

Answers

1. (*d*)	2. (*c*)	3. (*b*)	4. (*c*)	5. (*d*)
6. (*c*)	7. (*d*)	8. (*a*)	9. (*d*)	10. (*c*)

PART-II
SYSTEM OF GOVERNMENT

12. Parliamentary System
13. Federal System
14. Centre–State Relations
15. Inter-State Relations
16. Emergency Provisions

12

Parliamentary System

1. Which of the following are the principles on the basis of which the parliamentary system of government in India operates?
   1. Nominal Executive Head
   2. Vice-President as the Chairman of the Upper House
   3. Real executive authority with the Council of Ministers
   4. Executive responsibility to the Lower House

   Choose the correct answer from the codes given below:

   (*a*) 1, 2 and 3 (*b*) 1, 2 and 4
   (*c*) 1, 3 and 4 (*d*) 2, 3 and 4

2. The Constitution of India establishes parliamentary form of government and the essence of this form of government is its responsibility to the:
   (*a*) People of India
   (*b*) President
   (*c*) Prime Minister
   (*d*) Legislature

3. Under a cabinet form of government, the cabinet generally remains in office:
   (*a*) For a fixed term
   (*b*) So long as it enjoys the confidence of the popular chamber of Legislature
   (*c*) So long as it enjoys the confidence of the head of state
   (*d*) So long as it enjoys the confidence of the electorate

4. In the parliamentary form of government, the members of the Council of Ministers are collectively responsible to:
   (*a*) The Head of State
   (*b*) The Chairman of the Upper House and the Speaker of the Lower House
   (*c*) The popular House of the Parliament
   (*d*) The Prime Minister

5. The separation of powers is the characteristic of:
   (*a*) Parliamentary Government
   (*b*) Presidential Government
   (*c*) Federal System
   (*d*) Unitary System

6. Which of the following are the merits of the parliamentary system?
   1. Responsible government
   2. Wide representation
   3. Government by amateurs
   4. Prevents despotism

   Select the correct answer using the codes given below:
   (*a*) 1 and 2 only (*b*) 2 and 3 only
   (*c*) 3 and 4 only (*d*) 1, 2 and 4

7. Which one of the following is the main principle on which the parliamentary system operates?
   (*a*) Supremacy of the Parliament
   (*b*) Responsibility of the Executive to the Legislature
   (*c*) Supremacy of the Judiciary
   (*d*) Theory of Separation of Powers

8. In a parliamentary form of government, ministers are appointed by:
   (*a*) The head of state at his discretion
   (*b*) The head of government
   (*c*) The head of state on the recommendations of the head of government
   (*d*) The Legislature

9. Which one of the following is not an essential feature of the parliamentary system?
   (*a*) Fusion of the Executive and the Legislature
   (*b*) Nominal head of state
   (*c*) Collective responsibility
   (*d*) Fixed tenure of the executive

10. Which of the following are the reasons for adopting parliamentary system of India?
    1. Preference to more responsibility
    2. Heterogeneous nature of Indian society
    3. Need to avoid legislative – executive conflicts
    4. Familiarity with the system

    Select the correct answer using the codes given below:
    (*a*) 1 and 3 only (*b*) 2 and 4 only
    (*c*) 3 and 4 only (*d*) 1, 2, 3 and 4

11. Consider the following features:
    1. Presence of a nominal or titular head of state.
    2. Collective responsibility of cabinet
    3. Accountability of the executive to the Legislature
    4. Separation of Powers

Which of these are the features of a parliamentary form of Government?

(*a*) 2, 3 and 4 (*b*) 1, 2 and 4

(*c*) 1, 3 and 4 (*d*) 1, 2 and 3

Answers

1. (*c*)	2. (*d*)	3. (*b*)	4. (*c*)	5. (*b*)
6. (*d*)	7. (*b*)	8. (*c*)	9. (*d*)	10. (*d*)
11. (*d*)				

13

Federal System

1. Which of the following federal principles are not found in Indian federation?
    1. Bifurcation of the Judiciary between the Federal and State Governments
    2. Equality of representation of the states in the Upper House of the Federal Legislature
    3. The Union cannot be destroyed by any state seceding from the Union at its will
    4. Federal Government can redraw the map of the Indian Union by forming new states

    Select the correct answer using the codes given below:

    (*a*) 1, 2 and 3 (*b*) 2, 3 and 4
    (*c*) 1 and 2 only (*d*) 3 and 4 only

2. The Constitution of India is federal in character because:
    (*a*) The Head of the State (the President) is elected by an electoral college consisting of the elected members of both the Houses of the Parliament and the elected members of the Legislative Assemblies of the States.
    (*b*) The Governors of States are appointed by the President and they hold office during the pleasure of the President.
    (*c*) There is distribution of powers between the Union and the States.
    (*d*) The amendment of the Constitution can be made only by following the procedure laid down in the Constitution and in some cases the amendment requires ratification by Legislatures of the States.

3. Which of the following are the federal features of the Indian Constitution?
    1. Independent Judiciary
    2. Written Constitution
    3. Supremacy of the Constitution
    4. Bicameral Legislature

    Select the correct answer using the codes given below:

    (*a*) 1 and 3 only (*b*) 2 and 4 only
    (*c*) 2 and 3 only (*d*) 1, 2, 3 and 4

4. In the Constitution of India, the term "Federal":
    (*a*) Figures in the Preamble
    (*b*) Figures in Part III of the Constitution
    (*c*) Figures in Article 368
    (*d*) Does not figure anywhere

5. When can the Parliament legislate on a subject in the State List?
   (*a*) If the Parliament passes a resolution to that effect in the national interest.
   (*b*) If the Supreme Court grants necessary authority to the Parliament.
   (*c*) If the Rajya Sabha passes a resolution by two-thirds majority declaring that the subject in the State List under consideration is of national importance.
   (*d*) If the President issues an ordinance transferring the subject from the State List to the Union or the Concurrent Lists.

6. The quotation, "The Indian Constitution establishes, indeed, a system of government which is at the most quasi-federal, a unitary State with subsidiary federal features rather than the Federal State with unitary features" is attributed to:
   (*a*) I. Jennings (*b*) G. Austin
   (*c*) K.C. Wheare (*d*) H.J. Laski

7. What does the term "Federation" imply?
   (*a*) Fusion of powers
   (*b*) Separation of powers
   (*c*) Division of powers
   (*d*) Devolution of powers

8. Which of the following are the unitary features of the Indian Constitution?
   1. States not indestructible
   2. No equality of state representation
   3. Emergency Provisions
   4. All-India Services

   Select the correct answer using the codes given below:
   (*a*) 1, 2, 3 and 4 (*b*) 2 and 3 only
   (*c*) 1 and 3 only (*d*) 2 and 4 only

9. The best form of federalism suited for countries like India is:
   (*a*) Centralised federalism
   (*b*) Bargaining federalism
   (*c*) Cooperative federalism
   (*d*) Conflicting federalism

10. Under the Indian Constitution, the residuary powers are vested in the:
    (*a*) Executive (*b*) Judiciary
    (*c*) Parliament (*d*) State Legislatures

11. The structure of the Indian Constitution is:
    (*a*) Federal in form and unitary in spirit
    (*b*) Unitary
    (*c*) Unitary in form and federal in spirit
    (*d*) Pure federal

12. Indian federation closely resembles:
(*a*) U.S.A. (*b*) Canada
(*c*) Australia (*d*) Nigeria

13. Consider the following statements:
1. The term "federation" is derived from a Greek word "foedus" which means "treaty" or "agreement".
2. A federation can be formed by way of integration or by way of disintegration.

Which of the statements given above is/are correct?
(*a*) 1 only (*b*) 2 only
(*c*) Both 1 and 2 (*d*) Neither 1 nor 2

14. Parliament has power to legislate with respect to a matter in the State list provided it is in the:
(*a*) National interest (*b*) Interest of the State concerned
(*c*) Interest of the public (*d*) Interest of the minority

15. The concentration of powers is an essential feature of:
(*a*) Cabinet Government (*b*) Presidential Government
(*c*) Federal Government (*d*) Unitary Government

16. Which among the following is/are the feature(s) of a Federal State?
1. The powers of the Central and the State (Constituent Unit) Governments are clearly laid down.
2. It has an unwritten constitution.

Select the correct answer using the codes given below:
(*a*) 1 only (*b*) 2 only
(*c*) Both 1 and 2 (*d*) Neither 1 nor 2

17. Which Schedule of the Constitution of India contains the three lists that divide powers between the Union and the sates?
(*a*) Fifth Schedule (*b*) Sixth Schedule
(*c*) Seventh Schedule (*d*) Eighth Schedule

18. Which one among the following pairs of level of government and legislative power is not correctly matched?
(*a*) Central Government : Union List
(*b*) Local Governments : Residuary Powers
(*c*) State Governments : State List
(*d*) Central and State Governments : Concurrent List

19. Who, among the following, expressed the view that the Indian Constitution is federal in as much as it establishes what may be called a Dual Polity?
(*a*) H.M. Seervai (*b*) K.C. Wheare
(*c*) B.R. Ambedkar (*d*) Ivor Jennings

Answers

1. (*c*)	2. (*c*)	3. (*d*)	4. (*d*)	5. (*c*)
6. (*c*)	7. (*c*)	8. (*a*)	9. (*c*)	10. (*c*)
11. (*a*)	12. (*b*)	13. (*b*)	14. (*a*)	15. (*d*)
16. (*a*)	17. (*c*)	18. (*b*)	19. (*c*)	

14

Centre-State Relations

1. Consider the following statements:
   1. For the Parliament to make laws with respect to any matter enumerated in the State List, a resolution must be passed in both the Houses of the Parliament.
   2. A resolution passed as stated above can be extended beyond one year.

   Which of the statements given above is/are correct?

   (*a*) 1 only (*b*) 2 only
   (*c*) Both 1 and 2 (*d*) Neither 1 nor 2

2. Consider the following statements:

   The Article 73 of the Constitution of India which deals with the extent of executive power of the Union, provides that:
   1. The executive power of the Union extends to all matters with respect to which the Parliament has the power to make laws.
   2. The Government of India may also exercise such authority available under any treaty.

   Which of the statements given above is/are correct?

   (*a*) 1 only (*b*) 2 only
   (*c*) Both 1 and 2 (*d*) Neither 1 nor 2

3. Consider the following statements about Union-State relations:
   1. In case of overlapping of a matter between the three kinds of subjects of legislations, predominance has been given to the Union Legislation.
   2. In the concurrent sphere, in the case of repugnancy between a Union and a State law relating to the same subject, the former prevails, even if the State law was reserved for the assent of the President and has received such assent.
   3. The vesting of residual power under the Indian Constitution follows the precedent of Canada and not that of the Government of India Act, 1935.

   Which of the statements given above is/are correct?

   (*a*) 1 and 2 only (*b*) 1 and 3 only
   (*c*) 2 and 3 only (*d*) 1, 2 and 3

4. Consider the following statements:
   1. With the consent of the Government of India, the Governor of a State may entrust on the Union Government or to its officers functions relating to a State subject, to which executive power of that State extends.

2. The President of India cannot entrust to any State Government or to its officers, functions in relation to any matter to which the executive power of the Union extends.
3. There is a provision in the Constitution of India to create the National Integration Council.

Which of the statements given above is/are correct?

(*a*) 1, 2 and 3 (*b*) 2 and 3 only
(*c*) 1 and 3 only (*d*) 1 only

5. What is the implication of the Union Government giving "Special Status" to a State?
   (*a*) Subsequently large percentage of the Central assistance will be grants-in-aid.
   (*b*) Current account budgetary deficit will be bridged by the Union Government.
   (*c*) The extent of loan as a percentage of total assistance will be high.
   (*d*) The Union Government meets entire expenditure of the State during the period of "Special Status".

6. Who, among the following, can establish additional courts for better administration of any existing law with respect to a matter contained in the Union List?
   (*a*) Parliament by law
   (*b*) Parliament with the consent of states
   (*c*) Union Government by resolution
   (*d*) Supreme Court of India

7. Consider the following statements:
   1. The Parliament and the State Legislature have power to make laws with respect to Goods and Services Tax imposed by the Union or by the State.
   2. The Parliament has exclusive power to make laws with respect to Goods and Services Tax where the supply of goods or services or both takes place in the course of inter-state trade or commerce.

   Which of the statements given above is/are correct?

   (*a*) 1 only (*b*) 2 only
   (*c*) Both 1 and 2 (*d*) Neither 1 nor 2

8. Consider the following statements:
   1. Parliament shall, while a Proclamation Emergency is in operation, have the power to make laws for the whole or any part of territory of India with respect to any of the matters enumerated in the State List.
   2. Parliament has exclusive power to make any law with respect to any matter not enumerated in the Concurrent List or State List.
   3. Parliament has power to make any law for the whole or any part of the territory of India for implementing any treaty, agreement or convention with any other country.
   4. Parliament has power to legislate with respect to a matter in the State List in the national interest subject to the resolution passed by the Council of States by two-thirds majority.

   Which of the statements given above are correct?

   (*a*) 1, 2 and 3 (*b*) 1, 2, 3 and 4
   (*c*) 1, 3 and 4 (*d*) 2 and 4 only

9. A law made by the Parliament having extra-territorial operation shall:
   (*a*) not be deemed invalid (*b*) be deemed invalid
   (*c*) be deemed ultra vires (*d*) be deemed unconstitutional

10. Which of the following is not a principal source of non-tax revenue of the Union?
    (*a*) Posts and Telegraphs (*b*) Broadcasting
    (*c*) Forests (*d*) Opium

11. The taxes on the consignment of goods in the course of inter-state trade or commerce belongs to which of the following category?
    (*a*) Taxes levied by the Union but collected and appropriated by the states
    (*b*) Taxes levied, collected and retained by the states
    (*c*) Taxes levied and collected by the Centre but assigned to the states
    (*d*) Taxes levied and collected by the Centre and distributed between the union and the states

12. If any directions are issued by the Union Government to a State and they have not been complied with, then which one of the following statements is correct?
    (*a*) It shall be presumed that the constitutional machinery in the State had failed as per Article 365 of the Constitution.
    (*b*) It shall be presumed that the State had law and order problem and action under Article 365 is required.
    (*c*) The Union Government can appoint advisers to help the Governor for performing his functions.
    (*d*) The Parliament may make laws for that State.

13. Which one of the following is the correct statement?
    A resolution passed by the Council of States under Article 249 empowering the Parliament to legislate on State subjects in national interest remains in force for a period:
    (*a*) Not exceeding six months
    (*b*) Not exceeding two years
    (*c*) Not exceeding one year
    (*d*) Of unlimited time

14. Which of the following statements regarding the residuary powers in the Constitution of India are correct?
    1. Residuary powers have been given to the Union Parliament.
    2. In the matter of residuary powers, the Constitution of India follows the Constitution of Australia.
    3. The final authority to decide whether a particular matter falls under the residuary power or not is the Parliament.
    4. The Government of India Act, 1935 placed residuary powers in the hands of the Governor-General.

    Select the correct answer using the codes given below:
    (*a*) 1, 2 and 3 (*b*) 2 and 3 only
    (*c*) 1 and 4 only (*d*) 3 and 4 only

15. Consider the following statements:
    1. There are no tax entries in the Concurrent List.
    2. The 101st Amendment Act, 2016 has conferred concurrent power upon the Parliament and the State Legislatures to make laws governing Goods and Services Tax.

    Which of the statements given above is/are correct?

    (*a*) 1 only (*b*) 2 only
    (*c*) Both 1 and 2 (*d*) Neither 1 nor 2

16. Which of the following is/are correctly matched?

1. Duty levied by the Union but collected and appropriated by the States	:	Succession duty and estate duty in respect of property other than agricultural land
2. Taxes levied and collected by the Union but assigned to the States	:	Stamp duties on bills of exchange, cheques, promissory notes and others

    Choose the correct answer from the codes given below:

    (*a*) 1 only (*b*) 2 only
    (*c*) Both 1 and 2 (*d*) Neither 1 nor 2

17. Which of the following constitutional provisions facilitate Union control over States?
    1. All-India services
    2. Grants-in-aid
    3. Inter-State Councils

    Select the correct answer using the codes given below:

    (*a*) 1 and 2 only (*b*) 2 and 3 only
    (*c*) 1 and 3 only (*d*) 1, 2 and 3

18. The idea of the Union giving directions to the States was adopted by the makers of the Indian Constitution from:
    (*a*) The Government of India Act, 1935
    (*b*) The US Constitution
    (*c*) The Soviet Constitution
    (*d*) The Australian Constitution

19. Which one of the following statements is not correct?
    (*a*) Parliament has exclusive power to make law on any matter in the Union List.
    (*b*) Parliament and State Legislatures both have power to make law on any matter in the Concurrent List.
    (*c*) In certain exceptional circumstances, State Legislatures can make law on a subject given in the Union List.
    (*d*) Parliament can make law on State subjects in certain circumstances.

20. Consider the following statements:
    1. The Parliament has power to make laws with respect to any matter for any part of the territory of India not included in a Sate even though that matter is one which is enumerated in the State List.

2. The above provision has reference to the Union Territories or the Acquired Territories (if any).

Which of the statements given above is/are correct?

(*a*) 1 only
(*b*) 2 only
(*c*) Both 1 and 2
(*d*) Neither 1 nor 2

21. Who among the following said, "There can be no doubt that the standard of administration depends upon the caliber of civil servants who are appointed to these strategic posts"?

(*a*) Jawaharlal Nehru
(*b*) Dr. B.R. Ambedkar
(*c*) Sardar Vallabhbhai Patel
(*d*) Warren Hastings

22. On the subject of Income Tax:

(*a*) The Union Government has more powers than State Governments.
(*b*) The State Governments have more powers than the Union Government.
(*c*) Both Union and State Governments have equal powers but Union shall prevail in case of conflict.
(*d*) Only the Union Government has power.

23. Verdicts of the Supreme Court of India in which of the following cases have a direct bearing on Centre-State relations?

1. S.R. Bommai Case
2. Kesavananda Bharati Case
3. Menaka Case
4. Indra Sawhney Case

Select the correct answer using the codes given below:

(*a*) 1 only
(*b*) 1 and 2 only
(*c*) 1, 2 and 3
(*d*) 2, 3 and 4

24. Which one of the following is the correct statement?

The rule of repugnancy has application in a case where:

(*a*) both Union and State occupy two different fields in different Lists.
(*b*) both Union and State laws are enacted under the Concurrent List.
(*c*) the Union law is enacted under List III and State law is enacted under List II.
(*d*) the Union and State laws are enacted under the State List.

25. Consider the following statements:

1. The 101st Amendment Act, 2016 has paved the way for the introduction of Goods and Services Tax (GST) in the country.
2. The GST replaced a number of indirect taxes levied by the Union and the State Governments and is intended to remove cascading effect of taxes and provide for a common national market for goods and services.

Which of the statements given above is/are correct?

(*a*) 1 only
(*b*) 2 only
(*c*) Both 1 and 2
(*d*) Neither 1 nor 2

26. Which of the following taxes are levied and collected and retained by the States?
    1. Taxes on mineral rights
    2. Taxes on animals and boats
    3. Taxes on agricultural income
    4. Taxes on professions, trades, callings and employments

    Select the correct answer using the codes given below:

    (*a*) 1, 3 and 4 (*b*) 1, 2 and 3
    (*c*) 2 and 3 only (*d*) 1, 2, 3 and 4

27. Which of the following taxes belong to the Union exclusively?

    (*a*) Customs Duties (*b*) Land Revenue
    (*c*) Surcharge on Income Tax (*d*) Corporation Tax

28. Consider the following statements:

    The executive power of the Union extends to giving of directions to a State in respect of:
    1. Construction and maintenance of means of communication of national or military importance
    2. Maintenance of law and order in the State
    3. Protection of railways within the State
    4. Protection of secular character of the country

    Which of the statements given above are correct?

    (*a*) 1 and 2 only (*b*) 2 and 3 only
    (*c*) 1 and 3 only (*d*) 1, 2, 3 and 4

29. In case of inconsistency between laws made by the Parliament and the laws made by the State Legislatures, which one of the following shall prevail?

    (*a*) The law made by the Parliament before the law made by the Legislature of the State
    (*b*) The law made by the Parliament after the law made by the Legislature of the State
    (*c*) The law made by the Parliament before or after the law made by the Legislature of the State
    (*d*) The law made by the Legislature of the State

30. Consider the following pairs:
    1. Taxes levied by the Union but collected and appropriated by the States : Stamp duties
    2. Taxes levied and collected by the Centre but assigned to the States : Taxes on the sale of goods in the course of inter-state trade

    Which of the pairs given above is/are correctly matched?

    (*a*) 1 only (*b*) 2 only
    (*c*) Both 1 and 2 (*d*) Neither 1 nor 2

31. Which of the following formed a part of the terms of reference of the Punchhi Commission on Centre-State Relations constituted by the Government of India?
    1. Panchayati Raj institutions
    2. Communal violence

3. An integrated domestic market
4. Central Law Enforcement Agency

Select the correct answer using the codes given below:

(*a*) 1 and 4 only (*b*) 2 and 3 only
(*c*) 1, 2 and 3 (*d*) 1, 2, 3 and 4

32. Consider the following statements:

The Parliament becomes competent to make law on a matter enumerated in the State List only if the:

1. Council of States passes a resolution supported by not less than two-thirds majority of the members present and voting that it is in the national interest that the Parliament should make law on such matter.
2. Council of States and House of the People, both passes a resolution that it is in the national interest that the Parliament should make law on such matter.
3. President gives the prior permission for such legislation.
4. Speaker of the House of the People in consultation with Chairman of the Council of States gives the prior permission for such legislation.

Which of the statements given above is/are correct?

(*a*) 1 only (*b*) 1, 2 and 3
(*c*) 2 and 3 only (*d*) 1, 2, 3 and 4

33. In which of the following years, the Sarkaria Commission on Centre-State Relations submitted it's report?

(*a*) 1986 (*b*) 1887
(*c*) 1988 (*d*) 1989

34. Which one of the following statements is not correct?

(*a*) No law made by a State Legislature shall be treated as unconstitutional if it incidentally touches upon the jurisdiction provided for under List I or List III.
(*b*) The Legislature of a State cannot make a law to regulate "Water".
(*c*) The law made by the Parliament under Article 357 for a State continues its application after the expiry of President's rule.
(*d*) Parliament has full power to make law on a residuary matter.

35. Which one of the following is not correct?

(*a*) The executive power of every State shall be so exercised as to ensure compliance with the laws made by the Parliament
(*b*) Full faith and credit shall be given throughout the territory of India to Public Acts, records and judicial proceedings of the Union and of every State.
(*c*) The Governor of a State may entrust to the Government of India any matter to which the executive power of the State extends.
(*d*) The executive power of the Union extends to the giving of directions to a state to protect the railways within the State.

36. The division of legislative powers between the Centre and the States under the present Constitution of India is similar to between the Centre and the Provinces under the Government of India Act, 1935, in some of the following respects:
   1. In case of overlap of a matter as between the three lists or subjects, predominance in both is given to the Central Legislature.
   2. In case of repugnancy in the Concurrent field, in both a Central law prevails over a Provincial or State law.
   3. In both, residuary powers were vested in the Central Legislature.

   Which of the statements given above are correct?

   (*a*) 1, 2 and 3 (*b*) 1 and 2 only
   (*c*) 1 and 3 only (*d*) 2 and 3 only

37. The surcharges on taxes and duties referred to in Articles 269 and 270 belong to which of the following category?
   (*a*) Tax levied by the Union of India and assigned to the Centre
   (*b*) Tax levied by the Union of India but assigned to the States
   (*c*) Tax levied by the State and assigned to the State
   (*d*) Tax levied by the Union of India and distributed between the Union and the States

38. Which of the following Finance Commission recommended the "Alternative Scheme of Devolution"?
   (*a*) 8th Finance Commission (*b*) 9th Finance Commission
   (*c*) 10th Finance Commission (*d*) 11th Finance Commission

39. Consider the following statements:
   1. In extraordinary circumstances, the normal distribution of power between the Centre and the States is either suspended or the powers of the Union Parliament are extended over the state subjects.
   2. The Indian Constitution vests the residuary power in the Union Parliament and the final decision as to whether a particular matter falls under the residuary power or not is that of the Supreme Court.
   3. The Union Government has the power to give directions to the State Governments to ensure due compliance with Union laws.
   4. If the Legislatures of two or more states so resolve, Parliament can make laws with respect to any matter included in the State List relating to those states.

   Which of the above statements describe the nature of Indian Federalism?

   (*a*) 1, 2, 3 and 4 (*b*) 1, 2 and 3
   (*c*) 2 and 4 only (*d*) 1 and 3 only

40. Consider the following statements:
   1. Sarkaria Commission recommended that the Union Government may persuade the State Governments for constitution of an All-India Service for education.
   2. All-India Services are included in the Concurrent List of the Constitution of India.

Which of the statements given above is/are correct?

(*a*) 1 only (*b*) 2 only

(*c*) Both 1 and 2 (*d*) Neither 1 nor 2

41. In order to examine thoroughly the various issues in centre-state relations, the Administrative Reforms Commission of India constituted a study team under:

(*a*) A.K. Chanda (*b*) Mahavir Tyagi

(*c*) K. Santhanam (*d*) M.C. Setalvad

42. Which of the following Committee/Commission recommended the abolition of the IAS and IPS?

(*a*) Sarkaria Commission

(*b*) Administrative Reforms Commission of India

(*c*) Rajamannar Committee

(*d*) Punchhi Commission

Answers

1. (*b*)	2. (*c*)	3. (*b*)	4. (*d*)	5. (*a*)
6. (*a*)	7. (*c*)	8. (*b*)	9. (*a*)	10. (*c*)
11. (*c*)	12. (*a*)	13. (*c*)	14. (*c*)	15. (*c*)
16. (*d*)	17. (*d*)	18. (*a*)	19. (*c*)	20. (*c*)
21. (*b*)	22. (*d*)	23. (*a*)	24. (*b*)	25. (*c*)
26. (*d*)	27. (*c*)	28. (*c*)	29. (*c*)	30. (*c*)
31. (*d*)	32. (*a*)	33. (*c*)	34. (*b*)	35. (*c*)
36. (*b*)	37. (*a*)	38. (*c*)	39. (*a*)	40. (*a*)
41. (*d*)	42. (*c*)			

15

Inter-State Relations

1. Consider the following statements:
   1. The Inter-State Council is assisted by a secretariat called the Inter-State Council Secretariat.
   2. Since 2014, the Inter-State Council Secretariat is also functioning as the secretariat of the Zonal Councils.

   Which of the statements given above is/are correct?

   (*a*) 1 only (*b*) 2 only
   (*c*) Both 1 and 2 (*d*) Neither 1 nor 2

2. Consider the following statements:
   1. Parliament may by law provide that neither the Supreme Court nor any other court shall exercise jurisdiction in respect of any dispute with respect to the use, distribution or control of the waters of any Inter-State river or river valley.
   2. River Boards Act, 1956, provides for reference of an Inter-State river dispute for arbitration by a Water Dispute Tribunal.

   Which of the statements given above is/are correct?

   (*a*) 1 only
   (*b*) 2 only
   (*c*) Both 1 and 2
   (*d*) Neither 1 nor 2

3. Which of the following are duties of the Inter-State Council created under Article 263 of the Constitution of India?
   1. Inquiring into and advising upon disputes which may have arisen between/among States.
   2. Investigating and discussing subjects in which some or all of the States, or the Union and one or more of the States have a common interest.
   3. Making recommendations upon any such subject for the better coordination of policy and action with respect to that subject.
   4. Ensuring that officers belonging to All-India Services posted in various States are not punished by the Judiciary for acts of omission.

   Choose the correct answer from the codes given below:

   (*a*) 1, 2 and 3 (*b*) 1, 2 and 4
   (*c*) 1, 3 and 4 (*d*) 2, 3 and 4

4. Consider the following statements on Zonal Councils:
   1. Zonal Councils were set up under the provisions of the States Reorganisation Act.
   2. Zonal Councils discuss various issues of common interest in the field of planning, river waters, inter-state transport.
   3. They enable the Centre and States to co-operate in evolving uniform policies in social and economic matters.
   4. Their decisions are binding on Centre as well as on State Governments.

   Which of the statements given above are correct?

   (*a*) 1, 2 and 3 (*b*) 1, 3 and 4
   (*c*) 2, 3 and 4 (*d*) 1, 2 and 4

5. Consider the following statements regarding the constitutional provisions relating to trade, commerce and intercourse:
   1. Parliament may by law impose restrictions on the freedom of trade, commerce or intercourse between one state and another in the public interest.
   2. Bills imposing restrictions on the freedom of trade, commerce or intercourse within the state cannot be moved in the State Legislature without the sanction of the Central Government.
   3. Parliament may enact any law giving or authorizing any discrimination to deal with a situation arising from the scarcity of goods in any part of Indian Territory.
   4. Trade and commerce within the state is a subject in the Concurrent List.

   Which of the statements given above is/are correct?

   (*a*) 1, 2, 3 and 4
   (*b*) 3 and 4 only
   (*c*) 1 and 3 only
   (*d*) 2 only

6. Who among the following are the members of the Inter-State Council?

   (*a*) Chief Ministers of the States/Administrators of the Union Territories.
   (*b*) The Prime Minister, all the Chief Ministers of the States/Administrators of the Union Territories.
   (*c*) The Prime Minister, Six Union Cabinet Ministers and all the Chief Ministers of the States/Administrators of the Union Territories.
   (*d*) The Prime Minister, Leader of the Opposition in the Lok Sabha and all the Members of the Rajya Sabha.

7. Which one of the following is not correct?

   (*a*) The Governor of a State may entrust to the Government of India, functions in relation to any matter to which the executive power of the state extends.
   (*b*) The Governor of a state cannot entrust to the Government of India, functions in relation to any matter to which the executive power of the state extends unless there is consent of the Government of India.
   (*c*) The orders of Civil Courts are enforceable in the entire country.
   (*d*) Full faith and credit has to be given to every public act of every state.

8. The Chairman of Zonal Council is:
   (*a*) the Chief Minister and is nominated by the Prime Minister of India.
   (*b*) the Union Minister and is nominated by the President of India.
   (*c*) the Home Minister and is ex-officio.
   (*d*) the Vice-President of India.

9. The North-Eastern Council was created by which of the following?
   (*a*) A resolution of the Union Cabinet
   (*b*) An amendment to the Constitution
   (*c*) A resolution of the Parliament
   (*d*) An Act of the Parliament

10. Under which of the following regimes was the Inter-State Council (ISC) setup?
   (*a*) Congress Government in 1975
   (*b*) Janata Government in 1978
   (*c*) Janata Dal-led Government in 1990
   (*d*) United Front Government in 1996

11. Inter-State water disputes can be resolved by which one of the following?
   (*a*) Supreme Court only
   (*b*) Union Government only
   (*c*) Tribunals established by the Parliament by law
   (*d*) Special courts established by the President of India

12. Which one of the following is the correct statement?
   "Full Faith and Credit" clause of the Constitution does not apply to:
   (*a*) Public records
   (*b*) Judicial proceedings
   (*c*) Acts of corporations
   (*d*) Public Acts

13. An Inter-State Council may be established by:
   (*a*) The Parliament
   (*b*) The President
   (*c*) The Union Cabinet
   (*d*) The Zonal Council

14. Which of the following statements on Zonal Councils are correct?
   1. They owe their existence to the Constitution of India.
   2. There are five zonal councils.
   3. They coordinate relations among the governments of the States and Union territories and the Government of India.
   4. They are set up under the States Reorganisation Act, 1956.

   Select the correct answer using the codes given below:
   (*a*) 1, 2 and 3
   (*b*) 2, 3 and 4
   (*c*) 3 and 4 only
   (*d*) 2 and 4 only

15. Which of the following State was added as a member of the North-Eastern Council in 2002?
   (*a*) Tripura
   (*b*) Meghalaya
   (*c*) Sikkim
   (*d*) Nagaland

Answers

1. (*a*)	2. (*a*)	3. (*a*)	4. (*a*)	5. (*c*)
6. (*c*)	7. (*a*)	8. (*c*)	9. (*d*)	10. (*c*)
11. (*c*)	12. (*c*)	13. (*b*)	14. (*b*)	15. (*c*)

16

Emergency Provisions

1. Consider the following statements:
   1. No Proclamation of Emergency can be made by the President of India unless the Union Ministers of Cabinet rank, headed by the Prime Minister, recommended to him, in writing, that such a Proclamation should be issued.
   2. The President of India must issue a Proclamation of Revocation of Emergency any time that the Lok Sabha passes a resolution disapproving the proclamation or its continuance.

   Which of the statements given above is/are correct?

   (*a*) 1 only (*b*) 2 only
   (*c*) Both 1 and 2 (*d*) Neither 1 nor 2

2. Consider the following statements:

   If the financial emergency has been declared by the President under the Article 360, then its proclamation:
   1. may be revoked or varied by a subsequent proclamation.
   2. shall cease to operate at the expiration of two months, unless before the expiration of that period it has been approved by the resolution of both Houses of Parliament.

   Which of the statements given above is/are correct?

   (*a*) 1 only (*b*) 2 only
   (*c*) Both 1 and 2 (*d*) Neither 1 nor 2

3. Consider the following statements:
   1. While a Proclamation of Emergency is in operation, Article 359 of the Constitution of India does not come into operation till an order is issued by the President specifying the rights which are suspended.
   2. While a Proclamation of Emergency is in operation, Article 358 makes the restrictions imposed by Article 19 non-existent against the state.

   Which of the statements given above is/are correct?

   (*a*) 1 only (*b*) 2 only
   (*c*) Both 1 and 2 (*d*) Neither 1 nor 2

4. Which of the following are not necessarily the consequences of the proclamation of the President's Rule in a State?
   1. Dissolution of the State Legislative Assembly
   2. The removal of the Council of Ministers in the State

3. Dissolution of the local bodies
4. Takeover of the State administration by the Union Government

Choose the correct answer from the codes given below:

(*a*) 1, 2 and 4 (*b*) 1 and 3 only
(*c*) 2 and 3 only (*d*) 1, 3 and 4

5. Consider the following statements:

Proclamation of Emergency under Article 352 of the Constitution of India:

1. Requires written communication of the Union Cabinet to the President to that effect.
2. Can be issued for the whole of India or part thereof.
3. Lapses, if not approved by both Houses of Parliament within a month.
4. Requires a resolution, approving the proclamation passed by both Houses of Parliament only by a majority of the total membership of each House, and not less than 2/3rd members present and voting.
5. Once approved by the Parliament can last for six months.

Which of the statements given above are correct?

(*a*) 1, 2, 3, 4 and 5 (*b*) 2, 3 and 4
(*c*) 1, 4 and 5 (*d*) 1, 2, 3 and 5

6. In case of declaration of financial emergency:

(*a*) all the State Governments will be dissolved and management of economy will be taken over by the Union Government.
(*b*) all Money Bills of the states will be considered and passed only by the Parliament.
(*c*) all the State Assemblies will be put under suspended animation and laws on the State List will be enacted by the Parliament.
(*d*) the President may give such directions to the states as may be deemed necessary for economic recovery and salaries of officials may be temporarily reduced.

7. Law made by the Parliament with respect to any matter enumerated in State List, during a proclamation of national emergency, will cease to have effect in which one of the following conditions?

(*a*) When the Proclamation of Emergency has ceased to operate
(*b*) When it is repealed by the Parliament
(*c*) On the expiration of six months after the Proclamation of Emergency has ceased to operate
(*d*) On the expiration of one year after the Proclamation of Emergency has ceased to operate

8. Consider the following statements:

The Supreme Court judgement in S.R. Bommai vs. Union of India has been interpreted to mean that the Governor can dismiss a Council of Ministers or the Chief Minister:

1. At his pleasure on his subjective estimate of the strength of the Chief Minister in the Assembly.
2. When the Legislative Assembly has expressed its want of confidence in the Council of Ministers.

3. When a measure of the Council of Ministers has been defeated on the floor of the Assembly.
4. When a censure motion against the Council of Ministers has been rejected in the Legislative Assembly.

Which of the statements given above are correct?

(*a*) 1 and 2 only (*b*) 2 and 3 only
(*c*) 1 and 3 only (*d*) 3 and 4 only

9. Which of the following will be the consequences of the Proclamation of Financial Emergency by the President?
   1. The Centre can give directions to the States to observe the principles of financial propriety.
   2. The President can reduce the salaries and allowances of government employees excluding the judges of Supreme Court and High Courts.
   3. All money bills and other financial bills passed by a State Legislature can be reserved for the consideration of the President.
   4. The Parliament can authorise the President to sanction expenditure from the Consolidated Fund of the State.

   Select the correct answer using the codes given below:

   (*a*) 1, 2 and 3 (*b*) 1, 2, 3 and 4
   (*c*) 1 and 3 only (*d*) 1, 3 and 4

10. Which of the following statements is the correct one?
    (*a*) War, external aggression, internal disturbance and armed rebellion are the grounds for proclaiming emergency.
    (*b*) Words "armed rebellion" were replaced by the word "war" by the 44th Amendment.
    (*c*) Actual existence of any one or more grounds mentioned in Article 352 is necessary for proclaiming emergency.
    (*d*) The President proclaims emergency on the basis of any ground mentioned in Article 352 or possibility thereof.

11. If the President of India exercises his power as provided under Article 356 of the Constitution in respect of a particular State, then:
    (*a*) the Assembly of the State is automatically dissolved.
    (*b*) Article 19 is suspended in that State.
    (*c*) Parliament assumes the power to legislate on the subjects in the State List.
    (*d*) the President can make laws relating to that State.

12. When a Proclamation of Emergency is issued by the President under Article 352 of the Constitution of India:
    (*a*) Fundamental Rights are automatically suspended.
    (*b*) the freedoms under Article 19 are automatically suspended and other Fundamental Rights can be suspended by an order of the President.
    (*c*) the freedoms under Article 19 are automatically suspended and other Fundamental Rights, except those under Articles 20 and 21, can be suspended by an order of the President.
    (*d*) only the freedoms under Article 19 are suspended and other Fundamental Rights cannot be suspended.

13. Which one of the following is the correct statement?

Proclamation of Emergency in a State under Article 356 can continue beyond one year if:

(*a*) the High Court of the State certifies that the situation in the State is very serious.

(*b*) the Governor of the State certifies that the law and order situation is not under control.

(*c*) the Election Commission certifies that it is difficult to hold elections to the Assembly.

(*d*) the President is satisfied about the grave situation in the State through independent investigation.

14. Which of the following may be done under conditions of financial emergency?

1. Reduction in the number of districts in the country for effecting economy
2. Abolition of all State Legislative Assemblies to reduce expenditure
3. Reduction in the salaries of the judges of the High Court
4. Reservation of Money Bills of State Legislative Assemblies for the consideration of the President

Choose the correct answer from the codes given below:

(*a*) 1, 2 and 3 (*b*) 2, 3 and 4

(*c*) 3 and 4 only (*d*) 1 and 4 only

15. When a state fails to implement the administrative directions given by the Union under Article 256 of the Constitution of India:

(*a*) Parliament may compel the state to execute the said directions

(*b*) The Governor may dissolve the State Legislature

(*c*) The President may presume that Constitutional machinery in the State has failed

(*d*) The President may impose emergency under Article 352 of the Constitution

16. Proclamation of emergency by the President of India can be made on the written advice of the Cabinet only. This provision has been added:

(*a*) after 44th Constitutional Amendment.

(*b*) after 42nd Constitutional Amendment.

(*c*) by the Constituent Assembly in the Constitution of India.

(*d*) by the Supreme Court of India in 1975.

17. The President's Rule under Article 356 remains valid in a state for the maximum period of:

(*a*) One year (*b*) Two years

(*c*) Three years (*d*) Four years

18. Proclamation of Emergency under Article 352, when Lok Sabha stands dissolved has to be approved by:

(*a*) Rajya Sabha and then it will continue till the reconstitution of new Lok Sabha, which must approve it within 30 days of its first sitting.

(*b*) New Lok Sabha within six months of its constitution.

(*c*) Lok Sabha in the next session after six months.

(*d*) Rajya Sabha only.

19. On which of the following grounds, the second proclamation of national emergency was made in 1971?
   (*a*) War
   (*b*) External aggression
   (*c*) Internal disturbance
   (*d*) Armed rebellion

20. Which one of the following is not an automatic consequence of the Proclamation of Emergency?
   (*a*) Suspension of the enforcement of Fundamental Rights except those conferred by Articles 20 and 21.
   (*b*) Extension of the Union's executive power to the issue of directions to any State as to the manner in which its executive power has to be exercised.
   (*c*) Extension of the power of the Parliament to the making of legislation in regard to items of the State List
   (*d*) Suspension of Article 19.

21. Consider the following statements:

   Parliament may make law on a subject enumerated in State List only if the:
   1. President deems it proper that such law is necessary for all the States.
   2. Proclamation of Emergency under Article 352 is in operation.
   3. Lok Sabha passes a resolution by $2^{nd}/3^{rd}$ majority of its total membership.
   4. Governor of the State requests the President for such legislation.

   Which of the statements given above is/are correct?
   (*a*) 1 and 4 only
   (*b*) 2 only
   (*c*) 3 only
   (*d*) 3 and 4 only

22. The judgement in the S.R. Bommai vs. Union of India case pertained broadly to which Article of the Constitution of India?
   (*a*) Article 29
   (*b*) Article 32
   (*c*) Article 353
   (*d*) Article 356

23. Consider the following statements in respect of provisions as to financial emergency:
   1. A Proclamation of Financial Emergency has to be laid before each House of Parliament.
   2. A Proclamation of Financial Emergency ceases to operate at the expiration of six months, unless before the expiration of that period, it has been approved by resolutions of both Houses of Parliament.

   Which of the statements given above is/are correct?
   (*a*) 1 only (*b*) 2 only
   (*c*) Both 1 and 2 (*d*) Neither 1 nor 2

Answers

1. (*c*)	2. (*c*)	3. (*c*)	4. (*b*)	5. (*a*)
6. (*d*)	7. (*c*)	8. (*b*)	9. (*c*)	10. (*d*)
11. (*c*)	12. (*c*)	13. (*c*)	14. (*c*)	15. (*c*)
16. (*a*)	17. (*c*)	18. (*a*)	19. (*b*)	20. (*a*)
21. (*b*)	22. (*d*)	23. (*a*)		

PART-III CENTRAL GOVERNMENT

17. President
18. Vice-President
19. Prime Minister
20. Central Council of Ministers
21. Cabinet Committees
22. Parliament
23. Parliamentary Committees
24. Parliamentary Forums
25. Parliamentary Group
26. Supreme Court
27. Judicial Review
28. Judicial Activism
29. Public Interest Litigation

17

President

1. Consider the following statements:
   1. When the President of India is to be impeached for violation of the Constitution, the charge shall be preferred by either House of Parliament.
   2. An election to fill a vacancy in the office of the President of India occurring because of his death, resignation or removal or otherwise shall be held in no case later than nine months from the date of occurrence of the vacancy.

   Which of the statements given above is/are correct?

   (*a*) 1 only (*b*) 2 only
   (*c*) Both 1 and 2 (*d*) Neither 1 nor 2

2. Consider the following statements:
   1. The President nominates twelve members of the Rajya Sabha on the advice of the Council of Ministers.
   2. The President has absolute power to appoint and remove the Chairman and the members of statutory bodies at his discretion.

   Which of the statements given above is/are correct?

   (*a*) 1 only (*b*) 2 only
   (*c*) Both 1 and 2 (*d*) Neither 1 nor 2

3. Consider the following statements:
   1. On the expiry of the term of five years by the President of India, the outgoing President must continue to hold the office until his successor enters upon his office.
   2. The Electoral College for the President's election consists of the elected members of the Legislative Assemblies of Delhi and Puducherry also.

   Which of the statements given above is/are correct?

   (*a*) 1 only (*b*) 2 only
   (*c*) Both 1 and 2 (*d*) Neither 1 nor 2

4. The Executive power of the Union Government is vested in the President of India. The President shall exercise these powers:

   (*a*) Himself
   (*b*) Directly or through officers subordinate to him if he so desires
   (*c*) Either directly or through officers subordinate to him in accordance with the provisions of the Constitution
   (*d*) Only on the advice of the Prime Minister

5. Which one of the following statements is correct?
   (*a*) The Chief Election Commissioner of India holds his office during the pleasure of the President.
   (*b*) The Governor of a State holds his office during the pleasure of the President.
   (*c*) The Prime Minister can only be removed by a resolution passed by both Houses of the Parliament.
   (*d*) The speaker of the Lok Sabha can be removed at the pleasure of the President.

6. In which of the following cases the President of India is not bound by the advice of the Council of Ministers?
   1. The choice of the Prime Minister.
   2. The dismissal of the Government which refuses to quit after having lost its majority in the House of the People.
   3. The allocation of business.
   4. The dissolution of the House, when appeal to the electorate becomes necessary.

   Choose the correct answer from the codes given below:
   (*a*) 1, 2 and 3 (*b*) 1, 2 and 4
   (*c*) 1, 3 and 4 (*d*) 2, 3 and 4

7. Which of the following statements is not correct?
   (*a*) There shall be a Council of Ministers headed by the Prime Minister to aid and advise the President who shall act in accordance with such advice.
   (*b*) The President may require the Council of Ministers to reconsider such advice.
   (*c*) The President need not act in accordance with the advice tendered after such reconsideration.
   (*d*) The President shall act in accordance with the advice tendered after such reconsideration.

8. Which of the following powers of the President is contained in Article 72 of the constitution?
   (*a*) Power to grant pardon
   (*b*) Executive power of the Union
   (*c*) Power to appoint the Prime Minister
   (*d*) Appointment of the Attorney-General

9. Consider the following statements:
   1. The President can commute death sentence to life imprisonment.
   2. The Governor cannot commute death sentence to life imprisonment.
   3. The President's power to pardon extends to punishments or sentences by court martial.

   Which of the statements given above is/are correct?
   (*a*) 2 only (*b*) 1 and 3 only
   (*c*) 1, 2 and 3 (*d*) 2 and 3 only

10. Consider the following statements:
    1. The prior recommendation of the President is needed to introduce in the Parliament a Bill involving expenditure from the Consolidated Fund of India.
    2. The President decides on the questions as to disqualifications of the members of the parliament in consultation with the Supreme Court.

Which of the statements given above is/are correct?

(*a*) 1 only (*b*) 2 only
(*c*) Both 1 and 2 (*d*) Neither 1 nor 2

11. In which one of the following cases is the President of India not bound by the aid and advice of the Union Council of Ministers?
 (*a*) In deciding the question of removal of a Governor
 (*b*) In deciding the question whether a member of Lok Sabha has become disqualified to continue as a member
 (*c*) While exercising power to grant pardon
 (*d*) In dismissing a civil servant without any enquiry and hearing on the ground of security of state

12. Money can be advanced out of the Contingency Fund of India to meet unforeseen expenditure by the
 (*a*) Parliament (*b*) President
 (*c*) Finance Minister (*d*) Prime Minister

13. Consider the following statements:

 The charge of violation of the Constitution by the President of India for his impeachment cannot be preferred by a House unless:
 1. A resolution containing the proposal is moved after a seven days' notice in writing signed by not less than $1/4^{th}$ of the total number of the members of that House.
 2. The resolution is passed by a majority of not less than $2/3^{rd}$ of the total membership of that House.

 Which of the statements given above is/are correct?
 (*a*) 1 only (*b*) 2 only
 (*c*) Both 1 and 2 (*d*) Neither 1 nor 2

14. The Constitution (42nd Amendment) Act, 1976, made it obligatory for the President of India to act in accordance with the advice of the Council of Ministers.

 For the above purpose, which one of the following Articles of the Constitution of India was amended by the Constitution (42nd Amendment) Act, 1976?
 (*a*) Article 73 (*b*) Article 74
 (*c*) Article 75 (*d*) Article 77

15. Consider the following statements:
 1. Absolute veto power of the President implies overridden by a higher majority.
 2. The President has no veto power with respect to state legislation.

 Which of the statements given above is/are correct?
 (*a*) 1 only (*b*) 2 only
 (*c*) Both 1 and 2 (*d*) Neither 1 nor 2

16. Which of the following is a correct statement about the President of India?
 (*a*) He can address both Houses of the Parliament, can summon the Houses of the Parliament and can send messages to either House of the Parliament.

(*b*) He can summon the Houses of the Parliament but cannot send messages to either House of the Parliament.

(*c*) He can send messages to either House of the Parliament but cannot summon the Houses of the Parliament.

(*d*) He cannot send messages to either House of the Parliament or summon the Houses of the Parliament.

17. The President of India:

(*a*) Can be a member of the Parliament

(*b*) Is part of the Parliament

(*c*) Cannot stand for election for more than two terms

(*d*) Presides over joint sittings of both the Houses of the Parliament

18. Which one of the following statements about the impeachment of the President of India is not correct?

(*a*) The charge for violation of the Constitution shall be preferred by either House of the Parliament.

(*b*) The resolution has to be moved after at least thirty days' notice in writing.

(*c*) The resolution has to be signed by not less than one-fourth of the total number of members of the House.

(*d*) The resolution has to be passed by a majority of not less than two-thirds of the total membership of the House.

19. Who of the following presidential candidates was elected unopposed?

(*a*) Dr. S. Radhakrishnan (*b*) V. V. Giri

(*c*) N. Sanjeeva Reddy (*d*) Dr. Rajendra Prasad

20. Which of the following Articles of the constitution deals with the implement of the President?

(*a*) Article 61 (*b*) Article 54

(*c*) Article 52 (*d*) Article 56

21. The rule of passing resolution by two-thirds majority of the total number of members of the House of Parliament is applicable in case of:

(*a*) Amendment of the Constitution

(*b*) Approval of Proclamation of Emergency

(*c*) Impeachment of the President

(*d*) Disapproval of Proclamation of Emergency

22. Consider the following statements:

1. In the case of Puducherry, the President can legislate by making regulations but only the assembly is suspended or dissolved.

2. The President can make advances out of the Contingency Fund of India to meet any unforeseen expenditure.

Which of the statements given above is/are correct?

(*a*) 1 only (*b*) 2 only

(*c*) Both 1 and 2 (*d*) Neither 1 nor 2

23. As per provisions of the Constitution of India, who makes rules for more convenient transaction of the business of the Government of India and for allocation among the Ministers of the said business?
   (*a*) The President
   (*b*) The Union Law Minister
   (*c*) The Attorney-General of India
   (*d*) The Cabinet Secretariat

24. Which one of the following statements is correct?

   On receipt of a Constitutional Amendment Bill after its passing by each House of the Parliament, the President:
   (*a*) Shall give his assent
   (*b*) May give his assent
   (*c*) May withhold his assent
   (*d*) May return the Bill for reconsideration

25. "The President may require the Council of Ministers to reconsider the advice tendered by the latter and shall act in accordance with the advice tendered after such reconsideration."

   The above provision was inserted in the Indian Constitution by the:
   (*a*) 38th Amendment (*b*) 42nd Amendment
   (*c*) 44th Amendment (*d*) 52nd Amendment

26. Which of the following pardoning powers of the President implies reducing the period of sentence without changing its character?
   (*a*) Remission (*b*) Reprieve
   (*c*) Respite (*d*) Commutation

27. Which one of the following is not correct about the powers of the President of India to grant pardons, reprieves, respites or remissions of punishment or to suspend, remit or commute the sentence of any person convicted of any offence?
   (*a*) The President can do so in all cases where the punishment or sentence is by a Court Martial.
   (*b*) The President may exercise such powers in all cases where punishment or sentence is for an offence against any law falling within the executive power of the Union.
   (*c*) The President may exercise such powers in all cases where the sentence is a sentence of death.
   (*d*) The President may reject a petition for mercy but he must hear a petition for mercy before rejecting.

28. Which one of the following statements about the executive powers of the President is incorrect?
   (*a*) All important appointments are made by the President on the advice of the Council of Ministers.
   (*b*) The Prime Minister and all Union Ministers are appointed by the President.
   (*c*) The President has the absolute power to appoint and remove the Chairmen and the members of statutory bodies at his discretion.
   (*d*) The President is the supreme commander of the Armed Forces.

29. The President of India is elected by the "Electoral College" consisting of:
    (*a*) All Members of the Parliament.
    (*b*) Elected Members of the Parliament and the State Legislative Assemblies.
    (*c*) Members of the Parliament, the State Legislative Assemblies and the Legislative Councils.
    (*d*) All the Members of the Parliament and the State Legislative Assemblies.

30. Consider the following statements:
    1. If a Bill other than Money Bill is returned by the President for reconsideration of the Houses and the Bill is again passed by both the Houses of the Parliament with or without amendments and again presented to the President, then also it is not obligatory upon him to declare his assent to it.
    2. A Bill for the purpose of formation of new States and alteration of areas, boundaries or names of existing States can be introduced in either House of the Parliament and no recommendation of the President is required for the introduction of such a Bill.

    Which of the statements given above is/are correct?
    (*a*) 1 only (*b*) 2 only
    (*c*) Both 1 and 2 (*d*) Neither 1 nor 2

31. Which of the following explains the suspensive veto power of the President?
    (*a*) Overridden by a higher majority (*b*) Overridden by an ordinary majority
    (*c*) Withholding of the assent (*d*) Taking no action on the bill

32. The authority to declare war or peace under the Indian Constitutions is vested in:
    (*a*) The Prime Minister (*b*) The Defence Minister
    (*c*) The Parliament (*d*) The President

33. Which one of the following statements is correct?
    (*a*) The President may continue to be a member of the Parliament even after assuming charge of the Presidential office.
    (*b*) The President is not barred from holding any other office of profit even after assuming charge of Presidential office.
    (*c*) The President is entitled to use his official residence only on payment of the rent fixed.
    (*d*) The emoluments and allowances of the President shall not be diminished during his term of office.

34. Which one of the following is not a constitutional prerogative of the President of India?
    (*a*) Returning a Legislative Bill for reconsideration (*b*) Returning a Money Bill for reconsideration
    (*c*) Dissolving the Lok Sabha (*d*) Summoning the Rajya Sabha

35. Consider the following statements relating to the President of India:
    1. He may resign by writing to the Vice-President.
    2. He shall continue, notwithstanding the expiration of his term, to hold office until his successor enters upon his office.
    3. He is not entitled to hold the office for more than two terms.

Which of the statements given above are correct?

(*a*) 1 and 3 only (*b*) 1 and 2 only

(*c*) 1, 2 and 3 (*d*) 2 and 3 only

36. For which of the following Union Territories, the President cannot make regulations for the peace, progress and good government?

(*a*) Andaman and Nicobar Islands (*b*) Chandigarh

(*c*) Lakshadweep (*d*) Ladakh

37. The President of India is not the authority for the appointment of:

(*a*) Judges of the High Courts

(*b*) State Governors

(*c*) Union Ministers

(*d*) Chairman of a State Public Service Commission

38. Who among the following do not participate in the election of the President of India?

(*a*) Elected Members of the Rajya Sabha

(*b*) Elected Members of the Lok Sabha

(*c*) Elected Members of the Vidhan Sabhas

(*d*) Elected Members of the Vidhan Parishads

39. Consider the following statements:

1. Article 54 of the Constitution deals with the manner of election of the President.
2. Article 55 of the Constitution deals with the election of the President

Which of the statements given above is/are correct?

(*a*) 1 only (*b*) 2 only

(*c*) Both 1 and 2 (*d*) Neither 1 nor 2

40. Which of the following explains the reprieve powers of the President?

(*a*) Stay of the execution of a sentence for a temporary period

(*b*) Awarding a letter sentence in place of one originally awarded

(*c*) Substitution of one form of punishment for a lighter form

(*d*) Reducing the period of sentence without changing its character

41. Which one of the following is not correct regarding the executive powers of the President?

(*a*) He must be kept informed by the Prime Minister of all decisions of the Cabinet.

(*b*) He presides over the meetings of the Council of Ministers when he deems fit.

(*c*) He can ask the Prime Minister to submit a decision of any minister for the consideration of the Council of Ministers.

(*d*) He must be supplied with such other information about the administration of the country as he asks for it.

42. Which of the following veto powers of the President implies taking no action on the bill?

(*a*) Qualified Veto (*b*) Absolute Veto

(*c*) Suspensive Veto (*d*) Pocket Veto

43. The power of the President of India to issue an ordinance is a/an:
(*a*) Executive power
(*b*) Legislative power
(*c*) Constituent power
(*d*) Quasi-judicial power

44. The impeachment of the President of India can be initiated in:
(*a*) Either House of the Parliament
(*b*) A joint sitting of both Houses of the Parliament
(*c*) The Lok Sabha alone
(*d*) The Rajya Sabha alone

45. Who amongst the following decides about the disqualification of the Members of the Parliament?
(*a*) Election Commission
(*b*) Supreme Court
(*c*) Speaker
(*d*) President of India

46. Which of the following Articles of the Constitution deals with the appointment of the Attorney-General by the President?
(*a*) Article 77
(*b*) Article 75
(*c*) Article 76
(*d*) Article 78

47. Consider the following statements:
1. Respite implies the stay of the execution of a sentence for a temporary period.
2. The pardoning power of the President is independent of the Judiciary.

Which of the statements given above is/are correct?
(*a*) 1 only
(*b*) 2 only
(*c*) Both 1 and 2
(*d*) Neither 1 nor 2

48. In the event of occurrence of vacancies in the offices of both, the President and the Vice-President of India, who among the following shall discharge the functions of the President till a new President is elected?
(*a*) Speaker of the Lok Sabha
(*b*) Leader of the majority party in the Lok Sabha
(*c*) Chief Justice of India
(*d*) Senior most Governor

49. Which of the following Articles of the Constitution deals with the executive powers of the Union?
(*a*) Article 54
(*b*) Article 52
(*c*) Article 53
(*d*) Article 55

50. Consider the following statements in respect of an Ordinance promulgated by the President of India during the recess of the Parliament:
1. Such an Ordinance may be withdrawn at any time by the President.
2. Such an Ordinance shall be laid before both the Houses of Parliament and shall cease to operate at the expiration of six weeks from the reassembly of the Parliament, or before that period if disapproved by both the Houses.

Which of the statements given above is/are correct?
(*a*) 1 only
(*b*) 2 only
(*c*) Both 1 and 2
(*d*) Neither 1 nor 2

51. Which of the following pardoning powers of the President implies substitution of one form of punishment for a lighter form?

(*a*) Commutation (*b*) Reprieve

(*c*) Remission (*d*) Respite

52. Which of the following veto powers is not possessed by the President of India?

(*a*) Suspensive Veto (*b*) Qualified Veto

(*c*) Pocket Veto (*d*) Absolute Veto

53. Consider the following statements:

The President of India has the power to address both the Houses of the Parliament at the commencement of:

1. the first session after the general elections.
2. each session.
3. the first session of each year.
4. the budget session of each year.

Which of these are correct?

(*a*) 2 and 3 only (*b*) 1 and 4 only

(*c*) 1 and 3 only (*d*) 2 and 4 only

54. Consider the following statements:

1. When the Vice-President of India acts as the President of India, he performs simultaneously the functions of the Chairman of the Rajya Sabha.
2. The President of India can promulgate Ordinances at any time except when both the Houses of the Parliament are in session.

Which of the statements given above is/are correct?

(*a*) 1 only (*b*) 2 only

(*c*) Both 1 and 2 (*d*) Neither 1 nor 2

55. Consider the following statements:

1. An ordinance can be issued by the President only on those subjects on which the Parliament can make laws.
2. An ordinance issued by the President is not subject to the same constitutional limitation as an Act of the Parliament.

Which of the statements given above is/are correct?

(*a*) 1 only (*b*) 2 only

(*c*) Both 1 and 2 (*d*) Neither 1 nor 2

56. The Union Executive of India consists of

(*a*) the President, the Vice-President, the Lok Sabha Speaker and the Council of Ministers.

(*b*) the President, the Deputy Chairman of the Rajya Sabha, the Lok Sabha Speaker and the Prime Minister.

(*c*) the President and the Council of Ministers.

(*d*) the President, the Vice-President and the Council of Ministers.

Answers

1. (*a*)	2. (*a*)	3. (*c*)	4. (*c*)	5. (*b*)
6. (*b*)	7. (*c*)	8. (*a*)	9. (*b*)	10. (*a*)
11. (*b*)	12. (*b*)	13. (*b*)	14. (*b*)	15. (*d*)
16. (*a*)	17. (*b*)	18. (*b*)	19. (*c*)	20. (*a*)
21. (*c*)	22. (*c*)	23. (*a*)	24. (*a*)	25. (*c*)
26. (*a*)	27. (*d*)	28. (*c*)	29. (*b*)	30. (*d*)
31. (*b*)	32. (*d*)	33. (*d*)	34. (*b*)	35. (*b*)
36. (*b*)	37. (*d*)	38. (*d*)	39. (*d*)	40. (*a*)
41. (*b*)	42. (*d*)	43. (*b*)	44. (*a*)	45. (*d*)
46. (*c*)	47. (*b*)	48. (*c*)	49. (*c*)	50. (*c*)
51. (*a*)	52. (*b*)	53. (*c*)	54. (*b*)	55. (*a*)
56. (*d*)				

18

Vice-President

1. Consider the following statements:
   1. The Constitution of India provides that the Vice-President of India shall be the ex-officio Chairman of the Council of States.
   2. The Constitution of India has not fixed any emoluments for the Vice-President of India in that capacity.

   Which of the statements given above is/are correct?
   (*a*) 1 only (*b*) 2 only
   (*c*) Both 1 and 2 (*d*) Neither 1 nor 2

2. Consider the following statements:
   1. The Vice-President of India may be removed from his office by a resolution of the council of states passed by a majority of all the then members of the council and agreed to by the House of the People.
   2. An election to fill a vacancy caused by the expiration of the term of office of Vice-President shall be completed before the expiration of the term.
   3. The Vice-President shall, notwithstanding the expiration of his term, continue to hold office until his successor enters upon his office.

   Which of the statements given above are correct?
   (*a*) 1, 2 and 3 (*b*) 1 and 2 only
   (*c*) 2 and 3 only (*d*) 1 and 3 only

3. The Vice-President is elected by an electoral college consisting of:
   (*a*) Members of both Houses of the Parliament
   (*b*) Elected members of both Houses of the Parliament
   (*c*) Elected members of both Houses of the Parliament and the State Legislative Assemblies
   (*d*) Members of both Houses of the Parliament and the State Legislative Assemblies

4. Which of the following statements is/are correct with regard to the Vice-President of India?
   1. He must be a Member of the Parliament.
   2. He is elected by proportional representation.
   3. He should not hold any other office of profit.

   Select the correct answer using the codes given below:
   (*a*) 1 only (*b*) 1 and 3 only
   (*c*) 2 and 3 only (*d*) 1 and 2 only

5. Who of the following vice-presidential candidates was elected unopposed?
   (*a*) K. R. Narayanan
   (*b*) R. Venkataraman
   (*c*) Dr. Shankar Dayal Sharma
   (*d*) Krishna Kant

6. The Vice-President of India may be removed from his office by
   (*a*) impeachment.
   (*b*) a resolution passed by Lok Sabha and Rajya Sabha with a two-thirds majority.
   (*c*) a resolution passed with a two-thirds majority in a joint session of the Parliament.
   (*d*) a resolution passed by the Rajya Sabha with an effective majority and agreed to by a majority members of the Lok Sabha.

7. Which one of the following statements is not correct?
   (*a*) The Vice-President of India holds office for a period of five years.
   (*b*) The Vice-President of India is eligible for re-election.
   (*c*) The Vice-President of India can act as the President only for a maximum period of nine months.
   (*d*) The Supreme Court of India has to look into all disputes with regard to the election of the Vice-President of India.

8. Consider the following statements:
   1. The American Vice-President succeeds to the presidency when it falls vacant.
   2. The Indian Vice-President merely serves as an acting President until the new President assumes charge.

   Which of the statements given above is/are correct?
   (*a*) 1 only (*b*) 2 only
   (*c*) Both 1 and 2 (*d*) Neither 1 nor 2

9. The Vice-President of India can resign from his office at any time by addressing the resignation letter to the:
   (*a*) Deputy Chairman of Rajya Sabha
   (*b*) Chief Justice of India
   (*c*) President of India
   (*d*) Speaker of Lok Sabha

10. Consider the following statements:
    1. No ground has been mentioned in the constitution for the removal of Vice-President.
    2. No resolution for the removal of Vice-President can be moved unless at least 21 days' advance notice has been given.

    Which of the statements given above is/are correct?
    (*a*) 1 only (*b*) 2 only
    (*c*) Both 1 and 2 (*d*) Neither 1 nor 2

Answers

1. (*c*)	2. (*a*)	3. (*a*)	4. (*c*)	5. (*c*)
6. (*d*)	7. (*c*)	8. (*c*)	9. (*c*)	10. (*a*)

19

Prime Minister

1. Consider the following statements with respect to the duties of the Prime Minister according to the Constitution of India:
   1. To make rules for the more convenient transaction of business of the Government of India and for the allocation among the Ministers of the said business.
   2. If the President so requires to submit for consideration of the Council of Ministers any matter on which a decision has been taken by a Minister but which has not been considered by the Council.

   Which of the statements given above is/are correct?

   (*a*) 1 only (*b*) 2 only
   (*c*) Both 1 and 2 (*d*) Neither 1 nor 2

2. Which one of the following is constitutionally obligatory on the part of the Prime Minister of India?
   (*a*) As the President is the supreme commander of the defence forces, the Prime Minister has to take all major decisions regarding defence only after prior approval by the President.
   (*b*) The Prime Minister has to communicate to the President all decisions of the Cabinet relating to administration and proposals for legislation.
   (*c*) As the ministers are appointed by the President, the Prime Minister has to go by Presidential discretion in the allocation of business among the ministers.
   (*d*) The Prime Minister, if he happens to be the leader of a party not having the required majority, should prove his majority strength in both the Houses of the Parliament within the period stipulated by the President.

3. Which of the following bodies are headed by the Prime Minister?
   1. National Integration Council
   2. National Water Resources Council
   3. NITI Aayog
   4. Inter-State Council
   5. Zonal Councils

   Select the correct answer from the codes given below:

   (*a*) 1, 3, 4 and 5 (*b*) 3, 4 and 5
   (*c*) 1, 2, 3 and 4 (*d*) 2, 3 and 4

4. "If any functionary under our constitution is to be compared with the US President, he is the Prime Minister and not the President of the Union". This statement is attributed to:
   (*a*) Jawaharlal Nehru (*b*) B.R. Ambedkar
   (*c*) Rajendra Prasad (*d*) K.M. Munshi

5. Which one of the following is correct in terms of the Constitution of India?
   (*a*) The Prime Minister decides the allocation of portfolios among the ministers.
   (*b*) When the Prime Minister resigns, the Council of Ministers gets dissolved.
   (*c*) All the principal policy announcements of the government are made by the Prime Minister.
   (*d*) It shall be the duty of the Prime Minister to communicate to the President all decisions of the Council of Ministers relating to the administration of the affairs of the union.

6. Which of the following Articles of the Constitution broadly govern the relationship between the Prime Minister and the President?
   1. Article 75
   2. Article 73
   3. Article 78
   4. Article 76
   5. Article 74

   Select the correct answer using the codes given below:
   (*a*) 1, 2, 3 and 5 (*b*) 1, 3 and 5
   (*c*) 1, 3, 4 and 5 (*d*) 1, 2, 3, 4 and 5

7. The Constitution of India lays down that proposals for legislation are to be communicated to the President by the
   (*a*) Prime Minister
   (*b*) Speaker of the Lok Sabha and Chairman of the Rajya Sabha
   (*c*) Minister for Law
   (*d*) Minister for Parliamentary Affairs

8. Who among the following called the Prime Minister as "the captain of the ship of the state"?
   (*a*) Ramsay Muir (*b*) Lord Morely
   (*c*) H.J. Laski (*d*) Munro

9. Who of the following became the Prime Ministers after being Chief Ministers?
   1. P.V. Narasimha Rao
   2. Charan Singh
   3. H.D. Deve Gowda
   4. V.P. Singh
   5. Morarji Desai

   Select the correct answer from the codes given below:
   (*a*) 2, 3, 4 and 5 (*b*) 1, 2 and 4
   (*c*) 1, 2, 3, 4 and 5 (*d*) 2, 3 and 4

10. Consider the following statements:

The Prime Minister as the head of the Council of Ministers

1. has a free hand in the distribution of portfolios.
2. can reshuffle the Ministers and ask any Minister to resign.
3. is bound by the advice of the Ministers.
4. advises the Ministers in day-to-day administration of Ministries.

Which of the statements given above are correct?

(*a*) 1 and 2 only (*b*) 2 and 3 only
(*c*) 1, 2 and 4 (*d*) 3 and 4 only

11. Which of the following are included in Article 78 of the Indian Constitution, defining the duties of Prime Minister?

1. To communicate to the President all decisions of the Council of Ministers relating to the administration of the affairs of the Union and proposals for legislation.
2. To take prior presidential sanction for the budget before submitting it in the Parliament.
3. To furnish the information called for by the President regarding administration of affairs of the Union.
4. If the President so requires to submit for consideration of the Council of Ministers a matter on which a minister has taken a decision without submitting the same for consideration by the Council beforehand.

Choose the correct answer from the codes given below:

(*a*) 1 and 2 only (*b*) 1, 3 and 4 only
(*c*) 2 and 4 only (*d*) 1 and 3 only

Answers

1. (*b*)	2. (*b*)	3. (*c*)	4. (*b*)	5. (*d*)
6. (*b*)	7. (*a*)	8. (*d*)	9. (*c*)	10. (*a*)
11. (*b*)				

20 Central Council of Ministers

1. Which of the following are not mentioned in the Constitution of India?
   1. Council of Ministers
   2. Collective Responsibility
   3. Resignation of Ministers
   4. Office of the Deputy Prime Minister

   Select the correct answer from the codes given below:

   (*a*) 1 and 2 only (*b*) 2 and 3 only
   (*c*) 3 and 4 only (*d*) 1 and 3 only

2. Consider the following statements:
   1. The President cannot function without the Union Council of Ministers.
   2. The Solicitor-General is the highest legal authority of the Union Government.
   3. The Union Council of Ministers can function for some time even after the death or resignation of the Prime Minister.
   4. In the absence of the Prime Minister, only the Home Minister can preside over emergency meetings of the Union Council of Ministers.

   Which of the statements given above is/are correct?

   (*a*) 1 only (*b*) 3 and 4 only
   (*c*) 1, 2 and 4 (*d*) 1, 2, 3 and 4

3. According to the Article 74 of the Constitution, which of the following statements relating to the advice tendered by Ministers to the President would be correct?
   (*a*) It shall not be inquired into in any court.
   (*b*) It can be inquired into in the Supreme Court.
   (*c*) It can be inquired into in all the courts.
   (*d*) It cannot be inquired into in the High Courts.

4. How are the salaries and allowances of the Union Ministers determined?
   (*a*) By the Cabinet Secretariat (*b*) By the Parliament
   (*c*) By the Ministry of Finance (*d*) By the Ministry of the Parliamentary Affairs

5. Which of the following Constitutional Amendment Acts has/have made the decisions of the Council of Ministers binding on the President of India?
   (*a*) 42nd and 44th Amendment Acts (*b*) 43rd Amendment Act
   (*c*) 40th Amendment Act (*d*) 40th and 41st Amendment Acts

6. Which of the Articles of the Constitution of India are relevant to analyse the constitutional provisions that deal with the relationship of the President with the Council of Ministers?
   (*a*) Articles 71, 75 and 78
   (*b*) Articles 74, 75 and 78
   (*c*) Articles 73, 76 and 78
   (*d*) Articles 72, 73 and 76

7. The accountability or responsibility of the Prime Minister and the Cabinet to the Lok Sabha is:
   (*a*) Intermittent (*b*) Indirect
   (*c*) At the time of elections (*d*) Direct, continuous and collective

8. Consider the following statements:
   1. The Kitchen Cabinet helps the Prime Minister in maintaining secrecy in making decisions on important political issues.
   2. The Kitchen Cabinet, being a small unit, is much more efficient decision-making body than a large Cabinet.

   Which of the statements given above is/are correct?
   (*a*) 1 only (*b*) 2 only
   (*c*) Both 1 and 2 (*d*) Neither 1 nor 2

9. In which of the following Articles of the Constitution of India is the principle of collective responsibility of the Council of Ministers enshrined?
   (*a*) Article 75 (*b*) Article 74
   (*c*) Article 77 (*d*) Article 78

10. "There shall be a Council of Ministers with the Prime Minister at the head to aid and advice the President who shall in the exercise of his functions act in accordance with such advice". This provision in the Constitution has been laid down by which one of the following Constitutional Amendment Acts?
   (*a*) 41st Amendment (*b*) 42nd Amendment
   (*c*) 43rd Amendment (*d*) 72nd Amendment

11. Article 74 of the Constitution provides that:
   (*a*) There shall be a Council of Ministers with the Prime Minister at the head, to aid and advise the President in exercise of his functions.
   (*b*) There shall be a Council of Ministers with the Prime Minister at the head, to aid and advise the President, who shall in exercise of his functions, act in accordance with such advice.
   (*c*) There shall be a Council of Ministers with the Prime Minister at the head, to aid and advise the President, who shall in exercise of his functions act in accordance with such advice provided that the President may require the Council of Ministers to reconsider such advice, either generally or otherwise and the President shall act in accordance with the advice tendered after such reconsideration.
   (*d*) There shall be a Council of Ministers with the Prime Minister at the head, to aid and advise the President, who shall in exercise of his functions, act in accordance with such advice or otherwise on his own.

12. According to the Constitution of India, if the President so requires, it shall be the duty of the Prime Minister to submit for the consideration of the Council of Ministers any matter on which a decision has been taken by a Minister, but which has not been considered by the Council. This ensures
    (*a*) collective responsibility.
    (*b*) the status of the Prime Minister as the first among the equals.
    (*c*) the power of the President to nullify the decision of the Minister.
    (*d*) the inherent power of the Minister to take a decision independent of the Council of Ministers.

13. Consider the following statements:
    1. All decisions of the Council of Ministers relating to the administration of the Union must be communicated to the President.
    2. The President can call for information relating to proposals for legislation.
    3. The President can direct that any matter on which decision has been taken by a Minister should be placed before the Council of Ministers.
    4. The President has the right to address and send messages to the Council of Ministers to elicit specific information.

    Which of the statements given above is/are correct?
    (*a*) 1 only (*b*) 3 and 4 only
    (*c*) 1, 2 and 3 (*d*) 1, 2, 3 and 4

14. Which one among the following features of the Constitution of India is indicative of the fact that the real executive power is vested in the Council of Ministers headed by the Prime Minister?
    (*a*) Federalism (*b*) Representative Legislature
    (*c*) Universal adult franchise (*d*) Parliamentary democracy

15. Which one of the following is not correct in relation to the Council of Ministers?
    (*a*) It is recognised by the Constitution.
    (*b*) The number of its members is not specified in the Constitution.
    (*c*) Its working is as per the provisions in the Constitution.
    (*d*) Its members and their ranks are decided by the Prime Minister.

16. The executive power of the Union is vested in the:
    (*a*) Union Cabinet (*b*) President of India
    (*c*) Prime Minister (*d*) Union Council of Ministers

17. Whenever the Constitution requires the "satisfaction" of the President for the exercise of any power or function by him, it means:
    (*a*) The personal satisfaction of the President
    (*b*) The satisfaction of the Council of Ministers
    (*c*) The satisfaction of the Members of the Parliament
    (*d*) The satisfaction of the Members of the Lok Sabha

Answers

1. (*c*)	2. (*a*)	3. (*a*)	4. (*b*)	5. (*a*)
6. (*b*)	7. (*d*)	8. (*c*)	9. (*a*)	10. (*b*)
11. (*c*)	12. (*a*)	13. (*c*)	14. (*d*)	15. (*c*)
16. (*b*)	17. (*b*)			

21

Cabinet Committees

1. Consider the following statements:
    1. The non-cabinet ministers are debarred from the membership of the Cabinet Committees.
    2. The Cabinet Committees are an organisational device to reduce the enormous workload of the cabinet.

    Which of the statements given above is/are correct?

    (*a*) 1 only (*b*) 2 only
    (*c*) Both 1 and 2 (*d*) Neither 1 nor 2

2. Which of the following provides for the establishment of the Cabinet Committees?

    (*a*) Constitution of India (*b*) Parliamentary Statutes
    (*c*) Rules of Business (*d*) Presidential Orders

3. Consider the following statements:
    1. In addition to Cabinet Committees, several Group of Ministers (GOMs) are constituted to look into different issues/subjects.
    2. Some of these GOMs are empowered to take decisions on behalf of the Cabinet whereas the others make recommendations to the Cabinet.

    Which of the statements given above is/are correct?

    (*a*) 1 only (*b*) 2 only
    (*c*) Both 1 and 2 (*d*) Neither 1 nor 2

4. Which one of the following Cabinet Committees is described as a "Super-Cabinet"?

    (*a*) Economic Affairs Committee
    (*b*) Parliamentary Affairs Committee
    (*c*) Political Affairs Committee
    (*d*) Appointments Committee

5. Consider the following statements:
    1. The cabinet cannot review the decisions taken by the Cabinet Committees.
    2. The Cabinet Committees are based on the principles of division of labour and effective delegation.

    Which of the statements given above is/are correct?

    (*a*) 1 only (*b*) 2 only
    (*c*) Both 1 and 2 (*d*) Neither 1 nor 2

6. Which of the following cabinet committees is chaired by the Union Home Minister?
   (*a*) Parliamentary Affairs Committee
   (*b*) Economic Affairs Committee
   (*c*) Political Affairs Committee
   (*d*) Appointments Committee

7. Which of the following cabinet committee deals with all policy matters pertaining to domestic and foreign affairs?
   (*a*) Appointments Committee
   (*b*) Economic Affairs Committee
   (*c*) Parliamentary Affairs Committee
   (*d*) Political Affairs Committee

Answers

1. (*b*)	2. (*c*)	3. (*c*)	4. (*c*)	5. (*b*)
6. (*a*)	7. (*d*)			

22

Parliament

1. Consider the following statements:
   1. A Bill pending in the Rajya Sabha which has not been passed by the Lok Sabha shall lapse on the dissolution of the Lok Sabha.
   2. A Bill pending in the Parliament shall lapse by reason of the prorogation of the Houses.

   Which of the statements given above is/are correct?

   (*a*) 1 only (*b*) 2 only
   (*c*) Both 1 and 2 (*d*) Neither 1 nor 2

2. Consider the following statements:
   1. The Chairman of the Council of States or the Speaker of the House of the People, or person acting as such, shall not vote at any sitting of either House of the Parliament or joint sitting of the House in the first instance, but shall have and exercise a casting vote in the case of an equality of votes.
   2. A person is qualified to fill a seat in the Council of States or the House of the People if he is not less than twenty-five years of age.

   Which of the statements given above is/are correct?

   (*a*) 1 only (*b*) 2 only
   (*c*) Both 1 and 2 (*d*) Neither 1 nor 2

3. Consider the following statements:
   1. Since the sums required to meet expenditure described by the Constitution of India as expenditure charged upon the Consolidated Fund of India are not submitted to the vote the of Parliament, no House is competent to discuss these estimates.
   2. Annual Finance Bill provides the legal authority for the withdrawal of sums from the Consolidated Fund of India.

   Which of the statements given above is/are correct?

   (*a*) 1 only (*b*) 2 only
   (*c*) Both 1 and 2 (*d*) Neither 1 nor 2

4. Consider the following statements in respect of provisions for removing deadlock between the two Houses of the Parliament:

   After a bill has been passed by one House and transmitted to the other House, the President may notify to the Houses his intention to summon them for a joint sitting, if:
   1. the Bill is rejected by the other House.
   2. the Houses have finally disagreed as to the amendments to be made in the Bill.

3. more than three months have elapsed from the date of the receipt of the Bill by the other House without the Bill being passed by it.

Which of the statements given above are correct?

(*a*) 1, 2 and 3 (*b*) 1 and 2 only
(*c*) 2 and 3 only (*d*) 1 and 3 only

5. In India, the parliamentary control over government and administration is considerably reduced and restricted in effectiveness due to which of the following reasons?
   1. The expansion in the volume and variety of administrative work
   2. The Frequent use of Guillotine
   3. The large size of the Parliament
   4. The members of the Parliament are laymen
   5. The financial committees do post mortem work

   Select the correct answer using the codes given below:

   (*a*) 1, 2 and 5 (*b*) 2, 3 and 4
   (*c*) 2, 3, 4 and 5 (*d*) 1, 2, 3, 4 and 5

6. An exceptional grant under the Constitution of India is regarded as:
   (*a*) an advance on account of estimated expenditure for a part of any financial year pending completion of procedure for voting of grant.
   (*b*) a grant for meeting an unexpected demand on account of indefinite character of the service which cannot be stated with details.
   (*c*) a grant forming no part of current service of any financial year.
   (*d*) a grant made when a need has arisen during the current financial year for additional expenditure upon some new service.

7. The provision for the Contingency Fund of India results in:
   (*a*) absolving the executive from preparing the estimates of the expenditure.
   (*b*) compelling the Legislature to approve the expenditure.
   (*c*) reducing the legislative control over the executive.
   (*d*) providing a safety valve to tide over a crisis.

8. Which of the following tools of control may be adopted for raising a discussion in the House on a matter of urgent public importance?
   (*a*) Censure motion
   (*b*) Adjournment motion
   (*c*) Calling attention
   (*d*) Cut motion

9. Consider the following statements relating to the procedure of the election of the Speaker and the Deputy Speaker of the Lok Sabha:
   1. The election of the Speaker shall be held on such date as the Prime Minister may fix and the Secretary-General shall send to every member notice of this date.
   2. The election of the Deputy Speaker shall be held on such date as the Speaker may fix and the Secretary-General shall send to every member notice of this date.

Which of the statements given above is/are correct?

(*a*) 1 only (*b*) 2 only

(*c*) Both 1 and 2 (*d*) Neither 1 nor 2

10. Which one of the following statements is not correct?

(*a*) An Appropriation Act is not essential for passing a grant under a Vote of Credit.

(*b*) Re-appropriation does not involve any additional expenditure.

(*c*) The Rajya Sabha has no power to vote on the demands for grants.

(*d*) No amendment can be proposed in the Appropriation Bill in either House of the Parliament.

11. According to the Constitution, the Lok Sabha must meet at least:

(*a*) thrice each year with no more than two months between sessions.

(*b*) twice each year with no more than three months between sessions.

(*c*) twice each year with no more than four months between sessions.

(*d*) twice each year with no more than six months between sessions.

12. Consider the following statements:

1. The nature of a Bill, if it is certified by the Speaker of the House of People as a Money Bill, is not open to question in a Court of Law.
2. The President of India has the power to question the nature of a Bill to be taken as a Money Bill even if it is certified to be so by the Speaker of the House of People.

Which of the statements given above is/are correct?

(*a*) 1 only (*b*) 2 only

(*c*) Both 1 and 2 (*d*) Neither 1 nor 2

13. Consider the following statements:

1. The budget is placed in the Rajya Sabha at the end of the Finance Minister's Budget Speech in the Lok Sabha.
2. Since 2017, the budget is presented to the Lok Sabha on the first day of February.

Which of the statements given above is/are correct?

(*a*) 1 only (*b*) 2 only

(*c*) Both 1 and 2 (*d*) Neither 1 nor 2

14. What does the "Rule of Lapse" mean?

(*a*) All pending bills in the Parliament lapse with its prorogation.

(*b*) All appropriations voted by the Parliament expire at the end of the financial year.

(*c*) The demand for grants of a ministry lapses with criticism of its policy by the opposition.

(*d*) The appropriation bill lapses if it is not returned by the Rajya Sabha within 14 days.

15. Consider the following statements:

The expenditure charged on the Consolidated Fund of India comprises:

1. pension payable to Judges of a High Court.
2. debt charges for which the Government of India is liable.
3. salary, allowances and pension payable to Comptroller and Auditor-General of India.

Which of the statements given above are correct?

(*a*) 1, 2 and 3 (*b*) 1 and 3 only
(*c*) 2 and 3 only (*d*) 1 and 2 only

16. The object of the adjournment motion in the Parliament is to:
(*a*) collect information from the ministers.
(*b*) make a cut in the budget proposals.
(*c*) criticise a particular policy of the Government.
(*d*) topple the Government.

17. Which of the following parliamentary procedures implies the mode of arriving at a decision?
(*a*) Division (*b*) Guillotine
(*c*) Motion (*d*) Point of order

18. Which one of the following is the correct sequence of the given stages in relation to the enactment of the budget?
(*a*) Voting of demands for grants-General discussion-Consideration and passing of the Appropriation Bill-Consideration and passing of the Finance Bill
(*b*) General discussion-Voting of demands for grants-Consideration and passing of the Appropriation Bill-Consideration and passing of the Finance Bill
(*c*) Voting of demands for grants-Consideration and passing of the Appropriation Bill-Consideration and passing of the Finance Bill-General discussion
(*d*) General discussion-Consideration and passing of the Finance Bill-Consideration and passing of the Appropriation Bill-Voting of demands for grants

19. Which one of the following pairs is not correctly matched?

State		No. of members in the Rajya Sabha
(*a*) Maharashtra	:	19
(*b*) Tamil Nadu	:	18
(*c*) Bihar	:	18
(*d*) West Bengal	:	16

20. Which one of the following events is not considered to be an indication of loss of confidence of the lower House of the Parliament?
(*a*) Adjournment motion is carried.
(*b*) Vote of thanks on the President's address is not carried.
(*c*) Cut on Money Bill is passed.
(*d*) Censure motion is passed.

21. How much is the quorum of a House of the Parliament of India?
(*a*) One-half of the membership of the House
(*b*) One-third of the membership of the House
(*c*) Two-thirds of the membership of the House
(*d*) One-tenth of the membership of the House

22. Which of the following pairs are correctly matched?
    1. Article 266 – No tax shall be levied or collected except by the authority of law.
    2. Article 117 – No tax can be imposed unless asked for by the executive government.
    3. Article 113 – No expenditure can be sanctioned unless asked for by the executive government.
    4. Article 265 – No expenditure can be incurred except with the authorisation of the legislature.

    Select the correct answer using the codes given below:
    (*a*) 1, 2, 3 and 4 (*b*) 2, 3 and 4
    (*c*) 1, 3 and 4 (*d*) 2 and 3 only

23. Consider the following statements:
    A Bill is deemed to be a Money Bill if it contains only provisions dealing with the:
    1. alteration or regulation of any tax.
    2. regulation of the borrowing of money by the government.
    3. appropriation of money out of the Consolidated Fund of India.
    4. custody of the Contingency Fund of India.

    Which of the above statements are correct?
    (*a*) 1, 2 and 3 only (*b*) 2, 3 and 4 only
    (*c*) 1 and 4 only (*d*) 1, 2, 3 and 4

24. The Rajya Sabha has exclusive jurisdiction in:
    (*a*) approving a proclamation of emergency.
    (*b*) the creation and abolition of States.
    (*c*) the election of the Vice-President.
    (*d*) authorising the Parliament to legislate on a subject in the State List.

25. What is the maximum period that shall not intervene between last sitting in one session and the date appointed for first sitting in the next session for each House of the Parliament?
    (*a*) Four months (*b*) Five months
    (*c*) Six months (*d*) Eight months

26. When Demands for Grants are introduced in Lok Sabha, the Speaker applies the guillotine:
    (*a*) after the demands are discussed and approved.
    (*b*) after the demands are discussed and voted down by the Lok Sabha.
    (*c*) when the demands are discussed and reduced.
    (*d*) when the time allotted is coming to a close.

27. Which of the following parliamentary device is related to the drawing of attention of the speaker towards incorrect or incomplete answers by the Ministers?
    (*a*) Cut Motion
    (*b*) Call Attention Motion
    (*c*) Privilege Motion
    (*d*) Adjournment Motion

28. Which one of the following powers of the Rajya Sabha is provided in the Constitution of India?
    (*a*) To reject or amend a money bill
    (*b*) To decide whether a bill is a money bill
    (*c*) To vote for public expenditure
    (*d*) To delay a money bill for a period not exceeding fourteen days

29. The method of election of the members of the Rajya Sabha on the basis of proportional representation by the State Legislatures was borrowed from the:
    (*a*) Constitution of the U.S.A.
    (*b*) Constitution of Australia
    (*c*) Constitution of South Africa
    (*d*) Constitution of Ireland

30. Which one of the following statements is correct?
    Parliament can make a law with respect to a matter in the state list in the national interest if:
    (*a*) the President of India gives permission.
    (*b*) the Parliament passes a resolution.
    (*c*) a State makes a request.
    (*d*) the Rajya Sabha passes a resolution by a two-thirds majority.

31. Which one of the following statements is not correct?
    (*a*) There is a provision in the Constitution of India for readjustment of allocation of seats in the Lok Sabha upon the completion of each census.
    (*b*) If for a period of 60 days, a member of either House is absent without the permission of the House from all meetings thereof, the House may declare his seat vacant.
    (*c*) The Rajya Sabha approves Money Bill after it has been passed by the Lok Sabha.
    (*d*) The Attorney-General of India has the right to speak in, and otherwise to take part in the proceedings of either House of the Parliament.

32. Consider the following statements:
    1. The constitution of India has authorised the Parliament to create a Contingency Fund of India.
    2. The Contingency Fund of India enables the government to meet any unforeseen expenditure.

    Which of the statements given above is/are correct?
    (*a*) 1 only (*b*) 2 only
    (*c*) Both 1 and 2 (*d*) Neither 1 nor 2

33. Which one of the following schedules of the Constitution of India deals with allocation of seats in the Council of States?
    (*a*) Third Schedule
    (*b*) Fourth Schedule
    (*c*) Fifth Schedule
    (*d*) Sixth Schedule

34. Under Article 312 of the Constitution of India, the Rajya Sabha has exclusive power to recommend the establishment of which one of the following?
   (*a*) River-valley Development Authorities
   (*b*) Zonal Councils
   (*c*) Administrative Tribunals
   (*d*) New All-India Services

35. Payments from the Consolidated Fund of India are authorised by which of the following?
   (*a*) Money Bill (*b*) Appropriation Act
   (*c*) Finance Act (*d*) Consolidated Fund Act

36. Vote of Credit provides for making:
   (*a*) an exceptional grant which forms no part of current service of any financial year
   (*b*) any grant in advance in respect of estimated expenditure for a part of any financial year
   (*c*) a grant for meeting an unexpected demand upon resources of India
   (*d*) a grant for additional expenditure upon new service not contemplated in the financial year

37. Which one of the following is not a measure of control exercised by the Parliament over Government?
   (*a*) Asking questions (*b*) Committees system
   (*c*) Review of decision (*d*) No-confidence motion

38. Consider the following statements:
   1. A Bill returned by the President for reconsideration does not lapse on the dissolution of the Lok Sabha.
   2. A Bill passed by the Lok Sabha and pending in the Rajya Sabha lapses on the dissolution of the Lok Sabha.
   3. A Bill under consideration of the Lok Sabha lapses when the Lok Sabha is prorogued.
   4. A Bill pending in the Rajya Sabha but not passed by the Lok Sabha does not lapse on the dissolution of the Lok Sabha.

   Which of the statements given above are correct?
   (*a*) 2, 3 and 4 only (*b*) 1 and 2 only
   (*c*) 3 and 4 only (*d*) 1, 2 and 4 only

39. During the discussion on the Demands for Grants, cut motions can be moved to reduce the amount of a demand. Which of the following categories are classified as cut motion?
   1. Policy cut
   2. Economy cut
   3. Token cut
   4. Programme cut

   Select the correct answer using the codes given below:
   (*a*) 1 and 2 only (*b*) 2 and 4 only
   (*c*) 1, 2 and 3 (*d*) 3 and 4 only

40. Which one of the following statements holds good in respect of the Rajya Sabha?
   (*a*) One-third of its members retire after every three years.
   (*b*) Two-thirds of its members retire after every three years.
   (*c*) Two-thirds of its members retire after every two years.
   (*d*) One-third of its members retire after every two years.

41. Which one of the following is the correct sequence through which an Ordinary Bill passes through in the Parliament?
   (*a*) Authentication, Discussion of Principles, Clause-by-Clause consideration, Post-introduction motion, Assent
   (*b*) Post-introduction motion, Discussion of Principles, Clause-by-Clause consideration, Authentication, Assent
   (*c*) Discussion of Principles, Authentication, Post-introduction motion, Clause-by-Clause consideration, Assent
   (*d*) Discussion of Principles, Post-introduction motion, Clause-by-Clause consideration, Authentication, Assent

42. Who among the following decides whether a Bill is a Money Bill?
   (*a*) The Finance Minister
   (*b*) The Chairman of the Rajya Sabha
   (*c*) The President of India
   (*d*) The Speaker of the Lok Sabha

43. A non-money bill passed by the Parliament is returned by the President to the Parliament for reconsideration. It is passed once again by the Parliament without any change. Now, the:
   (*a*) President can again withhold his assent.
   (*b*) Bill will automatically lapse.
   (*c*) Bill will be referred to the Supreme Court.
   (*d*) President will give his assent.

44. The Lok Sabha Secretariat comes under the direct supervision of which of the following?
   (*a*) Ministry of Home Affairs
   (*b*) Ministry of Parliamentary Affairs
   (*c*) Prime Minister's Office
   (*d*) Speaker of the Lok Sabha

45. Consider the following statements regarding money bills:
   1. They originate in the Lok Sabha.
   2. They originate in the Rajya Sabha.
   3. The Rajya Sabha can recommend amendments.
   4. Both the Houses have equal powers over them.

   Which of the statements given above is/are correct?
   (*a*) 1 only (*b*) 1 and 3 only
   (*c*) 2 only (*d*) 4 only

46. If a member of either House of the Parliament is, without the permission of the House, absent from all meetings thereof for more than a certain period, the House may declare his seat vacant. What is the duration of this period?
(*a*) 60 days
(*b*) 45 days
(*c*) 30 days
(*d*) 15 days

47. Vote on account means:
(*a*) The expenditure charged on the Consolidated Fund of India is not submitted to the vote of the Parliament.
(*b*) A proposal submitted by the Finance Minister before presenting the budget.
(*c*) To bring a proposal related to the speech of the President before the joint session of the Parliament.
(*d*) If the budget is not passed before 1st April, the Parliament is authorised to sanction any grant in advance to meet the expenses.

48. Which of the following is a motion for the adjournment of the debate on a bill/motion/ resolution etc. or a motion to retard or delay the progress of a business under the consideration of the House?
(*a*) No-Day-Yet-Named Motion
(*b*) Closure Motion
(*c*) Adjournment Motion
(*d*) Dilatory Motion

49. Which one of the following statements related to Money Bills is not correct?
(*a*) It cannot be introduced in the Council of States.
(*b*) If any question arises whether the bill is Money Bill or not, the decision of the Lok Sabha Speaker is final.
(*c*) In case of a deadlock over a Money Bill, the President can summon a joint sitting of the Parliament.
(*d*) A Money Bill cannot be introduced except on the recommendation of the President.

50. Which one of the following statements is correct?

The estimates which relate to expenditure charged upon the Consolidated Fund of India:
(*a*) can be discussed in the House of the People only.
(*b*) can be discussed in the Council of the States only.
(*c*) can be discussed in either House of the Parliament.
(*d*) cannot be discussed in any House of the Parliament.

51. Which of the following is the subject of Article 110 of the constitution of India?
(*a*) Annual Financial Statement or Budget
(*b*) Supplementary, additional or excess grants
(*c*) Appropriation Bill
(*d*) Definition of "Money Bill"

52. Which one of the following is not applicable regarding the purpose of Cut Motion?
   (*a*) Raising questions of urgent public importance
   (*b*) Drawing attention to any lapse on the part of the administration
   (*c*) Drawing attention to specific problems
   (*d*) Concentrating discussion on some concrete points

53. Which of the following is the quorum requirement in the Rajya Sabha?
   (*a*) 25 (*b*) 50
   (*c*) 100 (*d*) 126

54. What will follow if a Money Bill is substantially amended by the Rajya Sabha?
   (*a*) The Lok Sabha may still proceed with the Bill, accepting or not accepting the recommendations of the Rajya Sabha.
   (*b*) The Lok Sabha cannot consider the Bill further.
   (*c*) The Lok Sabha may send the Bill to the Rajya Sabha for reconsideration.
   (*d*) The President may call a joint sitting for passing the Bill.

55. Which one of the following statements about the Speaker of the Lok Sabha is not correct?
   (*a*) He has the power to adjourn the House sine die.
   (*b*) He has the power to summon the House even after prorogation.
   (*c*) He continues to be in office even after the dissolution of the House and until immediately before the first meeting of the House.
   (*d*) He must vacate the office if he ceases to be a member of the Lok Sabha.

56. The Deputy Chairman of the Rajya Sabha is elected by:
   (*a*) elected members of the Rajya Sabha.
   (*b*) all members of the Rajya Sabha.
   (*c*) elected members of the Parliament.
   (*d*) all members of the Parliament.

57. In which of the following years, the Central Government merged the railway budget into the general budget?
   (*a*) 2016 (*b*) 2017
   (*c*) 2018 (*d*) 2019

58. Who chairs the Joint Session of the two Houses of the Parliament?
   (*a*) The Vice-President of India
   (*b*) The Speaker of the House of the People
   (*c*) The Chairman of the Rajya Sabha
   (*d*) The Prime Minister of India

59. Under Article 368 of the Constitution of India, a Constitutional Amendment Bill is passed by the Parliament by:
   (*a*) simple majority of members present and voting.
   (*b*) two-thirds majority of members present and voting.

(*c*) three-fourths majority of members present and voting.
(*d*) majority of total membership and majority of not less than two-thirds of the members present and voting.

60. Which of the following are correct about the contingency fund of India?
    1. It was created under the provisions of the Article 267.
    2. It was created in 1951.
    3. It is held by the Finance Secretary on behalf of the President.
    4. Its amount will be determined by the President.

    Select the correct answer using the codes given below:
    (*a*) 1 and 3 only (*b*) 1, 3 and 4
    (*c*) 2, 3 and 4 (*d*) 3 and 4 only

61. Which of the following is not correct with regard to the Speaker of the Lok Sabha?
    (*a*) The Speaker certifies whether a particular Bill is a Money Bill or not.
    (*b*) Discussion on a motion for the removal of the Speaker is presided over by the Vice-President.
    (*c*) The Speaker has power to curtail or cancel the zero hour.
    (*d*) The Speaker nominates chairpersons of various committees.

62. Which of the following statements are correct in respect of parliamentary debate on Appropriation Bill?
    1. No amendments can be moved on the amount of expenditure.
    2. Speaker is empowered to withhold permission on matters of repetitive nature.
    3. Rajya Sabha has power to amend or reject the Bill.

    Select the correct answer using the codes given below:
    (*a*) 1 and 2 only (*b*) 1 and 3 only
    (*c*) 2 and 3 only (*d*) 1, 2 and 3

63. According to parliamentary procedure, the term "guillotine" means that the Speaker:
    (*a*) stops the business on hand and puts the matter to vote.
    (*b*) adjourns the House before expiry of the time.
    (*c*) disallows voting on a motion.
    (*d*) reprimands a member for misbehaviour.

64. While discussing a budget, the Parliament cannot:
    (*a*) give assent to the demand. (*b*) reduce the demand.
    (*c*) refuse the demand. (*d*) increase the demand.

65. Which one of the following is not related to Adjournment Motion?
    (*a*) The matter is framed in general terms.
    (*b*) The matter is urgent.
    (*c*) The matter is of general public interest.
    (*d*) The matter does not raise a question of privilege.

66. Which one among the following carries out demarcation of electoral constituencies in each State and allocation of seats in the Lok Sabha to different States?
(*a*) Election Commission
(*b*) Register General
(*c*) Delimitation Commission
(*d*) States Reorganisation Commission

67. Which of the following is/are correct in respect of "Zero Hour" discussion?
1. It is not directed against an individual Minister.
2. It covers questions raised over matters of public importance.

Select the correct answer using the codes given below:
(*a*) 1 only (*b*) 2 only
(*c*) Both 1 and 2 (*d*) Neither 1 nor 2

68. Which one of the following is true of the Appropriation Act?
(*a*) It is the demand for grants approved by the Parliament.
(*b*) It applies to approval of the budget by the Parliament.
(*c*) Authorisation by the Parliament for withdrawal of money from the Consolidated Fund.
(*d*) Authorisation by the Parliament for withdrawal of money from the Contingency Fund.

69. Which one of the following statements is correct with regard to the power of The Parliament in enacting the Budget?
(*a*) It can increase a tax but not reduce it.
(*b*) It can increase a tax as well as reduce or abolish it.
(*c*) It cannot increase a tax but can reduce or abolish it.
(*d*) It can neither increase a tax nor reduce it.

70. Who among the following can establish additional courts for better administration of any existing law with respect to a matter contained in the Union List?
(*a*) Chief Justice of India
(*b*) High Court of the concerned State
(*c*) Parliament
(*d*) Concerned State Legislature

71. Which of the following statements is/are correct?
1. No Member of the Parliament shall be liable to any proceedings in any Court in respect of any vote given by him in any Committee of the Parliament.
2. A House of the Parliament can try anyone or any case directly, as a Court of Justice.
3. No Member of the Parliament shall be liable to any proceedings in any Court in respect of anything said in the Parliament.

Select the correct answer using the codes given below:
(*a*) 1, 2 and 3 (*b*) 2 and 3 only
(*c*) 1 and 3 only (*d*) 1 only

72. Rajya Sabha has equal powers with the Lok Sabha:
   (*a*) in the matter of creating new All India Services.
   (*b*) in amending the Constitution.
   (*c*) in the removal of the Government.
   (*d*) in making cut motions.

73. Who among the following chooses a member of the Council of States to be its Deputy Chairman?
   (*a*) The President
   (*b*) The Union Minister of Parliamentary Affairs
   (*c*) The Prime Minister
   (*d*) The Council of States

74. The Demands for Supplementary Grants must be presented to and passed by the House:
   (*a*) before the end of the respective financial year.
   (*b*) before the budget of the following year is passed.
   (*c*) after the withdrawal of money from the Consolidated Fund.
   (*d*) after the submission of report of C.A.G.

75. Which of the following expenditures shall be charged on the Consolidated Fund of India?
   1. The emoluments and allowances of the President and other expenditure relating to his office.
   2. The emoluments and allowances of the Prime Minister and other expenditure relating to his office.
   3. The salaries and allowances of the Chairman and the Deputy Chairman of the Council of States.
   4. The salaries and allowances of the Speaker and the Deputy Speaker of the Lok Sabha.

   Choose the correct answer from the codes given below:
   (*a*) 1, 2 and 3 (*b*) 2, 3 and 4
   (*c*) 1, 3 and 4 (*d*) 1, 2 and 4

76. Demands for grants can emanate only from:
   (*a*) the leader of the Opposition.
   (*b*) the Executive.
   (*c*) the Chairman of the Estimates Committee.
   (*d*) any member who is not a member of the ruling party.

77. Which of the following grants is related to the additional expenditure not covered in the approved budget?
   (*a*) Vote on account (*b*) Vote on credit
   (*c*) Supplementary demand for grants (*d*) Excess demand for grants

78. What is meant by "Zero Hour"?
   (*a*) Exact time when the question hour ends.
   (*b*) Time between the question hour and the next item on the agenda.

(*c*) Time allotted for informal discussion between two stages of discussion on a bill.
(*d*) Specific time allotted for a discussion on budget.

79. Which of the following regarding the Rajya Sabha are correct?
 1. It is not subject to dissolution.
 2. It has a term of six years.
 3. One-third of its members retire after every two years.
 4. Its members shall not be less than 25 years of age.

 Select the correct answer using the codes given below:
 (*a*) 1, 2 and 3 (*b*) 2, 3 and 4
 (*c*) 1 and 3 only (*d*) 2 and 4 only

80. Which one of the following has precedence over every other motion?
 (*a*) Calling attention motion
 (*b*) Half-an-hour discussion
 (*c*) Adjournment motion
 (*d*) A resolution by both the Houses jointly

81. A Money Bill deals with:
 1. the receipt of money on account of the public account of India.
 2. giving any guarantee by the Government of India for borrowing of money.
 3. custody of Consolidated Fund of India.
 4. withdrawal of money from Contingency Fund of India.

 Select the correct answer using the codes given below:
 (*a*) 1 and 2 only (*b*) 1, 2, 3 and 4
 (*c*) 1, 2 and 4 (*d*) 3 and 4 only

82. When an advance grant is made by the Parliament in pending the regular passage of the budget, it is called what of the following?
 (*a*) Vote on credit (*b*) Token grant
 (*c*) Vote on account (*d*) Supplementary grant

83. Consider the following statements:
 1. The allocation of seats in the Rajya Sabha to be filled by the representatives of the States and of the Union Territories is in accordance with the provisions in that behalf contained in the Fourth Schedule of the Constitution of India.
 2. The representatives of each State and Union Territory in the Rajya Sabha are elected by elected members of the Legislative Assembly of the State and the body functioning as Legislature for the Union Territory in accordance with the system of proportional representation by means of the single transferable vote.

 Which of the statements given above is/are correct?
 (*a*) 1 only (*b*) 2 only
 (*c*) Both 1 and 2 (*d*) Neither 1 nor 2

84. Consider the following statements:
   1. The nature of a Bill which is certified by the Speaker as a Money Bill shall not be open to question in the either House of the Parliament but can be taken up only in a court of law.
   2. After the grants included in the Annual Financial Statement are voted by the House of the People, the grants so made by the House of the People as well as the expenditure charged on the Consolidated Fund of India and the taxing proposals of the budget are incorporated in the Appropriation Bill.

   Which of the statements given above is/are correct?

   (*a*) 1 only (*b*) 2 only
   (*c*) Both 1 and 2 (*d*) Neither 1 nor 2

85. Which of the following motions has come up as a new procedural device to cope with the emerging situations of fractured mandates resulting in hung Parliament?

   (*a*) Confidence motion (*b*) Censure motion
   (*c*) No-confidence motion (*d*) Dilatory motion

86. When an Ordinary Bill is referred to a joint sitting of both the Houses of Parliament, it has to be passed by a:

   (*a*) simple majority of the total number of members of both the Houses present and voting.
   (*b*) two-thirds majority of the total number of members of both the Houses.
   (*c*) simple majority of the total number of members of both the Houses.
   (*d*) two-thirds majority of the total number of members of both the Houses present and voting.

87. Consider the following statements with respect to the Rajya Sabha:
   1. The origin of the Rajya Sabha can be traced back to 1919 when in pursuance to the Government of India Act, 1919, a second chamber known as the Council of States was created.
   2. The Rajya Sabha has special powers to declare that it is necessary and expedient in the national interest that the Parliament may make laws with respect to a matter in the State List.

   Which of the statements given above is/are correct?

   (*a*) 1 only (*b*) 2 only
   (*c*) Both 1 and 2 (*d*) Neither 1 nor 2

88. Charged expenditure upon the Consolidated Fund of India:

   (*a*) is submitted to the vote of the Parliament.
   (*b*) is not submitted to the vote of the Rajya Sabha.
   (*c*) is not submitted for the sanction of the President.
   (*d*) is not submitted to the vote of the Parliament.

89. "No tax shall be levied or collected except by authority of law." Which Article of the Constitution of India provides this?

   (*a*) Article 209 (*b*) Article 215
   (*c*) Article 256 (*d*) Article 265

90. The estimates of expenditure from the Consolidated Fund of India included in the budget and required to be voted by the Lok Sabha are submitted in the form of which of the following?

(*a*) Charged Expenditure (*b*) Capital Budget
(*c*) Demands for Grants (*d*) Revenue Budget

91. What is the question asked orally after the Question Hour in the House called?

(*a*) Supplementary question
(*b*) Short-notice question
(*c*) Starred question
(*d*) Unstarred question

92. The economy cut motion seeks to reduce the proposed expenditure of a demand for grant by:

(*a*) Rupees one hundred (*b*) Rupee one
(*c*) A specified amount (*d*) An unspecified amount

93. Which of the following terms can be described as an instrument of socio-economic change?

(*a*) Voting on the demands for grants
(*b*) Budget
(*c*) Money Bill
(*d*) Charged Expenditure

94. Pending the passage of Finance Bill in the Parliament, the Provisional Collection of Taxes Act, 1931 empowers the government to collect taxes for a period of:

(*a*) 50 days (*b*) 60 days
(*c*) 75 days (*d*) 90 days

95. The Consolidated Fund of India is made up of:

(*a*) the excise duty and the income tax.
(*b*) the income tax and the corporate tax.
(*c*) the money raised from all loans.
(*d*) all revenue receipts of the Government of India.

96. What is the grant provided by the Parliament in respect of the estimated expenditure for the part of the ensuing financial year pending the regular passage of the budget called?

(*a*) Appropriation account (*b*) Token cut
(*c*) Vote on account (*d*) Cut motion

97. In the context of the budget, the term "guillotine" is used with reference to which of the following?

(*a*) Appropriation Bill
(*b*) Consolidated Fund charges
(*c*) Voting of Demands
(*d*) Finance Bill

98. Which of the following items are included in the charged expenditure?
   1. Any sums required to satisfy any judgement, decree or award of any court or arbitral tribunals.
   2. Debt charges for which the Government of India is liable.
   3. The salaries and allowances of certain high officials.

   Select the correct answer using the codes given below:

   (*a*) 1 and 2 only (*b*) 2 and 3 only
   (*c*) 1 and 3 only (*d*) 1, 2 and 3

99. Which of the following factors have led to the decline of Indian Parliament?
   1. Growth of delegated legislation
   2. Low level of attendance in the Parliament
   3. Frequent promulgation of ordinances
   4. Frequent amendment of the constitution
   5. Set back in the parliamentary behaviour and ethics

   Select the correct answer using the codes given below:

   (*a*) 1, 2, 3 and 5 (*b*) 1, 3, 4 and 5
   (*c*) 2, 3 and 4 (*d*) 1, 3 and 5

100. Consider the following statements:
   1. After the demands for grants in the Annual Financial Statement are voted by the Lok Sabha, the grants so made as well as the expenditure charged on the Consolidated Fund of India are incorporated in the Annual Finance Bill.
   2. The taxing proposals of the budget are included in an Appropriation Bill.

   Which of the statements given above is/are correct?

   (*a*) 1 only (*b*) 2 only
   (*c*) Both 1 and 2 (*d*) Neither 1 nor 2

Answers

1. (*d*)	2. (*a*)	3. (*d*)	4. (*b*)	5. (*d*)
6. (*c*)	7. (*d*)	8. (*b*)	9. (*b*)	10. (*a*)
11. (*d*)	12. (*a*)	13. (*c*)	14. (*b*)	15. (*a*)
16. (*c*)	17. (*a*)	18. (*b*)	19. (*c*)	20. (*a*)
21. (*d*)	22. (*d*)	23. (*d*)	24. (*d*)	25. (*c*)
26. (*d*)	27. (*c*)	28. (*d*)	29. (*c*)	30. (*d*)
31. (*c*)	32. (*c*)	33. (*b*)	34. (*d*)	35. (*b*)
36. (*c*)	37. (*c*)	38. (*d*)	39. (*c*)	40. (*d*)
41. (*b*)	42. (*d*)	43. (*d*)	44. (*d*)	45. (*b*)
46. (*a*)	47. (*d*)	48. (*d*)	49. (*c*)	50. (*c*)

51. (*d*)	52. (*a*)	53. (*a*)	54. (*a*)	55. (*b*)
56. (*b*)	57. (*b*)	58. (*b*)	59. (*d*)	60. (*a*)
61. (*b*)	62. (*a*)	63. (*a*)	64. (*d*)	65. (*a*)
66. (*c*)	67. (*b*)	68. (*c*)	69. (*c*)	70. (*c*)
71. (*c*)	72. (*b*)	73. (*d*)	74. (*a*)	75. (*c*)
76. (*b*)	77. (*c*)	78. (*b*)	79. (*c*)	80. (*c*)
81. (*b*)	82. (*c*)	83. (*a*)	84. (*d*)	85. (*a*)
86. (*a*)	87. (*c*)	88. (*d*)	89. (*d*)	90. (*c*)
91. (*a*)	92. (*c*)	93. (*b*)	94. (*c*)	95. (*d*)
96. (*c*)	97. (*c*)	98. (*d*)	99. (*a*)	100. (*d*)

23

Parliamentary Committees

1. Consider the following statements:
   1. After the Annual Financial Statement is presented before the House of the People, it is examined by the Public Accounts Committee.
   2. The Public Accounts Committee examines the report of the Comptroller and Auditor-General of India after it is laid before the Parliament.

   Which of the statements given above is/are correct?

   (*a*) 1 only (*b*) 2 only
   (*c*) Both 1 and 2 (*d*) Neither 1 nor 2

2. Consider the following statements:
   1. The Parliamentary Committee on Empowerment of Women was constituted in 1997.
   2. The Parliamentary Committee on Empowerment of Women consists of 20 members of the Lok Sabha and 10 members of the Rajya Sabha.

   Which of the statements given above is/are correct?

   (*a*) 1 only (*b*) 2 only
   (*c*) Both 1 and 2 (*d*) Neither 1 nor 2

3. Which among the following are the merits of the Parliamentary Departmental Standing Committees constituted to scrutinise the budget proposals?
   1. Legislative control is now more legal because the committees are established by law.
   2. Experts and specialists have been nominated to help the members of the Parliament.
   3. Legislative control is now much more close, continuous and in-depth.
   4. The Rajya Sabha and the opposition parties can play a greater role in exercising financial control.

   Select the correct answer from the codes given below:

   (*a*) 1 and 2 only (*b*) 2 and 3 only
   (*c*) 3 and 4 only (*d*) 1 and 4 only

4. Which one of the following committees is not a Standing Committee of the Parliament?
   (*a*) Public Accounts Committee
   (*b*) Estimates Committee
   (*c*) Committee on Public Undertakings
   (*d*) Consultative Committee of the Ministry of Finance

5. Which of the following parliamentary committees scrutinises a bill clause by clause and suggests changes?
   (*a*) Select Committee (*b*) Committee on Petitions
   (*c*) Business Advisory Committee (*d*) Estimates Committee

6. The Chairman of the Public Accounts Committee of the Parliament is appointed by the:
   (*a*) Speaker of the Lok Sabha (*b*) Prime Minister of India
   (*c*) President of India (*d*) Chairman of Rajya Sabha

7. Which one of the following Parliamentary Committees exclusively consists of members of the Lok Sabha?
   (*a*) The Public Accounts Committee
   (*b*) The Estimates Committee
   (*c*) The Committee on Public Undertakings
   (*d*) The Committee on the Welfare of Scheduled Castes and Scheduled Tribes

8. Which of the following committees are helped by the CAG in their work of exercising Parliamentary control over the executive?
   1. Public Accounts Committee
   2. Committee of Privileges
   3. Estimates Committee
   4. Committee on Public Undertakings

   Select the correct answer by using the codes given below:
   (*a*) 1 and 4 only (*b*) 1, 2 and 4
   (*c*) 1, 2 and 3 (*d*) 2, 3 and 4

9. Which one of the following is the correct chronological order of the evolution of the given Committees?
   (*a*) Committee on Public Undertakings – Estimates Committee – Public Accounts Committee
   (*b*) Estimates Committee – Public Accounts Committee – Committee on Public Undertakings
   (*c*) Committee on Public Undertakings – Public Accounts Committee – Estimates Committee
   (*d*) Public Accounts Committee – Estimates Committee – Committee on Public Undertakings

10. Which one of the following is a Parliamentary Standing Committee?
    (*a*) Committee on Draft Five-Year Plan (*b*) Railway Convention Committee
    (*c*) Business Advisory Committee (*d*) Joint Committee on Fertilizer Pricing

11. Consider the following statements regarding Public Accounts Committee:
    1. it examines the Audit Report of the CAG.
    2. the suggestions made by the Committee are necessarily accepted by the Government.
    3. it ensures the observance of the canons of financial propriety in all transactions.
    4. the Committee functions in a non-partisan manner.

    Which of the statements given above are correct?
    (*a*) 1, 3 and 4 (*b*) 2, 3 and 4
    (*c*) 1 and 2 only (*d*) 1, 2, 3 and 4

12. Which one of the following committees recommended for the creation of Committee on Public Undertakings?
    (*a*) Krishna Menon Committee
    (*b*) Ashok Chanda Committee
    (*c*) Gorwala Committee
    (*d*) T. Krishnamachari Committee

13. Which one of the following pairs is not correctly matched?
    (*a*) Committee on Petitions: Standing Committee to inquire
    (*b*) Committee on Government Assurances: Standing Committee to scrutinise
    (*c*) Committee on Subordinate Legislation: Standing Committee to inquire
    (*d*) Select or Joint Committee on Bills: Ad hoc Committee

14. Which one of the following statements is not correct with regard to Parliamentary Committees?
    (*a*) The Public Accounts Committee and the Public Undertakings Committee are joint committees of both the Houses of the Parliament.
    (*b*) Seventeen Departmentally Related Committees were set up in the early 1990s.
    (*c*) There are Standing and Ad hoc Committees.
    (*d*) The Estimates Committee and the Public Accounts Committee are always headed by a senior leader of the ruling party/coalition.

15. Which one of the following committees scrutinises in detail the report of the Comptroller and Auditor-General of India?
    (*a*) Public Accounts Committee
    (*b*) Estimates Committee
    (*c*) Select Committee of Expenditure
    (*d*) Consultative Committee of the Finance Ministry

16. The Speaker is the ex-officio Chairman of which of the following Committees?
    (*a*) Rules Committee
    (*b*) Committee of privileges
    (*c*) Committee on public undertakings
    (*d*) Committee on government assurances

17. Which of the following Committees consists of representatives of both the Houses namely the Lok Sabha and the Rajya Sabha?
    1. Estimates Committee
    2. Committee on Subordinate Legislation
    3. Public Accounts Committee
    4. Committee on Public Undertakings

    Select the correct answer using the codes given below:
    (*a*) 1 and 4 only (*b*) 1, 2 and 3
    (*c*) 3 and 4 only (*d*) 2, 3 and 4

18. Which of the following statements does not reflect the jurisdiction of the Estimates Committee?
    (*a*) It suggests alternative policies in order to bring efficiency and economy in administration.
    (*b*) It examines whether the money is well laid out within the limits of the policy implied in the estimates.
    (*c*) It suggests the form in which estimates are to be presented to the Parliament.
    (*d*) It helps in checking Governmental extravagance in making demands as its report is debated in the House.

19. Which one of the following committees is constituted by the Lok Sabha but comprises the members of the Rajya Sabha also?
    (*a*) Business Advisory Committee (*b*) Committee of Privileges
    (*c*) Public Accounts Committee (*d*) Rules Committee

20. The report of Public Accounts Committee is presented to the:
    (*a*) Prime Minister (*b*) Finance Minister
    (*c*) President (*d*) Lok Sabha

21. Which of the following parliamentary committees considers matters of Procedure in the House?
    (*a*) Rules Committee (*b*) Public Accounts Committee
    (*c*) Committee on Subordinate (*d*) Committee on Public Undertakings

22. The Parliament exercises final control on public finance:
    (*a*) through the Public Accounts Committee.
    (*b*) through the Estimates Committee.
    (*c*) through the enactment of the Budget.
    (*d*) through the Comptroller and Auditor-General of India.

23. The issue of whether a commitment made by a Minister on the floor of the House has been fulfilled or not is decided by the:
    (*a*) Consultative Committee attached to the Ministry concerned.
    (*b*) Select Committee dealing with the Ministry concerned.
    (*c*) Political Affairs Committee of the Union Cabinet.
    (*d*) Committee on Government Assurances.

24. Which one of the following Parliamentary Committees act as a "watchdog" on departmental expenditures and irregularities?
    (*a*) Estimates Committee
    (*b*) Committee on Public Undertakings
    (*c*) Public Accounts Committee
    (*d*) Committee on Government Assurances

25. Which of the following is/are true with respect to the Public Accounts Committee?
    1. Its work is based on the audit reports of the CAG.
    2. It examines the accounts of the Government of India for appropriations made by the Lok Sabha.
    3. It examines the accounts of autonomous and semi-autonomous bodies.

Select the correct answer using the codes given below:

(*a*) 1, 2 and 3 (*b*) 2 and 3 only
(*c*) 1 and 2 only (*d*) 3 only

26. Consider the following statements:
    1. Members of Rajya Sabha are not associated with the Committee on Public Undertakings.
    2. Railway Convention Committee is an ad hoc Parliamentary Committee.

    Which of the statements given above is/are correct?

    (*a*) 1 only (*b*) 2 only
    (*c*) Both 1 and 2 (*d*) Neither 1 nor 2

27. Consider the following statements:
    1. The Public Accounts Committee consists of 10 members from the Lok Sabha and 5 members from the Rajya Sabha.
    2. The Public Accounts Committee examines both the Appropriation and Finance Reports submitted by the Comptroller and Auditor-General of India.

    Which of the statements given above is/are correct?

    (*a*) 1 only (*b*) 2 only
    (*c*) Both 1 and 2 (*d*) Neither 1 nor 2

28. When were 17 Departmental Related Standing Committees set up on the recommendations of the Rules Committee of the Lok Sabha?

    (*a*) 1964 (*b*) 1977
    (*c*) 1990 (*d*) 1993

29. Which one of the following is not a function of the Committee on Subordinate Legislation?

    (*a*) To evolve a systematic pattern of the terms of delegation
    (*b*) To improve the methods of publicity of the rules
    (*c*) To lay down rules and regulations on the table of the House
    (*d*) To achieve uniformity in rule-making procedures

30. Consider the following statements:
    1. The Estimates Committee has been described as a "continuous economy committee".
    2. The Estimates Committee is a means of parliamentary control over government and administration.

    Which of the statements given above is/are correct?

    (*a*) 1 only (*b*) 2 only
    (*c*) Both 1 and 2 (*d*) Neither 1 nor 2

31. Which one of the following statements is not correct?

    (*a*) The main function of the Public Accounts Committee is to examine the Report of the Comptroller and Auditor-General of India.
    (*b*) The Public Accounts Committee comprises the Members of the Lok Sabha only.
    (*c*) A member of opposition can also be appointed as the Chairman of the Public Accounts Committee.
    (*d*) A member of the Public Accounts Committee can be re-elected for a second term.

32. The Consultative Committees are constituted by which of the following?
    (*a*) Speaker of the Lok Sabha
    (*b*) Chairman of the Rajya Sabha
    (*c*) Ministry of Parliamentary Affairs
    (*d*) Cabinet Secretariat

33. The Estimates Committee of the Lok Sabha:
    (*a*) prepares estimates of expenditure of the Central Government.
    (*b*) examines the accounts of Departments of Government of India.
    (*c*) prevents unauthorised collection of taxes.
    (*d*) suggests economies to be made in the Central administration.

Answers

1. (*b*)	2. (*c*)	3. (*c*)	4. (*d*)	5. (*a*)
6. (*a*)	7. (*b*)	8. (*a*)	9. (*d*)	10. (*c*)
11. (*a*)	12. (*a*)	13. (*c*)	14. (*d*)	15. (*a*)
16. (*a*)	17. (*c*)	18. (*d*)	19. (*c*)	20. (*d*)
21. (*a*)	22. (*a*)	23. (*d*)	24. (*c*)	25. (*a*)
26. (*b*)	27. (*b*)	28. (*d*)	29. (*c*)	30. (*c*)
31. (*b*)	32. (*c*)	33. (*d*)		

24

Parliamentary Forums

1. Consider the following statements:
   1. The Parliamentary Forum on Population and Public Health is the first Parliamentary Forum.
   2. The first Parliamentary Forum was established in 2004.

   Which of the statements given above is/are correct?

   (*a*) 1 only (*b*) 2 only
   (*c*) Both 1 and 2 (*d*) Neither 1 nor 2

2. What is the maximum strength of the Rajya Sabha in a Parliamentary Forum?

   (*a*) 7 members (*b*) 10 members
   (*c*) 15 members (*d*) 21 members

3. The Speaker of Lok Sabha is the President of all the Parliamentary Forums except the:

   (*a*) Parliamentary Forum on Population and Public Health.
   (*b*) Parliamentary Forum on Global Warming and Climate Change.
   (*c*) Parliamentary Forum on Water Conservation and Management.
   (*d*) Parliamentary Forum on Children.

4. What is the strength of a Parliamentary Forum (excluding the President and ex-officio Vice-Presidents)?

   (*a*) 21 Members
   (*b*) 15 Members
   (*c*) 31 Members
   (*d*) 25 Members

5. Who was the Speaker of the Lok Sabha when the first Parliamentary Forum was constituted?

   (*a*) Ms. Meira Kumar
   (*b*) Manohar Joshi
   (*c*) Somnath Chatterjee
   (*d*) G.M.C. Balayogi

6. Which one of the following is not a sub-forum of the Parliamentary Forum on Youth?

   (*a*) Sub-Forum on Empowerment
   (*b*) Sub-Forum on Health
   (*c*) Sub-Forum on Education
   (*d*) Sub-Forum on Employment

7. Which of the following Parliamentary Forums was established in the year 2011?
   (*a*) Parliamentary Forum on Population and Public Health
   (*b*) Parliamentary Forum on Disaster Management
   (*c*) Parliamentary Forum on Water Conservation and Management
   (*d*) Parliamentary Forum on Global Warming and Climate Change

Answers

1. (*d*)	2. (*b*)	3. (*a*)	4. (*c*)	5. (*c*)
6. (*a*)	7. (*b*)			

25

Parliamentary Group

1. Consider the following statements:
   1. The Indian Parliamentary Group (IPG) Acts both as the National Group of the Inter-Parliamentary Union (IPU) as well as the India Branch of the Commonwealth Parliamentary Association (CPA).
   2. The associate members of the IPG are entitled to representation at meetings and conferences of the IPU and the CPA.

   Which of the statements given above is/are correct?

   (*a*) 1 only (*b*) 2 only
   (*c*) Both 1 and 2 (*d*) Neither 1 nor 2

2. Which of the following statements regarding the objectives of the IPG are correct?
   1. To arrange lectures on political reference, economic, social and educational problems by the Members of the Parliament
   2. To promote personal contacts amongst the Members of the Parliament
   3. To arrange visits to foreign countries with a view to develop contacts with the Members of other Parliaments
   4. To bring out publications for the dissemination of information to the members of the IPG

   Select the correct answer using the codes given below:

   (*a*) 1, 2 and 3 (*b*) 2 and 3 only
   (*c*) 1 and 4 only (*d*) 1, 2, 3, and 4

3. The IPG was formed in pursuance of a:

   (*a*) resolution passed by the Parliament.
   (*b*) direction issued by the Speaker of Lok Sabha.
   (*c*) resolution issued by the Ministry of Parliamentary Affairs.
   (*d*) motion adopted by the Constituent Assembly (Legislature).

4. Consider the following statements:
   1. The Chairman of the Rajya Sabha is the ex-officio President of the IPG.
   2. The Deputy Chairman of the Rajya Sabha and the Deputy Speaker of the Lok Sabha are the ex-officio Vice-Presidents of the IPG.

   Which of the statements given above is/are correct?

   (*a*) 1 only (*b*) 2 only
   (*c*) Both 1 and 2 (*d*) Neither 1 nor 2

5. Consider the following statements:
   1. The membership of the IPG is open to all the Members of the Parliament.
   2. The former Members of the Parliament cannot become associate members of the IPG.

   Which of the statements given above is/are correct?

   (*a*) 1 only (*b*) 2 only
   (*c*) Both 1 and 2 (*d*) Neither 1 nor 2

6. Who of the following acts as the ex-officio Secretary-General of the IPG?
   (*a*) Secretary-General of the Rajya Sabha
   (*b*) Secretary of the Parliamentary Affairs
   (*c*) Speaker of the Lok Sabha
   (*d*) Secretary-General of the Lok Sabha

7. Consider the following statements:
   1. The IPG is an autonomous body.
   2. The IPG was formed in the year 1948.

   Which of the statements given above is/are correct?

   (*a*) 1 only (*b*) 2 only
   (*c*) Both 1 and 2 (*d*) Neither 1 nor 2

8. Consider the following statements:
   1. The IPU is an international organisation of the parliaments of sovereign states.
   2. The CPA is an association of Commonwealth Parliamentarians spread over National, State, Provincial and Territorial Parliaments.

   Which of the statements given above is/are correct?

   (*a*) 1 only (*b*) 2 only
   (*c*) Both 1 and 2 (*d*) Neither 1 nor 2

Answers

1. (*a*)	2. (*d*)	3. (*d*)	4. (*b*)	5. (*a*)
6. (*d*)	7. (*a*)	8. (*c*)		

26

Supreme Court

1. Consider the following statements:
   1. A retired Supreme Court Judge cannot act as a Judge of the Supreme Court even for a temporary period.
   2. A High Court Judge may be appointed as an ad hoc Judge of the Supreme Court for a temporary period.

   Which of the statements given above is/are correct?

   (*a*) 1 only (*b*) 2 only
   (*c*) Both 1 and 2 (*d*) Neither 1 nor 2

2. Consider the following statements:
   1. The Supreme Court has original jurisdiction in any dispute between the Government of India and one or more States.
   2. The Supreme Court has original jurisdiction in any dispute between the Government of India and any State or States on one side and one or more other States on the other.
   3. The Supreme Court has original jurisdiction in any dispute between the Government of India and any corporation or individual on one side and one or more States on the other.
   4. The Supreme Court has original jurisdiction in any dispute between two or more States.

   Which of the statements given above are correct?

   (*a*) 1 and 2 only (*b*) 1, 2 and 4
   (*c*) 3 and 4 only (*d*) 1, 2, 3 and 4

3. In which of the following categories of cases, the Supreme Court of India has the power to decide?
   1. A reference made by the President on a question of law or fact
   2. A case involving interpretation of the Constitution
   3. A case involving a substantial question of law of general importance
   4. A case where the constitutionality of any law has been challenged

   Select the correct answer using the codes given below:

   (*a*) 1, 2 and 3 (*b*) 1, 3 and 4
   (*c*) 1, 2 and 4 (*d*) 2, 3 and 4

4. Consider the following statements:
   1. The Supreme Court of India can sit only in Delhi.
   2. The Supreme Court of India can sit in places other than Delhi which the Chief Justice of India may appoint with the approval of the President.

3. The Parliament may make provisions for conferring supplemental powers upon the Supreme Court.

Which of the statements given above is/are correct?

(*a*) 1 and 3 only (*b*) 2 and 3 only
(*c*) 2 only (*d*) 3 only

5. Consider the following statements:
    1. In 2015, the Supreme Court declared both the 99th Constitutional Amendment Act as well as the National Judicial Appointments Commission Act unconstitutional and void.
    2. This verdict was delivered by the Supreme Court in the Fourth Judges case.

    Which of the statements given above is/are correct?

    (*a*) 1 only (*b*) 2 only
    (*c*) Both 1 and 2 (*d*) Neither 1 nor 2

6. In the appointment of the Judges of the Supreme Court, the recommendations of the collegium consisting of the Chief Justice of India and four of the most senior Judges of the Supreme Court is binding on the President of India, because:
    (*a*) it is so provided in the Constitution of India.
    (*b*) it has been the consistent practice for a long time.
    (*c*) it has been laid down by the Parliament.
    (*d*) it has been laid down by the Supreme Court.

7. Consider the following statements:
    1. The constitutional cases or references made by the President under Article 143 are decided by a bench consisting of at least seven judges.
    2. All other cases are decided by a single judge and division benches.

    Which of the statements given above is/are correct?

    (*a*) 1 only (*b*) 2 only
    (*c*) Both 1 and 2 (*d*) Neither 1 nor 2

8. Article 141 of the Constitution lays down that the law declared by the Supreme Court shall be binding on all courts within the territory of India. Therefore, the Supreme Court:
    (*a*) is bound by its earlier decisions as the expression "all courts" include the Supreme Court also.
    (*b*) is not bound by its own decisions and may reverse a previous decision.
    (*c*) can reverse a previous decision only when a new legislation is enacted having the effect of abrogating decision.
    (*d*) can reverse a previous decision only when the previous decision was given as a result of overlooking another previous decision.

9. Which one of the following is directly related to the Appellate jurisdiction of the Supreme Court of India?
    (*a*) Appeals made in civil, criminal and constitutional cases
    (*b*) Appeals made in constitutional cases only

(*c*) Adjudication of disputes between the Union and the States
(*d*) Adjudication of disputes between the States

10. How can the number of Judges in the Supreme Court of India be increased?
(*a*) By a Presidential notification
(*b*) By a Parliamentary Act
(*c*) By an Amendment of the Constitution of India
(*d*) By a Representation from the Supreme Court

11. Who of the following remarked, "The Supreme Court of India has more powers than any other Supreme Court in any part of the world"?
(*a*) N. Gopalaswamy Ayyangar
(*b*) Dr. K. M. Munshi
(*c*) Alladi Krishnaswamy Ayyar
(*d*) T. T. Krishnamachari

12. Consider the following statements:
1. Parliament can extend, but cannot curtail the jurisdiction and power of the Supreme Court.
2. No discussion can take place in the Parliament with respect to the conduct of any judge of the Supreme Court in the discharge of his duties.
3. A retired judge of the Supreme Court cannot appear or plead in any court or before any authority within the territory of India.
4. The salaries and allowances of the judges of the Supreme Court are charged on the Consolidated Fund of India.

Which of the statements given above are correct?
(*a*) 1, 2, 3 and 4 (*b*) 1 and 2 only
(*c*) 1 and 3 only (*d*) 2 and 4 only

13. Which one of the following categories of disputes is excluded from the original jurisdiction of the Supreme Court?
(*a*) Between the Government of India and one or more States
(*b*) Between two or more States
(*c*) Between residents of two or more States
(*d*) Between the Government of India and one or more states on one side and one or more other States on the other side

14. In order to remove a judge of the Supreme Court, the President is required by the Constitution to receive an address by each House of the Parliament supported by a majority of the total membership of the House, and by a prescribed majority of members of the House present and voting. How much is the prescribed majority?
(*a*) One-third (*b*) One-half
(*c*) Two-thirds (*d*) Three-fourths

15. Which one of the following is not an essential condition for the appointment as a judge of the Supreme Court?
   (*a*) A citizen of India
   (*b*) At least five years' experience as judge of a High Court or of two or more such Courts in succession
   (*c*) Must have completed 35 years of age
   (*d*) At least ten years' experience as an advocate of a High Court or of two or more such Courts in succession

16. The rules for regulating the practice and procedure of the Supreme Court are made by the:
   (*a*) President of India.
   (*b*) Supreme Court with the approval of the President of India.
   (*c*) Supreme Court alone.
   (*d*) Supreme Court in consultation with the Bar Council of India.

17. Which of the following states brought the first suit against the Centre under the original jurisdiction of the Supreme Court?
   (*a*) Kerala (*b*) West Bengal
   (*c*) Tamil Nadu (*d*) Assam

18. When the Chief Justice of India is appointed by the President, he is required to consult:
   (*a*) the Council of Ministers and all the Judges of the Supreme Court.
   (*b*) the Prime Minister, the Law Minister and the Attorney-General of India.
   (*c*) such of the Ministers of the Cabinet and the Prime Minister as he deems necessary.
   (*d*) such of the Judges of the Supreme Court and High Courts as he deems necessary.

19. Which one of the following statements is not correct?
   (*a*) A retired judge of the Supreme Court is prohibited from appearing and pleading in any court within the territory of India.
   (*b*) Supreme Court may issue writs for the enforcement of any legal right within the territory of India.
   (*c*) Supreme Court has the power to punish any person for its contempt.
   (*d*) Salary of Judges of the Supreme Court is not subject to vote of the Legislature.

20. Consider the following statements regarding the Advisory Jurisdiction of the Supreme Court:
   1. The reference for advice may be made to the Supreme Court on a question of law or fact by the President of India.
   2. Disputes arising out of pre-constitution treaties and agreements excluded from the original jurisdiction of the Supreme Court may also be referred to it.
   3. The advice given by the Supreme Court is binding on the Government.
   4. One of the cases referred to the Supreme Court for its advice was the constitutionality of the Kerala Education Bill.

   Which of the statements given above are correct?
   (*a*) 1, 2 and 4 (*b*) 2 and 3 only
   (*c*) 1 and 2 only (*d*) 3 and 4 only

21. Appellate jurisdiction of the Supreme Court in appeals from High Courts in regard to civil matters pertains only to a:
    (*a*) substantial question of law.
    (*b*) question of law.
    (*c*) question of fact.
    (*d*) mixed question of fact and law.

22. The Supreme Court of India is different from its counterpart in the U.S.A.:
    (*a*) in its role as the guardian of the Constitution.
    (*b*) in its advisory role.
    (*c*) in its role as the supreme authority in the judicial field in the country.
    (*d*) in its writ jurisdiction.

23. Which of the following jurisdiction of the Supreme Court is related to its role as a federal court?
    (*a*) Appellate Jurisdiction
    (*b*) Advisory Jurisdiction
    (*c*) Miscellaneous Powers
    (*d*) Original Jurisdiction

24. Law declared by the Supreme Court shall be binding on all the courts within the territory of India. Here "courts" mean:
    (*a*) all courts including the Supreme Court of India.
    (*b*) all courts except the Supreme Court of India.
    (*c*) all courts including the Supreme Court except such benches of the Supreme Court which consists of seven judges or more.
    (*d*) all courts including the Supreme Court except a bench of the Supreme Court which consists of all the judges of the Supreme Court.

25. Which one of the following statements is correct?

    If the Chief Justice of India is to make a request for the attendance of a Judge of a High Court at the sitting of the Supreme Court as an ad hoc judge:
    (*a*) only previous consent of the President of India is required.
    (*b*) previous consent of the President of India and consultation with the Chief Justice of the concerned High Court is required.
    (*c*) only consultation with the Chief Justice of the concerned High Court is required.
    (*d*) neither previous consent of the President of India nor consultation with the Chief Justice of the concerned High Court is required.

26. Which of the following has jurisdiction to decide a dispute between the Central Government and a State Government?
    (*a*) Inter-State Council
    (*b*) High Court under Article 226 of the Constitution of India
    (*c*) Supreme Court under Article 143 of the Constitution of India
    (*d*) Supreme Court under Article 131 of the Constitution of India

27. Which of the following were referred to the Supreme Court by the President for its advisory opinion?
    1. 2G spectrum case verdict
    2. Election commissioner's decision on deferring the Gujarat Assembly elections
    3. Punjab Termination of Agreements Act
    4. Jurisdiction of Centre and States on the subject of natural gas

    Select the correct answer using the codes given below:

    (*a*) 1, 2 and 4 (*b*) 2 and 3 only
    (*c*) 2 only (*d*) 1, 2, 3 and 4

28. Which one of the following statements is correct?
    (*a*) The original jurisdiction of the Supreme Court is unlimited.
    (*b*) A dispute between one State and another can only be dealt with by the Supreme Court.
    (*c*) The Supreme Court must admit appeal from any judgement or order made by any court.
    (*d*) All courts including the Supreme Court are bound by a Supreme Court decision.

29. Which one of the following statements is correct?
    The power of judicial review means the power of the Supreme Court to:
    (*a*) set aside any executive decision if it is against statutory law.
    (*b*) set aside any provision of law if it is contrary to the Fundamental Rights.
    (*c*) examine constitutional validity of any administrative action as well as legislative provision and strike it down if not found in accordance with the constitutional provisions.
    (*d*) review its own decision or decisions of any court or tribunal within the territory of India.

30. What is the correct chronological sequence of the following advisory opinions given by the Supreme Court under Article 143 of the Constitution of India?
    1. Delhi Laws Act
    2. Berubari Union
    3. Sea Customs Act
    4. Special Courts Bill

    Select the correct answer using the codes given below:

    (*a*) 1, 2, 3, 4 (*b*) 2, 1, 3, 4
    (*c*) 2, 3, 4, 1 (*d*) 2, 4, 3, 1

31. The jurisdiction of the Supreme Court of India may be enlarged by:
    (*a*) the Parliament by law.
    (*b*) the Parliament by resolution.
    (*c*) the President.
    (*d*) the President in consultation with the Chief Justice of India.

32. What age is prescribed for a person to qualify for appointment as a Judge of the Supreme Court of India?
    (*a*) Not below 30 years on the date of appointment
    (*b*) Not below 35 years on the date of appointment
    (*c*) Not below 40 years on the date of appointment
    (*d*) No age is prescribed

33. Which of the following Articles of the Constitution of India declares the Supreme Court to be a court of record?
    (*a*) Article 128 (*b*) Article 129
    (*c*) Article 130 (*d*) Article 131

34. What was the original strength of the Supreme Court?
    (*a*) Chief Justice of India and six judges
    (*b*) Chief Justice of India and seven judges
    (*c*) Chief Justice of India and eight judges
    (*d*) Chief Justice of India and nine judges

35. Disputes between States come to the Supreme Court under which of the following?
    (*a*) Appellate jurisdiction
    (*b*) Original jurisdiction
    (*c*) Advisory jurisdiction
    (*d*) Writ jurisdiction

36. Consider the following statements:
    1. Supreme Court's power to issue writs is narrower than that of a High Court.
    2. A citizen is free to approach a High Court or the Supreme Court as he chooses whenever his Fundamental Rights are violated.
    3. The law declared by the Supreme Court is binding on all courts throughout India.

    Which of the statements given above is/are correct?
    (*a*) 1 only (*b*) 1 and 2 only
    (*c*) 1, 2 and 3 (*d*) 2 and 3 only

37. Which of the following statements regarding the Supreme Court of India are correct?
    1. It has the power to entertain appeal from any court or tribunal within India.
    2. It has the power to deliver advisory opinion on any question of fact or law referred to it by the President.
    3. Salaries of the Judges of the Supreme Court are subject to vote by the Parliament.
    4. Its jurisdiction is binding on all other courts within India.

    Select the correct answer from the codes given below:
    (*a*) 1 and 3 only (*b*) 2 and 4 only
    (*c*) 2, 3 and 4 (*d*) 1, 2 and 4

Answers

1. (*b*)	2. (*B*)	3. (*d*)	4. (*b*)	5. (*c*)
6. (*d*)	7. (*b*)	8. (*b*)	9. (*a*)	10. (*b*)
11. (*c*)	12. (*a*)	13. (*c*)	14. (*c*)	15. (*c*)
16. (*b*)	17. (*b*)	18. (*d*)	19. (*b*)	20. (*a*)
21. (*a*)	22. (*b*)	23. (*d*)	24. (*b*)	25. (*b*)
26. (*d*)	27. (*d*)	28. (*b*)	29. (*c*)	30. (*a*)
31. (*a*)	32. (*d*)	33. (*b*)	34. (*b*)	35. (*b*)
36. (*c*)	37. (*d*)			

27

Judicial Review

1. Consider the following statements:
   1. The doctrine of judicial review originated and developed in the U.S.A.
   2. The doctrine of judicial review was propounded in the USA in the year 1903.

   Which of the statements given above is/are correct?

   (*a*) 1 only (*b*) 2 only
   (*c*) Both 1 and 2 (*d*) Neither 1 nor 2

2. Which of the following are the reasons for judicial review?
   1. To uphold the principle of the supremacy of the Constitution
   2. To maintain federal equilibrium
   3. To protect the Fundamental Rights of the citizens

   Select the correct answer using the codes given below:

   (*a*) 1 and 2 only (*b*) 2 and 3 only
   (*c*) 1 and 3 only (*d*) 1, 2 and 3

3. Which of the following Constitutional Amendment Acts was declared unconstitutional and null and void by the Supreme Court?

   (*a*) 96th Amendment
   (*b*) 97th Amendment
   (*c*) 98th Amendment
   (*d*) 99th Amendment

4. Consider the following statements:
   1. Article 31B saves the acts and regulations included on the Ninth Schedule from being challenged on the ground of contravention of the Fundamental Rights.
   2. Originally in 1951, the Ninth Schedule contained only 14 acts and regulations.

   Which of the statements given above is/are correct?

   (*a*) 1 only (*b*) 2 only
   (*c*) Both 1 and 2 (*d*) Neither 1 nor 2

5. Consider the following statements:
   1. The phrase "Judicial Review" has been used in the Constitution in the provisions of several Articles.
   2. Article 13 declares that all laws that are inconsistent with the Fundamental Rights shall be null and void.

Which of the statements given above is/are correct?

(*a*) 1 only (*b*) 2 only

(*c*) Both 1 and 2 (*d*) Neither 1 nor 2

6. Who of the following former chief justices of the American Supreme Court propounded for the first time the doctrine of judicial Review?

(*a*) John Jay

(*b*) John Rutledge

(*c*) John Marshall

(*d*) Oliver Ellsworth

7. In which of the following cases, the Supreme Court used the power of Judicial Review?

1. Minerva Mills case
2. Bank Nationalisation case
3. Privy Purses Abolition case
4. Golaknath case
5. Kesavananda Bharati case

Select the correct answer using the codes given below:

(*a*) 1, 3 and 5 (*b*) 2, 4 and 5

(*c*) 1, 2, 3 and 4 (*d*) 1, 2, 3, 4 and 5

8. On which of the following grounds, the constitutional validity of a legislative enactment can be challenged in the Supreme Court?

1. It infringes Fundamental Rights.
2. It is not outside the competence of the authority which has framed it.
3. It is repugnant to the constitutional provisions.

Select the correct answer using the codes given below:

(*a*) 1 and 2 only (*b*) 2 and 3 only

(*c*) 1 and 3 only (*d*) 1, 2 and 3

9. Which of the following doctrines was propounded for the first time in the famous case of Marbury v. Madison?

(*a*) Judicial Activism

(*b*) Judicial Review

(*c*) Public Interest Litigation

(*d*) Rule of Law

10. Consider the following statements:

1. The scope of Judicial Review in India is wider than what exists in the U.S.A.
2. The American Constitution does not explicitly mention the concept of Judicial Review in any of its provisions.

Which of the statements given above is/are correct?

(*a*) 1 only (*b*) 2 only

(*c*) Both 1 and 2 (*d*) Neither 1 nor 2

11. In which of the following cases, the Supreme Court ruled that there could not be any blanket immunity from Judicial Review of laws included in the Ninth Schedule?
    (*a*) Privy Purses Abolition case
    (*b*) Golaknath case
    (*c*) Bank Nationalisation case
    (*d*) I.R. Coelho case

12. Which of the following are the categories of Judicial Review?
    1. Judicial Review of constitutional amendments
    2. Judicial Review of legislation of the Parliament
    3. Judicial Review of administrative action of the Union

    Select the correct answer using the codes given below:
    (*a*) 1 and 2 only (*b*) 2 and 3 only
    (*c*) 1 and 3 only (*d*) 1, 2 and 3

Answers

1. (*a*)	2. (*d*)	3. (*d*)	4. (*a*)	5. (*b*)
6. (*c*)	7. (*d*)	8. (*c*)	9. (*b*)	10. (*b*)
11. (*d*)	12 (*d*)			

28 Judicial Activism

1. Consider the following statements:
   1. The concept of Judicial Activism originated and developed in the U.S.A.
   2. The term "judicial activism" was first coined in 1957 by an American historian and educator.

   Which of the statements given above is/are correct?

   (*a*) 1 only (*b*) 2 only
   (*c*) Both 1 and 2 (*d*) Neither 1 nor 2

2. Consider the following statements:
   1. Judicial activism and Judicial Restraint are the two alternative judicial philosophies in the United States.
   2. Judicial Restraint does not hold that the "original intent" of the authors of the Constitution and its amendments are knowable and must guide the courts.

   Which of the statements given above is/are correct?

   (*a*) 1 only (*b*) 2 only
   (*c*) Both 1 and 2 (*d*) Neither 1 nor 2

3. Consider the following statements:
   1. Human Rights activists primarily focus on civil and political rights issues.
   2. Bar-based groups agitate for the issues concerning autonomy and accountability of the Indian Judiciary.

   Which of the statements given above is/are correct?

   (*a*) 1 only (*b*) 2 only
   (*c*) Both 1 and 2 (*d*) Neither 1 nor 2

4. Which of the following is not a type of fears generated by judicial activism?

   (*a*) Epistemic fears
   (*b*) Legitimation fears
   (*c*) Social fears
   (*d*) Democratic fears

5. Which of the following are the reasons for judicial activism?
   1. Legislative vacuum
   2. Judicial enthusiasm
   3. Failure on the part of Legislature
   4. Responsibility of the Judiciary to protect the rights of citizens

Select the correct answer using the codes given below:

(*a*) 1, 2 and 3 (*b*) 2, 3 and 4

(*c*) 1 and 4 only (*d*) 1, 2, 3, and 4

6. Consider the following statements:
   1. The concepts of Judicial Review and judicial activism are closely related to each other.
   2. There is no difference between the concepts of Judicial Review and judicial activism.

   Which of the statements given above is/are correct?

   (*a*) 1 only (*b*) 2 only

   (*c*) Both 1 and 2 (*d*) Neither 1 nor 2

7. Consider the following statements:
   1. Judicial activism can be defined as the process of law-making by judges.
   2. The concept of judicial activism is not closely related to the concept of Public Interest Litigation.

   Which of the statements given above is/are correct?

   (*a*) 1 only (*b*) 2 only

   (*c*) Both 1 and 2 (*d*) Neither 1 nor 2

8. Consider the following statements:
   1. In India, the doctrine of judicial activism was introduced in the mid-1960s.
   2. Justice V.R. Krishna Iyer, Justice P.N. Bhagwati, Justice O. Chinnappa Reddy and Justice D.A. Desai laid the foundation of judicial activism in India.

   Which of the statements given above is/are correct?

   (*a*) 1 only (*b*) 2 only

   (*c*) Both 1 and 2 (*d*) Neither 1 nor 2

9. Who of the following first coined the term "judicial activism"?

   (*a*) Joel B. Grossman (*b*) Richard S. Wells

   (*c*) Justice John Marshall (*d*) Arthur Schlesinger Jr.

10. Consider the following statements:
    1. The Supreme Court of India said that Judicial Restraint is consistent with and complementary to the balance of power among the three independent branches of the state.
    2. According to it, Judicial Restraint will not protect the independence of the Judiciary.

    Which of the statements given above is/are correct?

    (*a*) 1 only (*b*) 2 only

    (*c*) Both 1 and 2 (*d*) Neither 1 nor 2

Answers

1. (*a*)	2. (*a*)	3. (*b*)	4. (*c*)	5. (*d*)
6. (*a*)	7. (*a*)	8. (*b*)	9. (*d*)	10. (*a*)

29

Public Interest Litigation

1. Consider the following statements:
   1. The concept of Public Interest Litigation (PIL) originated in the U.S.A. in the 1970s.
   2. In India, the concept of PIL was introduced in the early 1980s.

   Which of the statements given above is/are correct?

   (*a*) 1 only (*b*) 2 only
   (*c*) Both 1 and 2 (*d*) Neither 1 nor 2

2. Which of the following guidelines are laid down by the Supreme Court for checking the misuse of PIL?
   1. The court must effectively discourage the PIL filed for extraneous considerations.
   2. The court should prima facie verify the credentials of the petitioner before entertaining the PIL.
   3. The court need not be satisfied regarding the correctness of the contents of the petition before entertaining the PIL.
   4. The court must ensure that the petition involving larger public interest should be given priority over other petitions.

   Select the correct answer using the codes given below:

   (*a*) 1 and 2 only (*b*) 2 and 3 only
   (*c*) 3 and 4 only (*d*) 1, 2 and 4

3. Which of the following categories of cases are not entertained under PIL?
   1. Admission to medical institution
   2. Neglected children
   3. Service matters
   4. Petitions for early hearing of cases pending in subordinate courts

   Select the correct answer using the codes given below:

   (*a*) 1 and 2 only (*b*) 1, 3 and 4
   (*c*) 2 and 3 only (*d*) 3 and 4 only

4. Which of the following statements regarding the purposes of PIL are correct?
   1. Meaningful realisation of the Fundamental Rights
   2. Facilitating effective access to justice to the socially and economically weaker sections of the society
   3. Vindication of the rule of law

Select the correct answer using the codes given below:

(*a*) 1 and 2 only (*b*) 2 and 3 only
(*c*) 1 and 3 only (*d*) 1, 2 and 3

5. Consider the following statements:
 1. In PIL, the role held by the court is more assertive than in traditional actions.
 2. In PIL, there is a determination on the adjudication of individual rights.

 Which of the statements given above is/are correct?

 (*a*) 1 only (*b*) 2 only
 (*c*) Both 1 and 2 (*d*) Neither 1 nor 2

6. Consider the following statements:
 1. PIL is an exception to the traditional rule of "locus standi".
 2. PIL is also known as the Class Action Litigation.

 Which of the statements given above is/are correct?

 (*a*) 1 only (*b*) 2 only
 (*c*) Both 1 and 2 (*d*) Neither 1 nor 2

7. Which of the following categories of cases are entertained under PIL?
 1. Petitions from riot victims
 2. Bonded-labour matters
 3. Landlord-tenant matters
 4. Family pension

 Select the correct answer using the codes given below:

 (*a*) 1 and 2 only (*b*) 3 and 4 only
 (*c*) 1, 2 and 4 (*d*) 1, 2, 3 and 4

8. Consider the following statements:
 1. In India, PIL is a product of the judicial activism role of the Supreme Court.
 2. In India, Justice V.R. Krishna Iyer and Justice P.N. Bhagwati were the pioneers of the concept of PIL.

 Which of the statements given above is/are correct?

 (*a*) 1 only (*b*) 2 only
 (*c*) Both 1 and 2 (*d*) Neither 1 nor 2

9. Consider the following statements:
 1. Ordinarily, the High Court should entertain a writ petition by way of PIL questioning the constitutionality or validity of a statute or a statutory rule.
 2. The dispute between two warring groups purely in the realm of private law would be allowed to be agitated as a PIL.

 Which of the statements given above is/are correct?

 (*a*) 1 only (*b*) 2 only
 (*c*) Both 1 and 2 (*d*) Neither 1 nor 2

Answers

1. (*b*)	2. (*d*)	3. (*b*)	4. (*d*)	5. (*a*)
6. (*c*)	7. (*c*)	8. (*c*)	9. (*d*)	

PART-IV
STATE GOVERNMENT

30. Governor
31. Chief Minister
32. State Council of Ministers
33. State Legislature
34. High Court
35. Tribunals
36. Subordinate Courts
37. Special Provisions for Some States

30

Governor

1. Consider the following statements:
   1. The Parliament by law may appoint the Governor of a state as the Administrator of an adjoining Union territory.
   2. If a Governor of a State is appointed to act as an Administrator of an adjoining Union territory, he shall exercise his functions as such an Administrator independently of his Council of Ministers.

   Which of the statements given above is/are correct?

   (*a*) 1 only (*b*) 2 only
   (*c*) Both 1 and 2 (*d*) Neither 1 nor 2

2. Consider the following statements:
   1. As regards legislative powers, the Governor of a State is not a part of the State Legislature.
   2. The Governor of a State has no emergency powers to meet the situation arising from external aggression.

   Which of the statements given above is/are correct?

   (*a*) 1 only (*b*) 2 only
   (*c*) Both 1 and 2 (*d*) Neither 1 nor 2

3. Consider the following statements with respect to the powers of the Governor of a State:
   1. The Governor can summon, prorogue and dissolve the State Assembly.
   2. The Governor can adjourn the sittings of the State Assembly.
   3. The Governor addresses the first session of the Legislative Assembly after elections.
   4. The Governor causes to lay the annual budget in the State Assembly.

   Which of the statements given above are correct?

   (*a*) 1 and 2 only (*b*) 1, 3 and 4
   (*c*) 2 and 3 only (*d*) 2 and 4 only

4. Consider the following statements:
   1. There is a bar to the selection of the Governor of a State from amongst the members of the Legislature of the State.
   2. The original plan in the Draft Constitution of India was to have an elected Governor but in the Constituent Assembly it was replaced by the method of appointment by the President of India.
   3. The method of appointment of a Governor of a State by the President of India is repugnant to the prevailing practice in the federal systems of the United States of America and Australia.

Which of the statements given above are correct?

(*a*) 1, 2 and 3 (*b*) 1 and 2 only

(*c*) 2 and 3 only (*d*) 1 and 3 only

5. Which one of the following statements is not correct?

(*a*) The Governor can issue Ordinances when the Legislative Assembly is not in session or only when two Houses are not in session.

(*b*) The Governor can at his discretion issue the Ordinances whether the Assembly is in session or not.

(*c*) The Governor must be satisfied that such circumstances exist which render it necessary for him to take immediate action.

(*d*) The Governor's Ordinance shall have the same force and effect as an Act of the Legislature.

6. When a Bill passed by the State Legislature attempts to take away the powers of the High Court and is presented before the Governor for his assent, he:

(*a*) may give his assent.

(*b*) may withhold his assent.

(*c*) is bound to return the Bill for reconsideration.

(*d*) is bound to reserve the Bill for the consideration of the President.

7. Which of the following are functions to which the scope of the discretionary powers of the Governor is limited?

1. The appointment of the Chief Minister
2. The dismissal of the Ministry
3. The dissolution of the Legislative Assembly
4. Assent to Bills

Choose the correct answer from the codes given below:

(*a*) 1, 2 and 3 (*b*) 1, 2, 3 and 4

(*c*) 1, 3 and 4 (*d*) 2, 3 and 4

8. Consider the following statements:

1. No person shall be eligible for the appointment as a Governor unless he is a citizen of India and has completed the age of thirty years.
2. The Governor shall not hold any other office of profit.

Which of the statements given above is/are correct?

(*a*) 1 only (*b*) 2 only

(*c*) Both 1 and 2 (*d*) Neither 1 nor 2

9. The de-jure head of a State Government is the:

(*a*) Chief Minister of the State.

(*b*) Law Minister of the State.

(*c*) Home Minister of the State.

(*d*) Governor of the State.

10. The Governor of a State has the power to appoint whom of the following?
    1. Judges of the High Court
    2. Members of the State Public Service Commission
    3. Members of the State Finance Commission
    4. Accountant-General

    Which of the statements given above are correct?
    (*a*) 1 and 2 only
    (*b*) 2 and 3 only
    (*c*) 1, 3 and 4
    (*d*) 1, 2, 3 and 4

11. On receipt of the report from the Governor of a State that the Government of the State cannot be carried on in accordance with the provisions of the Constitution, the President of India under Article 356:
    (*a*) has to proclaim President's Rule in the State.
    (*b*) has to dismiss the State Government and dissolve the Legislative Assembly.
    (*c*) has to dismiss the Government but keep that Legislative Assembly in a state of suspended animation.
    (*d*) may refuse to impose President's Rule in the State.

12. When can the Governor of a State issue an ordinance?
    (*a*) When the Union Government asks him to do so
    (*b*) Whenever there is a law and order problem in the State
    (*c*) Whenever the State Legislature is not in session and the Governor is satisfied that immediate action is needed
    (*d*) Whenever the Judiciary advises him to do so

13. Consider the following statements:

    Under Article 200 of the Constitution of India, the Governor may:
    1. withhold his assent to a Bill passed by the State Legislature.
    2. reserve the Bill passed by the State Legislature for the consideration of the President.
    3. return a Bill, other than a Money Bill, for reconsideration of the Legislature.

    Which of the statements given above are correct?
    (*a*) 1 and 2 only (*b*) 2 and 3 only
    (*c*) 1 and 3 only (*d*) 1, 2 and 3

14. The correct constitutional position regarding the Governor is that the:
    (*a*) Governor acts on the advice of the Prime Minister
    (*b*) Governor acts on the advice of the President of India
    (*c*) Governor acts on the advice of the Chief Minister of the State
    (*d*) Governor acts on the advice of the Council of Ministers of the State

15. Consider the following statements:
    1. The emoluments and allowances of the Governor shall not be diminished during his term of office.
    2. Where the same person is appointed as the Governor of two or more States, the emoluments and allowances payable to the Governor shall be allocated among the states in such proportion as the Parliament may by law determine.

    Which of the statements given above is/are correct?

    (*a*) 1 only (*b*) 2 only
    (*c*) Both 1 and 2 (*d*) Neither 1 nor 2

16. Consider the following statements:

    The Governor of a State:
    1. is vested with executive power under the Constitution of India.
    2. is needed because of the federal structure of the Government.
    3. was to be elected according to the original Draft Constitution of India.
    4. is chosen only from among the categories laid down in the Constitution of India.

    Which of the statements given above are correct?

    (*a*) 1 and 4 only (*b*) 2 and 3 only
    (*c*) 1, 2 and 3 (*d*) 2, 3 and 4

17. In the performance of his duties and in the exercise of his powers, the Governor:

    (*a*) is answerable in a court of law. (*b*) is not answerable in a court of law.
    (*c*) can be impeached in the Vidhan Sabha. (*d*) is answerable to the Vidhan Sabha.

18. Under Article 213, the Governor of a State is empowered to:

    (*a*) exercise discretionary powers.
    (*b*) promulgate ordinances during the recess of the Legislature.
    (*c*) appoint a Judge of the State High Court.
    (*d*) exercise his emergency powers.

19. On which of the following issues can a Governor make recommendation to the President?
    1. Dismissal of the State Council of Ministers
    2. Removal of the Judges of the High Court
    3. Dissolution of the State Legislative Assembly
    4. Declaration of the breakdown of the Constitutional Machinery in the State

    Select the correct answer using the codes given below:

    (*a*) 1, 2 and 3 (*b*) 2, 3 and 4
    (*c*) 1, 3 and 4 (*d*) 1, 2 and 4

20. Which one of the following statements is not correct?

    (*a*) The Council of Ministers is collectively responsible to the Governor.
    (*b*) Under Article 167 of the Constitution of India, the Chief Minister has to communicate to the Governor all decisions of the Council of Ministers relating to the administration of the affairs of the State and proposals for legislation.

(*c*) Once the Governor reserves a Bill for the consideration of the President, the subsequent enactment of the Bill is in the hands of the President and the Governor shall have no further part in its career.

(*d*) The executive power of the State is vested in the Governor and all executive actions of the State have to be taken in the name of the Governor.

21. In which one of the following states, it is not constitutionally obligatory for the Governor to appoint a minister in-charge of tribal affairs?
(*a*) Bihar
(*b*) Madhya Pradesh
(*c*) Odisha
(*d*) Jharkhand

22. Consider the following matters:
1. Reservation of the State Bill for the consideration of the President.
2. Delivery of Speech in the House of the Legislature.
3. Recommendation to the President to impose the President's Rule.

Under Article 163 of the Constitution of India, the Governor is required to act in accordance with the advice of the Council of Ministers; but in relation to which of the matters given above, the said rule is not applicable?
(*a*) 1 and 3 only (*b*) 1, 2 and 3
(*c*) 2 and 3 only (*d*) 2 only

23. Who of the following is not appointed by the Governor?
(*a*) State Council of Ministers
(*b*) State Advocate-General
(*c*) State Director-General of Police
(*d*) Members of State Public Service Commission

24. The Governor of a State may be removed from the office by the President:
(*a*) at the request of the Chief Minister.
(*b*) on the advice of the Lok Ayukta.
(*c*) on the advice of the Union Cabinet.
(*d*) on the advice of the Attorney-General of India.

25. Consider the following statements with respect to the Governor of a State:
1. A Governor shall, notwithstanding the expiration of his term, continue to hold office until his successor enters upon his office.
2. No person shall be eligible for the appointment as the Governor unless he has completed the age of thirty years.
3. The question whether any, and if so what, advice was tendered by Ministers to the Governor shall not be inquired into in any Court.

Which of the statements given above is/are correct?
(*a*) 1, 2 and 3 (*b*) 1 and 2 only
(*c*) 1 and 3 only (*d*) 3 only

26. Which of the following is not correctly matched?
    (*a*) Article 153 – Office of the Governor
    (*b*) Article 156 – Term of the Governor
    (*c*) Article 154 – Executive authority of the Governor
    (*d*) Article 155 – Removal of the Governor

27. Which one of the following is not correct in respect of the Governor's ordinance-making power?
    (*a*) It is exercised only when the Legislature is not in session.
    (*b*) It is a discretionary power which need not be exercised with the aid and advice of Ministers.
    (*c*) The Governor himself is competent to withdraw the ordinance at any time.
    (*d*) The scope of the ordinance-making power is limited to subjects in List II and List III of Schedule VII.

28. Under which Article of the Constitution of India, the State Governor can reserve a Bill for the consideration of the President?
    (*a*) Article 169 (*b*) Article 200
    (*c*) Article 201 (*d*) Article 257

29. Who makes the rules for more convenient transaction of business of the State Government?
    (*a*) The Chief Secretary
    (*b*) A Committee of Secretaries
    (*c*) The Department of Home of the concerned State Government
    (*d*) The Governor

30. Consider the following statements with regard to the powers enjoyed by the Governor of a State:
    1. He addresses the Legislative Assembly of the State at the commencement of the first session each year.
    2. He can send messages to the Legislative Assembly with respect to a Bill pending in the Assembly at that time.
    3. He can summon, prorogue and dissolve the Legislative Assembly of the State.
    4. He can give assent to a Bill to curtail the powers of the State High Court.

    Which of the statements given above are correct?
    (*a*) 1 and 4 only (*b*) 3 and 4 only
    (*c*) 1 and 2 only (*d*) 1, 2 and 3

31. Which one of the following Constitutional Amendments made it possible to appoint one person to hold the office of the Governor in two or more states simultaneously?
    (*a*) Constitution (Seventh Amendment) Act, 1956
    (*b*) Constitution (Forty-second Amendment) Act, 1976
    (*c*) Constitution (Forty-third Amendment) Act, 1977
    (*d*) Constitution (Forty-fourth Amendment) Act, 1978

32. Which one of the following statements is correct?
    (*a*) The same person can be appointed as the Governor of three states.
    (*b*) A Governor can be appointed only in consultation with the Chief Minister of the State concerned.
    (*c*) A Governor has no power to entrust any of the functions of the state to Government of India even with the latter's consent.
    (*d*) Only a person who has completed 30 years of age can be appointed as the Governor of a state.

Answers

1. (*b*)	2. (*b*)	3. (*b*)	4. (*c*)	5. (*b*)
6. (*d*)	7. (*a*)	8. (*b*)	9. (*d*)	10. (*b*)
11. (*a*)	12. (*c*)	13. (*d*)	14. (*d*)	15. (*a*)
16. (*c*)	17. (*b*)	18. (*b*)	19. (*c*)	20. (*a*)
21. (*a*)	22. (*a*)	23. (*c*)	24. (*c*)	25. (*c*)
26. (*d*)	27. (*b*)	28. (*b*)	29. (*d*)	30. (*d*)
31. (*a*)	32. (*a*)			

31

Chief Minister

1. Consider the following statements with regard to the Chief Minister of a State:
   1. He is appointed by the Governor of the State.
   2. He and his Council of Ministers are collectively responsible to the Governor.
   3. He must communicate to the Governor all the decisions of Council of Ministers relating to the administration of the State and proposals for legislation.
   4. If the Governor of the State so requires, the Chief Minister shall submit for the consideration of the Council of Ministers any matter on which a decision has been taken by a minister but which has not been considered by the Council of Ministers.

   Which of the statements given above is/are correct?

   (*a*) 1, 2, 3 and 4 (*b*) 4 only
   (*c*) 1, 3 and 4 (*d*) 1 and 3 only

2. Consider the following powers/functions:
   1. Appointing ministers and allocating portfolios to them
   2. Presiding over the meetings of the Cabinet
   3. Resolving conflicts between ministers
   4. Communicating with the Governor

   The powers/functions of the Chief Minister of a State include:

   (*a*) 2, 3 and 4 (*b*) 1 and 4 only
   (*c*) 1, 2 and 3 (*d*) 1, 2, 3 and 4

3. Which of the following are included in Article 167 of the Indian Constitution, defining the duties of the Chief Minister?
   1. To communicate to the Governor of the State all decisions of the Council of Ministers relating to the administration of the affairs of the State and proposals for legislation
   2. To take prior Governor's sanction for the budget before submitting it in the State Legislative Assembly
   3. To furnish the information called for by the Governor regarding the administration of affairs of the State
   4. If the Governor so requires, to submit for the consideration of the Council of Ministers a matter on which a Minister has taken a decision without submitting the same for consideration by the Council beforehand

   Choose the correct answer from the codes given below:

   (*a*) 1 and 2 only (*b*) 1, 3 and 4
   (*c*) 2 and 4 only (*d*) 1 and 3 only

4. Which one of the following is constitutionally obligatory on the part of the Chief Minister of a State?
   (*a*) As the Governor is the head of the State, the Chief Minister has to take all major decisions regarding administration only after prior approval by the Governor.
   (*b*) The Chief Minister has to communicate to the Governor all decisions of the cabinet relating to administration and proposals for legislation.
   (*c*) As the ministers are appointed by the Governor, the Chief Minister has to go by Governor's discretion in the allocation of business among the ministers.
   (*d*) The Chief Minister, if he happens to be the leader of a party not having the required majority, should prove his majority strength in the State Legislative Assembly within the period stipulated by the Governor.

5. Which one of the following is correct in terms of the Constitution of India?
   (*a*) The Chief Minister decides the allocation of portfolios among the Ministers.
   (*b*) When the Chief Minister resigns, the Council of Ministers gets dissolved.
   (*c*) All the principal policy announcements of the Government are made by the Chief Minister.
   (*d*) It shall be the duty of the Chief Minister to communicate to the Governor all decisions of the Council of Ministers relating to the administration of the affairs of the State.

6. The salary and allowances of the Chief Minister of a State are determined by the:
   (*a*) Governor of the State
   (*b*) President of India
   (*c*) Parliament of India
   (*d*) State Legislature

7. When there is no majority party in the State Legislative Assembly, the principal consideration governing the choice of the Chief Minister by the Governor of the State is the:
   (*a*) ability of the person who is most likely to command a stable majority in the House.
   (*b*) largest political party in the Legislative Assembly.
   (*c*) the combination of several parties as a unit.
   (*d*) the loyalty and support of the party members to their respective party programmes and policies.

8. The Constitution of India lays down that proposals for legislation are to be communicated to the Governor by whom of the following?
   (*a*) Chief Minister
   (*b*) Speaker of the Legislative Assembly
   (*c*) Minister for Law
   (*d*) Minister for Home Affairs

9. Which of the following Articles of the Constitution of India provides for the office of the Chief Minister in the States?
   (*a*) Article 164 (*b*) Article 167
   (*c*) Article 163 (*d*) Article 166

10. Consider the following statements:

The Chief Minister as the head of the State Council of Ministers:

1. has a free hand in the distribution of portfolios.
2. can reshuffle the Ministers and ask any Minister to resign.
3. is bound by the advice of the Ministers.
4. advises the Ministers in day-to-day administration of departments.

Which of the statements given above are correct?

(*a*) 1 and 2 only (*b*) 2 and 3 only
(*c*) 1, 2 and 4 (*d*) 3 and 4 only

11. Constitutionally, the Chief Minister holds office during the pleasure of whom of the following?

(*a*) Speaker of the State Legislative Assembly
(*b*) Chief Justice of the State High Court
(*c*) Governor of the State
(*d*) President of India

12. Consider the following statements with respect to the duties of the Chief Minister of a State according to the Constitution of India:

1. To make rules for the more convenient transaction of business of the State Government, and for the allocation among the Ministers of the said business.
2. If the Governor of the State so requires, to submit for consideration of the Council of Ministers any matter on which a decision has been taken by a Minister but which has not been considered by the Council.

Which of the statements given above is/are correct?

(*a*) 1 only (*b*) 2 only
(*c*) Both 1 and 2 (*d*) Neither 1 nor 2

13. In which of the following bodies, does the Chief Minister of a State hold membership?

1. National Integration Council
2. Governing Council of NITI Aayog
3. Inter-State Council
4. Zonal Council

Select the correct answer from the codes given below:

(*a*) 1, 3 and 4 (*b*) 2 and 3 only
(*c*) 1, 2, 3 and 4 (*d*) 2, 3 and 4

14. Consider the following statements:

1. There shall be a Council of Ministers with the Chief Minister as the head to aid and advise the Governor in the exercise of his functions, except in so far he is by or under the Constitution, required to exercise his functions, or any of them in his discretion.
2. The Chief Minister shall be appointed by the Governor and other ministers shall be appointed by the Governor on the advice of the President of the majority party.

Which of the statements given above is/are correct?

(*a*) 1 only (*b*) 2 only
(*c*) Both 1 and 2 (*d*) Neither 1 nor 2

Answers

1. (*c*)	2. (*a*)	3. (*b*)	4. (*b*)	5. (*d*)
6. (*d*)	7. (*a*)	8. (*a*)	9. (*c*)	10. (*a*)
11. (*c*)	12. (*b*)	13. (*c*)	14. (*a*)	

32

State Council of Ministers

1. Consider the following statements:
   1. The Governor cannot function without the State Council of Ministers.
   2. A person who is not a member of the State Legislature cannot be appointed as a minister.
   3. The State Council of Ministers can function for sometime even after the death or resignation of the Chief Minister.
   4. In the absence of the Chief Minister, only the Home Minister can preside over emergency meetings of the State Council of Ministers.

   Which of the statements given above is/are correct?

   (*a*) 1 only (*b*) 3 and 4 only
   (*c*) 1, 2 and 4 (*d*) 1, 2, 3 and 4

2. There is a constitutional requirement to have a Minister in-charge of Tribal Welfare for the States of:
   (*a*) Assam, Nagaland and Manipur.
   (*b*) Himachal Pradesh, Haryana and Rajasthan.
   (*c*) Madhya Pradesh, Odisha, Chhattisgarh and Jharkhand.
   (*d*) Manipur, Tripura and Meghalaya.

3. Some state governments have, besides Cabinet Ministers and Ministers of State, Parliamentary Secretaries also. These Parliamentary Secretaries who are also members of the State Legislature are appointed by whom of the following?
   (*a*) The Chief Minister (*b*) The Governor
   (*c*) The Chief Whip of the ruling party (*d*) The Speaker

4. Which of the following pays the salaries and allowances of the Council of Ministers of the State Government?
   (*a*) Reserve Bank of India
   (*b*) Treasury of the State Government
   (*c*) Contingency Fund of the State
   (*d*) Consolidated Fund of the state

5. Which of the Articles of the Constitution of India are relevant to analyse the constitutional provisions that deal with the relationship of the Governor with the State Council of Ministers?
   (*a*) Articles 161, 165 and 166
   (*b*) Articles 163, 164 and 167

(*c*) Articles 162, 163 and 168
(*d*) Articles 164, 165 and 169

6. Which of the following Constitutional Amendment Act provided that the total number of ministers, including the Chief Minister, in the Council of Ministers in a State shall not exceed 15 per cent of the total strength of the Legislative Assembly of that State?
(*a*) 94th Amendment Act
(*b*) 89th Amendment Act
(*c*) 91st Amendment Act
(*d*) 87th Amendment Act

7. Consider the following statements:
   1. All decisions of the State Council of Ministers relating to the administration of the State must be communicated to the Governor.
   2. The Governor can call for information relating to proposals for legislation.
   3. The Governor can direct that any matter on which decision has been taken by a Minister should be placed before the State Council of Ministers.
   4. The Governor has the right to address and send messages to the State Council of Ministers to elicit specific information.

   Which of the statements given above is/are correct?
   (*a*) 1 only (*b*) 3 and 4 only
   (*c*) 1, 2 and 3 (*d*) 1, 2, 3 and 4

8. In which of the following provisions of the Constitution of India is the principle of collective responsibility of the State Council of Ministers enshrined?
(*a*) Article 164 (*b*) Article 162
(*c*) Article 163 (*d*) Article 167

9. The ministers in the State could be prosecuted only with the approval of the Governor because they:
(*a*) are the heads of the ministries.
(*b*) are representatives of the people.
(*c*) enjoy certain immunities under the provisions of the Constitution.
(*d*) exercise executive powers on behalf of the Governor.

10. The ministers in the Council of Ministers at the state level are appointed by the?
(*a*) President of the majority party
(*b*) Governor
(*c*) Chief Minister
(*d*) Prime Minister

11. Which of the following Articles of the Constitution of India declares that the ministers shall have the right to speak and take part in the proceeding of the State Legislature?
(*a*) Article 167 (*b*) Article 164
(*c*) Article 177 (*d*) Article 166

12. Which of the following are not mentioned in the Constitution of India?
   1. Council of Ministers headed by a Chief Minister
   2. Collective Responsibility of the State Council of Ministers
   3. Resignation of State Ministers
   4. Office of the Deputy Chief Minister

   Select the correct answer from the codes given below:

   (*a*) 1 and 2 only (*b*) 2 and 3 only
   (*c*) 3 and 4 only (*d*) 1 and 3 only

13. According to the Constitution of India, if the Governor so requires, it shall be the duty of the Chief Minister to submit for the consideration of the State Council of Ministers any matter on which a decision has been taken by a Minister, but which has not been considered by the Council. This ensures:
   (*a*) collective responsibility.
   (*b*) the status of the Chief Minister as the first among the equals.
   (*c*) the power of the Governor to nullify the decision of the Minister.
   (*d*) the inherent power of the Minister to take a decision independent of the State Council of Ministers.

14. Which of the following is the accountability or responsibility of the Chief Minister and the Cabinet to the State Legislative Assembly?
   (*a*) Intermittent
   (*b*) Indirect
   (*c*) At the time of elections
   (*d*) Direct, continuous and collective

15. According to Article 163 of the Constitution, which of the following statements relating to the question whether any, and if so what, advice was tendered by Ministers to the Governor would be correct?
   (*a*) It shall not be inquired into in any court.
   (*b*) It can be inquired into in the Supreme Court.
   (*c*) It can be inquired into in all the courts.
   (*d*) It cannot be inquired into in the High Court.

16. How are the salaries and allowances of the State Ministers determined?
   (*a*) By the Home Department
   (*b*) By the State Legislature
   (*c*) By the Finance Department
   (*d*) By the Law Department

17. Which of the following Constitutional Amendment Acts freed Bihar from the obligation of having a tribal welfare minister?
   (*a*) 91st Amendment Act (*b*) 92nd Amendment Act
   (*c*) 93rd Amendment Act (*d*) 94th Amendment Act

Answers

1. (*a*)	2. (*c*)	3. (*b*)	4. (*d*)	5. (*b*)
6. (*c*)	7. (*c*)	8. (*a*)	9. (*c*)	10. (*b*)
11. (*c*)	12. (*c*)	13. (*a*)	14. (*d*)	15. (*a*)
16. (*b*)	17. (*d*)			

33

State Legislature

1. Consider the following statements:
   1. A bill pending in the Legislature of a State shall not lapse by reason of the prorogation of the House or Houses thereof.
   2. A bill pending in the Legislative Council of a State which has not been passed by the Legislative Assembly shall not lapse on dissolution of the Assembly.

   Which of the statements given above is/are correct?

   (*a*) 1 only (*b*) 2 only
   (*c*) Both 1 and 2 (*d*) Neither 1 nor 2

2. Consider the following statements:
   1. The parliament may by law provide for the abolition of the Legislative Council of a State having such a Council or for the creation of such a Council in a state having no such Council.
   2. The total number of members in the Legislative Council of a State having such a Council shall not exceed one half of the total number of members in the Legislative Assembly of that State.

   Which of the statements given above is/are correct?

   (*a*) 1 only (*b*) 2 only
   (*c*) Both 1 and 2 (*d*) Neither 1 nor 2

3. The Upper Chamber of the State Legislature, besides other members, consists of:
   (*a*) 1/12 elected by teachers' electorate; 1/3 elected by municipalities; 1/12 elected by registered graduates.
   (*b*) 1/12 elected by registered graduates; 1/12 elected by women; 1/3 elected by trade unions and co-operative institutions.
   (*c*) 1/12 elected by women; 1/12 elected by municipalities and other local bodies; 1/3 elected by teachers' electorate.
   (*d*) 1/3 directly elected by the people; 1/12 elected by registered graduates; 1/12 elected by co-operative banks, women's organisations and other co-operative bodies.

4. The quorum to hold a meeting of a House of the State Legislature shall be:
   (*a*) thirty members or one-tenth of total membership whichever is less.
   (*b*) one-half of the total membership of the House.
   (*c*) one-tenth of the total membership of the House.
   (*d*) ten members or one-tenth of total membership whichever is more.

5. The members of a State Legislature are entitled to receive such salaries and allowances as may be determined by which of the following?
   (*a*) State Governor (*b*) State Legislature
   (*c*) Parliament of India (*d*) President of India

6. Consider the following statements:
   A Bill is reserved by the Governor of a State for the consideration of the President. The President may:
   1. give his assent to the Bill.
   2. withhold his assent to the Bill.
   3. veto the Bill.
   4. direct the Governor of the State to return it to the House for reconsideration.

   Which of the statements given above are correct?
   (*a*) 1, 2 and 3 (*b*) 3 and 4 only
   (*c*) 1, 2 and 4 (*d*) 1, 2, 3 and 4

7. A House of the State Legislature can declare the seat of a member vacant if he absents himself (without its permission) from all its meeting for a period how many days?
   (*a*) Thirty days (*b*) Forty-five days
   (*c*) Sixty days (*d*) Ninety days

8. Consider the following statements:
   1. No discussion can take place in the Legislature of a State with respect to the conduct of any Judge of the Supreme Court as per the provisions of Constitution of India.
   2. There is no restriction on the discussion to take place in the Legislature of a State with respect to the conduct of any Judge of the State's High Court as per the provisions of the Constitution of India.
   3. Courts cannot enquire into any proceedings of the Legislatures as per the provisions of the Constitution of India.

   Which of the statements given above are correct?
   (*a*) 1 and 2 only (*b*) 2 and 3 only
   (*c*) 1 and 3 only (*d*) 1, 2 and 3

9. The Legislative Assembly of a State can pass a resolution to abolish or create a Legislative Council in the State by a:
   (*a*) majority of not less than 2/3 of the members of the Legislative Assembly present and voting.
   (*b*) majority of not less than 1/3 of the members of the Legislative Assembly present and voting.
   (*c*) majority of the total membership of the Legislative Assembly and by a majority of not less than 2/3 of the members present and voting.
   (*d*) simple majority of the members of the State Legislative Assembly.

10. The Speaker of a State Legislative Assembly submits his resignation letter to the:
    (*a*) Governor (*b*) Chief Minister
    (*c*) Chief Justice of the High Court (*d*) Deputy Speaker

11. What is the maximum permissible strength of the Legislative Assembly (Vidhan Sabha) of any State?
(*a*) 400 members (*b*) 425 members
(*c*) 500 members (*d*) 545 members

12. Consider the following statements:
1. Reservation of a State Bill for the assent of the President is a discretionary power of the Governor of a State.
2. President of India is not empowered to keep a bill of the State Legislature pending for an indefinite period of time, without expressing his mind.

Which of the statements given above is/are correct?
(*a*) 1 only (*b*) 2 only
(*c*) Both 1 and 2 (*d*) Neither 1 nor 2

13. What is the time-limit within which a non-money Bill has to be sent to the State Legislature by the Governor for reconsideration?
(*a*) 14 days (*b*) One month
(*c*) Three months (*d*) No time limit specified

14. Which one of the following is not correct with respect to the powers of the Governor regarding a Bill passed by the State Legislature?
(*a*) He may give his assent to the Bill.
(*b*) He may withhold the Bill.
(*c*) He may reserve the Bill for the consideration of the President.
(*d*) He shall have no alternative but to give his assent to the Bill.

Answers

1. (*c*)	2. (*a*)	3. (*a*)	4. (*d*)	5. (*b*)
6. (*c*)	7. (*c*)	8. (*c*)	9. (*c*)	10. (*d*)
11. (*c*)	12. (*a*)	13. (*d*)	14. (*d*)	

34

High Court

1. Consider the following statements:
   1. The maximum number of Judges in a High Court are specified in the Constitution of India.
   2. Every High Court has the power of superintendence over all courts and tribunals (except military tribunals) provided they are subject to appellate jurisdiction of the High Court.

   Which of the statements given above is/are correct?
   (*a*) 1 only (*b*) 2 only
   (*c*) Both 1 and 2 (*d*) Neither 1 nor 2

2. Consider the following statements:
   A high court has jurisdiction to:
   1. punish for its contempt.
   2. tender advice on a legal question referred to it by the President of India.
   3. tender advice on a legal question referred to it by the Governor of the State.
   4. issue certain writs for enforcement of Fundamental Rights or for other purposes.

   Which of the statements given above are correct?
   (*a*) 1 and 4 only (*b*) 1 and 2 only
   (*c*) 1, 2 and 3 (*d*) 2, 3 and 4

3. The transfer of Judges from one High Court to another High Court may be made by the:
   (*a*) President of India in consultation with the Chief Justice of that High Court.
   (*b*) Chief Justice of the concerned High Court.
   (*c*) Governor of the concerned State in consultation with the Chief Justice of India.
   (*d*) President of India after consultation with the Chief Justice of India.

4. A retired judge of a High Court cannot:
   (*a*) practise in the Supreme Court.
   (*b*) practise in any High Court in India.
   (*c*) practise in the High Court from where he has retired.
   (*d*) practise in any court in India.

5. The writ jurisdiction of the Supreme Court of India under Article 32 of the Constitution of India is not wider than that of the writ jurisdiction of the High Courts under Article 226 because the High Courts may exercise this power in relation to which of the following?
   (*a*) Civil and criminal matters (*b*) Fundamental and other legal rights
   (*c*) Fundamental Rights and matters in appeals (*d*) Fundamental Rights and stay matters

6. Who among the following extends the jurisdiction of a High Court to, or excludes from, any Union territory?
   (*a*) The Parliament by law
   (*b*) The President of India
   (*c*) The Chief Justice of India
   (*d*) The Legislature of the State in which the High Court is situated

7. The nature of "consultation" with the Chief Justice of India in matters of appointment of a judge to a High Court is correctly described as:
   (*a*) inspection of the file by the Chief Justice.
   (*b*) concurrence of the Chief Justice.
   (*c*) conformity with the opinion of the Chief Justice.
   (*d*) formal reference to the Chief Justice without any obligation to carry out his wishes.

8. The Institution of High Court originated in India in which of the following years?
   (*a*) 1886 (*b*) 1864
   (*c*) 1868 (*d*) 1862

9. Which one of the following statements is not correct?
   (*a*) The Supreme Court can over-rule itself.
   (*b*) A High Court can over-rule itself.
   (*c*) Judgements of the Supreme Court bind the lower courts.
   (*d*) Judgements of a High Court do not bind the lower courts of the State.

10. The High Court having the jurisdiction in judicial matters relating to the largest number of States/Union Territories is:
    (*a*) Calcutta High Court
    (*b*) Kerala High Court
    (*c*) Bombay High Court
    (*d*) Guwahati High Court

11. A Judge of a High Court can be removed from office during his tenure by:
    (*a*) the Governor, if the State Legislature passes a resolution to this effect by two-thirds majority.
    (*b*) the President, on the basis of a resolution passed by the Parliament by two-thirds majority.
    (*c*) the Chief Justice of the Supreme Court, on the recommendation of the Parliament.
    (*d*) the Chief Justice of the High Court, on the recommendation of the State Legislature.

12. The power of Judicial Review means:
    (*a*) the power of the courts to define and interpret constitution.
    (*b*) the power of the courts to declare null and void any legislative or executive act, which is against the provisions of the Constitution.
    (*c*) the power of the Judiciary to define and interpret laws.
    (*d*) the power of the courts to legislate when there is no statutory provision.

13. Under the provisions of the Constitution of India, who is entitled to be consulted by the President of India in the matter of the appointments of the Judges of the High Courts?
    (*a*) The Union Minister of Law and Justice
    (*b*) The Advocate-General of the State
    (*c*) The Attorney-General of India
    (*d*) The Governor

14. Under which Article(s) of the Constitution of India is the power to issue writs for the enforcement of the Fundamental Rights vested in the Supreme Court and the High Courts?
    (*a*) Article 32 only
    (*b*) Article 226 only
    (*c*) Both Article 32 and Article 226
    (*d*) Neither Article 32 nor Article 226

15. Which of the following are the main jurisdictions of the High Court of a State?
    1. Original jurisdiction
    2. Appellate jurisdiction
    3. Supervisory jurisdiction
    4. Advisory jurisdiction

    Choose the correct answer from the codes given below:
    (*a*) 1, 2 and 3 (*b*) 2, 3 and 4
    (*c*) 1, 3 and 4 (*d*) 1, 2 and 4

16. Where was a fourth High Court was establish in 1866?
    (*a*) Bombay (*b*) Madras
    (*c*) Allahabad (*d*) Calcutta

17. The salaries and allowances of the judges of a High Court are determined by which of the following?
    (*a*) Chief Justice of India (*b*) Legislature of the State
    (*c*) Parliament of India (*d*) President of India

Answers

1. (*d*)	2. (*a*)	3. (*d*)	4. (*c*)	5. (*b*)
6. (*a*)	7. (*c*)	8. (*d*)	9. (*d*)	10. (*d*)
11. (*b*)	12. (*b*)	13. (*d*)	14. (*c*)	15. (*a*)
16. (*c*)	17. (*c*)			

35

Tribunals

1. Part XIVA of the Constitution of India deals with which of the following?
   1. Administrative tribunals
   2. Adjudication or trial by tribunals in respect of enforcement of any tax
   3. Adjudication or trial by tribunals in respect of ceiling on urban property
   4. Adjudication or trial by tribunals in respect of industrial and labour disputes

   Select the correct answer using the codes given below:

   (*a*) 1, 2, 3 and 4 (*b*) 1, 2 and 3
   (*c*) 3 and 4 only (*d*) 1 and 4 only

2. The Central Administrative Tribunal adjudicates disputes and complaints with respect to the service of persons who are:
   (*a*) appointed to public services and posts in connection with the affairs of the Union except members of the Defence services.
   (*b*) officials and servants of the Supreme Court or the High Courts.
   (*c*) members of the Secretarial staff of the Parliament or the State Legislatures.
   (*d*) members of the Defence Services.

3. Which one of the following is a Quasi-judicial authority?
   (*a*) Central Vigilance Commission
   (*b*) National Commission for Women
   (*c*) Comptroller and Auditor-General of India
   (*d*) Administrative Tribunal

4. The Central Administrative Tribunal was set up on the recommendation of:
   (*a*) the Ministry of Law and Justice.
   (*b*) the First Administrative Reforms Commission of India.
   (*c*) the Law Commission.
   (*d*) the Sarkaria Commission.

5. In which one of the following cases did the Supreme Court rule that the power of judicial review vested in the High Courts in respect of the decisions given by the Service Tribunals, cannot be ousted or excluded even by a Constitutional Amendment?
   (*a*) High Court of Judicature at Bombay v. Shirish Kumar
   (*b*) Sampath Kumar v. Union of India
   (*c*) Chandra Kumar v. Union of India
   (*d*) All India Judges Association v. Union of India

6. The Parliament passed the Administrative Tribunals Act in which year?
(*a*) 1985 (*b*) 1975
(*c*) 1982 (*d*) 1987

7. The chairman of a State Administrative Tribunal is appointed by the:
(*a*) Governor of the State.
(*b*) Chief Justice of the State High Court.
(*c*) Speaker of the State Legislative Assembly.
(*d*) President of India.

8. Which Article of the Constitution of India deals with administrative tribunals?
(*a*) Article 322 (*b*) Article 323
(*c*) Article 323A (*d*) Article 323B

9. Which of the following Constitutional Amendment Acts included Part XIVA (entitled as "Tribunals") in the Constitution of India?
(*a*) 42nd Amendment Act (*b*) 44th Amendment Act
(*c*) 47th Amendment Act (*d*) 49th Amendment Act

Answers

1. (*a*)	2. (*a*)	3. (*d*)	4. (*b*)	5. (*c*)
6. (*a*)	7. (*d*)	8. (*c*)	9. (*a*)	

36

Subordinate Courts

1. Consider the following statements:
   1. The district judge exercises both judicial and administrative powers.
   2. The sessions judge has no power to impose capital punishment.

   Which of the statements given above is/are correct?

   (*a*) 1 only (*b*) 2 only
   (*c*) Both 1 and 2 (*d*) Neither 1 nor 2

2. Which of the following statements regarding subordinate courts are correct?
   1. They function at district and lower levels.
   2. The pattern and designation of subordinate courts in the States is not uniform.
   3. Munsiff's courts have both civil and criminal jurisdiction.
   4. The pattern of subordinate courts in metropolitan areas is the same as that in districts.

   Select the correct answer using the codes given below:

   (*a*) 1 and 2 only (*b*) 1 and 3 only
   (*c*) 2 and 3 only (*d*) 3 and 4 only

3. Who among the following appoints the district judge in a State?
   (*a*) The Governor of the State
   (*b*) The President of India
   (*c*) The Chief Minister of the State
   (*d*) Chief Justice of the High Court of the State

4. Who appoints the judicial officers of the subordinate judiciary other than the district judges?
   (*a*) Union Public Service Commission
   (*b*) State Public Service Commission
   (*c*) Governor in accordance with the rules made by him in consultation with the High Court and State Public Service Commission
   (*d*) Governor in consultation with the High Court exercising jurisdiction in relation to such state

5. Which one of the following is not a qualification for a person to be appointed as a district judge?
   (*a*) He should not already be in the service of the Central or the State Government.
   (*b*) He should have been an advocate or a pleader for seven years.
   (*c*) He should have completed the 30 years of age.
   (*d*) He should be recommended by the High Court for appointment.

6. In which of the following states, the first Lok Adalat camp in the post-independence era was organised?
   (*a*) Maharashtra (*b*) Kerala
   (*c*) Rajasthan (*d*) Gujarat

7. Which of the following recommended the establishment of Gram Nyayalayas?
   (*a*) Second Administrative Reforms Commission of India
   (*b*) Law Commission of India
   (*c*) Committee of the High Courts
   (*d*) National Legal Services Authority

Answers

1. (*a*)	2. (*a*)	3. (*a*)	4. (*c*)	5. (*c*)
6. (*d*)	7. (*b*)			

37 Special Provisions for Some States

1. Consider the following statements:
   1. The Governor of Arunachal Pradesh will have special responsibility for law and order in the state.
   2. The Arunachal Pradesh Legislative Assembly is to consist of not less than 40 members.

   Which of the statements given above is/are correct?

   (*a*) 1 only (*b*) 2 only
   (*c*) Both 1 and 2 (*d*) Neither 1 nor 2

2. Which of the Acts of the Parliament relating to the following matters would not apply to Nagaland unless the State Legislative Assembly so decides?
   1. Religious or social practices of the Nagas
   2. Naga customary law and procedure
   3. Administration of civil and criminal justice involving decisions according to Naga customary law
   4. Ownership and transfer of land and its resources

   Select the correct answer using the codes given below:

   (*a*) 2 and 3 only (*b*) 1 and 2 only
   (*c*) 1, 2, 3 and 4 (*d*) 3 and 4 only

3. Who/which of the following can extend (with restrictions or modifications) to Sikkim any law which is in force in a state of the Indian Union?

   (*a*) The Parliament of India
   (*b*) The President of India
   (*c*) The Governor of Sikkim
   (*d*) The Legislative Assembly of Sikkim

4. The temporary, transitional and special provisions mentioned in Part XXI of the Constitution of India relate to which of the following State(s)?
   1. Manipur
   2. Nagaland
   3. Assam
   4. Andhra Pradesh

   Select the correct answer using the codes given below:

   (*a*) 1 only (*b*) 3 and 4 only
   (*c*) 1, 2 and 3 (*d*) 1, 2, 3 and 4

5. Under the provisions of Article 371E of the Constitution of India, who/which of the following is empowered to provide for the establishment of a Central University in the State of Andhra Pradesh?
   (*a*) The President of India
   (*b*) The Parliament of India
   (*c*) The Legislative Assembly of Andhra Pradesh
   (*d*) The Governor of Andhra Pradesh

6. Who/which of the following is authorised to provide for the creation of a committee of the Manipur Legislative Assembly consisting of the members elected from the Hill areas of the State?
   (*a*) The Governor of Manipur
   (*b*) The Chief Minister of Manipur
   (*c*) The Parliament of India
   (*d*) The President of India

7. According to Article 371A of the Constitution of India, the Governor of which one of the following States has special responsibility with respect to law and order in the State?
   (*a*) Assam
   (*b*) Manipur
   (*c*) Nagaland
   (*d*) Andhra Pradesh

8. In respect to which of the following states, Article 371B contains the special provisions?
   (*a*) Goa
   (*b*) Mizoram
   (*c*) Assam
   (*d*) Andhra Pradesh

9. Article 371 of the Constitution of India provides for special provisions with respect to which of the following states?
   (*a*) Andhra Pradesh
   (*b*) Assam
   (*c*) Nagaland
   (*d*) Maharashtra and Gujarat

10. Consider the following statements:
    1. Article 371E of the Constitution of India contains special provisions with respect to Sikkim.
    2. The 38th Constitutional Amendment Act made Sikkim a full-fledged state of the Indian Union.

    Which of the statements given above is/are correct?
    (*a*) 1 only
    (*b*) 2 only
    (*c*) Both 1 and 2
    (*d*) Neither 1 nor 2

11. Which of the following Constitutional Amendments made special provisions for the state of Karnataka?
    (*a*) 96th Amendment
    (*b*) 97th Amendment
    (*c*) 98th Amendment
    (*d*) 99th Amendment

Answers

1. (*a*)	2. (*c*)	3. (*b*)	4. (*d*)	5. (*b*)
6. (*d*)	7. (*c*)	8. (*c*)	9. (*d*)	10. (*d*)
11. (*c*)				

PART-V LOCAL GOVERNMENT

38. Panchayati Raj

39. Municipalities

38

Panchayati Raj

1. Consider the following statements:
   1. A Panchayat elected in place of a dissolved one does not enjoy the full period but remains in office for the remaining period after the dissolution.
   2. In Panchayats, seats are reserved for the Scheduled Castes, Scheduled Tribes and women but not for Backward Classes of citizens.

   Which of the statements given above is/are correct?

   (*a*) 1 only (*b*) 2 only
   (*c*) Both 1 and 2 (*d*) Neither 1 nor 2

2. Consider the following statements:
   1. Courts have no jurisdiction to examine the validity of a law relating to the delimitation of constituencies or allotment of seats in respect of Panchayats.
   2. An election to a Panchayat can be called in question only by an election petition, which should be presented to such authority and in such manner as may be prescribed by the State Election Commission.

   Which of the statements given above is/are correct?

   (*a*) 1 only (*b*) 2 only
   (*c*) Both 1 and 2 (*d*) Neither 1 nor 2

3. Consider the following statements:
   1. The Eleventh Schedule was inserted in the Constitution of India by the Constitution (73rd Amendment) Act, 1992.
   2. The Eleventh Schedule of the Constitution of India corresponds to Article 243W of the Constitution of India.

   Which of the statements given above is/are correct?

   (*a*) 1 only (*b*) 2 only
   (*c*) Both 1 and 2 (*d*) Neither 1 nor 2

4. Consider the following statements:
   1. According to Article 243D, one-third of the seats are reserved for the Scheduled Castes and Scheduled Tribes in every Panchayat.
   2. Not less than one-third of the total number of seats reserved for the SCs and STs in every Panchayat are reserved for women belonging to the Scheduled Castes, or as the case may be, the Scheduled Tribes.
   3. Not less than one-third of the total number of offices of chairpersons in Panchayats at each level are reserved for women.

Which of the statements given above are correct?

(*a*) 1 and 2 only (*b*) 2 and 3 only

(*c*) 1 and 3 only (*d*) 1, 2 and 3

5. On which of the following subjects, does the Finance Commission of a State constituted under the Part IX of the Constitution of India make recommendations to the Governor?
   1. Distribution between the State and the Panchayats of the net proceeds of the taxes by the State.
   2. Determination of the taxes which may be assigned to or appropriated by the Panchayats.
   3. Grants-in-aid to the Panchayats from the Consolidated Fund of the State.

   Select the correct answer using the codes given below:

   (*a*) 1, 2 and 3 (*b*) 1 and 2 only

   (*c*) 2 and 3 only (*d*) 1 and 3 only

6. Which one of the following is not correct?

   (*a*) Part IX of the Constitution of India pertaining to the Panchayats provided for setting up of a Finance Commission.

   (*b*) Part IX of the Constitution of India pertaining to the Panchayats provided for vesting all elections to the Panchayats in a State Election Commission.

   (*c*) Part IX of the Constitution of India pertaining to the Panchayats provided for reservation of posts of chairpersons at the village level or any other level for the Scheduled Castes, Scheduled Tribes and women.

   (*d*) Organisation of Village Panchayats is not included in the Directive Principles of State Policy.

7. 73rd Amendment to the Constitution of India provides for the:

   (*a*) two tiers of Panchayati Raj institutions at the village and district levels.

   (*b*) two tiers of Panchayati Raj institutions at the village and block levels.

   (*c*) two tiers of Panchayati Raj institutions at the block and district levels.

   (*d*) three tiers of Panchayati Raj institutions at the village, block and district levels.

8. Who makes provisions with respect to the maintenance of accounts by the Panchayats and the auditing of such accounts?

   (*a*) Finance Commission of the concerned State

   (*b*) Legislature of the State

   (*c*) Comptroller and Auditor-General of India

   (*d*) District Collector

9. The State Election Commissioner can be removed:

   (*a*) by the Governor of the State.

   (*b*) by the State Assembly.

   (*c*) through an order issued by the Chief Minister.

   (*d*) through a procedure similar to that for removal of the judge of a High Court.

10. Consider the following statements:

    In the post-73rd Amendment era, there has to be decentralisation of:

    1. decision-making powers.
    2. system as a whole.
    3. judicial powers.
    4. administrative powers.

    Which of the statements given above are correct?

    (*a*) 1, 2 and 3 (*b*) 1, 2 and 4
    (*c*) 2, 3 and 4 (*d*) 1, 3 and 4

11. Which of the following Committees was appointed to review the existing Administrative Arrangements for Rural Development and Poverty Alleviation Programmes?

    (*a*) G.V.K. Rao Committee (*b*) L.M. Singhvi Committee
    (*c*) Thungon Committee (*d*) Gadgil Committee

12. Which one of the following about Article 243 (G) is correct?

    (*a*) Panchayats should be enabled by law to function as agents of the State Government
    (*b*) Panchayats should be enabled by law to function as institutions of the self-government
    (*c*) Panchayats will act as the implementing agencies for centrally sponsored schemes
    (*d*) Gram Panchayats will be answerable to the District Panchayats

13. Consider the following statements:

    1. The Chairperson of a Panchayat at district level is elected in such manner as the Legislature of the State may provide.
    2. Legislature of a State may provide for representation of members of the Legislative Assembly of the State representing constituencies which comprise wholly or partly a Panchayat area at a level other than the village level, in such Panchayat.
    3. The Lok Sabha may provide for the representation of its members representing constituencies which comprise wholly or partly a Panchayat area at a level other than the village level, in such Panchayat.

    Which of the statements given above is/are correct?

    (*a*) 1 and 2 only (*b*) 2 only
    (*c*) 3 only (*d*) 2 and 3

14. 73rd Constitutional Amendment does not apply to which of the following states?

    (*a*) Meghalaya (*b*) Goa
    (*c*) Sikkim (*d*) Himachal Pradesh

15. Which of the following Committees is related to the Devolution of Powers and Functions to the Panchayati Raj Institutions?

    (*a*) Ramachandra Committee (*b*) Lalit Mathur Committee
    (*c*) Mani Shankar Aiyar Committee (*d*) Rajwant Sandhu Committee

16. Consider the following statements with respect to the 73rd Constitutional Amendment:

    1. It envisages the Gram Sabha as the foundation of the Panchayati Raj System.
    2. It provides that Panchayat bodies will have a duration of five years.

3. It stipulates that the Chairperson of a Panchayat shall be elected by and from amongst the elected members thereof.
4. It has reserved 33 per cent of the seats to Other Backward Classes in Panchayati Raj Institutions.

Which of the statements given above are correct?

(*a*) 1, 2, 3 and 4 (*b*) 1, 2 and 3
(*c*) 2, 3 and 4 (*d*) 1 and 2 only

17. Under which one of the following provisions is reservation for the Scheduled Castes and the Scheduled Tribes in every Panchayat made?
(*a*) Article 243 (Q) of the Constitution of India
(*b*) Article 243 (V) of the Constitution of India
(*c*) Article 243 (S) of the Constitution of India
(*d*) Article 243 (D) of the Constitution of India

18. Which of the following provisions can be made by law by a State Legislature?
1. Representation of the members of the House of People in Panchayats subject to fulfilling certain conditions
2. Reservation of seats in any Panchayat in favour of backward class of citizens
3. Authorising a Panchayat to levy, collect and appropriate taxes

Select the correct answer using the codes given below:

(*a*) 1, 2 and 3 (*b*) 1 and 2 only
(*c*) 2 and 3 only (*d*) 1 and 3 only

19. What is the minimum population below which Panchayats at the intermediate level are not constituted as per the provision of the Constitution (73rd Amendment) Act?
(*a*) 20 lacs (*b*) 25 lacs
(*c*) 30 lacs (*d*) 35 lacs

20. State Finance Commission is appointed by a State Government every five years to determine:
(*a*) financial resources of the State for placing State's requirement before the Union Government.
(*b*) development requirements of the State for formulating State Plan.
(*c*) budgetary requirements of various departments of the State Government.
(*d*) pattern of distribution of State's tax revenue between the State Government and the local bodies (both rural and urban) and the pattern of grants-in-aid to local bodies.

21. Which of the following is/are correct with respect to the 73rd Amendment to the Constitution of India?
1. Constitutional status to Panchayats
2. Reservation of seats for women belonging to the Scheduled Castes or the Scheduled Tribes
3. Providing permanent structures for district planning

Select the correct answer from the codes given below:

(*a*) 1 and 2 only (*b*) 1 only
(*c*) 2 and 3 only (*d*) 3 only

22. Under which of the following Articles of the Constitution of India, the State Legislatures delegate powers and functions to the Panchayats?
    (*a*) 243 and 243A (*b*) 243A and 243B
    (*c*) 243G and 243H (*d*) 243D and 243F

23. In which of the following states, the intermediate Panchayat is known as the Kshetra Panchayat?
    (*a*) Madhya Pradesh (*b*) West Bengal
    (*c*) Uttar Pradesh (*d*) Gujarat

24. In 1977, under whose chairmanship, the Panchayati Raj Committee was formed?
    (*a*) Ashok Mehta (*b*) Sardar Swaran Singh
    (*c*) Balwant Rai Mehta (*d*) Madhu Dandawate

25. Which of the following statements are correct?
    Village Panchayats are responsible for:
    1. agricultural production.
    2. rural industrial development.
    3. maternity and child welfare.
    4. higher vocational education.

    Select the correct answer using the codes given below:
    (*a*) 1, 2 and 4 (*b*) 1 and 3 only
    (*c*) 1, 2 and 3 (*d*) 2, 3 and 4

26. Which one of the following States was the first to introduce the Panchayati Raj system?
    (*a*) Tamil Nadu (*b*) West Bengal
    (*c*) Rajasthan (*d*) Uttar Pradesh

27. Constitution (73rd Amendment) Act that provided for the establishment of Panchayats also made which of the following provisions?
    1. Addition of a new Schedule (XI) to the Constitution listing 29 subjects which are to be handled by the Panchayats.
    2. Addition of a new Schedule (XI) to the Constitution listing 18 subjects which are to be handled by the Panchayats.
    3. Bar on the courts to question the validity of laws relating to delimitation of constituencies.
    4. Reservation of not less than one-third of the total number of seats in Panchayats for women (excluding the number of seats reserved for women belonging to the Scheduled Castes and Scheduled Tribes).

    Select the correct answer using the codes given below:
    (*a*) 1, 3 and 4 (*b*) 1 and 3 only
    (*c*) 2 and 4 only (*d*) 1 only

28. Which one of the following Articles of the Indian Constitution lays down that the State shall take steps to organise Village Panchayats?
    (*a*) Article 40 (*b*) Article 26
    (*c*) Article 39 (*d*) Article 38

29. Which of the following Constitutional Amendment Acts provided that the reservation of seats in Panchayats for the scheduled castes is not applicable to the state of Arunachal Pradesh?
(*a*) 81st Amendment (*b*) 82nd Amendment
(*c*) 83rd Amendment (*d*) 84th Amendment

30. Consider the following features:
1. Panchayats have now been brought under the direct supervision of the Governor.
2. Finance Commission of the State now determines the distribution of taxes and duties between the State and the Panchayats.
3. Panchayats are now entitled to receive grants-in-aid directly from the Central Government.
4. 1/3 of the seats in the Panchayats are now reserved for women.

According to the 73rd Amendment of the Constitution, which of these are correct features of Panchayats?
(*a*) 1 and 3 only (*b*) 2 and 3 only
(*c*) 3 and 4 only (*d*) 2 and 4 only

31. The Panchayati Raj is included in which of the following?
(*a*) Union List (*b*) State List
(*c*) Concurrent List (*d*) Residuary List

32. The 73rd Amendment Act emanates from which of the following articles?
(*a*) Article 38 (*b*) Article 40
(*c*) Article 44 (*d*) Article 52

33. Who of the following comprise the Zila Parishad?
1. Chairmen/Presidents of the Panchayat Samitis within the jurisdiction of the district
2. MPs, MLAs and MLCs whose constituencies are in the district
3. Representatives of co-operative societies, municipalities, notified area committees, etc.
4. Healthcare specialists

Choose the correct answer from the codes given below:
(*a*) 1 and 2 only (*b*) 1, 2 and 3
(*c*) 1, 2 and 4 (*d*) 2, 3 and 4

34. Which of the following subjects is related to Mani Shankar Aiyar Committee (2012)?
(*a*) Planning at the Grassroots Level
(*b*) Restructuring of District Rural Development Agency
(*c*) Devolution of Powers and Functions to Panchayati Raj Institutions
(*d*) Leveraging Panchayats for Efficient Delivery of Public Goods and Services

35. Which of the following are within the mandate of the 73rd Amendment to the Constitution of India?
1. Disqualification provision for Panchayat membership
2. Setting up of a State Finance Commission
3. Empowering the State Election Commission to hold periodic local government elections
4. Constitution of a District Planning Committee

Select the correct answer using the codes given below:

(*a*) 1, 2 and 4 (*b*) 2 and 3 only

(*c*) 1 and 3 only (*d*) 1, 2 and 3

36. Under Article 243D, which one of the following categories enjoys reservation for Panchayat membership in proportion to their population?

(*a*) Scheduled Castes and Scheduled Tribes (*b*) Women

(*c*) Backward Classes (*d*) Physically handicapped persons

37. The members of a Panchayat Samiti are:

(*a*) directly elected by the people.

(*b*) indirectly elected by the members of the Village Panchayat.

(*c*) nominated by the Block Development Officer.

(*d*) nominated by the president/chairman of the Panchayat Samiti.

38. Which of the following is not a feature of Ashok Mehta Committee recommendations on Panchayati Raj Institutions (PRIs)?

(*a*) Constitutional recognition to the PRIs

(*b*) Non-involvement of political parties in elections to the PRIs

(*c*) Reservation of seats for SCs and STs

(*d*) A minister-in-charge of Panchayati Raj

39. Consider the following statements:

The 73rd Constitutional Amendment Act provided:

1. for 27% reservation of seats in the Panchayats for the Other Backward Castes (OBCs).
2. that the Chairpersons of the Panchayats at intermediate or district level shall be elected by and from amongst the elected members thereof.

Which of the statements given above is/are correct?

(*a*) 1 only (*b*) 2 only

(*c*) Both 1 and 2 (*d*) Neither 1 nor 2

40. Consider the following statements in reference to the Constitution (73rd Amendment) Act:

1. The Governor of a State shall constitute a Finance Commission every fifth year to review the financial position of the Panchayats.
2. The superintendence, direction and control of all elections to the Panchayats are vested in the State Election Commission.

Which of the statements given above is/are correct?

(*a*) 1 only (*b*) 2 only

(*c*) Both 1 and 2 (*d*) Neither 1 nor 2

41. Which one of the following committees had recommended people's participation in community development programmes?

(*a*) Ashok Mehta Committee (*b*) Balwant Rai Mehta Committee

(*c*) Rural-urban Relationship Committee (*d*) L.M. Singhvi Committee

42. Consider the following Statements:
    1. Balwant Rai Mehta Committee was appointed in 1957.
    2. Ashok Mehta Committee submitted its report in 1977.
    3. G.V.K. Rao Committee submitted its report in 1986.
    4. L.M. Singhvi Committee was appointed in 1986.

    Which of the statements given above are correct?

    (*a*) 1, 2 and 3 (*b*) 1, 2 and 4
    (*c*) 1, 3 and 4 (*d*) 1 and 4 only

43. Consider the following with reference to 73rd Constitutional Amendment in respect of Panchayati Raj:
    1. Direct elections of members at all levels
    2. Direct elections of chairpersons at the village level
    3. Indirect election of chairpersons at the intermediate levels and district levels
    4. Mandatory provision for holding elections

    Which of the statements given above are correct?

    (*a*) 1, 2 and 3 (*b*) 2, 3 and 4
    (*c*) 1, 2 and 4 (*d*) 1, 3 and 4

44. Which one of the following government documents first suggested for having elections of Panchayati Raj Institutions on political party basis?

    (*a*) Report of the First Administrative Reforms Commission of India
    (*b*) Ashok Mehta Committee Report
    (*c*) Balwant Rai Mehta Committee Report
    (*d*) Diwakar Committee Report

45. Consider the following with respect to the revolutionary features of the 73rd Constitutional Amendment:
    1. Bestowal of Constitutional status on Panchayati Raj Institutions (PRIs)
    2. Mandatory elections to PRIs
    3. Introduction of third tier of Government with powers in rural India
    4. 33% reservation of seats and chairpersonships for women in the Panchayats at each level

    Which of the statements given above are correct?

    (*a*) 1 and 4 only (*b*) 1, 2 and 3
    (*c*) 3 and 4 only (*d*) 1, 2, 3 and 4

46. Under which provision does the Governor of a State constitute a State Finance Commission to review the financial position of Panchayats?

    (*a*) Under the discretionary powers of the Governor
    (*b*) By a resolution passed in the Legislative Assembly
    (*c*) In accordance with the Article 243-I of the Constitution of India
    (*d*) In accordance with a resolution passed in the Rajya Sabha

47. Consider the following statements:

73rd Amendment of the Constitution has provided constitutional sanction for:

1. building a three-tier structure of Panchayati Raj.
2. reservation of seats for women.
3. withdrawal of the right of governments to hold elections to Panchayats.
4. taking away the right of State Governments to give grants to Panchayats.

Which of the statements given above are correct?

(*a*) 1 and 2 only (*b*) 1, 2 and 3
(*c*) 2, 3 and 4 (*d*) 1 and 4 only

48. In which part of the Indian Constitution has the provision for panchayats been made?

(*a*) Part IX (*b*) Part IV
(*c*) Part III (*d*) Part IXA

49. Which one of the following committees recommended the separation of regulatory and development functions at the district level?

(*a*) Dantwala Committee
(*b*) Hanumantha Rao Committee
(*c*) Kothari Committee
(*d*) G.V.K. Rao Committee

50. Who recommends to the Governor the principles which should govern the distribution between the State and the Panchayats of the net proceeds of the taxes, tolls and fees leviable by the state which may be divided between them?

(*a*) Zilla Parishad (*b*) Chief Minister
(*c*) Finance Minister of the State (*d*) State Finance Commission

51. Which of the following are provided for in the 73rd Constitutional Amendment?

1. Elections through the Chief Election Commissioner
2. Devolution of functions by the state government
3. Creation of the State Finance Commission
4. Setting up a three-tiered Indian Federation

Select the correct answer from the codes given below:

(*a*) 1 and 2 only (*b*) 2 and 3 only
(*c*) 3 and 4 only (*d*) 2, 3 and 4

52. The Ashok Mehta Committee (1977) has recommended for the establishment of which of the following?

(*a*) Mandal Panchayat (*b*) Nagar Panchayat
(*c*) Panchayat Samiti (*d*) Gram Panchayat

53. How many items does the Eleventh Schedule of the Constitution relating to the Panchayats contain?

(*a*) 18 items (*b*) 28 items
(*c*) 19 items (*d*) 29 items

54. Consider the following statements with respect to the 73rd Constitutional Amendment:
    1. For 27% reservation to the Other Backward Classes
    2. That the chairperson of the Panchayat at intermediate/district level shall be elected by, and from amongst the elected members thereof
    3. For reservation for SCs/STs
    4. For uniform five-year term for local bodies

    Which of the statements given above is/are correct?

    (*a*) 1 only (*b*) 1 and 2 only
    (*c*) 2, 3 and 4 (*d*) 1, 2, 3 and 4

55. As per Article 243H of 73rd Constitutional Amendment Act, the Legislature of a State, may by law, provide for making grants-in-aid to the Panchayats from:
    (*a*) contingency Fund of the President.
    (*b*) contingency Fund of the Governor.
    (*c*) consolidated Fund of the State.
    (*d*) consolidated Fund of India.

56. Which one of the following provisions has been left to the will of the State Governments in the 73rd Constitutional Amendment Act?
    (*a*) Providing reservation to the Backward Classes
    (*b*) All posts at all levels to be filled by direct elections
    (*c*) Reservation of seats for SC/ST in proportion to their population
    (*d*) Reservation up to 1/3 seats for women in Panchayats

57. Consider the following Committees set up to study the structure, powers and functions to be assigned to Panchayati Raj Institutions:
    1. Santhanam Committee
    2. Ashok Mehta Committee
    3. Balwant Rai Mehta Committee
    4. G.V.K. Rao Committee

    Which one of the following is their correct chronological order?

    (*a*) 3, 4, 2, 1 (*b*) 2, 1, 3, 4
    (*c*) 3, 1, 2, 4 (*d*) 2, 4, 3, 1

Answers

1. (*c*)	2. (*a*)	3. (*a*)	4. (*b*)	5. (*a*)
6. (*d*)	7. (*d*)	8. (*b*)	9. (*d*)	10. (*b*)
11. (*a*)	12. (*b*)	13. (*b*)	14. (*a*)	15. (*b*)
16. (*d*)	17. (*d*)	18. (*a*)	19. (*a*)	20. (*d*)
21. (*a*)	22. (*c*)	23. (*c*)	24. (*a*)	25. (*c*)
26. (*c*)	27. (*b*)	28. (*a*)	29. (*c*)	30. (*d*)
31. (*b*)	32. (*b*)	33. (*b*)	34. (*d*)	35. (*d*)

36. (*a*)	37. (*a*)	38. (*b*)	39. (*b*)	40. (*c*)
41. (*b*)	42. (*c*)	43. (*d*)	44. (*b*)	45. (*d*)
46. (*c*)	47. (*a*)	48. (*a*)	49. (*d*)	50. (*d*)
51. (*d*)	52. (*a*)	53. (*d*)	54. (*c*)	55. (*c*)
56. (*a*)	57. (*c*)			

39

Municipalities

1. Consider the following statements:
   1. The Chairperson of every District Planning Committee shall forward the development plan as recommended by such Committee to the Governor of the State.
   2. Not less than two-thirds of the total number of members of the District Planning Committee shall be elected from amongst the elected members of the Panchayat at the district level and the Municipalities in the district.

   Which of the statements given above is/are correct?

   (*a*) 1 only (*b*) 2 only
   (*c*) Both 1 and 2 (*d*) Neither 1 nor 2

2. Consider the following statements:
   1. In an urban area where municipal services are being provided by an industrial establishment, it is still mandatory to constitute a Municipality under the 74th Constitutional Amendment Act.
   2. It is obligatory to constitute Ward Committees for one or more wards within the territorial area of a Municipality having a population of 3 lacs or more.

   Which of the statements given above is/are correct?

   (*a*) 1 only (*b*) 2 only
   (*c*) Both 1 and 2 (*d*) Neither 1 nor 2

3. Which of the following statements regarding the 74th Amendment to the Constitution of India are correct?
   1. It provides for the insertion of a new Schedule to the Constitution.
   2. It restructures the working of the municipalities.
   3. It provides for the reservation of seats for women and Scheduled Castes in the municipalities.
   4. It is applicable only to some specified states.

   Select the correct answer using the codes given below:

   (*a*) 1, 2 and 3 (*b*) 1, 2 and 4
   (*c*) 1, 3 and 4 (*d*) 1, 2, 3 and 4

4. Consider the following:
   1. District Board
   2. Municipal Corporation
   3. Notified Area Authority and Town Area Committee
   4. Township Committee and Port Trust

Which of these is/are urban local body/bodies in India?

(*a*) 1 only (*b*) 2 and 3 only

(*c*) 1, 3 and 4 (*d*) 2, 3 and 4

5. As per the Constitution (74th Amendment) Act, Legislatures of States have not been conferred the power to empower municipalities with the responsibility of:

(*a*) Preparation of plans for economic development and social justice

(*b*) Management of law and order

(*c*) Implementation of schemes as may be entrusted to them

(*d*) Levy, collection and appropriation of taxes, duties, tolls, etc

6. Which one of the following is not correct?

Part IX-A of the Constitution of India pertaining to the Municipalities provides:

(*a*) that grants-in-aid be made to the Municipalities from the Consolidated Fund of the State.

(*b*) for setting up a separate Finance Commission for the Municipalities.

(*c*) for setting up Committee for District Planning.

(*d*) for setting up Committee for Metropolitan Planning.

7. The sources of revenue of urban local bodies in India are which of the following?

1. Taxes
2. Fees and fines
3. Grants
4. Loans

Select the correct answer from the codes given below:

(*a*) 1 and 2 only (*b*) 1 and 3 only

(*c*) 1, 2, 3 and 4 (*d*) 1, 3 and 4

8. "A transitional area", "a smaller urban area" or "a larger urban area" in the context of a Nagar Panchayat, a Municipal Council or a Municipal Corporation, are specified by the Governor after considering which of the following?

1. Density of population
2. Percentage of employment in non-agricultural activities
3. Number of hospitals in the area

Select the correct answer using the codes given below:

(*a*) 1, 2 and 3 (*b*) 1 and 2 only

(*c*) 2 and 3 only (*d*) 1 and 3 only

9. Which one of the following functions is not the concern of the Local Government in India?

(*a*) Public health (*b*) Sanitation

(*c*) Public utility services (*d*) Maintenance of public order

10. Which one of the following Constitution (Amendment) Acts provided for the formation of the Metropolitan Planning Committee?

(*a*) 42nd Constitution (Amendment) Act

(*b*) 44th Constitution (Amendment) Act

(*c*) 73rd Constitution (Amendment) Act

(*d*) 74th Constitution (Amendment) Act

11. Which of the following statements is not correct?
    (*a*) A Metropolitan area is specified by the Governor through a public notification.
    (*b*) A Metropolitan area means an area having a population of 8 lacs or more.
    (*c*) A Metropolitan area may be comprised in more than one district.
    (*d*) A Metropolitan area may consist of more than two Municipalities or Panchayats or other contiguous areas.

12. According to the Constitution of India, it is obligatory to constitute "Ward Committees" in the area of a municipality. How much should the population of such municipality be?
    (*a*) One lac or more (*b*) Two lacs or more
    (*c*) Three lacs or more (*d*) Five lacs or more

13. Consider the following objectives:
    1. Bringing about uniformity in the structure of local governments throughout the country
    2. Ensuring regular and rational flow of funds from the State's revenue
    3. Having properly elected governments at regular intervals
    4. Having single unified authority for the city's management and development

    Which of these did the 74th Amendment to the Constitution of India try to inject into the working of urban local bodies?
    (*a*) 1 and 2 only (*b*) 1, 3 and 4
    (*c*) 1, 2 and 3 (*d*) 2, 3 and 4

14. In 1989, the 64th and 65th Amendment Bills were not passed and the Amendment Acts could not come in force at that time because:
    (*a*) Lok Sabha was dissolved in November, 1989.
    (*b*) Lok Sabha could not pass the Bills for lack of required majority.
    (*c*) Rajya Sabha could not pass the Bills due to lack of required majority.
    (*d*) The President sent the Bills for reconsideration.

15. Which of the following items is dealt by Article 243T of the Constitution of India?
    (*a*) Constitution of Municipalities
    (*b*) Reservation of seats in Municipal Bodies
    (*c*) State Finance Commission
    (*d*) Duration of Municipalities

16. Which one of the following statements with regard to Finance Commission in States is not correct?
    (*a*) The 74th Amendment of the Constitution of India provides for the establishment of a Finance Commission by a State to review the financial position of the municipalities.
    (*b*) The Chief Minister of the State decides the composition of the Finance Commission and nominates the Chairman.
    (*c*) The Finance Commission is expected to recommend the division of resources between the State and the municipalities within the State.
    (*d*) The Finance Commission is authorised to make recommendations with regard to grants-in-aid to the Panchayats from the Consolidated Fund of a State.

17. Who among the following is hailed as the father of local self-government in India?
(*a*) Lord Mayo (*b*) Lord Ripon
(*c*) Jawaharlal Nehru (*d*) Mahatma Gandhi

18. Municipal Area means the territorial area of a Municipality as is notified by which of the following?
(*a*) Governor (*b*) Municipal Commissioner
(*c*) Municipal Council (*d*) Council of Ministers

19. To whom does the Chairperson of every Metropolitan Planning Committee forward the development plan as recommended by such a Committee?
(*a*) The NITI Aayog
(*b*) The Finance Minister, Government of India
(*c*) The Urban Development Minister, Government of India
(*d*) The Government of the State

20. The Constitution (74th Amendment) Act, 1992 provides for which of the following?
1. Municipal Committees
2. Ward Committees
3. Committee for District Planning
4. Committee for Metropolitan Planning

Select the correct answer using the codes given below:
(*a*) 1 and 3 only (*b*) 2 and 4 only
(*c*) 1, 2 and 3 (*d*) 2, 3 and 4

21. Nagar Palika bill was first introduced in the Parliament during the prime ministership of whom of the following?
(*a*) V.P. Singh (*b*) Chandrasekhar
(*c*) Rajiv Gandhi (*d*) Narasimha Rao

22. Which of the following is correct in respect of financial powers of local governments in India?
(*a*) Local Governments have constitutionally earmarked taxation powers.
(*b*) Local Governments are empowered to levy such taxes as are permitted under the law.
(*c*) Local Governments are empowered to levy charges on all items within their sphere of activities.
(*d*) Local Governments are empowered to levy taxes with the permission of the department concerned.

23. Under which Article of the Constitution of India did the District Planning Committee come into existence?
(*a*) Article 243ZD (*b*) Article 243ZE
(*c*) Article 244ZD (*d*) Article 242ZD

24. Which of the following functions have been laid down in the 12th Schedule of the Constitution of India for the municipalities?
1. Urban poverty alleviation
2. Planning for economic and social development

3. Regulation for tanneries
4. Urban forestry

Select the correct answer using the codes given below:

(*a*) 1, 2 and 3 (*b*) 2, 3 and 4
(*c*) 1 and 4 only (*d*) 1, 2, 3 and 4

25. Which of the following units of urban local self-government does not have a constitutional foundation?
(*a*) Cantonment Boards
(*b*) Municipal Councils
(*c*) Municipal Corporations
(*d*) Nagar Panchayats

26. 73rd and 74th Amendments to the Constitution of India provide for elections to the local bodies after which of the following periods?
(*a*) After every one year (*b*) After every three years
(*c*) After every five years (*d*) After every two years

27. Who of the following functionary belongs to the institution of Municipality?
(*a*) Sarpanch (*b*) Chairman
(*c*) Mayor (*d*) Councillor

28. An election to constitute a municipality has to be completed:
(*a*) immediately on completion of its term of five years.
(*b*) before the expiry of its fixed tenure.
(*c*) before the expiry of a period of six months from the date of its dissolution.
(*d*) before the expiry of a period of three months from the date of its dissolution.

29. To which of the following, the 74th Constitutional Amendment has not paid attention?
1. Municipal personnel system
2. Constitution and composition of municipality
3. Relations between elected executive and bureaucracy
4. Disqualifications for membership of municipality

Select the correct answer using the codes given below:

(*a*) 1 and 4 only (*b*) 1 and 3 only
(*c*) 2, 3 and 4 (*d*) 1, 2 and 3

30. Who consolidates the plans prepared by the Panchayats and Municipalities in the district?
(*a*) State Planning Board
(*b*) Public Accounts Committee
(*c*) District Planning Committee
(*d*) District Planning and Development Council

31. Where is the first municipal corporation that was established in India?
(*a*) Madras (*b*) Delhi
(*c*) Bombay (*d*) Hyderabad

32. The Metropolitan Planning Committee while preparing the draft plan has to give due regard to:
    1. matters of common interest between Municipalities and Panchayats.
    2. overall objectives and priorities set by the Union Government.
    3. plans prepared by Panchayats in Metropolitan area.
    4. contingent circumstances emerging out of natural calamities.

    Select the correct answer using the codes given below:

    (*a*) 1, 2, 3 and 4 (*b*) 2 and 4 only
    (*c*) 1 and 3 only (*d*) 1, 2 and 3

33. Consider the following pairs:

1.	Cantonment Board	:	Administered centrally by Defence Ministry
2.	Notified Area Committee	:	Administers newly developing towns
3.	Municipal Council	:	Administers big cities with complex problems
4.	Municipal Corporation	:	Headed by an elected Mayor

    Which of these pairs are correctly matched?

    (*a*) 1, 2, 3 and 4 (*b*) 1 and 4 only
    (*c*) 1, 2 and 4 (*d*) 2 and 3 only

34. Consider the following statements:
    1. The Constitution (73rd Amendment) Act, 1992 has added 16 Articles and a new Schedule in the Constitution of India.
    2. The Constitution (74th Amendment) Act, 1992 has added 18 Articles but no new Schedule in the Constitution of India.

    Which of the statements given above is/are correct?

    (*a*) 1 only (*b*) 2 only
    (*c*) Both 1 and 2 (*d*) Neither 1 nor 2

35. Which of the following urban body is a semi-municipal authority?

    (*a*) Town Area Committee (*b*) Port Trust
    (*c*) Township (*d*) Town Improvement Trust

36. The following are associated with well known local government policies:
    1. Balwant Rai Mehta
    2. Lord Mayo
    3. Lord Ripon
    4. Ashok Mehta

    Which is the correct chronological sequence of the above?

    Choose the correct answer from the codes given below:

    (*a*) 1, 2, 3 and 4 (*b*) 2, 3, 1 and 4
    (*c*) 3, 2, 4 and 1 (*d*) 4, 1, 3 and 2

37. Which of the following are the sources of revenue of urban local bodies?
    1. Property tax 2. Market tax
    3. Sales tax 4. Animal tax

Select the correct answer using the codes given below:

(*a*) 1 and 2 only (*b*) 2, 3 and 4

(*c*) 1, 3 and 4 (*d*) 1, 2 and 4

38. Consider the following statements:
    1. The State Finance Commissions receive grants directly from the Finance Commission set up by the Union Government.
    2. The State Finance Commissions review the economic conditions of the various Panchayati Raj Institutions and Municipal Bodies in the States.

    Which of the statements given above is/are correct?

    (*a*) 1 only (*b*) 2 only

    (*c*) Both 1 and 2 (*d*) Neither 1 nor 2

39. Which of the following is the most important tax revenue of the urban local bodies?

    (*a*) Entertainment tax (*b*) Professional tax

    (*c*) Property tax (*d*) Water tax

40. In which pair of Schedules of the Constitution, the functions of Panchayats and Municipalities are incorporated?

    (*a*) 8th and 9th (*b*) 9th and 10th

    (*c*) 10th and 11th (*d*) 11th and 12th

41. The Chairperson of a District Planning Committee forwards the development plan recommended by the Committee to which one of the following?

    (*a*) The State Government (*b*) The District Development Officer

    (*c*) The District Collector (*d*) Chairperson, Zilla Parishad

42. Consider the following statements:
    1. Local government including self-government institutions in both urban and rural areas is a subject under the Concurrent List of the Seventh Schedule of the Constitution of India.
    2. Provisions inserted in the Constitution of India by article 243-243ZG are in the nature of basic provisions.
    3. These provisions have to be supplemented by laws made by the respective State Legislatures.

    Which of the statements given above is/are correct?

    (*a*) 1 and 2 only (*b*) 2 and 3 only

    (*c*) 3 only (*d*) 1, 2 and 3

43. When was the first municipal corporation in India at Madras set up?

    (*a*) 1587 (*b*) 1688

    (*c*) 1787 (*d*) 1887

44. Regarding the Municipalities, who makes the provisions with respect to the composition and the territorial area of a Ward's Committee?

    (*a*) Municipal Commissioner (*b*) District Collector

    (*c*) State Legislature by law (*d*) State Election Commissioner

45. Which one of the following is not correct for the Local Government?
   (a) A constitutional obligation for the Village Panchayats to function as units of self-government
   (b) The Constitution's placing the subject of local self-government as a responsibility of the states
   (c) A constitutional obligation for the states to constitute Finance Commission to ensure financial viability of Municipalities
   (d) A constitutional obligation for the Municipalities to carry out schemes related to public distribution system

46. In which one of the following Schedules of the Constitution of India is the Urban Local Self-Government mentioned?
   (*a*) Seventh Schedule (*b*) Eighth Schedule
   (*c*) Eleventh Schedule (*d*) Twelfth Schedule

47. Which one of the following has the authority to constitute an area into a municipality or a municipal corporation or a Panchayat?
   (*a*) Central Government (*b*) Divisional Commissioner
   (*c*) District Collector (*d*) State Government

48. A metropolitan committee can be set up in an area having a population of how many?
   (*a*) 3 lacs – 4.99 lacs (*b*) 5 lacs – 9.99 lacs
   (*c*) Upto 10 lacs (*d*) Above 10 lacs

49. Consider the following statements with respect to the Constitutional (74th Amendment) Act, 1992:

   It provided for:
   1. three-tier municipalities.
   2. ward committees.
   3. district Planning Committees.
   4. direct election of chairperson of a municipality.

   Which of the statements given above is/are correct?
   (*a*) 1 only (*b*) 2 and 3 only
   (*c*) 1, 2 and 3 (*d*) 2, 3 and 4

50. Which of the following Articles of the Constitution of India deals with the Metropolitan Planning Committee?
   (*a*) Article 243ZB (*b*) Article 243ZC
   (*c*) Article 243ZD (*d*) Article 243ZE

51. The State Government's administrative control over municipalities does not include which of the following powers?
   (*a*) Power of inspection
   (*b*) Power of approving bye-laws and rules
   (*c*) Power of decide over-borrowings
   (*d*) Power of dissolution and supersession

52. Consider the following statements:
   1. The Constitution (74th Amendment) Act introduced a new part IXA in the Constitution of India.
   2. The provisions of the Constitution (74th Amendment) Act also apply to the Scheduled Areas and Tribal Areas.
   3. The Constitution (74th Amendment) Act specifies the manner and procedure of election of the Chairperson of a Municipal Corporation.

   Which of the statements given above is/are correct?

   (*a*) 1 only (*b*) 3 only
   (*c*) 1 and 2 only (*d*) 1, 2 and 3

Answers

1. (*d*)	2. (*b*)	3. (*a*)	4. (*d*)	5. (*b*)
6. (*b*)	7. (*c*)	8. (*b*)	9. (*d*)	10. (*d*)
11. (*b*)	12. (*c*)	13. (*c*)	14. (*c*)	15. (*b*)
16. (*b*)	17. (*b*)	18. (*a*)	19. (*d*)	20. (*d*)
21. (*c*)	22. (*b*)	23. (*a*)	24. (*d*)	25. (*a*)
26. (*c*)	27. (*b*)	28. (*b*)	29. (*b*)	30. (*c*)
31. (*a*)	32. (*d*)	33. (*c*)	34. (*a*)	35. (*a*)
36. (*b*)	37. (*d*)	38. (*b*)	39. (*c*)	40. (*d*)
41. (*a*)`	42. (*b*)	43. (*b*)	44. (*c*)	45. (*d*)
46. (*a*)	47. (*d*)	48. (*d*)	49. (*b*)	50. (*d*)
51. (*c*)	52. (*a*)			

PART-VI UNION TERRITORIES AND SPECIAL AREAS

40

Union Territories

1. Consider the following statements:
   1. An administrator of a union territory is an agent of the President of India and not the Head of State like a Governor.
   2. The Parliament can make laws on any subject of the three lists (including the State List) for the Union territories.

   Which of the statements given above is/are correct?

   (*a*) 1 only (*b*) 2 only
   (*c*) Both 1 and 2 (*d*) Neither 1 nor 2

2. The President can make regulations for the peace, progress and good government for which of the following?
   1. Andaman and Nicobar Islands
   2. Lakshadweep
   3. Ladakh
   4. Chandigarh

   Select the correct answer from the codes given below:

   (*a*) 1, 2, 3 and 4 (*b*) 1, 2 and 3
   (*c*) 2, 3 and 4 (*d*) 1, 2 and 4

3. Which of the following is correct regarding the union territories?
   1. Articles 239 to 241 contain provisions regarding the union territories.
   2. Part VIII of the Constitution deals with the union territories.
   3. Part VII of the Constitution deals with the union territories.
   4. Articles 238 to 242 contain provisions regarding the union territories.

   Select the correct answer from the codes given below:

   (*a*) 1 and 3 only (*b*) 1 and 2 only
   (*c*) 3 and 4 only (*d*) 2 and 4 only

4. Which of the following Constitutional Amendment Acts provides a special status to the Union Territory of Delhi and redesignated it the National Capital Territory of Delhi?

   (*a*) 59th Amendment Act (*b*) 62nd Amendment Act
   (*c*) 67th Amendment Act (*d*) 69th Amendment Act

5. Which of the following union territories is placed under the jurisdiction of the Calcutta High Court?

   (*a*) Andaman and Nicobar Islands (*b*) Ladakh
   (*c*) Lakshadweep (*d*) Puducherry

6. The Part 'C' states and Part 'D' territories were constituted as the "union territories" by which of the following acts?
   (*a*) 5th Constitutional Amendment Act
   (*b*) 16th Constitutional Amendment Act
   (*c*) 14th Constitutional Amendment Act
   (*d*) 7th Constitutional Amendment Act

7. Which of the following are the reasons for the creation of Union Territories?
   1. Special treatment of the tribal people
   2. Cultural distinctiveness
   3. Strategic importance
   4. Care of the backward people
   5. Political and administrative considerations

   Select the correct answer from the codes given below:
   (*a*) 1, 3 and 5 (*b*) 2, 3, 4 and 5
   (*c*) 1, 2, 3, 4 and 5 (*d*) 1, 2, 3 and 5

8. Who/which of the following can put a union territory under the jurisdiction of the high court of adjacent state?
   (*a*) The President of India
   (*b*) The Chief Justice of India
   (*c*) The Parliament of India
   (*d*) The Administrator of the concerned union territory

9. Which one of the following union territories has a high court of its own?
   (*a*) Puducherry (*b*) Chandigarh
   (*c*) Delhi (*d*) Lakshadweep

10. In the case of Puducherry, the President of India can legislate by making regulations only:
   (*a*) when the Parliament passes a resolution to that effect.
   (*b*) when the Assembly passes a resolution to that effect.
   (*c*) when the Assembly is suspended or dissolved.
   (*d*) when the Lt. Governor requests him to do so.

11. Consider the following statements:
   1. The Constitution of India contains separate provisions for the administration of acquired territories.
   2. The constitutional provisions for the administration of union territories also apply to the acquired territories.

   Which of the statements given above is/are correct?
   (*a*) 1 only (*b*) 2 only
   (*c*) Both 1 and 2 (*d*) Neither 1 nor 2

12. In which of the following years, the name of the union Territory of the Laccative, Minicoy and Amindivi Islands was Changed to that of the Union Territory of Lakshadweep?
   (*a*) 1968 (*b*) 1969
   (*c*) 1973 (*d*) 1974

Answers

1. (*c*)	2. (*b*)	3. (*b*)	4. (*d*)	5. (*a*)
6. (*d*)	7. (*c*)	8. (*c*)	9. (*c*)	10. (*c*)
11. (*b*)	12. (*c*)			

41

Scheduled and Tribal Areas

1. Who/Which of the following is empowered to declare an area to be a scheduled area?
   (*a*) The Governor of the State
   (*b*) The Legislative Assembly of the State
   (*c*) The Parliament of India
   (*d*) The President of India

2. Sixth Schedule to the Constitution of India makes special administrative provisions in regard to the tribal areas in:
   (*a*) Assam, Meghalaya, Tripura and Mizoram.
   (*b*) Meghalaya, Assam, Nagaland and Manipur.
   (*c*) Tripura, Manipur, Mizoram and Meghalaya.
   (*d*) Arunanchal Pradesh, Nagaland, Assam and Tripura.

3. What is the maximum number of members in a Tribes Advisory Council?
   (*a*) 20 members (*b*) 25 members
   (*c*) 28 members (*d*) 34 members

4. As per the sixth schedule to the Constitution of India, the rules for the first Constitution of District and Regional Councils are prepared by which of the following?
   (*a*) The Ministry of Home, Government of India
   (*b*) The Chief Minister in consultation with existing tribal councils or other representative tribal organisations of the region
   (*c*) The Governor in consultation with existing tribal councils or other representative tribal organisations of the region
   (*d*) The State Legislature

5. Which Article of the Constitution of India envisages a special system of administration for scheduled areas and tribal areas?
   (*a*) Article 242 (*b*) Article 244
   (*c*) Article 246 (*d*) Article 248

6. Which/Who of the following can appoint a commission to examine and report on any matter relating to the administration of the autonomous districts or regions?
   (*a*) The Legislative Assembly of the State (*b*) The Governor of the State
   (*c*) The President of India (*d*) The Parliament of India

7. Which schedule of the Constitution of India deals with the administration and the control of scheduled areas and scheduled tribes?
   (*a*) Fourth Schedule (*b*) Fifth Schedule
   (*c*) Sixth Schedule (*d*) Seventh Schedule

8. The Autonomous District Council, under the Sixth Schedule of the Constitution, is not operative in which of the following states of North-East India?
   (*a*) Assam (*b*) Tripura
   (*c*) Nagaland (*d*) Meghalaya

9. How many members of a district council are nominated by the Governor of the State?
   (*a*) 2 members (*b*) 4 members
   (*c*) 5 members (*d*) 7 members

10. Who/Which of the following is empowered to direct that a law of the Parliament does not apply to a scheduled area?
    (*a*) The President of India (*b*) The Supreme Court of India
    (*c*) The High Court of the State (*d*) The Governor of the State

11. In which of the following years, the Dilip Singh Bhuria Commission on the administration of scheduled areas was appointed?
    (*a*) 2000 (*b*) 2002
    (*c*) 2004 (*d*) 2006

12. The Chakma District is a tribal area of which of the following state?
    (*a*) Tripura (*b*) Assam
    (*c*) Mizoram (*d*) Meghalaya

Answers

1. (*d*)	2. (*a*)	3. (*a*)	4. (*c*)	5. (*b*)
6. (*b*)	7. (*b*)	8. (*c*)	9. (*b*)	10. (*d*)
11. (*b*)	12. (*c*)			

PART-VII
CONSTITUTIONAL BODIES

42. Election Commission
43. Union Public Service Commission
44. State Public Service Commission
45. Finance Commission
46. Goods and Services Tax Council
47. National Commission for SCs
48. National Commission for STs
49. National Commission for BCs
50. Special Officer for Linguistic Minorities
51. Comptroller and Auditor-General of India
52. Attorney-General of India
53. Advocate-General of the State

42

Election Commission

1. Consider the following statements:
   1. As per provisions of the Constitution of India, a Regional Commissioner shall not be removed from office except on the recommendation of the Governor of the State where the Regional Commissioner is posted.
   2. The number of the Election Commissioners in the Election Commission shall be fixed by the President from time to time.

   Which of the statements given above is/are correct?

   (*a*) 1 only (*b*) 2 only
   (*c*) Both 1 and 2 (*d*) Neither 1 nor 2

2. Consider the following statements with respect to the Election Commission of India:
   1. The term of office of the Election Commissioners is same as the Chairman of the Union Public Service Commission.
   2. In case of difference of opinion amongst the Chief Election Commissioner and/or other Election Commissioners, the matter is referred to the President of India.
   3. Independence of the Election Commission and its insulation from executive interference is ensured by a special provision under Article 324 of the Constitution of India.

   Which of the statements given above is/are correct?

   (*a*) 1 only (*b*) 3 only
   (*c*) 1 and 3 only (*d*) 2 and 3 only

3. In the Lok Sabha elections, who among the following can order adjournment of poll or countermanding of election on the ground of booth capturing?
   (*a*) Chief Election Commissioner
   (*b*) Election Commission of India
   (*c*) Chief Electoral Officer of the State
   (*d*) Returning Officer of the Constituency

4. The Chief Election Commissioner of India holds office for which period?
   (*a*) Six years
   (*b*) During the pleasure of the President
   (*c*) For six years or till the age of 65 years, whichever is earlier
   (*d*) For five years or till the age of 60 years, whichever is earlier

5. An Election Commissioner shall not be removed from office except on the recommendation of which of the following?
   (*a*) The President (*b*) The Supreme Court
   (*c*) The Chief Election Commissioner (*d*) The Law Minister

6. Which of the following commissions is created under Article 324 of the Constitution of India?
   (*a*) The Finance Commission
   (*b*) The Commission for Backward Classes
   (*c*) The Election Commission
   (*d*) The Official Language Commission

7. Before giving any decision on questions about disqualification of a member of either House of the Parliament, the President of India shall obtain the opinion of which one of the following?
   (*a*) Supreme Court (*b*) Election Commission
   (*c*) Attorney-General of India (*d*) Solicitor-General of India

8. Which one of the following statements is correct?
   The Chief Election Commissioner can be removed from office before expiry of his term:
   (*a*) in like manner and on like grounds as a member of the Union Public Service Commission.
   (*b*) in like manner and on like grounds as a Judge of the Supreme Court.
   (*c*) on the recommendations of the Supreme Court.
   (*d*) on the recommendations of the Cabinet.

9. The President may from time to time fix the number of Election Commissioners of the Election Commission on the basis of:
   (*a*) advice by the Chief Election Commissioner.
   (*b*) advice by the Prime Minister's Office.
   (*c*) recommendation of the Union Law Ministry.
   (*d*) the law made in that respect by the Parliament.

10. The responsibility of preparation of electoral rolls rests with which of the following?
   (*a*) The Parliament (*b*) The Local Administration
   (*c*) The Election Commission (*d*) The State Government

Answers

1. (*b*)	2. (*c*)	3. (*b*)	4. (*c*)	5. (*c*)
6. (*c*)	7. (*b*)	8. (*b*)	9. (*d*)	10. (*c*)

43 Union Public Service Commission

1. Consider the following statements:
   1. The President of India is empowered by the Constitution of India to make regulations specifying the matters on which it is not necessary to consult the Union Public Service Commission.
   2. The reasons for non-acceptance of the advice of the Union Public Service Commission have to be laid before each House of the Parliament.

   Which of the statements given above is/are correct?

   (*a*) 1 only (*b*) 2 only
   (*c*) Both 1 and 2 (*d*) Neither 1 nor 2

2. Which of the following are the functions of the Union Public Service Commission?
   1. To conduct examinations for recruitment to the services of the Union
   2. To advise on matters referred to it by the President or the Governor
   3. To advise on all disciplinary matters affecting a government servant
   4. To advise on the principles to be followed in respect of promotions and transfers

   Select the correct answer using the codes given below:

   (*a*) 1 and 2 only (*b*) 1, 2 and 3
   (*c*) 1, 3 and 4 (*d*) 2, 3 and 4

3. Consider the following statements:

   A member of the Union Public Service Commission is:
   1. debarred from re-appointment as a member.
   2. ineligible for any other employment under the Central or State Government.
   3. disqualified from becoming a constitutional functionary like a Governor.

   Which of the statements given above are correct?

   (*a*) 1, 2 and 3 (*b*) 2 and 3 only
   (*c*) 1 and 3 only (*d*) 1 and 2 only

4. Consider the following statements:
   1. The UPSC makes recruitment to Group A and Group B services.
   2. The Staff Selection Commission makes recruitment to Group C services.

   Which of the statements given above is/are correct?

   (*a*) 1 only (*b*) 2 only
   (*c*) Both 1 and 2 (*d*) Neither 1 nor 2

5. Which of the following statements is not true?
   (*a*) A member of the Union Public Service Commission (UPSC) holds office for a term of six years or until he attains the age of 65 years.
   (*b*) The Chairperson of UPSC is not eligible for further employment under the Government of India or Government of any State after retirement.
   (*c*) One half of the members of the UPSC should be persons who have held office for at least 10 years either under the Government of India or the Government of State.
   (*d*) The Chairperson and other members of the UPSC are appointed by the Prime Minister.

6. Under the Constitution of India, the power to extend functions of the Union Public Service Commission has been vested in which of the following?
   (*a*) The President of India (*b*) The Parliament
   (*c*) The Chairman of the Commission (*d*) The Ministry of Personnel

7. Who among the following is a Constitutional authority for whose removal from office by the President a reference to the Supreme Court is necessary?
   (*a*) Chairman of the Union Public Service Commission
   (*b*) Judge of the Supreme Court
   (*c*) Comptroller and Auditor-General of India
   (*d*) Chief Election Commissioner

8. Which one of the following statements is correct?
   (*a*) Union Public Service Commission may serve the needs of a State if requested by the Governor of that State and approved by the President.
   (*b*) Union Public Service Commission may serve the needs of a State if requested by the Chief Minister of that State.
   (*c*) Union Public Service Commission cannot serve the needs of a State.
   (*d*) Union Public Service Commission may serve the needs of a State simply on the request of the Governor and the approval of the President is not necessary.

9. The Constitution of India enjoins upon the government to consult the Union Public Service Commission in disciplinary matters. Which one of the following is an institution whose emergence cannot exactly be reconciled with the constitutionally prescribed role of the Union Public Service Commission?
   (*a*) The First Administrative Reforms Commission of India
   (*b*) The Central Bureau of Investigation
   (*c*) The Central Vigilance Commission
   (*d*) The Law Commission

10. Which one of the following is not a function of the Union Public Service Commission?
   (*a*) It conducts examinations for the appointments to the services of the union.
   (*b*) It shall be consulted on all matters relating to methods of recruitment to civil services.
   (*c*) It shall be consulted on all disciplinary matters affecting a person serving the Government of India.
   (*d*) It shall be consulted in cases as regards the reservation of posts for Backward Classes, Scheduled Castes and Scheduled Tribes.

11. Consider the following statements:
    1. The salaries and allowances of members of the UPSC are charged on the Consolidated Fund of India.
    2. Under the provisions of the Constitution, additional functions may be conferred on the UPSC by the President.

    Which of the statements given above is/are correct?

    (*a*) 1 only (*b*) 2 only
    (*c*) Both 1 and 2 (*d*) Neither 1 nor 2

12. Which one of the following statements about a member of the Union Public Service Commission on his ceasing to hold office is incorrect?
    (*a*) He is eligible to be appointed as the Chairman of the UPSC.
    (*b*) He is ineligible to be appointed as the Chairman of any State PSC.
    (*c*) He is ineligible for employment under the Government of India.
    (*d*) He is ineligible for employment under the State Governments.

13. Which of the following does not concern the Union Public Service Commission?
    (*a*) Recruitment (*b*) Classification of services
    (*c*) Disciplinary matters (*d*) Promotion

14. The annual report of the UPSC is submitted to which of the following?
    (*a*) The Ministry of Personnel (*b*) The Parliament
    (*c*) The Prime Minister (*d*) The President

15. Who/which of the following can exclude posts, services and matters from the purview of the UPSC?
    (*a*) The Parliament (*b*) The Supreme Court
    (*c*) The Prime Minister (*d*) The President

16. Consider the following statements:

    A member of the Union Public Service Commission:
    1. is appointed by the President of India.
    2. is ineligible for re-appointment to that office.
    3. holds office for a period of 6 years or till the age of 60 years, whichever is earlier.

    Which of the statements given above are correct?

    (*a*) 1, 2 and 3 (*b*) 1 and 2 only
    (*c*) 2 and 3 only (*d*) 1 and 3 only

17. Who/Which is vested with powers to make regulations as to conditions of service of members and staff of the Union Public Service Commission?
    (*a*) The President of India
    (*b*) The Parliament
    (*c*) The Union Minister of Law
    (*d*) The Chairman, Union Public Service Commission

18. Immediately before 26 January, 1950, the Union Public Service Commission was known as which of the following?
    (*a*) Public Service Commission
    (*b*) Federal Public Service Commission
    (*c*) Central Public Service Commission
    (*d*) Imperial Public Service Commission

19. According to which one of the following Articles of the Constitution of India is the Government bound to seek the advice of the UPSC?
    (*a*) Article 120
    (*b*) Article 220
    (*c*) Article 320
    (*d*) Article 420

20. The UPSC (Exemption from Consultation) regulations made by the President shall be laid before the Parliament for how many days?
    (*a*) 14 days
    (*b*) 21 days
    (*c*) 30 days
    (*d*) 60 days

21. In which of the following, does the Union Public Service Commission advise the Central Government?
    1. On matters relating to the methods of recruitment to the civil services.
    2. On the principles to be followed in making appointments to the civil services.
    3. On disciplinary matters in respect of persons serving in a civil capacity.
    4. On seniority cases when referred to it.

    Select the correct answer from the codes given below:
    (*a*) 1, 2 and 4
    (*b*) 2, 3 and 4
    (*c*) 1, 3 and 4
    (*d*) 1, 2, 3 and 4

22. In terms of Constitutional status, the Union Public Service Commission is:
    (*a*) an Advisory Body.
    (*b*) a Grievance Redressal Body.
    (*c*) a body incharge of directing recruitment at State level.
    (*d*) a body which supervises training of civil servants.

23. How can functions of the Union Public Service Commission be extended in respect of the services of the Union and also in respect of the services of any local authority or other body corporate constituted by law or of any public institution?
    (*a*) By the President
    (*b*) By the resolution of the Union Government
    (*c*) By an Act of the Parliament
    (*d*) By the Union Home Minister

24. Which one of the following statements is not correct in respect of the Union Public Service Commission?
    (*a*) The Constitution of India does not specify the number of Members of the Union Public Service Commission while it specifies the number in case of the Supreme Court judges.
    (*b*) As nearly as may be one-half of the Members of the Union Public Service Commission must have held office for at least ten years either under the Government of India or under the Government of a State prior to their joining the Commission.

(*c*) On ceasing to hold office, a Member of the Union Public Service Commission other than the Chairman is eligible for appointment as the Chairman of a State Public Service Commission.

(*d*) Before creation of a new Group 'A' post under the Central Government, a clearance from the Union Public Service Commission is required.

Answers

1. (*c*)	2. (*c*)	3. (*d*)	4. (*c*)	5. (*d*)
6. (*b*)	7. (*a*)	8. (*a*)	9. (*c*)	10. (*d*)
11. (*a*)	12. (*b*)	13. (*b*)	14. (*d*)	15. (*d*)
16. (*b*)	17. (*a*)	18. (*b*)	19. (*c*)	20. (*a*)
21. (*d*)	22. (*a*)	23. (*c*)	24. (*d*)	

44 State Public Service Commission

1. The State Public Service Commission is consulted on:
   1. all matters relating to methods of recruitment to civil services and for civil posts in the State.
   2. all disciplinary matters affecting a person in service under the State.

   Which of the statements given above is/are correct?

   (*a*) 1 only (*b*) 2 only
   (*c*) Both 1 and 2 (*d*) Neither 1 nor 2

2. Consider the following statements:

   A member of the State Public Service Commission can be removed only by the:
   1. Governor on the ground of his misbehaviour.
   2. President on the ground of his infirmity of body or mind.
   3. Governor when such member becomes insolvent.
   4. President on the ground of misbehaviour after receiving report of the Supreme Court after due enquiry.

   Which of the statements given above is/are correct?

   (*a*) 1, 2 and 3 (*b*) 2 and 4 only
   (*c*) 1 and 3 only (*d*) 2 only

3. Consider the following statements:

   The Constitution provides for the establishment of Public Service Commission:
   1. for the Union.
   2. for each State.
   3. common for Union Territories.
   4. common for two or more States.

   Which of the statements given above are correct?

   (*a*) 1, 2 and 4 (*b*) 1, 2 and 3
   (*c*) 2 and 3 only (*d*) 1 and 4 only

4. The number of members of a JSPSC and their conditions of service are determined by who/which of the following?

   (*a*) The Governors of the concerned states (*b*) The Legislature of the concerned states
   (*c*) The Chairman of the UPSC (*d*) The President of India

5. Which one of the following functions does not require consultation with the State Public Service Commission as per provisions of the Constitution of India?
   (*a*) Methods of recruitment to civil services and civil posts.
   (*b*) Principles to be followed in making appointments to civil services.
   (*c*) The manner in which any provision may be made for the reservation of appointments or posts in favour of any backward class of citizens.
   (*d*) Any claim for the award of a pension in respect of injuries suffered by a person while serving under the Government of the State in a civil capacity.

6. Which one of the following statements is correct?

   The Union Public Service Commission may agree to serve all or any of the needs of a State:
   (*a*) on request by the Governor of the State.
   (*b*) on request by the Governor of the State subject to approval of the President of India.
   (*c*) on request by the Chief Minister of the State.
   (*d*) only if Parliament by law, so prescribes.

7. A Joint Public Service Commission for two or more States can be established by:
   (*a*) the concerned States.
   (*b*) an Act of the Parliament.
   (*c*) the Union Public Service Commission.
   (*d*) the Government of India.

8. The State Public Service Commission submits its annual report to which of the following?
   (*a*) Parliament
   (*b*) State Legislature
   (*c*) President
   (*d*) Governor

9. When the report of the State Public Service Commission is not accepted, the reasons for such non-acceptance are to be laid before which of the following?
   (*a*) The Parliament
   (*b*) The President
   (*c*) The State Legislature
   (*d*) The Cabinet Committee presided over by the Chief Minister

10. Who/Which of the following determines the salaries, allowances and other service conditions of the SPSC members?
    (*a*) The Governor
    (*b*) The Chief Minister
    (*c*) The Chairman, SPSC
    (*d*) The State Legislature

11. A member of the State Public Service Commission can be removed on the ground of misbehaviour only after an inquiry has been held by:
    (*a*) a Joint Parliamentary Committee.
    (*b*) the Supreme Court of India.
    (*c*) the High Court of the concerned State.
    (*d*) a Committee constituted by the Governor of the State.

12. Which one of the following is the correct statement?

Parliament may by law provide for the appointment of a Joint State Public Service Commission to serve the needs of two or more States:

(*a*) when the President deems it to be necessary.
(*b*) when the Governors of those States request the Centre to appoint such Commission.
(*c*) when a resolution to that effect is passed by the legislatures of those States.
(*d*) when the Parliament deems it to be necessary.

Answers

1. (*c*)	2. (*b*)	3. (*a*)	4. (*d*)	5. (*c*)
6. (*b*)	7. (*b*)	8. (*d*)	9. (*c*)	10. (*a*)
11. (*b*)	12. (*c*)			

45

Finance Commission

1. On which of the following matters, does the Finance Commission make recommendations to the President of India?
   1. The distribution between Union and States of net proceeds of taxes and allocation between the States of their respective shares of such proceeds.
   2. The principles which should govern the grants-in-aid of the revenues of the States out of the Consolidated Fund of India.

   Select the correct answer using the codes given below:

   (*a*) 1 only (*b*) 2 only
   (*c*) Both 1 and 2 (*d*) Neither 1 nor 2

2. Consider the following statements with regard to the Finance Commission:
   1. The recommendations of the Finance Commission cover a period of five years.
   2. The Report of the Finance Commission is submitted to the Prime Minister.

   Which of the statements given above is/are correct?

   (*a*) 1 only (*b*) 2 only
   (*c*) Both 1 and 2 (*d*) Neither 1 nor 2

3. Which one of the following statements about the Finance Commission is not correct?
   (*a*) The Commission comprises a Chairman and four other members.
   (*b*) The Parliament is authorised to determine by law the qualifications of the members of the Commission.
   (*c*) All the appointments are made by the President of India.
   (*d*) All the members have to be from Indian Economic Service or Indian Statistical Service.

4. Which of the following bodies enjoy the constitutional status?
   1. Finance Commission
   2. NITI Aayog
   3. Zonal Councils
   4. North-Eastern Council
   5. Election Commission
   6. National Human Rights Commission

   Select the correct answer using the codes given below:

   (*a*) 1, 3 and 5 (*b*) 1 and 5 only
   (*c*) 1, 2, 5 and 6 (*d*) 1, 3, 5 and 6

5. Which of the following is/are the issue(s) on which recommendations to be made by the Finance Commission to the President of India are specified in the Constitution of India?
   1. The principles which should govern the grants-in-aid of the revenues of the States out of the Consolidated Fund of India.
   2. Measures needed to augment the Consolidated Fund of a State to supplement the resources of the Panchayats in the State.
   3. Measures needed to augment the Consolidated Fund of a State to supplement the resources of the Municipalities in the State.

   Select the correct answer using the codes given below:

   (*a*) 1, 2 and 3 (*b*) 2 and 3 only
   (*c*) 1 only (*d*) 2 only

6. Which of the following Finance Commissions was chaired by Dr. P. V. Rajamannar?
   (*a*) First Finance Commission (*b*) Fourth Finance Commission
   (*c*) Sixth Finance Commission (*d*) Eighth Finance Commission

7. Which one of the following is not correct about Finance Commission?
   (*a*) The members of the Commission are appointed by the President.
   (*b*) It is to act as a balancing wheel of Indian fiscal federalism.
   (*c*) The qualifications of members of the Commission are determined by the Parliament.
   (*d*) It is constituted under the provisions of Article 180 of the Constitution of India.

8. Who of the following was the Chairman of the Fifteenth Finance Commission appointed in 2017?
   (*a*) Y.V. Reddy (*b*) N.K. Singh
   (*c*) Dr. Vijay Kelkar (*d*) Dr. C. Rangarajan

9. On the recommendation of which of the following bodies, the statutory grants are given to the States by the Centre?
   (*a*) NITI Aayog (*b*) Inter-State Council
   (*c*) Finance Ministry (*d*) Finance Commission

10. The Finance Commission recommends the distribution of the net proceeds of the Union Government arising from:
    (*a*) all taxes between the Union and the States.
    (*b*) specified taxes among the States only.
    (*c*) all sources including taxes, fees and surcharges between the Union and the States.
    (*d*) specified taxes without the surcharge between the Union and the States.

11. The principles concerning the provisions of the grants-in-aid to the States out of the Consolidated Fund of India are recommended by which of the following?
    (*a*) Inter-State Council
    (*b*) First Administrative Reforms Commission of India
    (*c*) Finance Commission
    (*d*) Public Accounts Committee

12. The Article 281 of the Constitution deals with the recommendations of which of the following Constitutional bodies?
   (*a*) Finance Commission
   (*b*) Union Public Service Commission
   (*c*) Election Commission
   (*d*) Comptroller and Auditor-General of India

13. The Finance Commission is constituted to recommend criteria for:
   (*a*) framing a financial bill.
   (*b*) preparing the annual budget of Union Government.
   (*c*) distribution of financial resources between Union and the States.
   (*d*) auditing the receipts and expenditures of the Union Government.

14. Consider the following statements:

   The Finance Commission makes recommendation to the President in respect of:
   1. the distribution of net proceeds of taxes to be shared between the Union and the States.
   2. assessment of natural, capital and human resources.
   3. the principles governing grants-in-aid to the States.
   4. any other matter concerning financial relations between the Union and the States.

   Which of the statements given above are correct?
   (*a*) 1, 2, 3 and 4
   (*b*) 2 and 4 only
   (*c*) 1, 3 and 4
   (*d*) 1, 2 and 3

15. The qualifications for the members of Finance Commission:
   (*a*) are laid down in the Constitution of India.
   (*b*) can be prescribed by the Parliament of India.
   (*c*) can be prescribed by the President of India.
   (*d*) can be prescribed by the Union Finance Minister.

16. Consider the following statements about the Finance Commission:
   1. The duty of the Finance Commission is to make recommendations as to the distribution of revenue resources between the Union and the States.
   2. It is appointed every fifth year by the President of India.
   3. It raises revenue for central financial transfers to the States.
   4. It borrows money from the market for central grants to the States.

   Which of the statements given above is/are correct?
   (*a*) 1 and 2 only
   (*b*) 1, 2 and 3
   (*c*) 1 only
   (*d*) 2 and 4 only

17. Which of the following qualifications is prescribed for the Chairman of the Finance Commission?
   (*a*) A person having specialised knowledge of Government finance and accounts
   (*b*) A person having specialised knowledge of economics
   (*c*) A person having experience in public affairs
   (*d*) A person having wide experience in financial matters and in administration

18. Which one among the following is the function of the Finance Commission?
   (*a*) Preparation of the Central Budget
   (*b*) Assessing income tax proceeds
   (*c*) Determining the principles governing grants-in-aid the states
   (*d*) Exercising control over Government expenditure

19. Which of the following is/are the functions of the Finance Commission?
   1. Making recommendations as to the principles governing grants-in-aid of the revenues of the States
   2. To suggest measures to augment the Consolidated Fund of India

   Select the correct answer using the codes given below:
   (*a*) 1 only (*b*) 2 only
   (*c*) Both 1 and 2 (*d*) Neither 1 nor 2

20. In which Article of our Constitution is the Finance Commission dealt with?
   (*a*) Article 280 (*b*) Article 380
   (*c*) Article 281 (*d*) Article 381

21. The Finance Commission has the responsibility relating to which of the following?
   (*a*) Principles governing grants-in-aid to states
   (*b*) Coordination in the Central Secretariat
   (*c*) Appointment of High Court Judges
   (*d*) Alternative Expenditure Policy

Answers

1. (*c*)	2. (*a*)	3. (*d*)	4. (*b*)	5. (*a*)
6. (*b*)	7. (*d*)	8. (*b*)	9. (*d*)	10. (*d*)
11. (*c*)	12. (*a*)	13. (*c*)	14. (*c*)	15. (*b*)
16. (*a*)	17. (*c*)	18. (*c*)	19. (*a*)	20. (*a*)
21. (*a*)				

46

Goods and Services Tax Council

1. Consider the following statements:
   1. The 102nd Amendment Act provides for the establishment of the GST Council.
   2. The 102nd Amendment Act inserted a new Article 279A in the constitution.

   Which of the statements given above is/are correct?

   (*a*) 1 only (*b*) 2 only
   (*c*) Both 1 and 2 (*d*) Neither 1 nor 2

2. With reference to a decision taken in a meeting of the GST Council, consider the following statements:
   1. The vote of the central government shall have a weightage of two-thirds of the total votes cast in that meeting.
   2. The votes of all the state governments combined shall have a weightage of one-third of the total votes cast in that meeting.

   Which of the statements given above is/are correct?

   (*a*) 1 only (*b*) 2 only
   (*c*) Both 1 and 2 (*d*) Neither 1 nor 2

3. On which of the following matters, the GST Council makes recommendations?
   1. The threshold limit of turnover below which goods and services may be exempted from GST.
   2. Any special rate for a specified period to raise additional resources during a national calamity.
   3. The goods and services that may be subjected to GST.
   4. The rates including floor rates with bands of GST.

   Select the correct answer using the codes given below:

   (*a*) 1, 3 and 4 (*b*) 2 and 3 only
   (*c*) 1, 2, 3 and 4 (*d*) 3 and 4 only

4. The GST Council consists of the:
   1. Prime Minister.
   2. Union Finance Minister.
   3. Union Minister of State in-charge of Finance.
   4. Chief Ministers of all states.
   5. Ministers in-charge of Finance in all states.

Select the correct answer using the codes given below:

(*a*) 1, 2, 4 and 5 (*b*) 2, 3 and 5

(*c*) 2, 4 and 5 (*d*) 1, 2, 3 and 4

5. On which of the following grounds, any Act or proceedings of the GST Council will not become invalid?
   1. Any procedural irregularity of the Council not affecting the merits of the case
   2. Any defect in the appointment of a person as a member of the Council
   3. Any vacancy or defect in the constitution of the Council

   Select the correct answer using the codes given below:

   (*a*) 1 and 2 only (*b*) 2 and 3 only

   (*c*) 1 and 3 only (*d*) 1, 2 and 3

6. Who of the following Acts as the ex-officio Secretary to the GST Council?

   (*a*) Union Finance Secretary

   (*b*) Union Expenditure Secretary

   (*c*) Union Revenue Secretary

   (*d*) Union Financial Services Secretary

7. Consider the following statements:
   1. Article 279A empowers the President to constitute a GST Council by an order.
   2. The President issued the GST order in 2017.

   Which of the statements given above is/are correct?

   (*a*) 1 only (*b*) 2 only

   (*c*) Both 1 and 2 (*d*) Neither 1 nor 2

8. Consider the following statements:

   When there is a dispute with respect to GST Council's recommendations or their implementation, it shall establish a mechanism to adjudicate upon the dispute:
   1. Between the centre and one or more states
   2. Between the centre and any state or states on one side and one or more other states on the other side
   3. Between two or more states

   Which of the statements given above is/are correct?

   (*a*) 1, 2 and 3 (*b*) 1 and 2 only

   (*c*) 2 and 3 only (*d*) 2 only

9. Consider the following statements:
   1. The vice-chairperson of the GST Council is nominated by the Union Finance Minister.
   2. One-half of the total number of members of the GST Council is the quorum for conducting a meeting.

   Which of the statements given above is/are correct?

   (*a*) 1 only (*b*) 2 only

   (*c*) Both 1 and 2 (*d*) Neither 1 nor 2

10. With reference to the functions of the GST Council, consider the following statements:
    1. The Council has to recommend compensation to the states for the loss of revenue arising on account of the introduction of GST.
    2. The Council shall recommend the date on which the GST may be levied on petroleum and natural gas.

    Which of the statements given above is/are correct?

(*a*) 1 only	(*b*) 2 only
(*c*) Both 1 and 2	(*d*) Neither 1 nor 2

Answers

1. (*d*)	2. (*d*)	3. (*c*)	4. (*b*)	5. (*d*)
6. (*c*)	7. (*a*)	8. (*a*)	9. (*b*)	10. (*c*)

47 National Commission for SCs

1. Consider the following statements:
   1. The first National Commission for Scheduled Castes and Scheduled Tribes was constituted in the year 1992.
   2. The first National Commission for Scheduled Castes and Scheduled Tribes was constituted under the Constitution (Sixty-fifth Amendment) Act.
   3. The 87th Amendment bifurcated the combined National Commission for Scheduled Castes and Scheduled Tribes into two separate bodies.

   Which of the statements given above are correct?

   (*a*) 1 and 2 only (*b*) 2 and 3 only
   (*c*) 1 and 3 only (*d*) 1, 2 and 3

2. Which of the following were created under the provisions of the Constitution of India?
   1. North-Eastern Council
   2. Finance Commission
   3. National Commission for Scheduled Castes
   4. Commission to investigate the conditions of Backward Classes

   Select the correct answer using the codes given below:

   (*a*) 1, 2, 3 and 4 (*b*) 1, 2 and 3
   (*c*) 2, 3 and 4 (*d*) 1 and 4 only

3. Who of the following places the annual report of the National Commission for SCs before the Parliament?

   (*a*) The Union Minister for Social Justice (*b*) The Union Cabinet
   (*c*) The Prime Minister of India (*d*) The President of India

4. Which Article of the Constitution of India deals with the National Commission for SCs?

   (*a*) Article 336 (*b*) Article 337
   (*c*) Article 338 (*d*) Article 338 A

5. The National Commission for SCs consists of a chairperson, a vice-chairperson and how many other members?

   (*a*) Two other members (*b*) Three other members
   (*c*) Four other members (*d*) Five other members

6. The separate National Commission for SCs came into existence in which year?

   (*a*) 2000 (*b*) 2002
   (*c*) 2004 (*d*) 2006

7. The conditions of service of the members of the National Commission for SCs are determined by which of the following?
   (*a*) The Parliament of India
   (*b*) The President of India
   (*c*) The Union Cabinet
   (*d*) The Constitution of India

Answers

1. (*a*)	2. (*c*)	3. (*d*)	4. (*c*)	5. (*b*)
6. (*c*)	7. (*b*)			

48 National Commission for STs

1. Consider the following statements:
   1. The National Commission for Scheduled Tribes was constituted under the Constitution (Eighty-ninth Amendment) Act.
   2. The first National Commission for Scheduled Tribes was constituted in 2006.

   Which of the statements given above is/are correct?

   (*a*) 1 only (*b*) 2 only
   (*c*) Both 1 and 2 (*d*) Neither 1 nor 2

2. Which one of the following is a Constitutional Body?

   (*a*) National Commission for Scheduled Tribes
   (*b*) National Commission for Minorities
   (*c*) National Commission for Women
   (*d*) National Commission for Protection of Child Rights

3. The National Commission for STs submits its annual report to which of the following?

   (*a*) The Parliament of India (*b*) The Union Cabinet
   (*c*) The Ministry of Tribal Affairs (*d*) The President of India

4. Which Article of the Constitution of India deals with the National Commission for STs?

   (*a*) Article 338A (*b*) Article 339
   (*c*) Article 334 (*d*) Article 338

5. The members of the National Commission for STs are appointed by which of the following?

   (*a*) The Cabinet Committee on Appointments (*b*) The Parliament of India
   (*c*) The President of India (*d*) The Minister for Tribal Affairs

6. Consider the following statements:
   1. The National Commission for STs presents an annual report to the Parliament.
   2. The central government and the state governments are required to consult the National Commission for STs on all major policy matters affecting the STs.

   Which of the statements given above is/are correct?

   (*a*) 1 only (*b*) 2 only
   (*c*) Both 1 and 2 (*d*) Neither 1 nor 2

7. Consider the following statements:
    1. The National Commission for STs consists of a chairperson, a vice-chairperson and two other members.
    2. The Conditions of service of the members of the National Commission for STs are determined by the Parliament.

    Which of the statements given above is/are correct?

    (*a*) 1 only (*b*) 2 only
    (*c*) Both 1 and 2 (*d*) Neither 1 nor 2

Answers

1. (*a*) 2. (*a*) 3. (*d*) 4. (*a*) 5. (*c*)
6. (*b*) 7. (*d*)

49 National Commission for BCs

1. Consider the following statements:
   1. The National Commission for Backward Classes (BCs) presents an annual report to the central government.
   2. The National Commission for BCs can also submit a report as and when it thinks necessary.

   Which of the statements given above is/are correct?

   (*a*) 1 only (*b*) 2 only
   (*c*) Both 1 and 2 (*d*) Neither 1 nor 2

2. Which of the following are the constitutional bodies?
   1. National Commission for BCs
   2. National Commission for Protection of Child Rights
   3. National Commission for SCs
   4. National Human Rights Commission

   Select the correct answer using the codes given below:

   (*a*) 1 and 3 only (*b*) 2 and 3 only
   (*c*) 1 and 4 only (*d*) 2 and 4 only

3. Which of the following Articles of the Constitution of India enabled the President to specify the socially and educationally backward classes?

   (*a*) Article 340
   (*b*) Article 341
   (*c*) Article 342
   (*d*) Article 342A

4. Consider the following statements:
   1. The Central Government and State Government are required to consult the National Commission for BCs on all major policy matters affecting the socially and educationally backward classes.
   2. The National Commission for BCs is not vested with the power to regulate its own procedure.

   Which of the statements given above is/are correct?

   (*a*) 1 only (*b*) 2 only
   (*c*) Both 1 and 2 (*d*) Neither 1 nor 2

5. The conditions of service and tenure of office of the Chairperson, the Vice-Chairperson and members of the National Commission for BCs are determined by which of the following?
   (*a*) The Constitution of India
   (*b*) The Union Cabinet
   (*c*) The President of India
   (*d*) The Parliament of India

6. The Article of the Indian Constitution containing the provision for the National Commission for BCs is:
   (*a*) Article 338
   (*b*) Article 338A
   (*c*) Article 338B
   (*d*) Article 339

7. Consider the following statements:
   1. The National Commission for BCs consists of a Chairperson, a Vice-Chairperson and two other members.
   2. They are appointed by the central government.

   Which of the statements given above is/are correct?
   (*a*) 1 only
   (*b*) 2 only
   (*c*) Both 1 and 2
   (*d*) Neither 1 nor 2

8. Which of the following amendments conferred a constitutional status on the National Commission for BCs?
   (*a*) 101st Amendment Act
   (*b*) 102nd Amendment Act
   (*c*) 103rd Amendment Act
   (*d*) 104th Amendment Act

9. Consider the following statements:
   1. The National Commission for BCs was set up in 1992.
   2. The Commission ceased to be a statutory body and became a constitutional body in 2016.

   Which of the statements given above is/are correct?
   (*a*) 1 only
   (*b*) 2 only
   (*c*) Both 1 and 2
   (*d*) Neither 1 nor 2

Answers

1. (*b*)	2. (*a*)	3. (*d*)	4. (*a*)	5. (*c*)
6. (*c*)	7. (*d*)	8. (*b*)	9. (*d*)	

50

Special Officer for Linguistic Minorities

1. Which of the following committees/commissions recommended the establishment of the office of the Special Officer for Linguistic Minorities?
   (*a*) First Administrative Reforms Commission of India
   (*b*) Swaran Singh Committee
   (*c*) States Reorganisation Commission
   (*d*) Rajamannar Committee

2. The Commissioner for Linguistic Minorities submits his annual reports and other reports to which of the following?
   (*a*) The National Commission for Minorities (*b*) The Parliament of India
   (*c*) The President of India (*d*) The Union Cabinet

3. The Article of the Constitution of India containing the provision for the Special Officer for Linguistic Minorities is which of the following?
   (*a*) Article 350A (*b*) Article 351
   (*c*) Article 350 (*d*) Article 350B

4. At the central level, the Commissioner for Linguistic Minorities falls under which of the following?
   (*a*) The Ministry of Tribal Affairs
   (*b*) The Ministry of Home Affairs
   (*c*) The Ministry of Social Justice
   (*d*) The Ministry of Minority Affairs

5. The office of the Special Officer for Linguistic Minorities was created in which of the following years?
   (*a*) 1957 (*b*) 1956
   (*c*) 1964 (*d*) 1969

6. Who/which of the following appoints the Special Officer for Linguistic Minorities?
   (*a*) The Cabinet Committee on Appointments
   (*b*) The President of India
   (*c*) The Speaker of the Lok Sabha
   (*d*) The Chairman of the National Minorities Commission

7. Where is the headquarters of the Commissioner for Linguistic Minorities?
   (*a*) Kolkata (*b*) New Delhi
   (*c*) Allahabad (*d*) Lucknow

8. **Which of the following Constitutional Amendment Acts made a provision for the Special Officer for Linguistic Minorities?**
   (*a*) Fourth Amendment Act
   (*b*) Seventh Amendment Act
   (*c*) Thirteenth Amendment Act
   (*d*) Fifteenth Amendment Act

Answers

1. (*c*)	2. (*c*)	3. (*d*)	4. (*d*)	5. (*a*)
6. (*b*)	7. (*c*)	8. (*b*)		

51

Comptroller and Auditor-General of India

1. Consider the following statements:
   1. The Comptroller and Auditor-General of India has no control over the issue of money from the Consolidated Fund of India.
   2. The term of the office of the Comptroller and Auditor-General of India has been fixed by an Act enacted by the Parliament.

   Which of the statements given above is/are correct?

   (*a*) 1 only　　(*b*) 2 only
   (*c*) Both 1 and 2　　(*d*) Neither 1 nor 2

2. Which of the following statements regarding the Comptroller and Auditor-General of India is/are true?

   The Report of the Comptroller and Auditor-General of India:
   1. can be considered by the joint session of both the Houses of the Parliament.
   2. includes examination of income and expenditure of all public sector undertakings.
   3. is placed before the Lok Sabha with the comments of the Estimates Committee.
   4. constitutes the basis for scrutiny by the Public Accounts Committee of the Parliament.

   Select the correct answer using the codes given below:

   (*a*) 1 and 2 only　　(*b*) 1 and 3 only
   (*c*) 2 and 4 only　　(*d*) 4 only

3. Which one of the following statements is not correct with regard to the Comptroller and Auditor-General of India (CAG)?
   (*a*) The CAG has been awarded a fully independent status.
   (*b*) The CAG can only be removed on the recommendation of the President.
   (*c*) The salary and emoluments of the CAG are charged on the Consolidated Fund of India.
   (*d*) The tenure of CAG is fixed for six years.

4. Who/Which among the following performs the watchdog functions in the financial management in the Government of India?
   1. The Controller-General of Accounts
   2. The Comptroller and Auditor-General of India
   3. The Public Accounts Committee
   4. The Finance Minister

Choose the correct answer from the codes given below:

(*a*) 1 and 2 only (*b*) 2 and 3 only
(*c*) 3 only (*d*) 1 and 4 only

5. Which one of the following statements is not correct regarding the functions and powers of the Comptroller and Auditor-General of India?
   (*a*) He examines the accounts of the Union Government and submits his report to the President.
   (*b*) He examines the accounts of the State Governments and submits his report to the Governors of the respective States.
   (*c*) He does not exercise any administrative control over the offices of the auditors working in the States.
   (*d*) In case either House of the Parliament desires to have any information from him, it can do so through the Public Accounts Committee.

6. Which one of the following statements about Comptroller and Auditor-General of India is not correct?
   (*a*) No minister can represent him in the Parliament.
   (*b*) His salary and emoluments are chargeable on the Consolidated Fund of India.
   (*c*) He cannot disallow any expenditure which in his opinion violates the Constitution.
   (*d*) He has been debarred from holding any office of profit under the Union or State Governments after his retirement.

7. The Comptroller and Auditor-General of India submits his audit reports to which of the following?
   (*a*) The Prime Minister (*b*) The Parliament
   (*c*) The President (*d*) The Chief Justice of India

8. Consider the following statements:
   1. The duty of CAG is not merely to ensure the legality of expenditure but also its propriety.
   2. The CAG has to uphold the Constitution and the laws of the Parliament in the fields of financial administration.

   Which of the statements given above is/are correct?

   (*a*) 1 only (*b*) 2 only
   (*c*) Both 1 and 2 (*d*) Neither 1 nor 2

9. Consider the following statements:

   All the Reports of the Comptroller and Auditor-General of India:
   1. relating to accounts of the Union and accounts of States are submitted to the President of India.
   2. relating to accounts of a State are submitted to the Governor of the State.
   3. relating to accounts of States are submitted to the Union Minister of Finance.

   Which of the statements given above is correct?

   (*a*) 1 only (*b*) 2 only
   (*c*) 3 only (*d*) None

10. The ultimate responsibility of taking due action on the comments of the Comptroller and Auditor-General of India vests with which of the following?
(*a*) The President of India (*b*) The Supreme Court
(*c*) The Parliament (*d*) Inter-State Council

11. Consider the following statements:

The Comptroller and Auditor-General of India has to:
1. audit government expenditure.
2. make financial policy.
3. sanction grants to various departments.
4. see that public expenditure are in conformity with the government rules.

Which of the statements given above are correct?
(*a*) 2, 3 and 4 (*b*) 1 and 3 only
(*c*) 2 and 3 only (*d*) 1 and 4 only

12. Who among the following can only be removed from the office in like manner and on the like grounds as a Judge of the Supreme Court?
1. Comptroller and Auditor-General of India
2. Chief Election Commissioner
3. Chairman, Union Public Service Commission
4. Attorney-General for India

Select the correct answer using the codes given below:
(*a*) 1, 2, 3 and 4 (*b*) 1, 2 and 4
(*c*) 1 and 2 only (*d*) 2 and 3 only

13. The annual report of the Comptroller and Auditor-General of India is scrutinised in detail by which of the following?
(*a*) Public Accounts Committee
(*b*) Estimates Committee
(*c*) Consultative Committee of the Finance Ministry
(*d*) Select Committee on Expenditure

14. Which one of the following is not correct regarding the Comptroller and Auditor-General (CAG) of India?
(*a*) His salary and other service conditions are determined by the Parliament.
(*b*) He shall take an oath before the President.
(*c*) He may also take an oath before any other person appointed for that purpose by the President.
(*d*) He can be removed on the grounds as in case of a Judge of High Court.

15. The provisions of the Act relating to the duties of the Comptroller and Auditor-General of India are to audit and report on all the expenditure from which of the following?
1. Consolidated Fund of India
2. Consolidated Fund of each State

3. Contingency Fund of India
4. Public Account of India

Select the correct answer using the codes given below:

(*a*) 1, 2, 3 and 4 (*b*) 1, 2 and 3
(*c*) 2, 3 and 4 (*d*) 1, 3 and 4

16. Which of the following fall within the duties of the Comptroller and Auditor-General of India?
    1. To audit and report on the receipts and expenditure of all bodies and authorities substantially financed from the Union or State revenues
    2. To audit the receipts and expenditure of each State to satisfy himself that the rules and procedures in that behalf are designed to secure an effective check on the assessment, collection and proper allocation of revenue

    Select the correct answer using the codes given below:

    (*a*) 1 only (*b*) 2 only
    (*c*) Both 1 and 2 (*d*) Neither 1 nor 2

17. In prescribing the form in which the accounts of the Union and the states are to be kept, the Comptroller and Auditor-General is expected to take approval of which of the following?
    (*a*) The Parliament
    (*b*) The Legislature of the state concerned and the Parliament
    (*c*) The Finance Minister
    (*d*) The President of India

18. Consider the following statements:
    1. The Article 149 of the Constitution lays down the provisions with regard to the appointment and service conditions of the CAG.
    2. The CAG cannot function independently unless he enjoys the constitutional protection.

    Which of the statements given above is/are correct?

    (*a*) 1 only (*b*) 2 only
    (*c*) Both 1 and 2 (*d*) Neither 1 nor 2

19. The Comptroller and Auditor-General of India submits three reports to the Parliament/State Legislatures. Which one of the following reports does not come under that category?
    (*a*) Audit Report on Finance Accounts
    (*b*) Audit Report on Appropriation Accounts
    (*c*) Audit Report on Capital Accounts
    (*d*) Audit Report on Commercial and Public Sector Enterprises

20. The Comptroller and Auditor-General of India has the power to audit which of the following?
    1. All expenditure from the Contingency Fund and the Public Account of the Union
    2. All expenditure from the Contingency Fund and the Public Account of a State
    3. All expenditure from the Consolidated Fund of each Union Territory having a Legislative Assembly of its own
    4. Accounts of all government companies set up under the Indian Companies Act

Select the correct answer using the codes given below:

(*a*) 1, 2, 3 and 4
(*b*) 1 and 2 only
(*c*) 3 and 4 only
(*d*) 1, 2 and 3

Answers

1. (*c*)	2. (*c*)	3. (*b*)	4. (*b*)	5. (*c*)
6. (*c*)	7. (*c*)	8. (*c*)	9. (*b*)	10. (*c*)
11. (*d*)	12. (*c*)	13. (*a*)	14. (*d*)	15. (*a*)
16. (*c*)	17. (*d*)	18. (*b*)	19. (*c*)	20. (*a*)

52

Attorney-General of India

1. Which one of the following statements is correct with regard to the office of the Attorney-General of India?
   (*a*) He shall have the right of audience in all the courts within the territory of India.
   (*b*) He shall perform his duties only in the Supreme Court.
   (*c*) He enjoys a fixed tenure.
   (*d*) The President appoints a person who is qualified to be a judge of a High Court, to be the Attorney-General of India.

2. Who is the first Law Officer of the Government of India?
   (*a*) Chief Justice of India
   (*b*) Union Law Minister
   (*c*) Attorney-General of India
   (*d*) Law Secretary

3. Who among the following holds his office at the pleasure of the President?
   (*a*) Chairman of the Union Public Service Commission
   (*b*) Attorney-General of India
   (*c*) Speaker of the Lok Sabha
   (*d*) Comptroller and Auditor-General of India

4. Who among the following can attend the meetings of both Houses of the Parliament while being not a member of either of the Houses?
   (*a*) Solicitor-General of India
   (*b*) Vice-President of India
   (*c*) Comptroller and Auditor-General of India
   (*d*) Attorney-General of India

5. Which Article of the Constitution of India has provided for the office of the Attorney-General of India?
   (*a*) Article 76
   (*b*) Article 74
   (*c*) Article 78
   (*d*) Article 77

6. The remuneration of the Attorney-General of India is determined by which of the following?
   (*a*) Parliament of India
   (*b*) President of India
   (*c*) Prime Minister of India
   (*d*) Union Cabinet

7. The Solicitor-General of India provides assistance to which of the following?
   (*a*) Union Law Secretary
   (*b*) Chief Justice of India
   (*c*) Union Law Minister
   (*d*) Attorney-General of India

8. Which of the following office is not created by the Constitution of India?
   (*a*) The Attorney-General of India
   (*b*) The Comptroller and Auditor-General of India
   (*c*) The Chief Justice of India
   (*d*) The Solicitor-General of India

Answers

1. (*a*)	2. (*c*)	3. (*b*)	4. (*d*)	5. (*a*)
6. (*b*)	7. (*d*)	8. (*d*)		

53 Advocate-General of the State

1. Consider the following statements:
   1. Like the Judge of a High Court, the Advocate-General of a State is appointed by the President of India.
   2. A person who is qualified to be appointed as the judge of a High Court, can be appointed as the Advocate-General.

   Which of the statements given above is/are correct?

   (*a*) 1 only (*b*) 2 only
   (*c*) Both 1 and 2 (*d*) Neither 1 nor 2

2. Consider the following statements with regard to the Advocate-General of a State:
   1. He holds office during the pleasure of the President of India.
   2. He can take part in the proceedings of the State Legislative Assembly.
   3. His salary is paid from the Consolidated Fund of India.
   4. He advises the State Government on legal matters.

   Which of the statements given above is/are correct?

   (*a*) 2 and 4 only (*b*) 3 only
   (*c*) 1 only (*d*) 1, 2, 3 and 4

3. The Advocate-General of a State enjoys all the privileges and immunities that are available to:
   (*a*) a member of the State Legislature.
   (*b*) a member of the Parliament of India.
   (*c*) the Governor of the State.
   (*d*) the President of India.

4. Which Article of the Constitution of India has provided for the office of the Advocate-General of the States?
   (*a*) Article 163 (*b*) Article 168
   (*c*) Article 165 (*d*) Article 169

5. The term of office of the Advocate-General of a State is:
   (*a*) 4 years (*b*) 5 years
   (*c*) 6 years (*d*) Not fixed

6. The remuneration of the Advocate-General of a State is determined by which of the following?
   (*a*) The President of India
   (*b*) The State Legislature
   (*c*) The State Governor
   (*d*) The Parliament of India

Answers

1. (*b*) 2. (*a*) 3. (*a*) 4. (*c*) 5. (*d*)
6. (*c*)

PART-VIII
NON-CONSTITUTIONAL BODIES

54. NITI Aayog
55. National Human Rights Commission
56. State Human Rights Commission
57. Central Information Commission
58. State Information Commission
59. Central Vigilance Commission
60. Central Bureau of Investigation
61. Lokpal and Lokayuktas
62. National Investigation Agency
63. National Disaster Management Authority

54

NITI Aayog

1. With reference to the legal status of the NITI Aayog (National Institution for Transforming India), consider the following statements:
   1. It is a statutory body.
   2. It is a non-constitutional body.
   3. It is a non-statutory body.
   4. It is a constitutional body.

   Which of the statements given above are correct?

   (*a*) 1 and 2 only (*b*) 2 and 3 only
   (*c*) 3 and 4 only (*d*) 1 and 4 only

2. Consider the following statements:
   1. The NITI Aayog is the successor to the erstwhile Planning Commission.
   2. The NITI Aayog is a quasi-judicial body.

   Which of the statements given above is/are correct?

   (*a*) 1 only (*b*) 2 only
   (*c*) Both 1 and 2 (*d*) Neither 1 nor 2

3. With reference to the functions of the NITI Aayog, consider the following statements:
   1. Providing both directional and policy inputs to the Government of India
   2. Designing strategic and long-term policies and programmes for the Government of India
   3. Making recommendations to the President of India with regard to the distribution of proceeds of taxes between the Union and the States
   4. Providing technical advice to the Centre and the States

   Which of the statements given above are correct?

   (*a*) 1, 2 and 3 (*b*) 2, 3 and 4
   (*c*) 1, 2 and 4 (*d*) 1 and 2 only

4. Which of the following statements regarding the National Institute of Labour Economics Research and Development (NILERD) is not correct?

   (*a*) It is a central autonomous organisation attached to the NITI Aayog.
   (*b*) It is mainly funded by grants-in-aid from the NITI Aayog.
   (*c*) It was formerly known as the Institute of Applied Manpower Research (IAMR).
   (*d*) The IAMR has been renamed as NILERD in 2015.

5. Consider the following statements:
   1. The Vice-Chairperson of the NITI Aayog is appointed by the Prime Minister.
   2. The Chief Executive Officer of the NITI Aayog is appointed by the Prime Minister.

   Which of the statements given above is/are correct?

   (*a*) 1 only (*b*) 2 only
   (*c*) Both 1 and 2 (*d*) Neither 1 nor 2

6. With reference to the composition of the NITI Aayog, consider the following statements:
   1. Prime Minister of India
   2. Chief Minister of all the States
   3. Chief Ministers of the Union Territories with Legislatures
   4. Lieutenant Governors of all the Union Territories
   5. Special Invitees nominated by the Prime Minister

   Which of the statements given above are correct?

   (*a*) 1, 2, 4 and 5 (*b*) 1, 2 and 3
   (*c*) 1, 2 and 4 (*d*) 1, 2, 3 and 5

7. The NITI Aayog was created by:
   (*a*) an Act of the Parliament.
   (*b*) an Amendment to the Constitution.
   (*c*) a Resolution of the Union Cabinet.
   (*d*) a Resolution of the Parliament.

8. Which of the following statements regarding the Development Monitoring and Evaluation Office (DMEO) are correct?
   1. It is an attached office of the NITI Aayog.
   2. It was established in 2014.
   3. It was setup by merging the erstwhile Programme Evaluation Organisation and the Independent Evaluation Office.
   4. Its head has the rank of a Secretary to the Government of India.

   Select the correct answer using the codes given below:

   (*a*) 1, 2 and 3 (*b*) 1, 3 and 4
   (*c*) 1 and 3 only (*d*) 1, 2, 3 and 4

9. With reference to the Regional Councils of the NITI Aayog, consider the following statements:
   1. These are formed for a specified tenure.
   2. These are convened by the Prime Minister.
   3. They comprise the Chief Ministers of States and Lt. Governors of Union Territories in the region.
   4. These are chaired by the Chairperson of the NITI Aayog or his nominee.

   Which of the statements given above are correct?

   (*a*) 1, 2 and 3 (*b*) 2 and 3 only
   (*c*) 1 and 4 only (*d*) 1, 2, 3 and 4

10. The Chief Executive Officer of the NITI Aayog holds the rank of a/an:
    (*a*) Secretary to the Government of India.
    (*b*) Additional Secretary to the Government of India.
    (*c*) Joint Secretary to the Government of India.
    (*d*) Deputy Secretary to the Government of India.

11. Which of the following are the objectives of the NITI Aayog?
    1. To foster cooperative federalism
    2. To create a knowledge and innovation support system
    3. To execute the programmes and initiatives
    4. To maintain a state-of-the-art Resource Centre

    Select the correct answer using the codes given below:
    (*a*) 1 and 2 only (*b*) 2 and 3 only
    (*c*) 3 and 4 only (*d*) 1, 2 and 4

12. Consider the following statements:
    1. The full-time members of the NITI Aayog enjoy the rank of a Cabinet Minister.
    2. The part-time members of the NITI Aayog would be on a rotation.

    Which of the statements given above is/are correct?
    (*a*) 1 only (*b*) 2 only
    (*c*) Both 1 and 2 (*d*) Neither 1 nor 2

Answers

1. (*b*)	2. (*a*)	3. (*c*)	4. (*d*)	5. (*c*)
6. (*d*)	7. (*c*)	8. (*c*)	9. (*d*)	10. (*a*)
11. (*d*)	12. (*b*)			

55 National Human Rights Commission

1. Consider the following statements:
   1. The National Human Rights Commission is the watchdog of human rights in the country.
   2. The National Human Rights Commission is an independent body.

   Which of the statements given above is/are correct?

   (*a*) 1 only
   (*b*) 2 only
   (*c*) Both 1 and 2
   (*d*) Neither 1 nor 2

2. The chairperson and members of the National Human Rights Commission are appointed on the recommendations of a committee consisting of the:
   1. Speaker of the Lok Sabha.
   2. Deputy Chairman of the Rajya Sabha.
   3. Leader of the Opposition in the Lok Sabha.
   4. Leader of the Opposition in the Rajya Sabha.
   5. Prime Minister.
   6. Union Home Minister.

   Select the correct answer from the codes given below:

   (*a*) 1, 3, 5 and 6
   (*b*) 1, 2 and 5
   (*c*) 1, 3, 4 and 5
   (*d*) 1, 2, 3, 4, 5 and 6

3. The ex-officio members of the National Human Rights Commission are who of the following?
   1. The Chairperson of the National Commission for Minorities
   2. The Chairperson of the National Commission for SCs
   3. The Chairperson of the National Commission for STs
   4. The Chairperson of the National Commission for Women

   Select the correct answer from the codes given below:

   (*a*) 1, 2 and 3
   (*b*) 2, 3 and 4
   (*c*) 1, 2, 3 and 4
   (*d*) 1, 2 and 4

4. Who among the following can be the Chairperson of the National Human Rights Commission?

   (*a*) Only a retired Chief Justice of a High Court
   (*b*) A retired Chief Justice of India or a judge of the Supreme Court
   (*c*) Any serving judge of the High Court
   (*d*) Any serving judge of the Supreme Court

5. In which year was the Human Rights Protection Law passed in India?
   (*a*) 1986 (*b*) 1987
   (*c*) 1993 (*d*) 1995

6. The salaries, allowances and other service conditions of the members of the National Human Rights Commission are determined by who/which of the following?
   (*a*) The President of India (*b*) The Parliament of India
   (*c*) The Chairman, NHRC (*d*) The Central Government

7. The National Human Rights Commission consists of a chairperson and how many members?
   (*a*) Three members (*b*) Four members
   (*c*) Five members (*d*) Six members

8. The chairperson of the National Human Rights Commission holds office for:
   (*a*) 5 years or until the age of 65 years, whichever is earlier.
   (*b*) 6 years or until the age of 65 years, whichever is earlier.
   (*c*) 4 years or until the age of 70 years, whichever is earlier.
   (*d*) 3 years or until the age of 70 years, whichever is earlier.

9. Which of the following provided for the establishment of the National Human Rights Commission?
   (*a*) A resolution of the Parliament (*b*) A resolution of the Union Cabinet
   (*c*) An order of the Supreme Court (*d*) An Act of the Parliament

10. Consider the following statements:
    1. The National Human Rights Commission is not a constitutional body.
    2. The National Human Rights Commission is a statutory body.

    Which of the statements given above is/are correct?
    (*a*) 1 only (*b*) 2 only
    (*c*) Both 1 and 2 (*d*) Neither 1 nor 2

Answers

1. (*c*)	2. (*d*)	3. (*c*)	4. (*b*)	5. (*c*)
6. (*d*)	7. (*c*)	8. (*d*)	9. (*d*)	10. (*c*)

56

State Human Rights Commission

1. Consider the following statements:
   1. The State Human Rights Commission is a multi-member body.
   2. The State Human Rights Commission consists of a chairperson and three members.

   Which of the statements given above is/are correct?

   (*a*) 1 only (*b*) 2 only
   (*c*) Both 1 and 2 (*d*) Neither 1 nor 2

2. The Protection of Human Rights Act, 1993 provides for the creation of which of the following?
   1. National Human Rights Commission
   2. State Human Rights Commission
   3. Joint State Human Rights Commission
   4. Human Rights Courts

   Select the correct answer from the codes given below:

   (*a*) 1 and 2 only (*b*) 1, 2 and 4
   (*c*) 1, 2, 3 and 4 (*d*) 1, 2 and 3

3. The chairperson of a State Human Rights Commission can be removed by whom of the following?

   (*a*) The Governor of the State (*b*) The President of India
   (*c*) The Parliament of India (*d*) The State Legislature

4. A State Human Rights Commission submits its annual report to whom/which of the following?

   (*a*) The State Legislature (*b*) The Governor of the State
   (*c*) The State Government (*d*) The High Court of the State

5. A member of a State Human Rights Commission holds office for:

   (*a*) 4 years or until the age of 70 years, whichever is earlier.
   (*b*) 5 years or until the age of 65 years, whichever is earlier.
   (*c*) 3 years or until the age of 70 years, whichever is earlier.
   (*d*) 6 years or until the age of 65 years, whichever is earlier.

6. Who among the following can be the chairperson of a State Human Rights Commission?

   (*a*) Only a retired Chief Justice of India
   (*b*) Any serving judge of the Supreme Court
   (*c*) Any serving judge of a High Court
   (*d*) A retired Chief Justice or a judge of a High Court

7. Consider the following statements:
   1. The functions of a State Human Rights Commission are mainly recommendatory in nature.
   2. The recommendations of a State Human Rights Commission are binding on the State Government.

   Which of the statements given above is/are correct?

   (*a*) 1 only (*b*) 2 only
   (*c*) Both 1 and 2 (*d*) Neither 1 nor 2

Answers

1. (*a*) 2. (*b*) 3. (*b*) 4. (*c*) 5. (*c*)
6. (*d*) 7. (*a*)

57

Central Information Commission

1. Consider the following statements:
   1. The Central Information Commission can order inquiry into any matter if there are reasonable grounds.
   2. The Central Information Commission has the power to secure compliance of its decisions from the public authority.

   Which of the statements given above is/are correct?

   (*a*) 1 only (*b*) 2 only
   (*c*) Both 1 and 2 (*d*) Neither 1 nor 2

2. Who among the following are members of a committee that recommends the appointment of the Chief Information Commissioner?
   1. The Prime Minister
   2. The Leader of opposition in the Lok Sabha
   3. The Leader of opposition in the Rajya Sabha
   4. The Union Cabinet Minister nominated by the Prime Minister
   5. The Speaker of the Lok Sabha

   Select the correct answer using the codes given below:

   (*a*) 1, 2 and 4 (*b*) 1, 2, 3 and 5
   (*c*) 1, 2, 3 and 4 (*d*) 1, 2 and 5

3. The Central Information Commission entertains complaints and appeals pertaining to offices, financial institutions and public sector undertakings under which of the following?
   1. Central government
   2. State government
   3. Local government
   4. Union territories

   Select the correct answer using the codes given below:

   (*a*) 1 and 4 only (*b*) 1 only
   (*c*) 1, 2, 3 and 4 (*d*) 1, 2 and 3

4. The salary, allowances and other service conditions of the Chief Information Commissioner shall be such as prescribed by whom/which of the following?

   (*a*) The President of India
   (*b*) The Parliament of India

(*c*) The Central Government
(*d*) The Supreme Court of India

5. The Central Information Commission submits its annual report to whom/which of the following?
(*a*) The President (*b*) The Parliament
(*c*) The Supreme Court (*d*) The Central Government

6. An Information Commissioner can be removed from the office by the President on the advise /recommendation of which of the following?
(*a*) Supreme Court
(*b*) Parliament
(*c*) Central Vigilance Commission
(*d*) Union Public Service Commission

7. The Central Information Commission was established in which year?
(*a*) 2000 (*b*) 2002
(*c*) 2005 (*d*) 2006

8. The Central Information Commission consists of a Chief Information Commissioner and how many Information Commissioners?
(*a*) Five Information Commissioners
(*b*) Ten Information Commissioners
(*c*) Six Information Commissioners
(*d*) Eight Information Commissioners

9. What is the term of office of the Chief Information Commissioner and an Information Commissioner?
(*a*) 4 years (*b*) 3 years
(*c*) 6 years (*d*) As prescribed

10. Which of the following provided for the establishment of the Central Information Commission?
(*a*) An order of the Supreme Court
(*b*) A resolution of the Parliament
(*c*) An Act of the Parliament
(*d*) A resolution of the Union Cabinet

11. The Central Information Commission falls under which of the following?
(*a*) The Ministry of Law
(*b*) The Ministry of Home Affairs
(*c*) The Ministry of Personnel
(*d*) The Ministry of Communications and Information Technology

12. Consider the following statements:
1. The Central Information Commission is a high-powered independent body.
2. The Central Information Commission is a constitutional body.

Which of the statements given above is/are correct?

(*a*) 1 only (*b*) 2 only

(*c*) Both 1 and 2 (*d*) Neither 1 nor 2

Answers

1. (*c*)	2. (*a*)	3. (*a*)	4. (*c*)	5. (*d*)
6. (*a*)	7. (*c*)	8. (*b*)	9. (*d*)	10. (*c*)
11. (*c*)	12. (*a*)			

58

State Information Commission

1. Consider the following statements:

   1. The State Information Commission entertains complaints and appeals pertaining to offices, financial institutions and public sector undertakings under the concerned state government.
   2. The State Information Commission is a high-powered independent body.

   Which of the statements given above is / are correct?

   (*a*) 1 only
   (*b*) 2 only
   (*c*) Both 1 and 2
   (*d*) Neither 1 nor 2

2. The State Information Commission submits its annual report to whom/which of the following?

   (*a*) The Governor of the State
   (*b*) The High Court of the State
   (*c*) The State Legislature
   (*d*) The State Government

3. How can a State Information Commissioner be removed from office?

   (*a*) By the order of the State Chief Information Commissioner.
   (*b*) By the order of the Supreme Court of India.
   (*c*) By the order of the Governor after the Supreme Court, on a reference made to it by the Governor, has on inquiry reported that the State Information Commissioner ought to be removed.
   (*d*) In a manner similar to the removal of a Judge of a High Court.

4. Who of the following is not a part of the committee that recommends the appointment of the State Chief Information Commissioner and the State Information Commissioners?

   (*a*) A Judge of the State High Court
   (*b*) The Chief Minister
   (*c*) A State Cabinet Minister nominated by the Chief Minister
   (*d*) The Leader of Opposition in the State Legislative Assembly

5. The salary, allowances and other Service conditions of a State Information commissioner shall be such as prescribed by which of the following?

   (*a*) The Central Government
   (*b*) The State Government
   (*c*) The State Legislature
   (*d*) The Parliament of India

6. The State Chief Information Commissioner holds office for:

   (*a*) As prescribed or until the age of 65 years, whichever is earlier.
   (*b*) 4 years or until the age of 70 years, whichever is earlier.

(*c*) 6 years or until the age of 70 years, whichever is earlier.
(*d*) 6 years or until the age of 65 years, whichever is earlier.

7. The Right to Information Act, 2005, provides for the creation of the:
   1. Central Information Commission.
   2. State Information Commission.
   3. Joint State Information Commission.

   Select the correct answer using the codes given below:

   (*a*) 1, 2 and 3 (*b*) 1 and 2 only
   (*c*) 1 and 3 only (*d*) 2 and 3 only

Answers

1. (*c*) 2. (*d*) 3. (*c*) 4. (*a*) 5. (*a*)
6. (*a*) 7. (*b*)

59 Central Vigilance Commission

1. Consider the following statements:
   1. The Central Vigilance Commission was set up by an Act of the Parliament.
   2. The Central Vigilance Commission has been broadly given the measure of independence and autonomy as that given to the Union Public Service Commission.

   Which of the statements given above is / are correct?

   (*a*) 1 only (*b*) 2 only
   (*c*) Both 1 and 2 (*d*) Neither 1 nor 2

2. Which one of the following is the main function of the Central Vigilance Commission?
   (*a*) To keep a watch on the investigation agencies in the country
   (*b*) To expedite the disposal of criminal cases pending in the courts
   (*c*) To scrutinise the utilisation of developmental funds sanctioned by the Government
   (*d*) To inquire or cause an inquiry of alleged offence of a public servant

3. The Central Vigilance Commission was established on the recommendation of which of the following?
   (*a*) First Administrative Reforms Commission of India
   (*b*) Estimates Committee
   (*c*) Committee on Prevention of Corruption
   (*d*) Law Commission

4. The salary, allowances and other service conditions of the Central Vigilance Commissioner are similar to those of:
   (*a*) a member of the UPSC.
   (*b*) a judge of the Supreme Court.
   (*c*) the Chairman of the UPSC.
   (*d*) the Chief Election Commissioner.

5. The Parliament enacted a law conferring statutory status on the Central Vigilance Commission in which year?
   (*a*) 2000 (*b*) 2002
   (*c*) 2003 (*d*) 2005

6. The Central Vigilance Commission presents its annual report to the whom/which of the following?
   (*a*) The Parliament (*b*) The President
   (*c*) The Prime Minister (*d*) The Home Minister

7. Which of the following institutions have been set up by Government of India to check misconduct, malpractices, corruption and misdemeanour on the part of public servants?
   1. Central Vigilance Commission
   2. Lokpal
   3. Special Police Establishment
   4. Central Bureau of Investigation

   Choose the correct answer by using the codes given below:

   (*a*) 2 and 3 only (*b*) 1 and 4 only
   (*c*) 3 and 4 only (*d*) 1, 2, 3 and 4

8. The Government of India appointed a Committee on the Prevention of Corruption under the chairmanship of whom of the following?

   (*a*) Ananthaswamy Ayyangar (*b*) P.V. Subbaiah
   (*c*) K. Santhanam (*d*) K. Hanumanthayya

9. In which of the following years, the Central Vigilance Commission was set up?

   (*a*) 1962 (*b*) 1966
   (*c*) 1967 (*d*) 1964

10. Who of the following is not a member of the committee that recommends the appointment of the Central Vigilance Commissioner?

    (*a*) The Prime Minister
    (*b*) The Home Minister
    (*c*) The Leader of the Opposition in the Lok Sabha
    (*d*) The Speaker of the Lok Sabha

Answers

1. (*b*)	2. (*d*)	3. (*c*)	4. (*c*)	5. (*c*)
6. (*b*)	7. (*d*)	8. (*c*)	9. (*d*)	10. (*d*)

60

Central Bureau of Investigation

1. Consider the following statements:
   1. The Director of Central Bureau of Investigation as Inspector-General of Police, Delhi Special Police Establishment, is responsible for the administration of the organisation.
   2. With the enactment of CVC Act, 2003, the superintendence of Delhi Special Police Establishment vests with the Central Government save investigations of offences under the Prevention of Corruption Act, 1988, in which, the superintendence vests with the Central Vigilance Commission.

   Which of the statements given above is/are correct?

   (*a*) 1 only　　(*b*) 2 only
   (*c*) Both 1 and 2　　(*d*) Neither 1 nor 2

2. The Central Bureau of Investigation was setup by which of the following?

   (*a*) An Act of the Parliament　　(*b*) An Amendment to the Constitution
   (*c*) A Resolution of the Home Ministry　　(*d*) A Resolution of the Personnel Ministry

3. Who among the following are members of a committee that recommends the appointment of the Director of CBI?
   1. The Prime Minister
   2. The Leader of Opposition in the Lok Sabha
   3. The Chief Justice of India
   4. The Leader of Opposition in the Rajya Sabha

   Select the correct answer using the codes given below:

   (*a*) 1, 3 and 4　　(*b*) 1, 2 and 4
   (*c*) 1, 2 and 3　　(*d*) 1, 2, 3 and 4

4. The Central Bureau of Investigation was setup in which year?

   (*a*) 1962　　(*b*) 1963
   (*c*) 1964　　(*d*) 1965

5. The Central Bureau of Investigation comes under the administrative control of which of the following?

   (*a*) Ministry of Home Affairs　　(*b*) Cabinet Secretariat
   (*c*) Prime Minister's Office　　(*d*) Ministry of Personnel

6. Which of the following Committees/Reports recommended for the establishment of the Central Bureau of Investigation?

   (*a*) Santhanam Committee
   (*b*) First Administrative Reforms Commission of India

(*c*) P.H. Appleby Report
(*d*) A.D. Gorwala Report

7. What is the security of tenure of office of the Director of CBI as per the CVC Act, 2003?
(*a*) Two years
(*b*) Three years
(*c*) Four years
(*d*) Five years

Answers

1. (*c*) 2. (*c*) 3. (*c*) 4. (*b*) 5. (*d*)
6. (*a*) 7. (*a*)

61

Lokpal and Lokayuktas

1. Where was the Institution of Ombudsman was first introduced?
   (*a*) New Zealand
   (*b*) Norway
   (*c*) Finland
   (*d*) Sweden

2. Which one of the following committees recommended the establishment of the institutions of Lokpal and Lokayukta?
   (*a*) Gorwala Committee
   (*b*) Appleby Committee
   (*c*) First Administrative Reforms Commission of India
   (*d*) Ashok Mehta Committee

3. Which of the following are the institutions for the redressal of citizen's grievances in India?
   1. Lokpal
   2. Lokayukta
   3. Administrative Tribunals
   4. Central Vigilance Commission

   Select the correct answer using the codes given below:
   (*a*) 1 and 2 only
   (*b*) 1, 2 and 4
   (*c*) 1 and 4 only
   (*d*) 1, 2, 3 and 4

4. Which of the following are major features of the institutions of Lokpal and Lokayukta as recommended by the First Administrative Reforms Commission of India?
   1. They should be demonstrably independent and impartial.
   2. They should compare with the highest judicial functionary in the country.
   3. They should be directly accountable to the Parliament.
   4. Their appointments should as far as possible be non-political.

   Select the correct answer by using the codes given below:
   (*a*) 1 and 4 only
   (*b*) 1, 2 and 4
   (*c*) 1, 2, 3 and 4
   (*d*) 2 and 3 only

5. According to the First Administrative Reforms Commission of India, the Lokpal would be appointed by the President after Consultation with whom of the following?
   1. The Chief Justice of India
   2. The Leader of Opposition in the Lok Sabha
   3. The Speaker of the Lok Sabha
   4. The Chairman of the Rajya Sabha

Select the correct answer using the codes given below:

(*a*) 1, 2, 3 and 4 (*b*) 1, 2 and 3
(*c*) 1, 3 and 4 (*d*) 2, 3 and 4

6. The Lokayukta and Uplokayuktas Act was first passed in which state?
   (*a*) Maharashtra (*b*) West Bengal
   (*c*) Karnataka (*d*) Odisha

7. The First Administrative Reforms Commission of India (1966), recommended the establishment of "Lokpal" in India on the lines of Ombudsman of which of the following countries?
   1. Finland 2. Denmark
   3. Norway 4. Switzerland

   Select the correct answer using the codes given below:
   (*a*) 1, 2 and 4 (*b*) 1 and 2 only
   (*c*) 1, 2 and 3 (*d*) 3 and 4 only

8. The specific purpose of the institution of Lokpal is to:
   (*a*) strengthen legislative control over administration.
   (*b*) supplement judicial control over administration.
   (*c*) protect and promote integrity in administration.
   (*d*) enable effective popular control over administration.

9. Which of the following States require(s) judicial qualifications for the appointment of Lokayukta?
   1. Maharashtra 2. Rajasthan
   3. Bihar 4. Andhra Pradesh

   Select the correct answer using the codes given below:
   (*a*) 1 only (*b*) 2 and 3 only
   (*c*) 4 only (*d*) 1 and 4 only

10. The office of Lokpal and Lokayukta in India is based on which one of the following?
    (*a*) Parliamentary Commissioner of UK
    (*b*) Ombudsman in Scandinavia
    (*c*) Procurator-General of Russia
    (*d*) Council of State in France

11. In which of the following stated years, the Lokpal Bill was not introduced in the Parliament?
    (*a*) 1968 (*b*) 1971
    (*c*) 1978 (*d*) 1985

Answers

1. (*d*)	2. (*c*)	3. (*d*)	4. (*b*)	5. (*c*)
6. (*d*)	7. (*c*)	8. (*c*)	9. (*c*)	10. (*b*)
11. (*c*)				

62 National Investigation Agency

1. Consider the following statements:
   1. In 2019, the jurisdiction of the National Investigation Agency (NIA) was extended.
   2. The NIA (Amendment) Act, 2019, inserted certain new offences in the schedule of the NIA Act.

   Which of the statements given above is/are correct?

   (*a*) 1 only (*b*) 2 only
   (*c*) Both 1 and 2 (*d*) Neither 1 nor 2

2. With reference to the functions of the NIA, consider the following statements:
   1. It is mandated to investigate and prosecute offences under the various Acts mentioned in the schedule of the NIA Act.
   2. It shares inputs with other intelligence and investigation agencies of the Central Government and the State Governments.
   3. It is the central counter-terrorism law enforcement agency in the country.

   Which of the statements given above are correct?

   (*a*) 1 and 2 only (*b*) 2 and 3 only
   (*c*) 1 and 3 only (*d*) 1, 2 and 3

3. The NIA was set up by:

   (*a*) a Resolution of the Cabinet Secretariat. (*b*) a Constitutional Amendment Act.
   (*c*) an Act of the Parliament. (*d*) a Resolution of the Union Home Ministry.

4. Consider the following statements:
   1. The NIA is headed by a Director-General.
   2. He is appointed by the President of India.

   Which of the statements given above is/are correct?

   (*a*) 1 only (*b*) 2 only
   (*c*) Both 1 and 2 (*d*) Neither 1 nor 2

5. Consider the following statements:
   1. The NIA was constituted in the year 2008.
   2. The NIA was established under the provisions of the NIA Act, 2008.

   Which of the statements given above is/are correct?

   (*a*) 1 only (*b*) 2 only
   (*c*) Both 1 and 2 (*d*) Neither 1 nor 2

6. The NIA works under the administrative control of which of the following?
   (*a*) The Cabinet Secretariat
   (*b*) The Prime Minister's Office
   (*c*) The Union Ministry of Personnel
   (*d*) The Union Ministry of Home Affairs

7. With reference to the legal status of the NIA, consider the following statements:
   1. It is a statutory body.
   2. It is a constitutional body.
   3. It is a non-statutory body.
   4. It is a non-constitutional body.

   Which of the statements given above are correct?
   (*a*) 1 and 2 only
   (*b*) 2 and 3 only
   (*c*) 1 and 4 only
   (*d*) 3 and 4 only

Answers

1. (*c*) 2. (*d*) 3. (*c*) 4. (*a*) 5. (*b*)
6. (*d*) 7. (*c*)

63 National Disaster Management Authority

1. Consider the following statements:
   1. The National Disaster Management Authority (NDMA) consists of a chairperson and other members, not exceeding eight.
   2. The other members of the NDMA are nominated by the chairperson of the NDMA.

   Which of the statements given above is/are correct?

   (*a*) 1 only (*b*) 2 only
   (*c*) Both 1 and 2 (*d*) Neither 1 nor 2

2. With reference to the legal status of the National Disaster Management Authority (NDMA), consider the following statements:
   1. It is a constitutional body.
   2. It is a statutory body.
   3. It is a non-constitutional body.
   4. It is a non-statutory body.

   Which of the statements given above are correct?

   (*a*) 2 and 3 only (*b*) 1 and 2 only
   (*c*) 3 and 4 only (*d*) 1 and 4 only

3. Consider the following statements:
   1. The District Disaster Management Authority (DDMA) consists of a chairperson and other members, not exceeding five.
   2. The Collector of the district is the ex-officio chairperson of the DDMA.
   3. The elected representative of the local authority is the ex-officio co-chairperson of the DDMA.

   Which of the statements given above is/are correct?

   (*a*) 1 and 2 only (*b*) 2 and 3 only
   (*c*) 2 only (*d*) 1, 2 and 3

4. The National Disaster Management Authority (NDMA) was set up by:

   (*a*) a resolution of the Union Ministry of Home Affairs.
   (*b*) a resolution of the Cabinet Secretariat.
   (*c*) an amendment to the Constitution.
   (*d*) an Act of the Parliament.

5. With reference to the functions of the National Disaster Management Authority (NDMA), consider the following statements:
   1. The NDMA exercises the general superintendence, direction and control of the National Disaster Response Force.
   2. The NDMA prepares an annual report on its activities and submits it to the President of India.

   Which of the statements given above is/are correct?

   (*a*) 1 only (*b*) 2 only
   (*c*) Both 1 and 2 (*d*) Neither 1 nor 2

6. The chief executive officer of the District Disaster Management Authority (DDMA) is appointed by whom/which of the following?
   (*a*) Collector of the District
   (*b*) State Disaster Management Authority (SDMA)
   (*c*) State Government
   (*d*) State Governor

7. Consider the following statements:
   1. Initially, the National Disaster Management Authority (NDMA) was constituted in 2004 by the Executive Order of the Government of India.
   2. Subsequently, the NDMA was notified in 2005 under the provisions of the Disaster Management Act, 2005.

   Which of the statements given above is/are correct?

   (*a*) 1 only (*b*) 2 only
   (*c*) Both 1 and 2 (*d*) Neither 1 nor 2

8. The National Disaster Management Authority (NDMA) works under the administrative control of which of the following?
   (*a*) The Prime Minister's Office
   (*b*) The Cabinet Secretariat
   (*c*) The Union Ministry of Home Affairs
   (*d*) The NITI Aayog

9. Consider the following statements:
   1. The chairperson of the State Disaster Management Authority (SDMA) designates one of the members as the vice-chairperson of the SDMA.
   2. An SDMA consists of a chairperson and other members, not exceeding six.

   Which of the statements given above is/are correct?

   (*a*) 1 only (*b*) 2 only
   (*c*) Both 1 and 2 (*d*) Neither 1 nor 2

10. Consider the following statements:
    1. The Vice-Chairperson of the National Disaster Management Authority (NDMA) has the status of a Minister of State.
    2. The National Institute of Disaster Management is located in Bhopal.

Which of the statements given above is/are correct?

(*a*) 1 only (*b*) 2 only

(*c*) Both 1 and 2 (*d*) Neither 1 nor 2

Answers

1. (*b*)	2. (*a*)	3. (*b*)	4. (*d*)	5. (*a*)
6. (*c*)	7. (*d*)	8. (*c*)	9. (*a*)	10. (*d*)

PART-IX OTHER CONSTITUTIONAL DIMENSIONS

64. Co-operative Societies

65. Official Language

66. Public Services

67. Rights and Liabilities of the Government

68. Special Provisions Relating to Certain Classes

64

Co-operative Societies

1. Consider the following statements:
   1. The Parliament may make provisions for the incorporation and regulation of co-operative societies.
   2. The maximum number of directors of a co-operative society shall not exceed twenty-five.

   Which of the statements given above is/are correct?

   (*a*) 1 only (*b*) 2 only
   (*c*) Both 1 and 2 (*d*) Neither 1 nor 2

2. Which of the following constitutional amendment acts gave a constitutional status and protection to the co-operative societies?

   (*a*) 95th Amendment (*b*) 96th Amendment
   (*c*) 97th Amendment (*d*) 98th Amendment

3. Which part of the Constitution of India contain provisions with respect to the co-operative societies?

   (*a*) Part IX (*b*) Part IXB
   (*c*) Part IXA (*d*) Part XI

4. Which of the following sets of the Articles of the Constitution of India deal with the co-operative societies?

   (*a*) Articles 243ZH to 243ZT (*b*) Articles 243ZI to 243ZT
   (*c*) Articles 243ZH to 243ZS (*d*) Articles 243ZG to 243ZS

5. Which/Who of the following can make provisions for the offences relating to the co- operative societies and penalties for such offences?

   (*a*) The State Governor (*b*) The State High Court
   (*c*) The Parliament of India (*d*) The State Legislature

6. Which of the following Articles of the Constitution deals with the application to Multi- state Co- operative Societies?

   (*a*) Article 243ZI (*b*) Article 243ZO
   (*c*) Article 243ZR (*d*) Article 243ZL

Answers

1. (*d*) 2. (*c*) 3. (*b*) 4. (*a*) 5. (*d*)
6. (*c*)

65

Official Language

1. Consider the following statements:

   1. The Parliament of India may make any one or more of the languages in use in a State or Hindi as the official language of that State.
   2. The Official Language Act lays down that English should be used for purposes of communication between the Union and non-Hindi States.

   Which of the statements given above is/are correct?

   (*a*) 1 only (*b*) 2 only
   (*c*) Both 1 and 2 (*d*) Neither 1 nor 2

2. Which of the following sets of Articles of the Constitution of India contain provisions pertaining to the official language?

   (*a*) Articles 347 to 353 (*b*) Articles 346 to 354
   (*c*) Articles 342 to 352 (*d*) Articles 343 to 351

3. What is the strength of Rajya Sabha in the Committee of the Parliament on Official Language?

   (*a*) 10 members (*b*) 15 members
   (*c*) 7 members (*d*) 20 members

4. In which of the following years, the Parliament enacted the Official Language Act?

   (*a*) 1963 (*b*) 1965
   (*c*) 1957 (*d*) 1955

5. Sindhi was included in the Eight Schedule of the Constitution of India by which of the following?

   (*a*) 21st Amendment Act
   (*b*) 15th Amendment Act
   (*c*) 27th Amendment Act
   (*d*) 23rd Amendment Act

6. Which Part of the Constitution of India deals with the official language?

   (*a*) Part XVI (*b*) Part XVII
   (*c*) Part XVIII (*d*) Part XIV

7. Which of the following states has Konkani as its official language?

   (*a*) Meghalaya (*b*) Nagaland
   (*c*) Jharkhand (*d*) Goa

8. **In 1955, the President appointed an Official Language Commission under the chairmanship of whom of the following?**

   (*a*) G.B. Pant
   (*b*) S.K. Dhar
   (*c*) B.G. Kher
   (*d*) H.N. Kunzru

Answers

1. (*b*)	2. (*d*)	3. (*a*)	4. (*a*)	5. (*a*)
6. (*b*)	7. (*d*)	8. (*c*)		

66

Public Services

1. Consider the following statements:
   1. A new all-India service can be created if both the Lok Sabha and Rajya Sabha declare by a resolution supported by not less than two-thirds of the members present and voting that it is necessary or expedient in the national interest to do so.
   2. There is no provision in the Constitution of India as to what level of authority can dismiss a member of a civil service of the Union or an all-India service or a civil service of a State.

   Which of the statements given above is/are correct?

   (*a*) 1 only (*b*) 2 only
   (*c*) Both 1 and 2 (*d*) Neither 1 nor 2

2. Consider the following statements:
   1. The personnel of the All-India Services serve in the Central Government, Union Territories and States.
   2. They bring a national perspective to their jobs.

   Which of the statements given above is/are correct?

   (*a*) 1 only (*b*) 2 only
   (*c*) Both 1 and 2 (*d*) Neither 1 nor 2

3. In the context of All-India Service, which one of the following finds mention in Article 312 of the Constitution of India?

   (*a*) All-India Service of Engineers
   (*b*) All-India Revenue Service
   (*c*) All-India Judicial Service
   (*d*) All-India Medical and Health Service

4. A new All-India service can be created by:

   (*a*) An amendment of the Constitution
   (*b*) An executive order
   (*c*) A resolution under Article 312 of the Constitution
   (*d*) A statute

5. The constitutional safeguards to civil servants are ensured by which of the following articles?

   (*a*) Article 310 (*b*) Article 315
   (*c*) Article 312 (*d*) Article 311

6. According to the Constitution of India, a new All India Service can be instituted with the initiative taken by:
   (*a*) more than two-thirds of the States. (*b*) the Inter-State Council.
   (*c*) the Lok Sabha. (*d*) the Rajya Sabha.

7. Which of the following services under the Government of India are termed as All-India Services?
   (*a*) IAS, IPS and Indian Foreign Service (*b*) IAS only
   (*c*) IAS and IPS only (*d*) IAS, IPS and Indian Forest Service

8. The Article in the Constitution of India that says that the Parliament may by law provide for the creation of an All India Service is which of the following?
   (*a*) Article 300 (*b*) Article 312
   (*c*) Article 320 (*d*) Article 420

9. Which of the following Amendments made a provision for the creation of All-India Judicial Service?
   (*a*) 44th Amendment (*b*) 38th Amendment
   (*c*) 57th Amendment (*d*) 42nd Amendment

10. Which one of the following is a State service?
    (*a*) Indian Statistical Service (*b*) Indian Postal Service
    (*c*) Indian Meteorological Service (*d*) Public Health Service

11. Which one of the following is a Central Service?
    (*a*) Educational Service (*b*) Agricultural Service
    (*c*) Overseas Communication Service (*d*) Cooperative Service

12. Consider the following statements:
    1. The Constitution (42nd Amendment) Act, 1976, provides the right of the government servant to make a representation against the penalty proposed to be imposed on him.
    2. The right of the Government of India to dismiss a government servant at its pleasure cannot be fettered by any contract.

    Which of the statements given above is/are correct?
    (*a*) 1 only (*b*) 2 only
    (*c*) Both 1 and 2 (*d*) Neither 1 nor 2

13. In pursuance of which Article of the Constitution of India are the conditions of service including recruitment to the Central Services regulated by a large number of rules?
    (*a*) Article 309 (*b*) Article 310
    (*c*) Article 311 (*d*) Article 312

14. In which of the following years, the classification of Central Services into Class-I, Class-II, Class-III and Class-IV was changed to Group A, Group B, Group C and Group D respectively?
    (*a*) 1972 (*b*) 1974
    (*c*) 1976 (*d*) 1978

15. The Articles in the Indian Constitution that are grouped under Services under the Union and the States are:
   (*a*) Articles 310 to 323
   (*b*) Articles 308 to 323
   (*c*) Articles 306 to 323
   (*d*) Articles 305 to 323

16. Which among the following is empowered to create more All-India Services?
   (*a*) Rajya Sabha
   (*b*) Union Parliament
   (*c*) Lok Sabha
   (*d*) Union Cabinet

17. Which one of the following Articles of the Constitution of India provides that every person who is a member of a defence service or of civil service of the Union or of All-India Services holds the office during the pleasure of the President of India?
   (*a*) Article 310
   (*b*) Article 315
   (*c*) Article 323
   (*d*) Article 323A

Answers

1. (*d*)	2. (*c*)	3. (*c*)	4. (*d*)	5. (*d*)
6. (*d*)	7. (*d*)	8. (*b*)	9. (*d*)	10. (*d*)
11. (*c*)	12. (*d*)	13. (*a*)	14. (*b*)	15. (*b*)
16. (*b*)	17. (*a*)			

67

Rights and Liabilities of the Government

1. Which one of the following was affirmed by the Supreme Court with respect to the sovereign immunity of the State?
   (*a*) Doctrine of sovereign immunity has relevance in the present day context.
   (*b*) State can succeed in pleading its immunity by showing that the tort was committed by its servants in the course of discharge of statutory functions.
   (*c*) State cannot claim sovereign immunity if its officers are negligent in exercise of their powers.
   (*d*) State can claim sovereign immunity even if its officers are negligent in exercise of their powers.

2. Article 361 of the Constitution of India guarantees the privilege to the President of India that he shall:
   (*a*) not participate in Parliamentary proceedings.
   (*b*) only be answerable to the Chief Justice of India.
   (*c*) address both the Houses of the Parliament at the time of joint session.
   (*d*) not be answerable to any court for the exercise of the powers of his office.

3. Which part of the Constitution of India deals with the rights and liabilities of the Government?
   (*a*) Part XII (*b*) Part XI
   (*c*) Part IX (*d*) Part XIII

4. Which Article of the Indian Constitution deals with the suability of the Union of India?
   (*a*) Article 100 (*b*) Article 200
   (*c*) Article 300 (*d*) Article 330

5. No criminal proceedings shall be instituted or continued against which one of the following in any court during the term of his office?
   (*a*) President, Vice-President and Governor
   (*b*) President, Prime Minister and Governor
   (*c*) President and Governor only
   (*d*) President, Vice-President and Prime Minister

Answers

1. (*c*) 2. (*d*) 3. (*a*) 4. (*c*) 5. (*c*)

68

Special Provisions Relating to Certain Classes

1. Consider the following statements:
   1. There was a special provision for the Anglo-Indian community in certain services.
   2. The Scheduled Castes and Scheduled Tribes (Prevention of Atrocities) Act was passed in 1955.
   3. The Untouchability (Offences) Act was renamed as the Protection of Civil Rights Act.

   Which of the statements given above are correct?

   (*a*) 1, 2 and 3 (*b*) 1 and 2 only
   (*c*) 2 and 3 only (*d*) 1 and 3 only

2. Which one of the following is the correct chronological order of setting up of the given Commissions concerning weaker sections of the Indian society?

   (*a*) Kaka Saheb Kalelkar Commission – National Commission for Minorities – National Commission for Scheduled Castes and Scheduled Tribes – Mandal Commission
   (*b*) National Commission for Scheduled Castes and Scheduled Tribes – National Commission for Minorities – Kaka Saheb Kalelkar Commission – Mandal Commission
   (*c*) Kaka Saheb Kalelkar Commission – Mandal Commission – National Commission for Scheduled Castes and Scheduled Tribes – National Commission for Minorities
   (*d*) National Commission for Scheduled Castes and Scheduled Tribes – Mandal Commission – Kaka Saheb Kalelkar Commission – National Commission for Minorities

3. The constitutional authority vested with the power of declaring castes or tribes as the Scheduled Castes or Scheduled Tribes is which/who of the following?

   (*a*) The Parliament (*b*) The Home Minister
   (*c*) The President of India (*d*) The Chairman, SC/ST Commission

4. Which of the following constitutional amendment acts conferred a constitutional status on the National Commission for BCs?

   (*a*) 101st Amendment (*b*) 102nd Amendment
   (*c*) 103rd Amendment (*d*) 99th Amendment

5. Which of the following constitutional amendment acts provide for making of any provision in favour of the SCs and STs for relaxation in qualifying marks in any examination or lowering the standards of evaluation for reservation in matters of promotion to the public services of the Centre and the States?

   (*a*) 74th Amendment (*b*) 82nd Amendment
   (*c*) 86th Amendment (*d*) 94th Amendment

6. What is the main object of protective discrimination in India?
   (*a*) To give special advantages to a particular group
   (*b*) To raise a disadvantaged group to a level where it can compete with other sections of society on equal footing
   (*c*) To give financial assistance to the poor
   (*d*) To promote class interest

Answers

1. (*d*) 2. (*c*) 3. (*c*) 4. (*b*) 5. (*b*)
6. (*b*)

PART-X
POLITICAL DYNAMICS

69. Political Parties
70. Role of Regional Parties
71. Elections
72. Election Laws
73. Electoral Reforms
74. Voting Behaviour
75. Coalition Government
76. Anti-Defection Law
77. Pressure Groups
78. National Integration
79. Foreign Policy

69 Political Parties

1. Which one of the following scholars described the party system prevailing in India in the early years of independence as one-party-dominant system?
(*a*) Bhikhu Parekh (*b*) Paul Brass
(*c*) Granville Austin (*d*) Rajni Kothari

2. What was the number of national parties and state parties on the eve of the first general elections (1952)?
(*a*) 12 and 36 (*b*) 14 and 39
(*c*) 8 and 32 (*d*) 16 and 28

3. On the basis of the criterion issued by the Election Commission of India, what is the minimum number of states in which a political party must be recognised to be termed as a "national party" throughout India?
(*a*) 3 states (*b*) 4 states
(*c*) 5 states (*d*) 6 states

4. Which one of the following functions pertains only to political party and not to pressure group?
(*a*) Collecting money for the organisation
(*b*) Contesting political election with own symbol
(*c*) Organising public meetings and rallies
(*d*) Publishing pamphlets and leaflets

5. Consider the following political parties of India:
1. DMK 2. CPI (*M*)
3. AGP 4. TDP
Which one of the following is the correct chronology of their formation?
(*a*) 1, 2, 4, 3 (*b*) 1, 2, 3, 4
(*c*) 2, 1, 4, 3 (*d*) 4, 3, 2,1

6. Who among the following advocated party-less democracy in India?
(*a*) Mahatma Gandhi
(*b*) M.N. Roy
(*c*) Jayaprakash Narayan
(*d*) Acharya Vinoba Bhave

7. The basic problem in the working of parliamentary system in India arises out of:
   (*a*) lack of a cohesive and viable party system.
   (*b*) the absence of an efficient and independent bureaucracy.
   (*c*) lack of clear constitutional provisions.
   (*d*) weak political executive on account of its dependence on the legislature.

8. Which one of the following statements is not correct?
   (*a*) Communist Party of India was formed in 1925.
   (*b*) Bharatiya Janata Party was formed in 1978.
   (*c*) Shiromani Akali Dal was formed in 1920.
   (*d*) AIADMK was formed in 1972.

9. In which of the following years, Bahujan Samaj Party (BSP) was formed?
   (*a*) 1984 (*b*) 1982
   (*c*) 1985 (*d*) 1980

Answers

1. (*d*)	2. (*b*)	3. (*b*)	4. (*b*)	5. (*a*)
6. (*c*)	7. (*a*)	8. (*b*)	9. (*a*)	

70 Role of Regional Parties

1. Consider the following statements:
   1. Regional parties have come to play a vital role in Indian politics at all levels i.e., local, state and national.
   2. A regional party focuses on local, regional as well as national issues.

   Which of the statements given above is/are correct?

   (*a*) 1 only (*b*) 2 only
   (*c*) Both 1 and 2 (*d*) Neither 1 nor 2

2. Which of the following are the reasons for the emergence of regional parties in India?
   1. Reorganisation of states on the basis of language
   2. Role of caste and religion in the political process
   3. Economic disparities and regional imbalances in the development
   4. Alienation and discontentment among the tribal groups
   5. Absence of a strong opposition party at the central level

   Select the correct answer using the codes given below:

   (*a*) 1, 3 and 4 (*b*) 1, 4 and 5
   (*c*) 2, 3 and 4 (*d*) 1, 2, 3, 4 and 5

3. Rashtriya Janata Dal is an example of which of the following categories of regional parties?
   (*a*) Those regional parties which have been formed by a split in national parties.
   (*b*) Those regional parties which are based on the regional culture or ethnicity.
   (*c*) Those regional parties which have been formed by individual leaders on the basis of their charismatic personality.
   (*d*) Those regional parties which have an all-India outlook but lack a national electoral base.

4. Consider the following statements:
   1. Regional parties have joined the coalition governments formed at the centre and have shared power with the national parties.
   2. Regional parties bring in regional factor in the decision-making and the policy-making by the coalition government at the centre.

   Which of the statements given above is/are correct?

   (*a*) 1 only (*b*) 2 only
   (*c*) Both 1 and 2 (*d*) Neither 1 nor 2

5. Which of the following are the features of a regional party?
   1. It is primarily concerned with exploiting the local resources of discontent.
   2. It has a political desire for greater regional autonomy of states in the Indian Union.
   3. Its electoral base is limited to a single region.

   Select the correct answer using the codes given below:

   (*a*) 1 and 2 only (*b*) 2 and 3 only
   (*c*) 1 and 3 only (*d*) 1, 2 and 3

6. Which of the following political parties belongs to the category of those regional parties which have an all-India outlook but lack a national electoral base?

   (*a*) Asom Gana Parishad (*b*) Trinamool Congress
   (*c*) Lok Janshakti Party (*d*) Samajwadi Party

7. Consider the following statements:
   1. Regional parties have increased the political consciousness of the people and also their interest in politics.
   2. Regional parties have neglected the implications and consequences of their narrow approach to the resolution of national issues.

   Which of the statements given above is/are correct?

   (*a*) 1 only (*b*) 2 only
   (*c*) Both 1 and 2 (*d*) Neither 1 nor 2

8. Which of the following is not a feature of a regional party?

   (*a*) It identifies itself with a particular cultural, religious, linguistic or ethnic group.
   (*b*) It is primarily concerned with preserving a variety of primordial demands.
   (*c*) It generally operates within a particular state or specific region.
   (*d*) It has an inclination to expand and control the central government.

9. Consider the following statements:
   1. Centralising tendencies of the congress party contributed to the rise of regional parties.
   2. Regional parties have made a significant contribution for the successful functioning of parliamentary democracy.

   Which of the statements given above is/are correct?

   (*a*) 1 only (*b*) 2 only
   (*c*) Both 1 and 2 (*d*) Neither 1 nor 2

Answers

1. (*a*)	2. (*d*)	3. (*a*)	4. (*c*)	5. (*d*)
6. (*d*)	7. (*c*)	8. (*d*)	9. (*c*)	

71

Elections

1. Consider the following statements:
   1. The party system and the elections in India are based on single member constituencies, first-past-the-post system and a bicameral legislature.
   2. The first general elections (Parliamentary Elections) were held in India in the year 1950 following the ratification of the Constitution.

   Which of the statements given above is/are correct?

   (*a*) 1 only (*b*) 2 only
   (*c*) Both 1 and 2 (*d*) Neither 1 nor 2

2. In which of the following circumstances are the courts debarred from interfering in electoral matters?
   1. Delimitation of constituencies
   2. Allotment of seats to the constituencies

   Select the correct answer using the codes given below:

   (*a*) 1 only (*b*) 2 only
   (*c*) Both 1 and 2 (*d*) Neither 1 nor 2

3. Which of the following set of Articles of the Constitution make the provisions with regard to the electoral system in India?

   (*a*) Articles 324 to 332 (*b*) Articles 324 to 329
   (*c*) Articles 324 to 328 (*d*) Articles 324 to 331

4. In which of the following years, the Model Code of Conduct was agreed to by all the political parties?

   (*a*) 1968 (*b*) 1962
   (*c*) 1978 (*d*) 1991

5. Which of the following are the true functions of the electoral process in a democracy like India?
   1. To keep the government responsive to the popular will
   2. To bring together citizens to choose public decision makers
   3. To change the government periodically if necessary
   4. To support a competitive party system

   Select the correct answer from the codes given below:

   (*a*) 1 and 2 only (*b*) 1, 2 and 3
   (*c*) 1, 3 and 4 (*d*) 2, 3 and 4

6. The "first-past-the-post" electoral system prevalent in India, refers to:
   (*a*) a system of proportional representation of weighted voting in a multi-member constituency.
   (*b*) single ballot, plural member majority voting system.
   (*c*) an electoral system in which the person winning the most votes of the votes cast in a constituency (single ballot, single member) is declared elected.
   (*d*) a system in which the winning candidate has to secure a plurality as well as majority of the votes cast.

Answers

1. (*a*)	2. (*c*)	3. (*b*)	4. (*a*)	5. (*b*)
6. (*c*)				

72

Election Laws

1. Consider the following statements:
   1. Articles 81 and 170 of the Constitution of India lay down the maximum number of seats in the Parliament and the Legislative Assemblies of States.
   2. Article 172 of the Constitution of India lays down the maximum and the minimum number of seats in the Legislative Council of a State.

   Which of the statements given above is/are correct?

   (*a*) 1 only (*b*) 2 only
   (*c*) Both 1 and 2 (*d*) Neither 1 nor 2

2. Consider the following statements:
   1. The Representation of the People Act, 1950, makes the provisions relating to the allocation of seats in the House of the People, the State Legislative Assemblies and the State Legislative Councils.
   2. The Representation of the People Act, 1951, makes the provisions relating to the manner of filling seats in the Council of States to be filled by representatives of union territories.

   Which of the statements given above is/are correct?

   (*a*) 1 only (*b*) 2 only
   (*c*) Both 1 and 2 (*d*) Neither 1 nor 2

3. Which of the following statements relating to the Delimitation Act, 2002, are correct?
   1. It was enacted to set up a Delimitation Commission for the purpose of effecting delimitation on the basis of the 2001 Census.
   2. It did not lay down any guidelines as to the manner in which such delimitation would be undertaken.
   3. Under it, the new Delimitation Commission was given the task of carrying out the delimitation of Parliamentary and Assembly constituencies.

   Select the correct answer using the codes given below:

   (*a*) 1 and 2 only (*b*) 2 and 3 only
   (*c*) 1 and 3 only (*d*) 1, 2 and 3

4. Which of the following matters are included in the conduct of elections, as per the provisions of the Representation of the People Act, 1951?
   1. Counting of votes
   2. Publication of election results
   3. Disputes regarding elections
   4. Declaration of assets and liabilities

Select the correct answer using the codes given below:

(*a*) 1, 2 and 4 (*b*) 1, 2, and 3
(*c*) 2, 3 and 4 (*d*) 1 and 2 only

5. Consider the following statements:
   1. The Parliament (Prevention of Disqualification) Act, 1959, declares that certain offices of profit under the Government shall disqualify the holders thereof for being chosen as or for being members of the Parliament.
   2. The Scheduled castes and Scheduled Tribes Orders (Amendment) Act, 1976, provides for the inclusion in, and the exclusion from, the lists of certain castes and tribes, for the readjustment of representation of parliamentary and assembly constituencies.

   Which of the statements given above is/are correct?

   (*a*) 1 only (*b*) 2 only
   (*c*) Both 1 and 2 (*d*) Neither 1 nor 2

6. Which of the following provisions are made by the Representation of the People Act, 1951?
   1. Qualifications and disqualifications for the membership of the Parliament and the State Legislatures
   2. Electoral rolls for Parliamentary, Assembly and Council constituencies
   3. Registration of political parties
   4. Corrupt practices and electoral offences

   Select the correct answer using the codes given below:

   (*a*) 1, 2 and 3 (*b*) 1, 3, and 4
   (*c*) 1, 2 and 4 (*d*) 2, 3 and 4

7. Consider the following statements:
   1. Registration of Electors Rules 1960, facilitates the conduct of fair and free elections to the Parliament and the State Legislatures.
   2. Conduct of Elections Rules, 1961, provides for the preparation and publication of electoral rolls.

   Which of the statements given above is/are correct?

   (*a*) 1 only (*b*) 2 only
   (*c*) Both 1 and 2 (*d*) Neither 1 nor 2

8. Which of the following provisions are made by the Representation of the People Act, 1950?
   1. Local authorities for the purposes of elections to the State Legislation Councils
   2. Election officers like chief electoral officers, district election officers, electoral registration officers and so on
   3. Administrative machinery for the conduct of elections
   4. Delimitation of Parliamentary, Assembly and Council Constituencies

   Select the correct answer using the codes given below:

   (*a*) 1, 2 and 3 (*b*) 2, 3 and 4
   (*c*) 1, 2 and 4 (*d*) 1, 2, 3 and 4

9. Consider the following statements:
   1. The Representation of the People Act, 1951 makes the provisions relating to the bye-elections and time limits for filling vacancies.
   2. The Representation of the People Act, 1950 makes the provision relating to the power of the Election Commission in connection with inquiries as to the disqualifications of members.

   Which of the statements given above is/are correct?

   (*a*) 1 only (*b*) 2 only
   (*c*) Both 1 and 2 (*d*) Neither 1 nor 2

Answers

1. (*a*)	2. (*a*)	3. (*c*)	4. (*a*)	5. (*b*)
6. (*b*)	7. (*d*)	8. (*c*)	9. (*a*)	

73

Electoral Reforms

1. The Representation of the People (Amendment) Act, 2003, passed by the Parliament of India sought to:
   (*a*) provide the facility to opt to vote through proxy to the service voters belonging to armed forces.
   (*b*) introduce open ballot system for elections to the Council of States.
   (*c*) insert provision regarding supply of copies of electoral rolls to candidates of recognised political parties.
   (*d*) make it mandatory for political parties to report all cases of contributions received above Rs. 20,000 to Election Commission.

2. Indrajit Gupta Committee is related to which of the following?
   (*a*) Registration of political parties
   (*b*) Criminalisation of politics
   (*c*) State funding of elections
   (*d*) Anti-defection law

3. The Electronic Voting Machines (EVMs) were used for the first time in 1999 in the general elections (entire state) to the Legislative Assembly of which of the following?
   (*a*) Goa
   (*b*) Rajasthan
   (*c*) Madhya Pradesh
   (*d*) Kerala

4. Which of the following Constitutional Amendment Acts reduced the voting age from 21 years to 18 years for the Lok Sabha as well as the assembly elections?
   (*a*) 56th Amendment
   (*b*) 59th Amendment
   (*c*) 61st Amendment
   (*d*) 63rd Amendment

5. What was the subject of the Vohra Committee?
   (*a*) Reform of the electoral laws
   (*b*) Nexus between crime and politics
   (*c*) Registration of political parties
   (*d*) Judicial interference in electoral matters

6. Which of the following are included in booth capturing?
   1. Seizure of a polling station and making polling authorities surrender ballot papers or voting machines
   2. Taking possession of polling station and allowing only one's own supporters to exercise their franchise
   3. Threatening and preventing any elector from going to polling station
   4. Seizure of the place being used for counting of votes

Select the correct answer by using the codes given below:

(*a*) 1 and 2 only (*b*) 2 and 3 only
(*c*) 1, 2, 3 and 4 (*d*) 3 and 4 only

7. Dinesh Goswami Committee on electoral reforms was appointed by which of the following?
(*a*) United Front Government
(*b*) BJP-led coalition Government
(*c*) United Progressive Alliance Government
(*d*) National Front Government

8. In which of the following years, the Tankha Committee (Core Committee) was appointed to look into the whole gamut of the election laws and electoral reforms?
(*a*) 2006 (*b*) 2010
(*c*) 2008 (*d*) 2012

Answers

1. (*b*)	2. (*c*)	3. (*a*)	4. (*c*)	5. (*b*)
6. (*c*)	7. (*d*)	8. (*b*)		

74

Voting Behaviour

1. Consider the following statements:
   1. Psephology, a branch of political science, deals with the scientific study of voting behaviour.
   2. The term "Psephology" was popularised by the British political scientists and sociologists.

   Which of the statements given above is/are correct?

   (*a*) 1 only (*b*) 2 only
   (*c*) Both 1 and 2 (*d*) Neither 1 nor 2

2. Consider the following statements:
   1. The media can sensitise the political functionaries and the electorate about the Model Code of Conduct and relevant laws governing the conduct of elections.
   2. During elections, media is present and active at all stages which means that they do not confirm to various laws governing the elections.

   Which of the statements given above is/are correct?

   (*a*) 1 only (*b*) 2 only
   (*c*) Both 1 and 2 (*d*) Neither 1 nor 2

3. Which of the following are the determinants of voting behaviour in India?
   1. Political events preceding an election
   2. Performance of the ruling party
   3. Ideology professed by a political party
   4. Economic conditions at the time of election
   5. Charismatic personality of the party leader

   Select the correct answer using the codes given below:

   (*a*) 2, 3 and 5 (*b*) 1, 2, 3 and 5
   (*c*) 1, 3 and 4 (*d*) 1, 2, 3, 4 and 5

4. Consider the following statements:
   1. The study of voting behaviour enables us to throw light as to how far electoral politics continues or breaks with the past.
   2. The study of voting behaviour helps in examining the internalisation of democracy as a value among the elite as well as the masses.

   Which of the statements given above is/are correct?

   (*a*) 1 only (*b*) 2 only
   (*c*) Both 1 and 2 (*d*) Neither 1 nor 2

5. Consider the following statements:
   1. Section 127A of the Representation of the People Act, 1951 prohibits the conduct of exit polls and dissemination of their results during the period mentioned therein.
   2. Section 171G of the Indian Penal Code prohibits incurring expenditure on advertisement without the authority of the contesting candidate.

   Which of the statements given above is/are correct?

   (*a*) 1 only (*b*) 2 only
   (*c*) Both 1 and 2 (*d*) Neither 1 nor 2

6. Which of the following are the reasons for the study of voting behaviour?
   1. It emphasises the real impact of the revolutionary ballot box.
   2. It helps to measure whether it is modern or primordial in the context of political development.
   3. It helps in comprehending the process of political socialisation.

   Select the correct answer using the codes given below:

   (*a*) 1 and 2 only (*b*) 2 and 3 only
   (*c*) 1 and 3 only (*d*) 1, 2 and 3

7. Consider the following statements:
   1. Rajni Kothari said, "Indian politics is casteist, and caste is politicised."
   2. Regionalism and sub-regionalism play an important role in voting behaviour.
   3. Personal and emotional association with political parties does not play any role in determining voting behaviour.

   Which of the statements given above are correct?

   (*a*) 1 and 2 only (*b*) 2 and 3 only
   (*c*) 1 and 3 only (*d*) 1, 2 and 3

8. Voting behaviour can be regarded as:
   1. instancing an Act of decision-making.
   2. a direct relation of the individual citizens to the formal government.
   3. a mode of legitimising the democratic rule.

   Select the correct answer using the codes given below:

   (*a*) 1 and 2 only
   (*b*) 2 and 3 only
   (*c*) 2 only
   (*d*) 1, 2 and 3

9. Consider the following statements:
   1. Money can influence the decisions of the voters not only in normal circumstances but also in a wave election.
   2. Despite India being a secular nation, no political party ignores the influence of religion in electoral politics.
   3. During elections, political parties arouse the linguistic feelings of the people and try to influence their decision-making.

Which of the statements given above are correct?

(*a*) 1 and 2 only (*b*) 2 and 3 only

(*c*) 1 and 3 only (*d*) 1, 2 and 3

10. Consider the following statements:
    1. Voting behaviour can be regarded as a role-action involving definite political orientation embedded in a particular type of political culture.
    2. Voting behaviour can be regarded as instancing participation in the political process involving integration into the political community.

    Which of the statements given above are correct?

    (*a*) 1 only (*b*) 2 only

    (*c*) Both 1 and 2 (*d*) Neither 1 nor 2

Answers

1. (*a*)	2. (*a*)	3. (*d*)	4. (*c*)	5. (*d*)
6. (*d*)	7. (*a*)	8. (*d*)	9. (*b*)	10. (*c*)

75

Coalition Government

1. Consider the following statements:
   1. The term "coalition" is derived from a Greek word.
   2. Coalition is a direct descendant of the exigencies of a multi-party system in a democratic set-up.

   Which of the statements given above is/are correct?

   (*a*) 1 only (*b*) 2 only
   (*c*) Both 1 and 2 (*d*) Neither 1 nor 2

2. Which of the following were the partners in the National Democratic Alliance (NDA) government formed at the Centre in 1999 under the leadership of A.B. Vajpayee?
   1. Trinamool Congress
   2. National Conference
   3. Shiv Sena
   4. Akali Dal
   5. DMK

   Select the correct answer using the codes given below:

   (*a*) 1, 3, 4 and 5 (*b*) 2, 3 and 4
   (*c*) 3 and 4 only (*d*) 1, 2, 3, 4 and 5

3. Consider the following statements:
   1. There is consensual decision-making in coalition governments.
   2. The members of coalition governments assume responsibility for the administrative failures.

   Which of the statements given above is/are correct?

   (*a*) 1 only (*b*) 2 only
   (*c*) Both 1 and 2 (*d*) Neither 1 nor 2

4. Which of the following are the features of coalition government or coalition politics?
   1. Pragmatism and not ideology is the hall-mark of coalition politics.
   2. The keynote of coalition politics is the compromise, and the rigid dogma has no place in it.
   3. Coalition politics is not a static but a dynamic affair as the coalition players and groups dissolve to form new ones.
   4. A coalition government works on the basis of a minimum programme which must be ideal for each partner of the coalition.

Select the correct answer using the codes given below:

(*a*) 1 and 3 only (*b*) 1, 2 and 3

(*c*) 2, 3 and 4 (*d*) 1, 2, 3 and 4

5. Consider the following statements:
   1. A coalition government acts as a channel to meet the expectations and redress the grievances of different groups.
   2. There is the possibility of smaller constituents of the coalition government playing the role of a "King-maker".
   3. A coalition government increases the tyranny of the government.

   Which of the statements given above is/are correct?

   (*a*) 1 and 2 only (*b*) 2 only

   (*c*) 3 only (*d*) 1, 2 and 3

6. Which of the following was not a partner in the United Front government formed at the Centre in 1997 and headed by I.K. Gujral?

   (*a*) DMK (*c*) TDP

   (*b*) Congress (*d*) AGP

7. Consider the following statements:
   1. The purpose of a coalition adjustment is to seize power.
   2. A coalition implies the existence of at least three partners.
   3. Coalitions are formed for the sake of some reward, material or psychic.

   Which of the statements given above is/are correct?

   (*a*) 1 and 2 only (*b*) 2 and 3 only

   (*c*) 1 and 3 only (*d*) 1, 2 and 3

8. Consider the following statements:
   1. A coalition government is more sensitive and responsive to regional demands and concerns than a single-party government.
   2. A coalition government represents a much broader spectrum of public opinion than a single-party government.

   Which of the statements given above is/are correct?

   (*a*) 1 only (*b*) 2 only

   (*c*) Both 1 and 2 (*d*) Neither 1 nor 2

Answers

1. (*b*) 2. (*d*) 3. (*a*) 4. (*b*) 5. (*a*)

6. (c) 7. (c) 8. (c)

76

Anti-Defection Law

1. Disqualification on the ground of defection for a Member of Parliament will not apply:
   (*a*) if he goes out of his party as a result of a merger of the party with another party.
   (*b*) if he has voluntarily given up his membership of the political party.
   (*c*) if he abstains from voting in the house contrary to the direction of the political party.
   (*d*) if a nominated member of a House joins a political party after six months.

2. Which one of the following Amendments to the Constitution of India sought to curb the political defection?
   (*a*) 42nd Amendment (*b*) 52nd Amendment
   (*c*) 62nd Amendment (*d*) 70th Amendment

3. Which one of the following Schedules of the Constitution of India includes the disqualification of a Legislator on grounds of defection?
   (*a*) 8th Schedule (*b*) 7th Schedule
   (*c*) 9th Schedule (*d*) 10th Schedule

4. What is the subject of the 91st Constitutional Amendment Act, 2003?
   (*a*) Right to Information
   (*b*) Limiting the size of Council of Ministers
   (*c*) Right to Education
   (*d*) Elimination of Corruption at all Levels

5. Who/Which of the following decides the question of disqualification of a member of the Parliament, arising on the ground of defection?
   (*a*) The President of India (*b*) The Supreme Court
   (*c*) The Presiding Officer of the House (*d*) The Election Commission

6. Consider the following statements:
   1. The anti-defection law is intended to strengthen the fabric of Indian Parliamentary democracy.
   2. The anti-defection law was enacted during the Prime Ministership of P.V. Narasimha Rao.

   Which of the statements given above is/are correct?
   (*a*) 1 only (*b*) 2 only
   (*c*) Both 1 and 2 (*d*) Neither 1 nor 2

7. Which of the following constitutional amendment Acts deleted the provision of the Tenth Schedule pertaining to exemption from disqualification in case of spilt by one- third members of legislative party?
(*a*) 91st Amendment (*b*) 89th Amendment
(*c*) 94th Amendment (*d*) 92nd Amendment

Answers

1. (*a*)	2. (*b*)	3. (*d*)	4. (*b*)	5. (*c*)
6. (*a*)	7. (*a*)			

77

Pressure Groups

1. Which one of the following statements is not an explanation of the general characteristics of a pressure group?
   (*a*) A major objective of a pressure group is to acquire, consolidate and extend political power.
   (*b*) A pressure group aims at projecting and fulfilling specific interests.
   (*c*) A pressure group seeks to influence decision-makers in a manner favourable to its specific interests.
   (*d*) A pressure group is generally too limited in its organisation and goals to be mistaken for a bonafide political party.

2. To which one of the following major political parties is the Centre of Indian Trade Unions (CITU) attached?
   (*a*) Indian National Congress
   (*b*) Communist Party of India (Marxist)
   (*c*) Communist Party of India
   (*d*) Bharatiya Janata Party

3. Which one of the following is the primary purpose of a pressure group?
   (*a*) To criticise the government
   (*b*) To contest the elections
   (*c*) To formulate policy
   (*d*) To bring pressure on government to influence policy decision

4. Which one of the following was the first country-wide pressure group of the organised Indian working class?
   (*a*) All India Trade Union Congress
   (*b*) Indian National Trade Union Congress
   (*c*) United Trade Union Congress
   (*d*) Hind Mazdoor Sabha

5. A pressure group is distinct from a political party in as much as it does not directly:
   (*a*) Contest elections
   (*b*) Finance a candidate
   (*c*) Propagate a policy
   (*d*) Resort to mobilisation of opinion

6. In which of the following countries, the term "pressure group" originated?
   (*a*) France
   (*b*) UK
   (*c*) USA
   (*d*) Germany

7. The Students Federation of India (SFI) is affiliated to which of the following political parties?
   (*a*) Indian National Congress
   (*b*) Bhartiya Janata Party
   (*c*) Communist Party of India
   (*d*) Communist Party of India (Marxist)

Answers

1. (*a*)	2. (*b*)	3. (*d*)	4. (*a*)	5. (*a*)
6. (*c*)	7. (*d*)			

78

National Integration

1. Consider the following statements:
   1. The National Integration Council is a recommendatory body.
   2. The National Integration Council is a constitutional body.

   Which of the statements given above is/are correct?

   (*a*) 1 only (*b*) 2 only
   (*c*) Both 1 and 2 (*d*) Neither 1 nor 2

2. Communalism in Indian context means:
   (*a*) serving the community in a befitting manner.
   (*b*) using communal identity for political gains.
   (*c*) a group of people bound by ethnic feelings.
   (*d*) creating friendly relations with the other communities.

3. In which of the following years, was the National Integration Council constituted first?
   (*a*) 1950 (*b*) 1956
   (*c*) 1961 (*d*) 1963

4. In which of the following years, the National Foundation for Communal Harmony was set up?
   (*a*) 1968 (*b*) 1992
   (*c*) 1976 (*d*) 1982

5. Who of the following is the Chairman of the National Integration Council?
   (*a*) The President of India (*b*) The Chief Justice of India
   (*c*) The Speaker of the Lok Sabha (*d*) The Prime Minister of India

6. The National Foundation for Communal Harmony is under the administrative control of:
   (*a*) Minority Affairs Ministry (*b*) Home Affairs Ministry
   (*c*) Cabinet Secretariat (*d*) Prime Minister's Office

7. Which of the following issues of the National Integration is related to the "sons of the soil theory"?
   (*a*) Regionalism (*b*) Linguism
   (*c*) Communalism (*d*) Casteism

Answers

1. (*a*) 2. (*b*) 3. (*c*) 4. (*b*) 5. (*d*)
6. (*b*) 7. (*a*)

79

Foreign Policy

1. Which of the following are the principles of the Panchsheel?
   1. Peaceful co-existence
   2. Mutual protection of the environment
   3. Mutual protection of indigenous population
   4. Mutual non-aggression

   Select the correct answer using the codes given below:

   (*a*) 2 and 3 only (*b*) 1 and 2 only
   (*c*) 1, 2 and 4 (*d*) 1 and 4 only

2. Which one of the following does not come under the concept of Non-alignment?
   (*a*) Foreign aid from all available sources
   (*b*) Non-involvement in military alliances formulated in the context of Cold War
   (*c*) Faith in isolationism
   (*d*) A demand for a better deal from the North Countries or South Countries

3. Despite being a Republican State, India is a member of the Commonwealth of Nations whose head is the British Monarch. This is because:
   (*a*) this membership does not affect the sovereign nature of the Indian Republic.
   (*b*) this membership only shows that the British ruled over India.
   (*c*) members of the association are sovereign and independent.
   (*d*) it is a symbol of the unity among the members of the association.

4. Where was the First Asian Relations Conference held?
   (*a*) Manila
   (*b*) Tokyo
   (*c*) New Delhi
   (*d*) Colombo

5. In which of the following years, was the Indo-China Treaty on Tibet signed?
   (*a*) 1950 (*b*) 1954
   (*c*) 1957 (*d*) 1962

6. Which of the following Commonwealth Summit was hosted by India?
   (*a*) 15th Summit (*b*) 18th Summit
   (*c*) 24th Summit (*d*) 27th Summit

7. Consider the following statements:
   1. India's "Act East" policy lays emphasis on improving cooperation with India's neighbouring south-east and east Asian countries.
   2. The "Act East" policy of India was initiated by the Prime Minister Atal Bihari Vajpayee.

   Which of the statements given above is/are correct?

   (*a*) 1 only (*b*) 2 only
   (*c*) Both 1 and 2 (*d*) Neither 1 nor 2

8. In which of the following years, India adopted its nuclear doctrine?

   (*a*) 2000 (*b*) 2002
   (*c*) 2003 (*d*) 2004

9. Consider the following statements:
   1. The Gujral Doctrine of India is formulated on India's accommodating approach towards its smaller neighbours on the basis of the principle of non-reciprocity.
   2. The Gujral Doctrine of India was initiated in 1994.

   Which of the statements given above is/are correct?

   (*a*) 1 only (*b*) 2 only
   (*c*) Both 1 and 2 (*d*) Neither 1 nor 2

Answers

1. (*d*) 2. (*c*) 3. (*a*) 4. (*c*) 5. (*b*)
6. (*c*) 7. (*a*) 8. (*c*) 9. (*a*)

80. National Commission to Review the Working of the Constitution

PART-XI
WORKING OF THE CONSTITUTION

80

National Commission to Review the Working of the Constitution

1. Which of the following in respect of the enlargement of Fundamental Rights were recommended by the "National Commission to Review the Working of the Constitution" constituted by the Government of India in the year 2000?
   1. Every person has a right to respect for his private and family life.
   2. Every person has a right to leave the territory of India and every citizen shall have the right to return to India.
   3. Every person who has been illegally deprived of his right to life or liberty shall have an enforceable right to compensation.

   Select the correct answer using the codes given below:

   (*a*) 1 and 2 only (*b*) 2 and 3 only
   (*c*) 1 and 3 only (*d*) 1, 2 and 3

2. Which of the following were the main areas of concern for the "National Commission to Review the Working of the Constitution" constituted by the Government of India in the year 2000?
   1. Electoral Reforms
   2. Union-State Relations
   3. Enlargement of Fundamental Rights
   4. Administrative System and Standards in Public Life

   Select the correct answer using the codes given below:

   (*a*) 1 and 2 only (*b*) 2 and 3 only
   (*c*) 1 and 3 only (*d*) 1, 2, 3 and 4

3. Who among the following was not a member of the "National Commission to Review the Working of the Constitution" constituted by the Government of India in the year 2000?

   (*a*) Soli J. Sorabjee (*b*) C.R. Irani
   (*c*) P.A. Sangma (*d*) Somnath Chatterjee

4. Which of the following were suggested by the National Commission to Review the Working of the Constitution (2002)?
   1. The Governor should be appointed only after consultation with the Chief Minister of the concerned state.
   2. A person with fair knowledge of Constitution and Indian polity should be preferred as the Governor.

3. The Governor should not be allowed to dismiss the ministry, so long as it enjoys the confidence of the Assembly.

Select the correct answer using the codes given below:

(*a*) 1, 2 and 3 (*b*) 1 and 2 only

(*c*) 2 and 3 only (*d*) 1 and 3 only

5. Who among the following was the Chairman of the "National Commission to Review the Working of the Constitution" constituted by the Government of India in the year 2000?

(*a*) A.M. Ahmadi (*b*) A.S. Anand

(*c*) M.N. Venkatachalaiah (*d*) J.S. Verma

Answers

1. (*d*) 2. (*d*) 3. (*d*) 4. (*d*) 5. (*c*)

PART-XII
APPENDICES-1

I. Articles of the Constitution (1-395)

II. Subjects of the Union, State and Concurrent Lists

III. Table of Precedence

IV. Constitutional Amendments

V. Presidents, Vice-Presidents, Prime Ministers, etc.

Appendix I

Articles of the Constitution (1-395)

1. Which of the following is/are provided by Article 249 of the Constitution of India?
   1. Residuary powers of legislation
   2. Power of the Parliament to legislate with respect to a matter in the state list in the national interest
   3. Legislation for giving effect to international agreements

   Select the correct answer using the codes given below:

   (*a*) 1 only (*b*) 1 and 2 only
   (*c*) 2 and 3 only (*d*) 2 only

2. Which one of the following pairs is correctly matched?
   (a) Reservation of seats for SCs and STs in the Lok Sabha : Article 330
   (b) Constitutional Amendment Procedure : Article 268
   (c) Public Service Commissions for the Union and States : Article 313
   (d) Special Provisions with respect to the State of Nagaland : Article 371D

3. Which of the following Articles of the Constitution of India deals with the promotion of international peace and security?
   (*a*) Article 51 (*b*) Article 39
   (*c*) Article 44 (*d*) Article 265

4. Which of the following Articles of the Constitution of India gives the right to Ministers and Attorney-General to speak in or to take part in the proceedings of either House of the Parliament?
   (*a*) Article 84 (*b*) Article 85
   (*c*) Article 87 (*d*) Article 88

5. Which of the following provisions is contained in Article 22 of the Constitution?
   (*a*) Prohibition of discrimination on the grounds of religion, race, caste, sex, place of birth
   (*b*) Prohibition of employment of children in factories
   (*c*) Protection against arrest and detention in certain cases
   (*d*) Abolition of untouchability

6. Under which Article of the Indian Constitution has the State been empowered to protect and improve the environment, forests and wildlife?
   (*a*) Article 43A (*b*) Article 48A
   (*c*) Article 44 (*d*) Article 46

7. Which one of the following is correctly matched?
   (*a*) Article 141 : Advisory jurisdiction of the Supreme Court
   (*b*) Article 136 : Power of the Supreme Court to grant special leave to appeal
   (*c*) Article 226 : Power of the superintendence of the High Court
   (*d*) Article 131 : Appellate jurisdiction of the Supreme Court

8. Which of the following Articles of the Constitution deals with the matter of Uniform Civil Code for the citizens?
   (*a*) Article 39A (*b*) Article 43
   (*c*) Article 44 (*d*) Article 50

9. Article 359 of the Constitution of India deals with which one of the following?
   (*a*) Declaration of financial emergency
   (*b*) Promulgation of President's rule in a State
   (*c*) Suspension of the enforcement of fundamental rights except a few during emergency
   (*d*) Terms and conditions of service of Members of the Union Public Service Commission

10. Which Article of the Constitution of India directs the State to make effective provision for securing the Right to work?
   (*a*) Article 16 (*b*) Article 38
   (*c*) Article 41 (*d*) Article 43

11. Which of the following Articles of the constitution deals with the subject of the functions of Public Service Commissions?
   (*a*) Article 50 (*b*) Article 143
   (*c*) Article 61 (*d*) Article 320

12. Which one of the following Articles of the Constitution of India deals with the saving of laws giving effect to certain directive principles?
   (*a*) Article 32 (*b*) Article 31A
   (*c*) Article 31B (*d*) Article 31C

13. Which one of the following pairs is not correctly matched?
   (*a*) Protection of childhood and youth from exploitation : Article 39
   (*b*) Right to work, to education and to public assistance in certain cases : Article 41
   (*c*) Provision for early childhood care and education to children below six years : Article 45
   (*d*) Protection of monuments and places and objects of national importance : Article 48A

14. Which Article of the Constitution of India has the provisions in respect of the amendment of any provision of the Constitution of India and procedure thereof?
   (*a*) Article 361 (*b*) Article 364
   (*c*) Article 366 (*d*) Article 368

15. Which of the following provisions is contained in Article 32 of the Constitution?
    (*a*) Right to Equality
    (*b*) Right to Freedom
    (*c*) Right to Freedom of Religion
    (*d*) Right to Constitutional Remedies

Answers

1. (*d*)	2. (*a*)	3. (*a*)	4. (*d*)	5. (*c*)
6. (*b*)	7. (*b*)	8. (*c*)	9. (*c*)	10. (*c*)
11. (*d*)	12. (*d*)	13. (*d*)	14. (*d*)	15. (*d*)

Appendix II

Subjects of the Union, State and Concurrent Lists

1. Which of the following are the matters covered under List-I of Seventh Schedule of the Constitution of India?
   1. Foreign loans
   2. Atomic energy
   3. Insurance
   4. Public health

   Select the correct answer using the codes given below:

   (*a*) 1, 2, 3 and 4 (*b*) 1, 2 and 3
   (*c*) 1 and 4 only (*d*) 2, 3 and 4

2. Which one of the following is not a part of the State List in the Seventh Schedule of the Constitution of India?
   (*a*) Relief of the disabled and unemployable
   (*b*) Taxes on lands and buildings
   (*c*) Prisons
   (*d*) Stock exchanges

3. Which of the following subjects is included in the concurrent list of the constitution of India?
   (*a*) Citizenship (*b*) Inter-state rivers
   (*c*) Trade unions (*d*) All-India services

4. In which List is the subject of Preventive Detention enumerated?
   (*a*) Union List
   (*b*) Both Union List and Concurrent List
   (*c*) State List
   (*d*) Concurrent List

5. Public Order is included in the Constitution as an item in which of the following?
   (*a*) Union list (*b*) State list
   (*c*) Concurrent list (*d*) Both Union and State lists

6. Which one among the following pairs is not correctly matched?
   (*a*) Union List : Banking
   (*b*) State List : Agriculture
   (*c*) Concurrent List : Marriage
   (*d*) Residuary List : Education

7. Which one of the following is mentioned in the Union List?
   (*a*) Excise duties on alcoholic liquor, opium, Indian hemp and other narcotic drugs
   (*b*) Taxes on animals and boats
   (*c*) Corporation tax
   (*d*) Professional tax

8. Which one of the following is not included in the State List in the Constitution of India?
   (*a*) Police (*b*) Law and Order
   (*c*) Prisons (*d*) Criminal Procedure Code

9. The entry "Public Health and Sanitation" is included in the Constitution of India in which of the following?
   (*a*) Union List (*b*) State List
   (*c*) Concurrent List (*d*) Both Union and State Lists

10. Which one of the following items come under the concurrent list of Indian Constitution?
    (*a*) Inter-State rivers (*b*) Trade Unions
    (*c*) Citizenship (*d*) Local Government

11. Taxation on imports and exports, and taxation on sales in the course of inter-state trade and commerce are exclusive to which of the following?
    (*a*) Union subjects
    (*b*) State subjects
    (*c*) Concurrent subjects
    (*d*) State subjects upon which Union may legislate

12. Which one of the following issues come under the Concurrent List?
    (*a*) Taxes on Professions, trades, callings and employments
    (*b*) Capitation Taxes
    (*c*) Adulteration of foodstuffs and other goods
    (*d*) Corporation Tax

Answers

1. (*b*)	2. (*d*)	3. (*c*)	4. (*b*)	5. (*b*)
6. (*d*)	7. (*c*)	8. (*d*)	9. (*b*)	10. (*b*)
11. (*a*)	12. (*c*)			

Appendix III

Table of Precedence

1. Consider the following statements:
   1. The Table of Precedence is related to the rank and order of the officials of the Union and State Governments.
   2. The order in the Table of Precedence is meant for state and ceremonial occasions and has no application in the day-to-day business of Government.

   Which of the statements given above is/are correct?

   (*a*) 1 only (*b*) 2 only
   (*c*) Both 1 and 2 (*d*) Neither 1 nor 2

2. What is the correct sequence of the following functionaries in the Order of Precedence?
   1. Judges of Supreme Court
   2. Comptroller and Auditor-General of India
   3. Governors of States within their respective states
   4. Former Prime Ministers

   Select the correct answer using the codes given below:

   (*a*) 4, 1, 3, 2 (*b*) 3, 4, 1, 2
   (*c*) 4, 3, 2, 1 (*d*) 3, 1, 2, 4

3. Who among the following ranks lowest in the Warrant of Precedence?

   (*a*) Attorney-General of India
   (*b*) Members of the NITI Aayog
   (*c*) Chairperson of the UPSC
   (*d*) Leader of Opposition in the Lok Sabha

4. In which of the following years, the present notification on the Warrant of Precedence (Order of Precedence) was issued by the government?

   (*a*) 1963 (*b*) 1976
   (*c*) 1979 (*d*) 1967

5. Who of the following is placed at the fifth position in the Order of Precedence?

   (*a*) Chief Justice of India
   (*b*) Deputy Prime Minister
   (*c*) Speaker of the Lok Sabha
   (*d*) Former Presidents

6. Who of the following is not placed at the same rank in the Table of Precedence?
   (*a*) Leader of Opposition in the Rajya Sabha
   (*b*) Cabinet Minister of the Union
   (*c*) Vice-Chairperson of NITI Aayog
   (*d*) Chief Election Commissioner

7. Consider the following officials:
   1. Cabinet Secretary
   2. Deputy Chairman of the Rajya Sabha
   3. Members of Parliament
   4. Chairperson of National Commission for SCs

   What is the correct sequence of the above officials in the Table of Precedence? Select the correct answer using the codes given below:

   (*a*) 2, 4, 3, 1 (*b*) 1, 4, 2, 3
   (*c*) 2, 1, 4, 3 (*d*) 1, 2, 4, 3

Answers

1. (*c*)	2. (*b*)	3. (*a*)	4. (*c*)	5. (*d*)
6. (*d*)	7. (*c*)			

Appendix IV Constitutional Amendments

1. The first Amendment to the Constitution (1951) made changes in relation to which of the following provisions?
   1. Special provisions for advancement of socially and educationally backward classes
   2. Validation of certain Acts and Regulations specified in the Ninth Schedule
   3. Saving of certain laws giving effect to certain Directive Principles
   4. Saving of laws providing for acquisition of estates

   Select the correct answer using the codes given below:
   (*a*) 1, 2 and 3 (*b*) 1, 2 and 4
   (*c*) 2, 3 and 4 (*d*) 1, 3 and 4

2. Which of the following Constitutional Amendment Acts curtailed the fundamental rights to property?
   (*a*) 19th Amendment (*b*) 25th Amendment
   (*c*) 31st Amendment (*d*) 45th Amendment

3. What does the Constitution (Ninety-second Amendment) Act, 2003, deal with?
   (*a*) Creation of a separate National Commission for Scheduled Tribes
   (*b*) Cyber crimes
   (*c*) Inclusion of Bodo, Dogri, Maithili and Santhali languages in the Eighth Schedule
   (*d*) Making right to free and compulsory education a Fundamental Right

4. Which of the following Constitutional Amendment Acts is related to the extension of the reservation of seats for the SCs and STs in the Lok Sabha and the Legislative Assemblies?
   (*a*) 42nd Amendment Act, 1976
   (*b*) 52nd Amendment Act, 1985
   (*c*) 62nd Amendment Act, 1989
   (*d*) 21st Amendment Act, 1966

5. 86th Amendment to the Constitution of India has:
   (*a*) made free and compulsory primary education a fundamental right.
   (*b*) incorporated provision of right to inheritance in the Directive Principles of State Policy.
   (*c*) enhanced the scope of reservation for backward communities in educational institutions.
   (*d*) brought minority educational institutions under strict control of the Central Government.

6. Which of the following pairs are correctly matched?

1.	24th Amendment	:	Asserted the right of the Parliament to amend any part of the Constitution including Part III.
2.	39th Amendment	:	Election of President, Vice-President, Prime Minister and Speaker is beyond the purview of the Judiciary.
3.	42nd Amendment	:	Political defections made illegal and reservations for SC/ST extended for another 10 years.
4.	70th Amendment	:	Granting of statehood to the Union Territory of Delhi.

Select the correct answer using the codes given below:

(*a*) 1 and 4 only (*b*) 1 and 2 only
(*c*) 2 and 3 only (*d*) 3 and 4 only

7. The Constitution (93rd Amendment) Act deals with:
(*a*) local self-government.
(*b*) extension of reservation in educational institutions.
(*c*) basic structure of the Constitution of India.
(*d*) appointment of judges in the Supreme Court of India.

8. Which of the following Constitutional Amendment Acts provided for reservations in promotions in government jobs for SCs and STs?
(*a*) 37th Amendment (*b*) 49th Amendment
(*c*) 58th Amendment (*d*) 77th Amendment

9. Part IVA was added to the Constitution of India by which of the following?
(*a*) Twenty-fifth Amendment Act (*b*) Forty-second Amendment Act
(*c*) Forty-fourth Amendment Act (*d*) Fifty-second Amendment Act

10. Select the correct sequence of the following constitutional amendments:
1. Voting age reduced from 21 years to 18 years
2. Right to property deleted from the list of Fundamental Rights
3. Sikkim became a State of the Indian Union
4. Hindi version of the Constitution was accepted officially

Select the correct answer using the codes given below:
(*a*) 3, 1, 4, 2 (*b*) 4, 2, 3, 1
(*c*) 3, 2, 4, 1 (*d*) 4, 1, 3, 2

11. Which of the following Constitutional Amendment Acts made special provisions in respect of Mizoram?
(*a*) 53rd Amendment (*b*) 61st Amendment
(*c*) 74th Amendment (*d*) 79th Amendment

Answers

1. (*b*)	2. (*b*)	3. (*c*)	4. (*c*)	5. (*a*)
6. (*b*)	7. (*b*)	8. (*d*)	9. (*b*)	10. (*c*)
11. (*a*)				

Appendix V

Presidents, Vice-Presidents, Prime Ministers, etc.

1. Consider the following Vice-Presidents of India:

   1. V.V. Giri
   2. M. Hidayatullah
   3. B.D. Jatti
   4. G.S. Pathak

   Which one of the following is the correct chronology of their tenures?

   (*a*) 1, 4, 3, 2 (*b*) 2, 1, 3, 4

   (*c*) 3, 2, 1, 4 (*d*) 4, 1, 3, 2

2. Who among the following was never a Deputy Prime Minister of India?

   (*a*) Devi Lal (*b*) G.L. Nanda

   (*c*) L.K. Advani (*d*) Y.B. Chavan

3. Who among the following had the longest tenure as the Prime Minister of India?

   (*a*) Morarji Desai (*b*) Charan Singh

   (*c*) V.P. Singh (*d*) Lal Bahadur Shastri

4. Who has been the only Lok Sabha Speaker to have become the President of India?

   (*a*) Giani Zail Singh

   (*b*) V.V. Giri

   (*c*) Neelam Sanjiva Reddy

   (*d*) K.R. Narayanan

5. Who among the following was the first Speaker of the Lok Sabha?

   (*a*) M.A. Ayyangar (*b*) G.V. Mavalankar

   (*c*) Sardar Hukam Singh (*d*) N. Sanjiva Reddy

6. Who among the following was the fourth President of India?

   (*a*) Zakir Hussain (*b*) Zail Singh

   (*c*) V.V. Giri (*d*) Neelam Sanjiva Reddy

7. Who of the following has not been a Chief Justice of India?

   (*a*) R.C. Lahoti (*b*) G.B. Pattanaik

   (*c*) M.S. Gill (*d*) V.N. Khare

8. Consider the following statements:

   1. A.K. Chanda was the first Comptroller and Auditor-General of India.
   2. K.V.K. Sundaram was the first Chief Election Commissioner of India.

Which of the statements given above is/are correct?

(*a*) 1 only (*b*) 2 only
(*c*) Both 1 and 2 (*d*) Neither 1 nor 2

9. Consider the following statements:
   1. M.C. Setalvad was the first Attorney-General of India.
   2. Sir Ross Barker was the first Chairman of the UPSC.

   Which of the statements given above is/are correct?

   (*a*) 1 only (*b*) 2 only
   (*c*) Both 1 and 2 (*d*) Neither 1 nor 2

Answers

1. (*a*)	2. (*b*)	3. (*a*)	4. (*c*)	5. (*b*)
6. (*c*)	7. (*c*)	8. (*d*)	9. (*c*)	

PART-XIII
APPENDICES-2

VI. Oath by the Constitutional and other Authorities

VII. Definitions Under the Constitution

VIII. Allied Amending Acts

IX. Model Code of Conduct Relating to Elections

X. Flag Code of India

Appendix VI Oath by the Constitutional and other Authorities

1. Consider the following statements:
   1. Every member of either House of the Parliament shall, before taking his seat, make and subscribe before the Speaker, an oath or affirmation.
   2. Every person appointed to be the Comptroller and Auditor-General of India shall, before he enters upon his office, make and subscribe before the President an oath or affirmation.

   Which of the statements given above is/are correct?

   (*a*) 1 only (*b*) 2 only
   (*c*) Both 1 and 2 (*d*) Neither 1 nor 2

2. Which of the following are contained in the form of oath of the President of India?
   1. To faithfully execute the office
   2. To preserve, protect and defend the Constitution and the law
   3. To devote himself to the service and well-being of the people of India
   4. To uphold the sovereignty and integrity of India

   Select the correct answer using the codes given below:

   (*a*) 2, 3 and 4 (*b*) 1, 2 and 3
   (*c*) 1, 2 and 4 (*d*) 1, 2, 3 and 4

3. In the absence of the Chief Justice of the State High Court, who among the following administers the oath of office to the Governor of a State?

   (*a*) The Speaker of the State Legislative Assembly
   (*b*) The Law Minister of the State
   (*c*) The senior most Judge of the State High Court available
   (*d*) The Chief Justice of India

4. Who of the following administers the oath of office to the State Chief Information Commissioner?

   (*a*) The President of India
   (*b*) The Chief Justice of India
   (*c*) The Governor of the State
   (*d*) The Chief Justice of the State High Court

5. Which one of the following is not a part of the form of oath or affirmation for the judges of High Courts?
   (*a*) To bear true faith and allegiance to the Constitution of India
   (*b*) To uphold the sovereignty and integrity of India
   (*c*) To uphold the Constitution and the laws
   (*d*) To devote himself to the service and well-being of the people of the state

Answers

1. (*b*) 2. (*b*) 3. (*c*) 4. (*c*) 5. (*d*)

Appendix VII

Definitions Under the Constitution

1. With reference to the definitions under the Constitution, consider the following statements:
    1. Indian state means any territory which the Government of the Dominion of India recognised as such a state.
    2. Union territory means any union territory specified in the First Schedule and does not include any other territory comprised within the territory of India but not specified in that Schedule.

    Which of the statements given above is/are correct?

    (*a*) 1 only
    (*b*) 2 only
    (*c*) Both 1 and 2
    (*d*) Neither 1 nor 2

2. Which of the following Amendment Acts is related to the definition of "Ruler"?

    (*a*) 26th Amendment Act
    (*b*) 16th Amendment Act
    (*c*) 19th Amendment Act
    (*d*) 24th Amendment Act

3. Which of the following Articles of the Constitution of India contains the definitions of various terms used in different provisions of the Constitution?

    (*a*) Article 363
    (*b*) Article 369
    (*c*) Article 366
    (*d*) Article 362

4. In the context of the definitions under the Constitution, the "Federal Court" means the Federal Court constituted under the:

    (*a*) Government of India Act, 1919
    (*b*) Government of India Act, 1935
    (*c*) Indian Independence Act, 1947
    (*d*) Constitution of India, 1950

5. Article 342 of the Constitution deals with the definition of which of the following?

    (*a*) Scheduled Castes
    (*b*) Scheduled Tribes
    (*c*) Backward Classes
    (*d*) Minorities

6. With reference to the definitions under the Constitution, consider the following statements:
    1. Proclamation of emergency means a proclamation issued under Article 356.
    2. Railway does not include any other line of communication wholly situated in one state and declared by the State Legislature by law not to be a railway.

Which of the statements given above is/are correct?

(*a*) 1 only (*b*) 2 only

(*c*) Both 1 and 2 (*d*) Neither 1 nor 2

Answers

1. (*a*) 2. (*a*) 3. (*c*) 4. (*b*) 5. (*b*)

6. (*d*)

Appendix VIII

Allied Amending Acts

1. Consider the following statements:
   1. The Sixth Schedule to the Constitution (Amendment) Act, 1988 included certain modifications in the Sixth Schedule of the Constitution in its application to the State of Assam.
   2. The Sixth Schedule to the Constitution (Amendment) Act, 1995 included certain modifications in the Sixth Schedule of the Constitution in its application to the states of Tripura and Mizoram.

   Which of the statements given above is/are correct?
   (*a*) 1 only (*b*) 2 only
   (*c*) Both 1 and 2 (*d*) Neither 1 nor 2

2. Where was the high court of Andhra State, formed in 1953, located?
   (*a*) Guntur (*b*) Tirupathi
   (*c*) Kurnool (*d*) Nellore

3. The Chandernagore (Merger) Act, 1954 merged the territory of Chandernagore (a former enclave of French India) into the state of:
   (*a*) Odisha (*b*) Andhra Pradesh
   (*c*) Tamil Nadu (*d*) West Bengal

4. The Assam (Alteration of Boundaries) Act, 1951 altered the boundaries of the State of Assam by ceding a strip of territory comprised in that state to which of the following countries?
   (*a*) Pakistan (*b*) Nepal
   (*c*) Bhutan (*d*) Myanmar

5. Which of the following statements with respect to the Sixth Schedule to the Constitution (Amendment) Act, 2003 are correct?
   1. It specified the Bodoland Territorial Areas District in the list of the tribal areas of the State of Assam.
   2. It created an autonomous self-governing body known as the Bodoland Territorial Council (BTC) within the state of Assam.
   3. It provided for adequate safeguards for the non-tribals in the BTC area.

   Select the correct answer using the codes given below:
   (*a*) 1 and 2 only (*b*) 2 and 3 only
   (*c*) 1 and 3 only (*d*) 1, 2 and 3

6. Consider the following statements:
   1. The Fifth Schedule to the Constitution (Amendment) Act, 1976 empowered the President of India to increase the area of any Scheduled Area in a state after consultation with the Governor of that state.
   2. The Fifth Schedule to the Constitution (Amendment) Act, 1976 empowered the President of India to rescind any order made for the designation of an area in any state to be a Scheduled Area, or in consultation with the Governor of the state concerned, make fresh order redefining the area which is to be a Scheduled Area.

   Which of the statements given above is/are correct?

   (*a*) 1 only (*b*) 2 only
   (*c*) Both 1 and 2 (*d*) Neither 1 nor 2

Answers

1. (*d*) 2. (*a*) 3. (*d*) 4. (*c*) 5. (*d*)
6. (*c*)

Appendix IX

Model Code of Conduct Relating to Elections

1. Consider the following statements:

   According to the Model Code of Conduct Relating to Elections, all political parties and candidates shall:

   1. refrain from serving or distributing liquor on polling day and during the twenty-eight hours preceding it.
   2. supply to their authorised workers suitable badges or identity cards.

   Which of the statements given above is/are correct?

   (*a*) 1 only (*b*) 2 only
   (*c*) Both 1 and 2 (*d*) Neither 1 nor 2

2. In which of the following years, the Election Commission first effectively put to use the Model Code of Conduct (MCC) to ensure fair elections and a level playing field?

   (*a*) 1991 (*b*) 1968
   (*c*) 1977 (*d*) 1990

3. Consider the following statements with respect to the Model Code of Conduct Relating to Elections:

   1. Ministers shall not sanction grants/payments out of discretionary funds from the time elections are announced by the Election Commission.
   2. Ministers shall not enter any polling station or place of counting except in their capacity as a candidate or voter or authorised agent.

   Which of the statements given above is/are correct?

   (*a*) 1 only (*b*) 2 only
   (*c*) Both 1 and 2 (*d*) Neither 1 nor 2

4. Which of the following formulates the "Model Code of Conduct for the Guidance of Political Parties and Candidates"?

   (*a*) Parliament (*b*) Law Ministry
   (*c*) Supreme Court (*d*) Election Commission

5. Consider the following statements with respect to the Model Code of Conduct Relating to Elections:

   1. The Ministers shall not combine their official visit with electioneering work.
   2. The Ministers shall not make use of official machinery or personnel during the electioneering work.

Which of the statements given above is/are correct?

(*a*) 1 only (*b*) 2 only

(*c*) Both 1 and 2 (*d*) Neither 1 nor 2

Answers

1. (*a*) 2. (*a*) 3. (*c*) 4. (*d*) 5. (*c*)

Appendix X

Flag Code of India

1. Consider the following statements:

    1. The Flag Code of India, 2002, took effect from January 26, 2002 and superseded the "Flag Code-India" as it existed earlier.
    2. For the sake of convenience, the Flag Code of India, 2002, has been divided into four parts.

    Which of the statements given above is/are correct?

    (*a*) 1 only (*b*) 2 only
    (*c*) Both 1 and 2 (*d*) Neither 1 nor 2

2. Who of the following dignitaries may fly the national flag on their cars, whenever they consider it necessary or advisable?

    1. Deputy Minister of a State
    2. Chairman of a State Legislative Council
    3. Union Cabinet Minister
    4. Head of Indian Mission

    Select the correct answer using the codes given below:

    (*a*) 2 and 3 only (*b*) 1 and 4 only
    (*c*) 1, 2 and 3 (*d*) 2, 3 and 4

3. Consider the following statements:

    1. The National Flag shall be rectangular in shape.
    2. The ratio of the length to the height (*width*) of the flag shall be 4:3.

    Which of the statements given above is/are correct?

    (*a*) 1 only (*b*) 2 only
    (*c*) Both 1 and 2 (*d*) Neither 1 nor 2

4. The privilege of flying the national flag on motor cars is limited to which of the following?

    1. President
    2. Vice-President
    3. Governors
    4. Lieutenant Governors

    Select the correct answer using the codes given below:

    (*a*) 1 and 2 only (*b*) 1, 2 and 3
    (*c*) 1, 2, 3 and 4 (*d*) 1 and 3 only

5. In the event of the death of which of the following dignitary, the national flag shall be half-masted at Delhi and State Capitals?
   (*a*) Union Cabinet Minister
   (*b*) Chief Justice of India
   (*c*) Vice-President
   (*d*) Governor

Answers

1. (*a*)	2. (*c*)	3. (*a*)	4. (*c*)	5. (*a*)

PART-XIV MODEL TEST PAPERS

Model Test Paper – 1

Model Test Paper – 2

Model Test Paper – 3

Model Test Paper – 4

Model Test Paper – 5

Model Test Paper – 6

Model Test Paper – 7

Model Test Paper – 8

Model Test Paper – 9

Model Test Paper – 10

Model Test Paper – I

1. Consider the following statements:

   Article 20 of the Constitution of India provides that:

   1. no person shall be prosecuted and punished for the same offence more than once.
   2. no person accused of any offence shall be compelled to be a witness against himself.

   Which of the statements given above is/are correct?

   (*a*) 1 only (*b*) 2 only

   (*c*) Both 1 and 2 (*d*) Neither 1 nor 2

2. Consider the following statements about elections:

   1. The Constitution provides that elections to the House of the People and the Legislative Assemblies of States are to be held on the basis of universal adult suffrage.
   2. The Constitution stipulates that there will be separate electoral rolls for Parliamentary and State Assembly elections.

   Which of the statements given above is/are correct?

   (*a*) 1 only (*b*) 2 only

   (*c*) Both 1 and 2 (*d*) Neither 1 nor 2

3. Consider the following statements:

   1. Zonal Councils have been established under an Article of the Constitution of India.
   2. There is a provision under an Article of the Constitution of India that the President can establish an Inter-State Council.
   3. The Union Home Minister has been nominated to be the common Chairman of all the Zonal Councils.

   Which of the statements given above are correct?

   (*a*) 1, 2 and 3 (*b*) 1 and 2 only

   (*c*) 2 and 3 only (*d*) 1 and 3 only

4. The Parliament does not have exclusive power to make any law with respect to which one of the following subjects?

   (*a*) Shipping and navigation (*b*) Stock exchanges

   (*c*) Trade and commerce in foodstuffs (*d*) Insurance

5. Which of the following statements is/are correct in relation to the legislative procedure regarding bills in the Parliament?

   1. A bill pending in the Parliament shall not lapse by reason of prorogation of the Houses.

2. A bill pending in the Council of States, which has not been passed by the House of the People, shall not lapse on dissolution of the House of the People.
3. A bill which is pending in the House of the People, or which having been passed by the House of the People is pending in the Council of States, shall, subject to the provisions of Article 108 (joint sitting of both Houses), lapse on dissolution of the House of the People.

Select the correct answer using the codes given below:

(*a*) 1 and 2 only (*b*) 1 only
(*c*) 2 and 3 only (*d*) 1, 2 and 3

6. Which one among the following is the distinguishing factor between a pressure group and a political party?
(*a*) Pressure groups are confined to a few, while political parties involve larger number of people.
(*b*) Pressure groups do not seek active political power, while political parties do.
(*c*) Pressure groups do not politically motivate people, while political parties do.
(*d*) Political parties take political stance, while pressure groups do not bother about political issues.

7. Which one of the following propositions is a correct description of the powers of the President of India under Article 356 of the Constitution?
(*a*) If the Chief Minister inspite of commanding the confidence of the Legislative Assembly, cannot run his government in accordance with the Constitution, the President can proclaim emergency.
(*b*) If the law and order in a state completely breaks down, the President can proclaim emergency.
(*c*) The President can refer the matter to the Supreme Court for advice and act in accordance with such advice.
(*d*) The President cannot make a proclamation of emergency if the governor refuses to make a report.

8. Consider the following statements:

A municipal corporation's income (revenue) is derived from:
1. Local taxes
2. Grants from State Government
3. Income from remunerative enterprises
4. Tax sharing between State Government and the Municipal Corporation concerned

Which of the statements given above are correct?

(*a*) 1, 2 and 4 (*b*) 1, 2 and 3
(*c*) 2, 3 and 4 (*d*) 1, 2, 3 and 4

9. According to the Constitution of India, a New All-India Service can be created if:
(*a*) The Parliament of India enacts a law by a special majority prescribed under Article 312 of the Constitution.
(*b*) The Rajya Sabha passes a resolution by a two-thirds majority of its members present and voting and an absolute majority of the whole House.

(*c*) The President of India so desires and issues a proclamation to that effect.
(*d*) The State Governments initiate such a proposal.

10. Which of the following writs is issued to quash the order of the tribunal?
(*a*) Mandamus
(*b*) Prohibition
(*c*) Certiorari
(*d*) Quo-Warranto

11. Consider the following statements:
1. The First Finance Commission was constituted in 1950.
2. The Finance Commission recommends the principles which should govern the grants-in-aid of the revenues of the States out of the Consolidated Fund of India.
3. The Finance Commission recommends the distribution between the Union and the States of the net proceeds of taxes which are to be divided between them.

Which of the statements given above are correct?
(*a*) 1, 2 and 3 (*b*) 1 and 2 only
(*c*) 2 and 3 only (*d*) 1 and 3 only

12. Provisions of the Constitution relating to the formation of new States can be amended by:
(*a*) two-thirds majority of the members present and voting in each House of the Parliament provided they also constitute majority of the total membership in each house.
(*b*) a Parliamentary resolution which should be ratified by a majority of State legislatures.
(*c*) a simple majority in each House of the Parliament.
(*d*) a three-fourth majority in each House of the Parliament.

13. Consider the following statements:
1. The Chief Information Commissioner is appointed by the President on the recommendation of a committee of which the Leader of Opposition in the Lok Sabha is one of the members.
2. The Headquarters of the Central Information Commission is at Bengaluru.

Which of the statements given above is/are correct?
(*a*) 1 only (*b*) 2 only
(*c*) Both 1 and 2 (*d*) Neither 1 nor 2

14. Which one of the following Prime Ministers did not head a minority government?
(*a*) I.K. Gujaral (*b*) V.P. Singh
(*c*) Chandrashekhar (*d*) Morarji Desai

15. Which of the following are the advantages of the 73rd amendment to the Constitution of India?
1. Constitutional protection to panchayats
2. Holding of panchayat elections at regular intervals
3. Reservation of seats for SCs and STs
4. Reservation of seats for Backward Classes

Select the correct answer from the codes given below:

(*a*) 1, 2 and 4
(*b*) 1, 3 and 4
(*c*) 2, 3 and 4
(*d*) 1, 2 and 3

16. Which Article of the Constitution empowers the Parliament to legislate on a matter of the State List in the national interest?

(*a*) Article 115
(*b*) Article 183
(*c*) Article 221
(*d*) Article 249

17. Which of the following pairs is correctly matched?

(*a*) Amendment procedure – Article 268
(*b*) Duties of the Prime Minister – Article 74
(*c*) President's rule – Article 365
(*d*) Inter-state Council – Article 264

18. Consider the following statements associated with Fundamental Duties in Part IVA of the Constitution.

It shall be the duty of every citizen of India:

1. to owe allegiance to the nation and to uphold and protect the sovereignty and security of India.
2. to uphold and protect the sovereignty, unity and integrity of India.
3. to defend the country and render national service when called upon to do so.

Which of the statements given above are correct?

(*a*) 1, 2 and 3
(*b*) 2 and 3 only
(*c*) 1 and 2 only
(*d*) 1 and 3 only

19. The creation of the office of the Lokpal was first recommended by the:

(*a*) National Police Commission
(*b*) States Reorganisation Commission
(*c*) First Administrative Reforms Commission of India
(*d*) Inter-State Council

20. Consider the following statements about the Attorney-General of India:

1. He is appointed by the President of India.
2. He has the right to take part in the proceedings of the Parliament.
3. He has the right of audience in all courts in India.

Which of the statements given above are correct?

(*a*) 1 and 2 only
(*b*) 1 and 3 only
(*c*) 2 and 3 only
(*d*) 1, 2 and 3

21. Which one of the following pairs is not correctly matched?

(a) Equality before law : Guaranteed to both citizens and non-citizens
(b) Altering the name of a state : Power of a state legislature

(c) Creating a new state : Power of the Parliament
(d) Equality of opportunity : Guaranteed only to Indian citizens

22. Which of the following statements regarding the advisory jurisdiction of the Supreme Court are correct?
    1. The opinion of the Supreme Court may be sought by the President on any question of law or fact.
    2. In case the opinion of the Supreme Court is sought, it is bound to give it.
    3. The advice given by the Supreme Court on a matter referred to it is binding on the President since the 42nd amendment.
    4. Advisory jurisdiction of the Supreme Court can also be exercised over disputes arising out of references made over pre-constitutional treaties.

    Select the correct answer from the codes given below:

    (*a*) 1 and 3 only (*b*) 2 and 3 only
    (*c*) 1 and 4 only (*d*) 1, 2, 3 and 4

23. Which of the following political events took place in 1990?
    (*a*) Formation of the Bharatiya Janata Party
    (*b*) Acceptance of the Mandal Commission Report
    (*c*) Formation of the First Communist Government in an Indian State
    (*d*) Passing of the 42nd Amendment Act

24. According to the Anti-Defection Law, a legislator attracts disqualification under the Tenth Schedule if:
    1. he voluntarily gives up the membership of the party on whose ticket he was elected.
    2. he votes or abstains from voting contrary to any direction issued by his political party.
    3. a nominated member joins any political party after six months.
    4. a member who has been elected as an independent member joins any political party.

    Select the correct answer using the codes given below:

    (*a*) 2 and 3 only (*b*) 1, 2 and 4
    (*c*) 1 and 3 only (*d*) 1, 2, 3 and 4

25. What is the procedure required to be followed for the abolition of an existing Legislative Council in a State?
    1. The Rajya Sabha must pass a resolution to that effect.
    2. The State Legislative Assembly must pass a resolution to that effect by a special majority as prescribed in the Constitution.
    3. Parliament must enact a law abolishing the Legislative Council.
    4. The State Legislative Assembly must pass a resolution with an ordinary majority as in the case of a bill.

Select the correct answer using the codes given below:

(a) 2 and 3 only (b) 1 and 2 only

(c) 1 and 4 only (d) 3 and 4 only

Answers

1. (c)	2. (a)	3. (c)	4. (c)	5. (d)
6. (b)	7. (a)	8. (d)	9. (a)	10. (c)
11. (c)	12. (c)	13. (a)	14. (d)	15. (d)
16. (d)	17. (c)	18. (b)	19. (c)	20. (d)
21. (b)	22. (c)	23. (b)	24. (d)	25. (a)

Model Test Paper – 2

1. Which of the following statements is/are correct in respect of the Constitution of India?
   1. The Constitution received signature of the President of the Constituent Assembly on 26 November, 1949.
   2. The provisions relating to citizenship were given immediate effect from 26 November, 1949.

   Select the correct answer using the codes given below:

   (*a*) 1 only (*b*) 2 only
   (*c*) Both 1 and 2 (*d*) Neither 1 nor 2

2. Consider the following political events:
   1. Inclusion of Ninth Schedule in the Constitution
   2. Passing of Anti-defection Bill
   3. First non-Congress government at the Centre
   4. Reorganisation of the State of Punjab

   The correct chronological sequence of these political events is:

   (*a*) 1, 2, 3, 4 (*b*) 4, 3, 2, 1
   (*c*) 1, 4, 3, 2 (*d*) 2, 3, 1, 4

3. Once the proclamation of emergency is made, the right of a citizen to move the Supreme Court for enforcement of his fundamental rights is suspended by the:

   (*a*) Prime Minister of India
   (*b*) President of India
   (*c*) Speaker of the Lok Sabha
   (*d*) Chief Justice of India

4. Consider the following statements:
   1. The Committee on Public Accounts examines the report of the Comptroller and Auditor-General of India before it is presented before each House of the Parliament.
   2. The President of India causes the reports of the Comptroller and Auditor-General of India to be laid before each House of the Parliament.
   3. After the Annual Financial Statement is presented before the Lok Sabha, the Committee on Public Accounts examines the estimates.

   Which of the statements given above is/are correct?

   (*a*) 1, 2 and 3 (*b*) 1 and 3 only
   (*c*) 1 only (*d*) 2 only

5. Which of the following Committee/Commission was related to the backward classes?
   (*a*) Rajamannar Committee
   (*b*) Fazl Ali Commission
   (*c*) Kaka Kalelkar Commission
   (*d*) Santhanam Committee

6. According to Article 78 of the Constitution of India, the Prime Minister has to furnish information to the President in respect of:
   1. all decisions of Council of Ministers relating to administration of the affairs of the Union.
   2. submitting for consideration of Council of Ministers any matter on which a decision has been taken by a Minister, but not considered earlier by the Council of Ministers.
   3. submitting proposals for legislation as the President may call for.
   4. international treaties.

   Select the correct answer using the codes given below:
   (*a*) 1, 2 and 4 (*b*) 1 and 4 only
   (*c*) 2 and 3 only (*d*) 1, 2 and 3

7. Which one among the following items was not added to the Concurrent List of the Constitution of India under the provisions of the 42nd Amendment Act, 1976?
   (*a*) Family Planning (*b*) Forests
   (*c*) Education (*d*) Railways

8. In which among the following cases, can the joint session of both the Houses of Parliament be summoned?
   1. To amend the Constitution.
   2. When a Bill has been pending with one House for more than six months after it was passed by the other.
   3. When both the Houses disagree on the amendments to be made in a Bill.
   4. When a bill is passed by one House and is rejected by the other.

   Select the correct answer using the codes given below:
   (*a*) 1, 2 and 3 (*b*) 2, 3 and 4
   (*c*) 2 and 3 only (*d*) 1 and 4 only

9. Consider the following statements:
   1. There is no provision in the Constitution of India to provide for immunity of the Union property from State taxation, and property and income of a State from Union taxation.
   2. There is a provision in the Constitution of India which empowers the President of India to establish an Inter-State Council for coordination between States.

   Which of the statements given above is/are correct?
   (*a*) 1 only (*b*) 2 only
   (*c*) Both 1 and 2 (*d*) Neither 1 nor 2

10. Which of the following statements regarding the exercise of judicial review is not correct?
    (*a*) A case must be brought before the Supreme Court regarding the validity of a law.
    (*b*) Unanimous opinion of all the judges is necessary for declaring a law null and void.

(*c*) Legislative enactments and executive orders may be struck down by the Supreme Court.
(*d*) The power is implicit in the provision of Article 13 of the Constitution.

11. Which one of the following is not a function of a State Finance Commission?
(*a*) Determination of taxes, duties and tolls which may be assigned to Panchayats
(*b*) Grants-in-aid to Panchayats from Consolidated Fund of the Union Government
(*c*) Measures to improve financial position of Panchayats
(*d*) Distribution of the net proceeds of fees leviable by the State between the State and Panchayats

12. The Montague's Declaration of 20th August, 1917, contained:
1. Increasing association of Indians in every branch of administration
2. Gradual development of self-government institutions
3. Realisation of responsible government independent of the British Empire
4. Progress in this policy to be achieved in successive stages

Select the correct answer using the codes given below:
(*a*) 1, 2 and 3 (*b*) 2 and 4 only
(*c*) 1, 2 and 4 (*d*) 1, 2, 3 and 4

13. Article 15 of the Constitution of India empowers the State to make special provisions for:
(*a*) reservation in employment for freedom fighters.
(*b*) women and children.
(*c*) reservation in employment for physically handicapped persons.
(*d*) relaxation of minimum qualifying marks for admission to those belonging to SC and ST categories.

14. Which of the following Schedules of the Constitution contains the forms of oaths and affirmations?
(*a*) Third Schedule
(*b*) Seventh Schedule
(*c*) Ninth Schedule
(*d*) Twelfth Schedule

15. Consider the following statements:
1. Salary and allowances of the Speaker of the Lok Sabha are charged on the Consolidated Fund of India.
2. In the Warrant of Precedence, the Speaker of Lok Sabha ranks higher than all the Union Cabinet Ministers other than the Prime Minister.

Which of the statements given above is/are correct?
(*a*) 1 only (*b*) 2 only
(*c*) Both 1 and 2 (*d*) Neither 1 nor 2

16. Consider the following statements:
1. No person is eligible for appointment as the Governor unless he has completed the age of thirty years.
2. The same person can be appointed as the Governor for three States.

Which of the statements given above is/are correct?

(*a*) 1 only (*b*) 2 only

(*c*) Both 1 and 2 (*d*) Neither 1 nor 2

17. Which one of the following pairs is correctly matched?

(*a*) Writ of Habeas Corpus : Issued only to the state

(*b*) Writ of Mandamus : Issued to the public servant

(*c*) Writ of Quo-Warranto : Issued to the subordinate courts

(*d*) Writ of Prohibition : Issued to the private individual

18. Consider the following statements:

1. The President shall appoint a person who is qualified to be appointed a judge of a High Court to be Attorney-General for India.
2. In the performance of his duties, the Attorney-General shall have right of audience in all courts in India.
3. The Attorney-General shall hold office during the pleasure of the President and shall receive such remuneration as the President may determine.

Which of the statements given above is/are correct?

(*a*) 1 only (*b*) 2 and 3 only

(*c*) 1 and 2 only (*d*) 1, 2 and 3

19. The authority to specify which castes shall be deemed to be Scheduled Castes rests with whom/which of the following?

(*a*) The President (*b*) The Governor

(*c*) The Prime Minister (*d*) The National Commission for Scheduled Castes

20. Consider the following statements:

1. There shall be council of Ministers with the Prime Minister at the head to aid and advise the President who shall, in the exercise of his functions, act in accordance with such advise.
2. The question whether any, and if so what, advise was tendered by ministers to the President shall not be inquired in any court.

Which of the statements given above is/are correct?

(*a*) 1 only (*b*) 2 only

(*c*) Both 1 and 2 (*d*) Neither 1 nor 2

21. On which of the following grounds, can a Judge of a High Court be impeached?

1. Violation of the Constitution
2. Proved misbehaviour
3. Incapacity

Select the correct answer using the codes given below:

(*a*) 1 only (*b*) 2 only

(*c*) 1, 2 and 3 (*d*) 2 and 3 only

22. The Legislative Council in a State can be created or abolished by the:
    (*a*) President on the recommendation of the Governor of the State.
    (*b*) Parliament on the recommendation of the Chief Minister of the State.
    (*c*) Parliament after the State Assembly passes a resolution to that effect.
    (*d*) Governor of the State on the recommendation of the Council of Ministers.

23. Which among the following statements with respect to the Comptroller and Auditor-General of India is/are correct?
    1. The procedure and grounds for his removal from the office are the same as that of a Judge of the Supreme Court.
    2. He prescribes the form in which accounts of the Union and the States are to be kept.

    Select the correct answer using the codes given below:
    (*a*) 1 only (*b*) 2 only
    (*c*) Both 1 and 2 (*d*) Neither 1 nor 2

24. The Vice-President of India can be removed from the office:
    (*a*) by a resolution initiated in the Council of States and approved by the Lok Sabha.
    (*b*) by a resolution passed in the Lok Sabha and agreed to by the Council of States.
    (*c*) by a resolution adopted by the two Houses meeting in a joint session.
    (*d*) following a formal process of impeachment.

25. Which of the following statements regarding the Preamble of the Constitution of India is/are correct?
    1. The Preamble is an integral part of the Constitution.
    2. The words "Secular" and "Socialist" have been a part of the Preamble since its inception.

    Select the correct answer from the codes given below:
    (*a*) 1 only (*b*) 2 only
    (*c*) Both 1 and 2 (*d*) Neither 1 nor 2

Answers

1. (*c*)	2. (*c*)	3. (*b*)	4. (*d*)	5. (*c*)
6. (*d*)	7. (*d*)	8. (*b*)	9. (*b*)	10. (*b*)
11. (*b*)	12. (*c*)	13. (*b*)	14. (*a*)	15. (*a*)
16. (*b*)	17. (*b*)	18. (*b*)	19. (*a*)	20. (*c*)
21. (*d*)	22. (*c*)	23. (*c*)	24. (*a*)	25. (*a*)

Model Test Paper – 3

1. Consider the following statements:
   1. Attorney-General of India has the right of audience in all courts in the territory of India.
   2. Attorney-General of India has the right to take part in the proceedings of the Parliament without the right to vote.

   Which of the statements given above is/are correct?

   (*a*) 1 only (*b*) 2 only
   (*c*) Both 1 and 2 (*d*) Neither 1 nor 2

2. Which of the following expenditures are charged on the Consolidated Fund of India?
   1. Emoluments and allowances of the President of India
   2. Salaries and allowances of the Chairman of the Council of States
   3. Salaries and allowances of the Speaker of the House of the People
   4. The pensions payable to or in respect of Judges of any High Court

   Select the correct answer using the codes given below:

   (*a*) 1, 2, 3 and 4 (*b*) 1, 2 and 3
   (*c*) 1, 3 and 4 (*d*) 2 and 4 only

3. The Chief Election Commissioner of India can be removed from office during his tenure:

   (*a*) by the Chief Justice of India if some charges are proved against him.
   (*b*) by the President on the basis of a resolution of the Union Cabinet.
   (*c*) by a Committee consisting of Chief Justice of India, Law Minister of India and the Vice-President of India.
   (*d*) by the President on the basis of resolution passed by the Parliament by two-thirds majority.

4. Which of the statements given below is/are correct?
   1. The Speaker immediately vacates his office whenever the State Legislative Assembly is dissolved.
   2. No Member of a State Legislative Assembly shall be liable to any proceedings in any court in respect of anything said or any vote given by him in the legislature.

   Select the correct answer using the codes given below:

   (*a*) 1 only (*b*) 2 only
   (*c*) Both 1 and 2 (*d*) Neither 1 nor 2

5. Which one of the following pairs is correctly matched?

(*a*) Republic	:	Head of the State is hereditary monarch
(*b*) Sovereign	:	Constitution rests on the people's will
(*c*) Democratic	:	Constitution does not recognise legal supremacy of another country
(*d*) Secular	:	State is without any religion of its own

6. Which of the following statements with regard to financial emergency is/are correct?
   1. It is required to be approved by both the Houses of Parliament within one month.
   2. Once approved by both the Houses of Parliament, it remains valid for six months.
   3. Salary of any government official including the Supreme Court judges can be reduced during financial emergency.
   4. During financial emergency, the executive authority of the Union shall extend to the giving of directions to any State to observe such canons of financial propriety as may be specified in the directions.

   Select the correct answer using the codes given below:

   (*a*) 1, 2, 3 and 4 (*b*) 1 and 4 only
   (*c*) 3 and 4 only (*d*) 3 only

7. The purpose of Directive Principles of State Policy is to:

   (*a*) lay down positive instructions which would guide State Policy at all levels.
   (*b*) implement Gandhiji's idea for a decentralised state.
   (*c*) check the use of arbitrary powers by the Government.
   (*d*) promote welfare of the backward sections of the society.

8. Which of the following issues were included in the terms of reference of the second Commission on Centre-State Relations set up by the Government of India?
   1. Inter-linking of rivers
   2. Devolution of powers and autonomy to Panchayati Raj Institutions
   3. Freeing Inter-State trade

   Select the correct answer using the codes given below:

   (*a*) 1 and 2 only (*b*) 2 and 3 only
   (*c*) 1 and 3 only (*d*) 1, 2 and 3

9. Article 368 of the Constitution of India lays down:

   (*a*) power of the Parliament to amend the Constitution.
   (*b*) power of the Parliament to amend the Constitution and procedure therefore.
   (*c*) procedure for amendment of the Constitution.
   (*d*) limitation on the power of the Parliament to amend the Constitution.

10. Consider the following statements:

1. Ministry of Parliamentary Affairs constitutes Consultative Committees of Members of both the Houses of Parliament.
2. The main purpose of these Committees is to provide a forum for formal discussions between the Government and Members of the Parliament on policies and programmes of the Government.

Which of the statements given above is/are correct?

(*a*) 1 only (*b*) 2 only
(*c*) Both 1 and 2 (*d*) Neither 1 nor 2

11. Which of the following Articles of the Constitution is related to the retrospective operation of criminal law?

(*a*) Article 20
(*b*) Article 30
(*c*) Article 16
(*d*) Article 15

12. Which of the following correctly indicates the features of regional political parties in India?:

1. They identify with region's culture.
2. They use regional language for their electoral gains.
3. They enter into electoral alliance with national parties.
4. They are a post-independence political phenomenon.

Select the correct answer using the codes given below:

(*a*) 1 and 2 only (*b*) 1, 2 and 3
(*c*) 1, 3 and 4 (*d*) 2 only

13. Which one of the following matters stands excluded from the jurisdiction of Inter-State Council?

(*a*) Enquiring into and advising upon disputes which may have arisen between the States
(*b*) Adjudication of any dispute or complaint with respect to the use, distribution or control of water of any inter-state river or river-valley
(*c*) Investigation and discussion of subjects in which some or all of the States or the Union and one or more States, have a common interest
(*d*) Recommendation on any such subject, in particular, recommendation for a better coordination of policy and action with respect to that subject

14. Consider the following duties:

1. To value and preserve the rich heritage of our composite culture
2. To safeguard private property
3. To develop scientific temper, humanism and spirit of enquiry and reform

Which of the above are fundamental duties include?

(*a*) 1, 2 and 3 (*b*) 1 and 2 only
(*c*) 2 and 3 only (*d*) 1 and 3 only

15. Which one of the following statements is correct?

The members of the Constituent Assembly were:

(*a*) elected through indirect election by the members of the Provincial Legislative Assemblies.
(*b*) elected directly by the people.
(*c*) nominated by the Government.
(*d*) elected by the local self-government bodies.

16. Which of the following are the provisions of Article 75 of the Constitution?

1. Ministers shall be appointed by the President on the advice of the Prime Minister.
2. The Council of Ministers shall be collectively responsible to the Lok Sabha.
3. The question whether any, and if so what, advice was tendered by Ministers do the President shall not be inquired in any court.
4. The salaries and allowances of Ministers shall be determined by the Parliament.

Select the correct answer using the codes given below:

(*a*) 1, 2 and 3 (*b*) 1, 2 and 4
(*c*) 2, 3 and 4 (*d*) 2 and 4 only

17. Which of the following features is/are contrary to the norms of a federal polity?

1. Common All-India Services
2. Single integrated judiciary

Select the correct answer using the codes given below:

(*a*) 1 only (*b*) 2 only
(*c*) Both 1 and 2 (*d*) Neither 1 nor 2

18. Which of the following constitutional amendment acts is related with the reservation of seats for the STs in the Legislative Assemblies of Nagaland, Meghalaya, Mizoram and Arunachal Pradesh?

(*a*) 52nd Amendment Act
(*b*) 57th Amendment Act
(*c*) 61st Amendment Act
(*d*) 65th Amendment Act

19. Judicial Review in the Indian Constitution is based on which of the following?

(*a*) Procedure established by law
(*b*) Due process of law
(*c*) Rule of law
(*d*) Precedents and conventions

20. Consider the following statements with respect to the Comptroller and Auditor-General of India:

1. He shall only be removed from office in like manner and on the like grounds as a judge of the Supreme Court.
2. He shall not be eligible for further office either under the Government of India or under the Government of any State after he has ceased to hold his office.

Which of the statements given above is/are correct?

(*a*) 1 only (*b*) 2 only

(*c*) Both 1 and 2 (*d*) Neither 1 nor 2

21. Which one of the following is not within the purview of the functions of a State Public Service Commission?
    (*a*) Consultation relating to recruitment to civil services
    (*b*) Consultation in relation to promotions and transfers from one service to the other
    (*c*) Consultation in relation to reservation of appointments or posts in favour of any backward class of citizens
    (*d*) Consultation in relation to disciplinary matters affecting civil servants

22. Consider the following statements:
    1. The President of India may be removed from his office before expiry of his term for violation of the Constitution.
    2. The impeachment charge against the President may be preferred by either House of the Parliament.
    3. For the resolution of impeachment, votes of two-thirds of the Members of the House present and voting are required.

    Which of the statements given above is/are correct?

    (*a*) 1 and 2 only (*b*) 1 and 3 only

    (*c*) 2 and 3 only (*d*) 1 only

23. A writ of Prohibition is an order issued by the Supreme Court or High Court which:
    (*a*) Affects the subject of production and consumption of liquor
    (*b*) Prohibits the police from arresting a person
    (*c*) Forbids the administrative authority from taking a particular action
    (*d*) Prohibits a quasi-judicial authority from proceeding with a case

24. Which of the following statements with respect to the judiciary in India is/are correct?
    1. Unlike in the United States, India has not provided for a double system of courts.
    2. Under the Constitution of India, there is a single integrated system of courts for the Union as well as the States.
    3. The organisation of the subordinate judiciary varies slightly from State to State.

    Select the correct answer using the codes given below:

    (*a*) 1 only (*b*) 1 and 2 only

    (*c*) 1, 2 and 3 (*d*) 2 and 3 only

25. Consider the following statements:
    1. The Preamble of the Constitution of India can be amended by the Parliament up to any extent barring its basic features.
    2. The Preamble can be amended only by a special majority of the Parliament and ratification by legislatures of half of the States.
    3. The Preamble has no role to play in the interpretation of any provision of the Constitution.

Which of the statements given above is/are correct?

(*a*) 1, 2 and 3 (*b*) 1 only

(*c*) 2 and 3 only (*d*) 2 only

Answers

1. (*c*)	2. (*a*)	3. (*d*)	4. (*b*)	5. (*d*)
6. (*c*)	7. (*a*)	8. (*d*)	9. (*b*)	10. (*a*)
11. (*a*)	12. (*b*)	13. (*b*)	14. (*d*)	15. (*a*)
16. (*b*)	17. (*c*)	18. (*b*)	19. (*a*)	20. (*c*)
21. (*c*)	22. (*a*)	23. (*d*)	24. (*c*)	25. (*b*)

Model Test Paper – 4

1. Consider the following statements:
   1. There is no provision in the Constitution of India under which the President of India may entrust, with the consent of the Government of a State, to that Government, functions in relation to any matter to which the executive power of the Union extends.
   2. Under the provisions of the Constitution of India, only legislature of a State can by law alter the name of that State.

   Which of the statements given above is/are correct?

   (*a*) 1 only (*b*) 2 only
   (*c*) Both 1 and 2 (*d*) Neither 1 nor 2

2. The President is recommended by the Finance Commission as to the:
   1. distribution of net proceeds of taxes between the Union and States.
   2. principles governing grants-in-aid of the revenues of States out of Contingency Fund of India.
   3. measures to augment Consolidated Fund of a State to supplement resources of Municipalities.
   4. measures to augment Consolidated Fund of a State to supplement resources of Panchayats.

   Select the correct answer using the codes given below:

   (*a*) 1, 2 and 3 (*b*) 1, 3 and 4
   (*c*) 1 and 4 only (*d*) 3 and 4 only

3. Who was the President of India at the time of proclamation of emergency in the year 1975?
   (*a*) V.V. Giri
   (*b*) Giani Zail Singh
   (*c*) Fakhruddin Ali Ahmed
   (*d*) Shankar Dayal Sharma

4. Which of the following statements as per the Constitution of India is/are correct?
   1. The State shall endeavour to provide early childhood care and education for all children until they complete the age of 6 years.
   2. It is a fundamental duty of every citizen who is the parent or guardian to provide opportunities for education to his child or, as the case may be, ward between the age of 6 and 14 years.
   3. The State shall provide free and compulsory education to all children of the age of 6 to 14 years.

Select the correct answer using the codes given below:

(*a*) 1 and 2 only (*b*) 2 and 3 only
(*c*) 1 only (*d*) 1, 2 and 3

5. Which of the following Commissions was headed by Veerappa Moily?
(*a*) Second Administrative Reforms Commission
(*b*) Second Commission on Centre-State Relations
(*c*) Thirteenth Finance Commission
(*d*) National Commission to Review the Working of the Constitution

6. Consider the following Committees/Commissions appointed in the post-Independence period to examine and report on local governments:
1. Committee of Ministers on Augmentation of Financial Resources of Urban Local Bodies
2. Rural-Urban Relationship Committee
3. National Commission on Urbanisation
4. Local Finance Enquiry Committee

The correct chronological sequence in which these Committees/Commissions were set up is:

(*a*) 1, 4, 3, 2 (*b*) 1, 4, 2, 3
(*c*) 4, 1, 3, 2 (*d*) 4, 1, 2, 3

7. Which of the following statements is correct regarding the procedure of passing of Bills in the Parliament?
(*a*) A Bill pending in Parliament shall not lapse because of the prorogation of the two Houses of the Parliament.
(*b*) A Bill pending in the Rajya Sabha which has not been passed by the Lok Sabha shall lapse on the dissolution of the Lok Sabha.
(*c*) A Bill passed by the Lok Sabha and pending in the Rajya Sabha shall not lapse on the dissolution of the Lok Sabha.
(*d*) A Bill passed by both Houses but returned by the President for reconsideration of Houses shall lapse on the dissolution of the Lok Sabha.

8. Consider the following statements:
1. The Union Executive consists of the President and the Council of Ministers with the Prime Minister as the head.
2. The President may, by writing in his hand, addressed to the Vice-President, resign his office.
3. The executive power of the Union is vested in the Prime Minister.

Which of the statements given above is/are correct?

(*a*) 1 and 3 only (*b*) 2 and 3 only
(*c*) 1, 2 and 3 (*d*) 2 only

9. The Sachar Committee Report pertains to which of the following?
(*a*) Indian federalism
(*b*) Economic development of backward regions
(*c*) Indian Muslims
(*d*) Backward Classes

10. Consider the following statements:
    1. The Comptroller and Auditor-General of India has no control over the issue of money from the Consolidated Fund unlike his British counterpart.
    2. Government companies do not fall within the duties of the Comptroller and Auditor-General of India to audit and report on their receipts and expenditure.

    Which of the statements given above is/are correct?

    (*a*) 1 only (*b*) 2 only
    (*c*) Both 1 and 2 (*d*) Neither 1 nor 2

11. Who of the following is not a part of the Committee that recommends the appointment of the Chief Information Commissioner to the President?
    (*a*) The Prime Minister
    (*b*) The leader of the opposition in the Lok Sabha
    (*c*) The Chief Justice of the Supreme Court
    (*d*) A Union Cabinet Minister, nominated by the Prime Minister

12. When the President of India is satisfied that the financial credit of the Government of India is threatened, he may:
    (*a*) direct reduction in the members in the Finance Commission.
    (*b*) proclaim financial emergency.
    (*c*) impose President's Rule in any state.
    (*d*) direct the Parliament to pass a special financial bill.

13. Which of the following statements is/are correct?

    Under the provisions of Article 200 of the Constitution of India, the Governor of a State may:
    1. withhold his assent to a Bill passed by the State Legislature.
    2. reserve the Bill passed by the State Legislature for consideration of the President.
    3. return the Bill, other than a money Bill, for reconsideration of the State Legislature.

    Select the correct answer using the codes given below:

    (*a*) 1 only (*b*) 1 and 2 only
    (*c*) 2 and 3 only (*d*) 1, 2 and 3

14. Which of the following provisions are contained in the Sixth Schedule of the Constitution?
    (a) The tribal areas in the states of Assam, Meghalaya, Tripura and Mizoram
    (b) All-India services
    (c) Control of scheduled areas and scheduled tribes
    (d) Comptroller and Auditor-General of India

15. Consider the following statements:
    1. Zonal Councils have been set up under a provision of the Constitution of India.
    2. The Parliament may by law provide for the exclusion of the jurisdiction of all Courts, except the Supreme Court for the adjudication of any dispute with respect to use, distribution or control of waters of, or in, any inter-State river or river valley.

Which of the statements given above is/are correct?

(*a*) 1 only (*b*) 2 only

(*c*) Both 1 and 2 (*d*) Neither 1 nor 2

16. Which one of the following is not correctly matched?

(a) Abolition of Untouchability : Article 17

(b) Reservation of appointments or posts in favour of any backward class of citizens : Article 16

(c) Prohibition of discrimination on grounds of religion, race, caste, sex or place of birth : Article 18

(d) Laws inconsistent with or in derogation of the fundamental rights : Article 13

17. Consider the following statements:

1. The Annual Appropriation Bill is passed by the Lok Sabha in the same manner as an Ordinary Bill.
2. An amendment to the Constitution of India can be initiated by an introduction of a Bill in either Lok Sabha or Rajya Sabha.

Which of the statements given above is/are correct?

(*a*) 1 only (*b*) 2 only

(*c*) Both 1 and 2 (*d*) Neither 1 nor 2

18. Consider the following statements:

1. In the Lok Sabha, 12 members are nominated by he President of India.
2. The Third Schedule of the Constitution deals with the allocation of seats in the Rajya Sabha to the states and union territories.

Which of the statements given above is/are correct?

(*a*) 1 only (*b*) 2 only

(*c*) Both 1 and 2 (*d*) Neither 1 nor 2

19. A member of the UPSC may be removed on the ground of misbehaviour by:

(*a*) Both the Houses of Parliament by way of impeachment

(*b*) The President on the basis of enquiry by the Supreme Court

(*c*) The Chairman of the UPSC

(*d*) The Prime Minister on the basis of the recommendation of the Cabinet

20. Consider the following statements:

Judicial review under the Constitution of India:

1. is a part of the basic structure of the Constitution.
2. can only be ousted or excluded by a constitutional amendment.

Which of the statements given above is/are correct?

(*a*) 1 only (*b*) 2 only

(*c*) Both 1 and 2 (*d*) Neither 1 nor 2

21. Which one of the following procedures is valid for passing a Bill seeking abolition of the Vidhan Parishad?
    (*a*) Resolution in the Rajya Sabha and consent of each House of the Parliament by majority of the members present and voting.
    (*b*) Resolution in the Vidhan Sabha by a majority of the total membership of the House and by majority of not less than two-thirds of the members of the House present and voting, followed by consent of each House of the Parliament by the majority of the members present and voting.
    (*c*) Resolution in either House of the Parliament and consent of each House of Parliament by absolute majority of the whole House, coupled with two-thirds majority of members present and voting.
    (*d*) Resolution in the Vidhan Parishad and consent of the Vidhan Sabha by simple majority, followed by consent of each House of the Parliament by simple majority.

22. Consider the following statements on Parliamentary Committees:
    1. Members of the Rajya Sabha are not associated with the Committees on Public Accounts and Public Undertakings.
    2. Members of the Committee on Estimates are drawn from both the Lok Sabha and the Rajya Sabha.

    Which of the statements given above is/are correct?
    (*a*) 1 only (*b*) 2 only
    (*c*) Both 1 and 2 (*d*) Neither 1 nor 2

23. Which one among the following is a function of the Pro-Tem Speaker of the Lok Sabha?
    (*a*) Conduct of the proceedings of the House in the absence of the Speaker
    (*b*) To check if the election certificates of the members of the House are in order
    (*c*) Swear-in the members of the House and hold the charge till a regular Speaker is elected
    (*d*) Give his assent to the Bills passed by the House

24. Which among the following are listed in the Eleventh Schedule?
    1. Minor irrigation
    2. Animal husbandry
    3. Women and child development
    4. Fire services
    5. Cattle ponds, prevention of cruelty to animals

    Select the correct answer using the codes given below:
    (*a*) 1, 2 and 3 (*b*) 1, 4 and 5
    (*c*) 2, 3 and 4 (*d*) 3, 4 and 5

25. Which of the following provisions of the Constitution of India need ratification by the legislatures of not less than one-half of the States to effect amendment?
    1. The manner of election of the President of India
    2. Extent of the executive power of the Union and the States

3. The Supreme Court and High Courts
4. Any of the Lists in the 7th Schedule

Select the correct answer using the codes given below:

(*a*) 1, 2, 3 and 4 (*b*) 1, 2 and 3
(*c*) 3 and 4 only (*d*) 1 and 2 only

Answers

1. (*d*)	2. (*b*)	3. (*c*)	4. (*d*)	5. (*a*)
6. (*d*)	7. (*a*)	8. (*d*)	9. (*c*)	10. (*a*)
11. (*c*)	12. (*b*)	13. (*d*)	14. (*a*)	15. (*d*)
16. (*c*)	17. (*b*)	18. (*d*)	19. (*b*)	20. (*a*)
21. (*b*)	22. (*d*)	23. (*c*)	24. (*a*)	25. (*a*)

Model Test Paper – 5

1. Consider the following statements:
   1. For election of the President of India, each elected member of either House of the Parliament shall have such number of votes as may be obtained by dividing the total number of votes assigned to the members of the Legislative Assemblies of the States by the number of the members of the Lok Sabha.
   2. The Vice-President of India is elected by the members of an electoral college consisting of the members of both the Houses of Parliament and the elected members of the Legislative Assemblies of each State.

   Which of the statements given above is/are correct?

   (*a*) 1 only (*b*) 2 only
   (*c*) Both 1 and 2 (*d*) Neither 1 nor 2

2. Consider the following Commissions:
   1. Kaka Kalelkar Commission on Backward Classes
   2. Sarkaria Commission on Centre-State Relations
   3. Shah Commission on Emergency Excesses

   Which one of the following is the correct chronological order of the above?

   (*a*) 2, 3, 1 (*b*) 1, 2, 3
   (*c*) 2, 1, 3 (*d*) 1, 3, 2

3. The Speaker of the Lok Sabha has been empowered to exercise the "Guillotine":

   (*a*) after demands are discussed.
   (*b*) after demands are discussed and passed.
   (*c*) when the time allotted for budget discussions is exhausted.
   (*d*) when the demands are passed with a cut.

4. Which of the following statements regarding the residuary powers of legislation are correct?
   1. The Lok Sabha has the exclusive power to make laws on any matter not enumerated in the Concurrent List.
   2. Residuary powers of legislation are laid down in Article 248 of the Constitution.
   3. Residuary powers include the power of imposing taxes not mentioned in any of the three lists.
   4. Article 248 of the Constitution provides for the establishment of additional courts.

   Select the correct answer using the codes given below:

   (*a*) 1 and 2 only (*b*) 1 and 3 only
   (*c*) 2 and 4 only (*d*) 2 and 3 only

5. With reference to the Constitution of India, which one of the following pairs is not correctly matched?

(*a*) Stock Exchanges	:	The State List
(*b*) Forests	:	The Concurrent List
(*c*) Insurance	:	The Union List
(*d*) Marriage and Divorce	:	The Concurrent List

6. Which of the following statements with regard to Inter-State Council is/are correct?
   1. It was established under the provisions of the Constitution of India.
   2. The Council is a recommendatory body.
   3. There is a standing committee of the Council under the Chairmanship of the Prime Minister of India to process matters for consideration of the Council.

   Select the correct answer using the codes given below:

   (*a*) 1 and 3 only (*b*) 2 only
   (*c*) 1 and 2 only (*d*) 1, 2 and 3

7. The institution of Lokayukta was created first in Maharashtra in which of the following years?

   (*a*) 1970 (*b*) 1972
   (*c*) 1973 (*d*) 1971

8. India's "Act East Policy":
   1. was articulated during the reign of H.D. Deve Gowda as India's Prime Minister.
   2. is directed towards South-East Asian countries.
   3. is about controlling terrorism.
   4. seeks to develop a bond among various countries on the basis of economic cooperation.

   Select the correct answer using the codes given below:

   (*a*) 1 and 2 only
   (*b*) 2 and 3 only
   (*c*) 2 and 4 only
   (*d*) 3 and 4 only

9. The growth of regional political parties in India is attributed to which of the following factors?
   1. Diversified nature of Indian society
   2. Inability to accommodate demands of various sections of society
   3. Regional imbalances in the development
   4. Factional fight within the larger parties

   Select the correct answer using the codes given below:

   (*a*) 1, 2, 3 and 4 (*b*) 1, 3 and 4
   (*c*) 1, 2 and 3 (*d*) 2, 3 and 4

10. The right to "freedom of speech and expression" is restricted on the grounds of:
    1. the sovereignty and integrity of India.
    2. contempt of court.
    3. friendly relations with foreign states.
    4. protection of minorities.

Select the correct answer using the codes given below:

(*a*) 1, 2 and 3 (*b*) 2, 3 and 4
(*c*) 1 and 3 only (*d*) 1, 2 and 4

11. Which of the following provisions is contained in Part XVII of the Constitution of India?
    (*a*) Provisions concerning administration of Tribal Areas
    (*b*) Language of the Union
    (*c*) Trade and Commerce within India
    (*d*) The Executive of the Union

12. Which one of the following is not the role of Pressure Groups?
    (*a*) To contest elections to promote their interest
    (*b*) To help candidates favourable to them to get elected
    (*c*) To patronise legislators to secure their help in furthering their cause
    (*d*) To try to influence public opinion and enlist its support

13. Consider the following statements:
    1. Emergency is always imposed throughout the nation.
    2. Emergency can be imposed not only on the grounds of actual war, external aggression or armed rebellion, but also in anticipation thereof.
    3. Every proclamation of Emergency will not remain in force after one month unless it is approved by both the Houses of Parliament.

    Which of the statements given above is/are correct?
    (*a*) 2 and 3 only
    (*b*) 1 and 2 only
    (*c*) 3 only
    (*d*) 1, 2 and 3

14. The registration of political parties is done as per the provisions/decision of which of the following?
    (*a*) Article 324 of the Constitution
    (*b*) The Representation of the People Act, 1951
    (*c*) The Election Commission by itself
    (*d*) The Election Commission in consultation with cabinet committee on political affairs

15. Which of the following statements is correct?

    A joint session of the Parliament shall be:
    1. convened by the Speaker.
    2. presided over by the senior most member of the Parliament.
    3. convened by the President.

    Select the correct answer using the codes given below:
    (*a*) 1 only (*b*) 2 only
    (*c*) 3 only (*d*) 2 and 3 only

16. According to the Cabinet Mission Plan, which one of the following was the method of electing the Constituent Assembly?
   (*a*) Universal Adult Franchise
   (*b*) Partly elected by the Provincial Assemblies and partly nominated by the Governor-General
   (*c*) Nominated by the Princely States
   (*d*) Partly elected by the Provincial Assemblies and partly nominated by the Princess

17. Consider the following statements with respect to the Attorney-General of India:
   1. He is appointed by the President
   2. He must have the same qualifications as are required by a Judge of a High Court.
   3. In the performance of his duties, he shall have the right of audience in all courts of India.

   Which of the statements given above is/are correct?
   (*a*) 1 only (*b*) 1 and 3 only
   (*c*) 2 and 3 only (*d*) 1, 2 and 3

18. Which one of the following Articles of the Constitution of India provides for the creation of the All-India Services?
   (*a*) Article 300 (*b*) Article 312
   (*c*) Article 320 (*d*) Article 321

19. Consider the following statements:
   1. A Money Bill cannot be introduced in the Council of States.
   2. The Council of States cannot reject a Money Bill nor amend it.

   Which of the statements given above is/are correct?
   (*a*) 1 only (*b*) 2 only
   (*c*) Both 1 and 2 (*d*) Neither 1 nor 2

20. Which of the following subject is related to the Indian Councils Act, 1861?
   (*a*) Dyarchy in the provinces
   (*b*) Inclusion of Non-official members in the Governor-General's Executive Council
   (*c*) Separate electorates
   (*d*) Federation and provincial autonomy

21. A part of the Preamble of the Constitution reads as under:

   "We the people of India, having solemnly resolved to constitute India into a Sovereign Socialist Secular Democratic Republic ....."

   Certain words in the above part were inserted by:
   (*a*) The Constitution (Seventh Amendment) Act, 1956
   (*b*) The Constitution (Eighteenth Amendment) Act, 1966
   (*c*) The Constitution (Thirty-fifth Amendment) Act, 1974
   (*d*) The Constitution (Forty-second Amendment) Act, 1976

22. Which of the following are the sources of municipal revenue?
    1. Revenue from taxation by the municipal bodies
    2. Revenue from non-tax sources under the control of municipal bodies
    3. Loans
    4. Share from income tax

    Select the correct answer from the codes given below:

    (*a*) 1, 2, 3 and 4
    (*b*) 1, 2 and 4
    (*c*) 1, 2 and 3
    (*d*) 2, 3 and 4

23. Which of the following are the Fundamental Duties mentioned in the Constitution of India?
    1. To follow the principles of morality
    2. To uphold and protect the sovereignty, unity and integrity of India
    3. To value and preserve the rich heritage of our composite culture
    4. To safeguard public property and to abjure violence

    Choose the correct answer from the codes given below:

    (*a*) 1, 2, 3 and 4
    (*b*) 1 and 4 only
    (*c*) 1, 2 and 3
    (*d*) 2, 3 and 4

24. Which of the following Committee/Task Force was headed by Mani Shankar Aiyer?
    (*a*) Committee on Restructuring of District Rural Development Agency
    (*b*) Task Force on Devaluation of Powers and Functions to Panchayati Raj Institutions
    (*c*) Expert Committee on Leveraging Panchayats for Efficient Delivery of Public Goods and Services
    (*d*) Task Force for Preparation of a Manual for District Planning

25. Which of the following is/are not the function(s) of the UPSC and State Public Service Commissions?
    1. Advising the appropriate governments on matters relating to methods of recruitment to civil services and for civil posts
    2. Consultation in creation of All-India Services
    3. Consultation on disciplinary matters affecting a person serving the Government of India or of a person serving the Government of a State in a civil capacity

    Select the correct answer using the codes given below:

    (*a*) 1 only
    (*b*) 1 and 2 only
    (*c*) 2 only
    (*d*) 2 and 3 only

Answers

1. (*d*)	2. (*d*)	3. (*c*)	4. (*d*)	5. (*a*)
6. (*c*)	7. (*d*)	8. (*c*)	9. (*a*)	10. (*a*)
11. (*b*)	12. (*a*)	13. (*a*)	14. (*b*)	15. (*c*)
16. (*d*)	17. (*b*)	18. (*b*)	19. (*c*)	20. (*b*)
21. (*d*)	22. (*c*)	23. (*d*)	24. (*c*)	25. (*c*)

Model Test Paper – 6

1. Consider the following statements:
   1. The First Amendment to the Constitution of India was made in 1955.
   2. The First Amendment to the Constitution of India made some changes in Article 19 and Article 31.

   Which of the statements given above is/are correct?

   (*a*) 1 only (*b*) 2 only
   (*c*) Both 1 and 2 (*d*) Neither 1 nor 2

2. Which of the following statements is/are correct?
   1. The constitutional remedy under Article 32 is available only in case of fundamental rights, not in the case of rights which follow from some other provision in the Constitution.
   2. Both the Supreme Court and High Courts can issue the writs of habeas corpus, mandamus, prohibition, certiorari and quo-warranto only for the purpose of enforcement of fundamental rights.

   Select the correct answer from the codes given below:

   (*a*) 1 only (*b*) 2 only
   (*c*) Both 1 and 2 (*d*) Neither 1 nor 2

3. Consider the following statements:
   1. The Chairman and the members of the UPSC are appointed by the President.
   2. The Chairman and the members of the UPSC are eligible for further employment under the Government.

   Which of the statements given above is/are correct?

   (*a*) 1 only (*b*) 2 only
   (*c*) Both 1 and 2 (*d*) Neither 1 nor 2

4. Where was the first position of ombudsman instituted to safeguard the rights of citizens?

   (*a*) Austria (*b*) Sweden
   (*c*) Finland (*d*) Denmark

5. Consider the following statements:
   1. The Constitution of India classifies the members of the Council of Ministers at the Centre into different ranks.
   2. A member of one House of the Parliament who has been chosen as a Union Minister does not have the right to vote in the House of which he is not a member.

Which of the statements given above is/are correct?

(*a*) 1 only (*b*) 2 only

(*c*) Both 1 and 2 (*d*) Neither 1 nor 2

6. Which of the following provisions of the Constitution of India is adopted from the Constitution of Canada?
   (*a*) Amendment of the Constitution
   (*b*) Directive Principles
   (*c*) Emergency Powers of the President
   (*d*) The Union-State Relations

7. Which of the following is not reserved by the Governor for the consideration of the President?
   (*a*) Bills affecting powers of the High Courts
   (*b*) Bills relating to compulsory acquisition of property
   (*c*) Bills seeking to impose restrictions on the inter-state trade
   (*d*) Bills relating to imposition of taxes on agricultural income

8. The Supreme Court does not have original jurisdiction regarding a dispute between:
   (*a*) the Government of India and a State or States.
   (*b*) the Government of India and one State on one side and one or more States on the other side.
   (*c*) two States.
   (*d*) a citizen and a State.

9. Which of the following are included in the non-tax revenue of the municipal bodies?
   1. Toll on new bridges
   2. Fees and fines
   3. Income from enterprises
   4. Taxes on advertisements

   Select the correct answer from the codes given below:

   (*a*) 1 and 3 only (*b*) 2, 3 and 4

   (*c*) 2 and 4 only (*d*) 2 and 3 only

10. The President of India has power to declare emergency under Article 352 on which of he following grounds?
    1. War
    2. Internal disturbance
    3. External aggression
    4. Armed rebellion

    Select the correct answer using the codes given below:

    (*a*) 1, 2 and 3 (*b*) 1, 3 and 4

    (*c*) 1, 2 and 4 (*d*) 2, 3 and 4

11. Which one of the following pairs is not correctly matched?

(*a*) L.M. Singhvi Committee, 1986	:	Constitutional Status for Panchayati Raj
(*b*) Santhanam Committee, 1964	:	Prevention of Corruption
(*c*) Satish Chandra Committee, 1988	:	Civil Services Examination, Union Public Service Commission
(*d*) Verma Committee, 1999	:	Parliamentary control over public expenditure

12. Which one of the following is not expressly covered as a Fundamental Right under the Constitution of India?
    (*a*) Right to form association
    (*b*) Right to equality before law
    (*c*) Right to freedom of press
    (*d*) Right to assemble peaceably and without arms

13. Consider the following statements:
    The Committee on Public Undertakings:
    1. is a creation of the Parliament.
    2. is a constitutional body.
    3. was created by the Cabinet.
    4. has 22 members.

    Which of the statements given above are correct?
    (*a*) 1 and 2 only (*b*) 2 and 3 only
    (*c*) 3 and 4 only (*d*) 1 and 4 only

14. Who among the following determines the authority who shall readjust the allocation of seats in the Lok Sabha to the states, and division of each State into territorial constituencies?
    (*a*) The President of India
    (*b*) The Parliament of India
    (*c*) The Chief Election Commissioner of India
    (*d*) The Lok Sabha alone

15. Which of the following are the functions of the Chief Minister?
    1. To communicate to the Central Government all the decisions of the Council of Ministers relating to the administration of the State
    2. To instruct District Collectors to carry out all the decisions of the Council of Ministers relating to the administration of the State
    3. To communicate to the Governor all decisions of the Council of Ministers relating to the administration of the State
    4. To communicate to the Governor all decisions of the Council of Ministers regarding proposals for legislation

Select the correct answer from the codes given below:

(*a*) 1 and 2 only (*b*) 1 and 4 only

(*c*) 2 and 3 only (*d*) 3 and 4 only

16. Ashok Mehta Committee Report, 1978 recommended Constitution of:
(*a*) two tiers of Panchayati Raj institutions at the village and block levels.
(*b*) two tiers of Panchayati Raj institutions at Mandal (group of villages) and district levels.
(*c*) three tiers of Panchayati Raj institutions at the village, block and district levels.
(*d*) three tiers of Panchayati Raj institutions at the village, district and regional levels.

17. Who of the following officials examines the financial operation of the executive?
(*a*) The Speaker
(*b*) The Finance Minister
(*c*) The President
(*d*) The Comptroller and Auditor-General

18. In which one of the following cases, the Supreme Court gave verdict which has a direct bearing on the Centre-State relations?
(*a*) Kesavananda Bharati case
(*b*) Vishakha case
(*c*) S.R. Bommai case
(*d*) Indra Sawhney case

19. Consider the following statements:

The Comptroller and Auditor-General of India is responsible for the audit of the accounts of:

1. the Union Government.
2. the state Governments.
3. the Governments of Union Territories.
4. the urban and rural local bodies.

Which of the statements given above are correct?

(*a*) 1, 2 and 3 (*b*) 2, 3 and 4

(*c*) 1, 3 and 4 (*d*) 1, 2 and 4

20. Who among the following come under the jurisdiction of the Central Vigilance Commission?

1. Members of All-India Services serving in connection with the affairs of the Union and Group A officers of the Central Government
2. Senior officers in the Public Sector Undertakings of the Central Government
3. Senior officers in the Public Sector Banks
4. Senior officers in the Insurance Companies in the Public Sector

Select the correct answer using the codes given below:

(*a*) 1 only (*b*) 2, 3 and 4

(*c*) 1 and 2 only (*d*) 1, 2, 3 and 4

21. Which one of the following statements is not correct?
(*a*) A Minister is appointed by the Governor on the advice of the Chief Minister.
(*b*) Before a Minister enters upon his office, the Governor shall administer to him the oath of office and of secrecy.
(*c*) There shall be a Council of Ministers with the Chief Minister at the head to aid and advise the Governor who shall, in the exercise of his functions, act in accordance with such advice.
(*d*) A Minister shall hold office during the pleasure of the Governor.

22. The Legislative Council of a state can be abolished or created by the:
(*a*) President of India on the recommendation of the Parliament.
(*b*) Legislative Assembly of the state concerned.
(*c*) Parliament on the recommendation of the Governor of the State concerned.
(*d*) Parliament on the recommendation of the Legislative Assembly of the state concerned.

23. Consider the following statements with regard to All-India Services:
1. Article 312 of the Constitution specifies the procedure for their creation.
2. The All-India Services Act was enacted in 1950.
3. Indian Forest Services was established in 1966.
4. A new All-India Services can be created by the Rajya Sabha.

Which of the statements given above is/are correct?
(*a*) 1 only (*b*) 2 and 3 only
(*c*) 1 and 3 only (*d*) 2 and 4 only

24. For the purpose of inquiring into and advising upon inter-state dispute, if at any time, it appears to the President that the public interest would be served by the establishment of such council, he is empowered to establish which one of the following?
(*a*) Zonal Council
(*b*) Inter-State Council
(*c*) Inter-State Zonal Council
(*d*) The Central Inter-Zonal Council

25. Consider the following statements:
1. A Bill pending in the Parliament shall not lapse by reason of the prorogation of the Houses.
2. A Bill pending in the Council of States which has not been passed by the House of the People shall not lapse on dissolution of the House of the People.

Which of the statements given above is/are correct?
(*a*) 1 only (*b*) 2 only
(*c*) Both 1 and 2 (*d*) Neither 1 nor 2

Answers

1. (*d*) 2. (*a*) 3. (*a*) 4. (*b*) 5. (*b*)
6. (*d*) 7. (*d*) 8. (*d*) 9. (*d*) 10. (*b*)
11. (*d*) 12. (*c*) 13. (*d*) 14. (*b*) 15. (*d*)
16. (*b*) 17. (*d*) 18. (*c*) 19. (*a*) 20. (*d*)
21. (*c*) 22. (*d*) 23. (*c*) 24. (*b*) 25. (*c*)

Model Test Paper – 7

1. Consider the following statements:
   1. After the President has asked the Council of Ministers to reconsider the advice given by the Council of Ministers, the President may not act in accordance with the advice rendered after such reconsideration.
   2. The President can grant pardon under Article 72 of the Constitution of India to any person convicted of any offence.

   Which of the statements given above is/are correct?

   (*a*) 1 only (*b*) 2 only
   (*c*) Both 1 and 2 (*d*) Neither 1 nor 2

2. Consider the following statements:
   1. The legislation passed by the Parliament is subject to judicial review.
   2. The Constitution of India lays down the mechanism for the enforcement of Fundamental Rights.

   Which of the statements given above is/are correct?

   (*a*) 1 only (*b*) 2 only
   (*c*) Both 1 and 2 (*d*) Neither 1 nor 2

3. Consider the following statements:
   1. Administrative expenses of the Supreme Court of India are not subject to a vote in the Parliament.
   2. No discussion on the conduct of a Judge of the Supreme Court of India can take place in Parliament except upon a motion for an address to the President of India for removal of the judge.

   Which of the statements given above is/are correct?

   (*a*) 1 only (*b*) 2 only
   (*c*) Both 1 and 2 (*d*) Neither 1 nor 2

4. Which one of the following does not fall within the scope of the Committee on Public Undertakings?

   (*a*) Examination of the reports and accounts of such public undertakings as have been specifically allotted to the committee
   (*b*) Matters of major government policy as distinct from business or commercial functions of the public undertakings

(*c*) Examination of the reports of the Comptroller and Auditor-General
(*d*) Examination of the autonomy and efficiency of the public undertakings

5. Which one of the following statements is correct?
Emergency is proclaimed by the President under Article 352 of the Constitution of India when:
(*a*) he is of the opinion that security of India is under threat.
(*b*) the Prime Minister advises him to issue such a proclamation.
(*c*) parliament passes a resolution.
(*d*) written decision of the cabinet is communicated to him.

6. Consider the following statements:
1. If the Rajya Sabha has declared by resolution supported by not less than two-thirds of the members present and voting that it is necessary or expedient in the national interest to do so, the Parliament may by law provide for the creation of one or more all-India services.
2. Article 311 of the Constitution of India deals with the dismissal or removal of a person who is a member of a civil service of the Union or an all-India service or a civil service of a State or holds a civil post under the Union or a State.

Which of the statements given above is/are correct?
(*a*) 1 only (*b*) 2 only
(*c*) Both 1 and 2 (*d*) Neither 1 nor 2

7. A new Panchayat constituted upon the dissolution of a Panchayat before the expiration of its term shall continue:
(*a*) for next five years from the date of its first meeting and no longer.
(*b*) for the remainder of the period for which the dissolved Panchayat would have continued had it not been so dissolved.
(*c*) till it enjoys the pleasure of the Governor.
(*d*) till State Legislative Assembly allows it to continue.

8. Which of the following writs is regarded as a directive to a lower court or judicial body not to exceed its Limits?
(*a*) Habeas Corpus (*b*) Certiorari
(*c*) Mandamus (*d*) Quo-Warranto

9. Which one of the following is not the occasion for criticising the government in the Lok Sabha?
(*a*) General discussion on the budget
(*b*) Voting on demands for grants
(*c*) Motion of thanks to the President
(*d*) Discussion on the Finance Bill

10. Consider the following Committees appointed to examine and report on local governments:
1. Balwant Rai Mehta Committee
2. Ashok Mehta Committee

3. Smt. Daya Choubey Committee
4. R.K. Khanna Committee

Which one of the following is the correct chronological sequence in which these Committees were set up?

(*a*) 2, 3, 4, 1 (*b*) 1, 4, 3, 2
(*c*) 2, 4, 3, 1 (*d*) 1, 3, 4, 2

11. If the Union Parliament is to assume legislative power over any subject included in the State List, the resolution to that effect has to be passed by which of the following?
(*a*) Lok Sabha
(*b*) Rajya Sabha
(*c*) Both Lok Sabha and Rajya Sabha
(*d*) Lok Sabha, Rajya Sabha and the legislatures of the concerned States

12. Which of the following pairs is not correctly matched?
(*a*) Central Bureau of Investigation –1963
(*b*) Special Police Establishment –1942
(*c*) Prevention of Corruption Act –1947
(*d*) Central Vigilance Commission –1964

13. Which one of the following is not a function of the Election Commission?
(*a*) To superintend, direct and control elections to the office of the President
(*b*) To select candidates for election
(*c*) To recognise and derecognise political parties
(*d*) To prepare electoral rolls

14. Which of the following are provided for by the 74th Constitutional Amendment in respect of Municipal Corporations?
1. Seats to be filled by direct elections on the basis of wards
2. Reservation of seats for SC/ST
3. Reservation of seats for backward classes
4. One-third reservation of seats for women

Choose the correct answer from the codes given below:

(*a*) 1, 2 and 3 (*b*) 1, 2 and 4
(*c*) 2, 3 and 4 (*d*) 1, 2, 3 and 4

15. Which one of the following is not the duty of the Prime Minister?
(*a*) To communicate to the President all the decisions of the Council of Ministers
(*b*) To furnish to the President information relating to the administration of the affairs of the State
(*c*) To submit to the President the agenda of the Cabinet meeting for his approval
(*d*) To submit any matter for the consideration of the Council of Ministers, if the President so requires

16. Which of the following are not subject to the detailed audit of the Comptroller and Auditor-General of India?

1. All cooperative societies
2. All public corporations
3. All civil expenditure
4. All defence expenditure

Select the correct answer from the codes given below:

(*a*) 1 and 2 only (*b*) 2 and 3 only
(*c*) 3 and 4 only (*d*) 1 and 4 only

17. In the Constitution of India, economic and social planning is included in which of the following?

(*a*) Union List of the VII Schedule
(*b*) State List of the VII Schedule
(*c*) Concurrent List of the VII Schedule
(*d*) Both Union and State Lists of the VII Schedule

18. Which of the following institutions is dealt by Article 323A of the Constitution of India?

(*a*) Comptroller and Auditor-General of India
(*b*) Finance Commission
(*c*) Administrative Tribunals
(*d*) Union Public Service Commission

19. When the name of a state is changed or a new state is created, the Constitution of India is required to be amended by the Parliament by a:

(*a*) simple majority.
(*b*) majority of total number of members of both the Houses.
(*c*) special majority.
(*d*) special majority after obtaining opinion of concerned state.

20. Consider the following statements:

President's Rule in a State can be proclaimed if:

1. there is constitutional breakdown in a State.
2. the Governor sends a report to the President to that effect.
3. the Governor of a State fails to perform his constitutional functions.
4. the State Administration fails to function in accordance with the provisions of the Constitution.

Which of the statements given above are correct?

(*a*) 1, 2 and 3 (*b*) 1, 2 and 4
(*c*) 2, 3 and 4 (*d*) 1, 3 and 4

21. The area of a Lok Sabha constituency for the purpose of general elections is determined by which of the following?

(*a*) Delimitation Commission (*b*) Election Commission of India
(*c*) Census Commission (*d*) President

22. For which one of the following judgements of the Supreme Court, the Kesavananda Bharati case is considered a landmark?
   (*a*) The religion cannot be mobilised for political ends.
   (*b*) Abolishing untouchability from the country.
   (*c*) The basic structure of the Constitution cannot be changed.
   (*d*) Right to life and liberty cannot be suspended under any circumstance.

23. In which one of the following states, is provision relating to reservation for Scheduled Castes in panchayats under 73rd Constitutional Amendment not applicable?
   (*a*) Nagaland (*b*) Mizoram
   (*c*) Meghalaya (*d*) Arunachal Pradesh

24. Consider the following statements:
   1. The Constitution of India grants personal immunity to the President of India and the Governor of a State for official acts, but no such immunity is granted to the Ministers.
   2. Civil proceedings may be brought against the President of India or the Governor of a State in respect of their personal acts only if six months' notice has been delivered to them.

   Which of the statements given above is/are correct?
   (*a*) 1 only (*b*) 2 only
   (*c*) Both 1 and 2 (*d*) Neither 1 nor 2

25. Consider the following statements:
   1. The Parliament has exclusive power to make any law with respect to any matter enumerated in List I.
   2. State Legislatures have exclusive power to make any law with respect to any matter enumerated in List II.
   3. The Parliament as well as State Legislatures have concurrent power to make any law with respect to any matter not enumerated in any of the three lists.

   Which of the statements given above is/are correct?
   (*a*) 1 and 2 only (*b*) 1 only
   (*c*) 2 only (*d*) 1 and 3 only

Answers

1. (*b*)	2. (*c*)	3. (*c*)	4. (*b*)	5. (*d*)
6. (*c*)	7. (*b*)	8. (*b*)	9. (*a*)	10. (*b*)
11. (*b*)	12. (*b*)	13. (*b*)	14. (*b*)	15. (*c*)
16. (*d*)	17. (*c*)	18. (*c*)	19. (*a*)	20. (*b*)
21. (*a*)	22. (*c*)	23. (*d*)	24. (*a*)	25. (*a*)

Model Test Paper – 8

1. Consider the following statements:
   1. The powers of the High Court under Article 226 of the Constitution of India are wider than those of Supreme Court under Article 32 of the Constitution of India.
   2. Both High Court and Supreme Court have concurrent power to enforce the fundamental rights.

   Which of the statements given above is/are correct?

   (*a*) 1 only (*b*) 2 only
   (*c*) Both 1 and 2 (*d*) Neither 1 nor 2

2. What is the correct chronological order in which the following provisions were incorporated into the Constitution of India through amendments?
   1. Directive Principle on Free Legal Aid
   2. Relaxation for SCs and STs in promotions
   3. Twelfth Schedule
   4. Article 51-A (k)

   Select the correct answer using the codes given below:

   (*a*) 1, 3, 2, 4 (*b*) 2, 1, 4, 3
   (*c*) 2, 3, 4, 1 (*d*) 4, 2, 1, 3

3. Which of the following are the provisions of Article 18 of the Constitution of India which pertains to the Right to Equality?
   1. No title, not being military or academic distinction, shall be conferred by the State.
   2. No citizen of India shall accept any title from any foreign State.
   3. No person holding any office of profit or trust under the State, shall without the consent of the President, accept any present, emolument or office of any kind from or under any foreign State.

   Select the correct answer using the codes given below:

   (*a*) 1 and 2 only (*b*) 2 and 3 only
   (*c*) 1 and 3 only (*d*) 1, 2 and 3

4. Consider the following statements:
   1. The Council of Ministers of a State in India is collectively as well as individually responsible to the Legislative Assembly of the State.
   2. The Governor of a State has the power to appoint the Members of the State Public Service Commission as well as the State High Court Judges.

Which of the statements given above is/are correct?

(*a*) 1 only (*b*) 2 only

(*c*) Both 1 and 2 (*d*) Neither 1 nor 2

5. Which of the following schedules of the Constitution of India deals with the validation of certain Acts and Regulations?

(*a*) Tenth Schedule (*b*) Eighth Schedule

(*c*) First Schedule (*d*) Ninth Schedule

6. The expression "Prime Ministerial form of government" indicates a form of government in which:

(*a*) the Prime Minister is directly elected by the people.

(*b*) the Prime Minister heads a coalition.

(*c*) the Prime Minister is the Head of the State.

(*d*) the Prime Minister is no longer the first among equals but is dominant.

7. Consider the following statements:

1. The Comptroller and Auditor-General of India/the Chairman and the Members of the Union Public Service Commission are appointed by the President by warrant under his hand and seal and shall be removed from office in like manner and on the like grounds as a Judge of the Supreme Court.

2. A Judge of the Supreme Court can be removed from his office on grounds of proved misbehaviour or incapacity after an address by each House of Parliament is supported by a majority of total membership of that House.

Which of the statements given above is/are correct?

(*a*) 1 only (*b*) 2 only

(*c*) Both 1 and 2 (*d*) Neither 1 nor 2

8. With reference to the conduct of government business in the Parliament, the term "closure" refers to:

(*a*) suspension of debate at the termination of a day's sitting of the Parliament.

(*b*) a rule of legislative procedure under which further debate on a motion can be halted.

(*c*) the termination of a Parliamentary session.

(*d*) refusal on the part of the Government to have the opposition look at important documents.

9. Whenever the Governor of a State has to address the State Legislature, who among the following prepares his address?

(*a*) Chief Secretary of the State

(*b*) Chief Minister and his Council of Ministers

(*c*) Speaker of the Legislative Assembly

(*d*) Governor himself

10. Which of the following taxes belong to the States exclusively?
    1. Taxes on lands and buildings
    2. Taxes on mineral rights
    3. Taxes on vehicles
    4. Taxes on income other than agricultural income

    Select the correct answer using the codes given below:

    (*a*) 1, 2 and 3 only (*b*) 2 and 3 only
    (*c*) 1 and 4 only (*d*) 1, 2, 3 and 4

11. The Constitutional Amendment relating to the declaration of emergency (1978) requires the President of India to act in accordance with the:
    (*a*) collective advice of the entire Council of Ministers.
    (*b*) advice of the Union Cabinet.
    (*c*) advice of the Attorney-General for India.
    (*d*) advice of the Supreme Court.

12. Which one among the following statements about the States Re-organisation Act is not correct?
    (*a*) The Act dealt with the issue of redrawing of the boundaries of States.
    (*b*) It was passed in the year 1956.
    (*c*) It created fourteen States and six Union Territories.
    (*d*) The State boundaries were drawn for administrative convenience.

13. Which of the following are provided for by the Constitution (74th Amendment) Act in respect of planning of urban and rural local governments?
    1. Constitution of the District Planning Committee
    2. Not less than 2/3rd of the total members of the District Planning Committee should be elected by, from amongst, the elected members of district panchayats and municipalities
    3. All other details regarding the composition of the District Planning Committee are left to the State Legislatures
    4. Constitution of the Metropolitan Planning Committee

    Select the correct answer using the codes given below:

    (*a*) 1, 2 and 3 (*b*) 2 and 4 only
    (*c*) 1, 3 and 4 (*d*) 1, 2, 3 and 4

14. Which one of the following statements regarding secularism is not correct?
    (*a*) "Secular Republic" implies a republic in which there is equal respect for all religions.
    (*b*) It was decided in the S.R. Bommai case that secularism is a basic feature of the Constitution of India.
    (*c*) According to the Supreme Court, the concept of secularism means that the "State" will have no religion.
    (*d*) The word "secular" was introduced under the Constitution by the 44th Amendment.

15. The President enjoys the right to issue regulations with regard to which of the following?
   (*a*) Andaman and Nicobar Islands
   (*b*) Lakshadweep
   (*c*) Both Andaman and Nicobar Islands, and Lakshadweep
   (*d*) Neither Andaman and Nicobar Islands nor Lakshadweep

16. Which of the following statements are correct with regard to the prohibition as to the holding of offices by members of Public Service Commissions on ceasing to be such members?
   1. The Chairman of the UPSC shall be ineligible for further employment either under the Government of India or under the Government of a state.
   2. The Chairman of an SPSC shall be eligible for appointment as chairman or any other member of the UPSC or as Chairman of any other SPSC, but not for any other employment either under the Government of India or under the Government of a state.
   3. A member other than Chairman of the UPSC shall be eligible for appointment as Chairman of an SPSC, but not for any other employment, either under the Government of India or under the Government of a state.
   4. A member other than Chairman of the SPSC shall be eligible for appointment as Chairman or any other member of the UPSC or as Chairman of that or any other SPSC, but not for any other employment either under the Government of India or under the Government of a state.

   Select the correct answer using the codes given below:
   (*a*) 1 only (*b*) 2 and 4 only
   (*c*) 1 and 3 only (*d*) 1, 2, 3 and 4

17. Which of the following funds contain receipts through provident fund, small savings and other deposits?
   (*a*) Consolidated Fund (*b*) Contingency Fund
   (*c*) Public Account (*d*) National Renewal Fund

18. What is "Act East Policy" of India?
   (*a*) Government of India's initiative for the infrastructural development in the North-Eastern States
   (*b*) India's search for oil and gas in its Eastern shoreline
   (*c*) India's collaboration with some East Asian countries in the exploration of oil and gas
   (*d*) India's continuing pursuit of close relations with South-East Asian countries

19. Consider the following statements:
   1. The Estimates Committee of Parliament lacks the expert assistance of the Comptroller and Auditor-General of India which is available to the Public Accounts Committee of Parliament.
   2. All the Ministries/Departments of the Union Government are not taken up for examination every year by the Estimates Committee, but only a few of them are selected for this purpose.

   Which of the statements given above is/are correct?
   (*a*) 1 only (*b*) 2 only
   (*c*) Both 1 and 2 (*d*) Neither 1 nor 2

20. Consider the following statements:
    1. The members of All- India Services can give independent and impartial advise to political executives in the states.
    2. The members of All-India Services enjoy constitutional safeguards with regard to security of service.

    Which of the statements given above is/are correct?
    (*a*) 1 only (*b*) 2 only
    (*c*) Both 1 and 2 (*d*) Neither 1 nor 2

21. What is the purpose of issue of Mandamus?
    (*a*) Directing an official for the performance of a duty
    (*b*) Release of an illegally detained person
    (*c*) Transferring of a case from an inferior court to a court of higher jurisdiction
    (*d*) Calling upon one to show as to by what authority he holds or claims a franchise or office

22. At the time of becoming the Prime Minister of our country one:
    (*a*) must be a member of one of the Houses of Parliament. If not, must become a member of one of the Houses within six months.
    (*b*) need not necessarily be a member of one of the Houses of Parliament but must get elected as a member of Lok Sabha within six months.
    (*c*) must be a member of one of the Houses of Parliament prior to appointment.
    (*d*) must be a member of Rajya Sabha.

23. In which one of the following States, is unified personnel system operating in municipal corporations?
    (*a*) Andhra Pradesh (*b*) West Bengal
    (*c*) Gujarat (*d*) Kerala

24. What is the correct chronological sequence of the following events?
    1. Montagu-Chelmsford Reforms
    2. Inauguration of Provincial Autonomy
    3. Morley-Minto Reforms Bill

    Select the correct answer using the codes given below:
    (*a*) 1, 2, 3 (*b*) 2, 3, 1
    (*c*) 3, 2, 1 (*d*) 3, 1, 2

25. Which of the following are not the functions of Union Public Service Commission?
    1. Disciplinary matters relating to Union civil servants.
    2. Matters referred to under Article 16(4).
    3. Manner in which Article 335 may be given effect.
    4. Principles to be followed in making appointments to Union civil servants.

    Select the correct answer using the codes given below:
    (*a*) 1 and 2 only (*b*) 1 and 3 only
    (*c*) 2 and 3 only (*d*) 2 and 4 only

Answers

1. (*c*)	2. (*a*)	3. (*d*)	4. (*d*)	5. (*d*)
6. (*d*)	7. (*d*)	8. (*b*)	9. (*b*)	10. (*a*)
11. (*b*)	12. (*d*)	13. (*c*)	14. (*d*)	15. (*c*)
16. (*d*)	17. (*c*)	18. (*d*)	19. (*c*)	20. (*c*)
21. (*a*)	22. (*a*)	23. (*a*)	24. (*d*)	25. (*c*)

Model Test Paper – 9

1. Which of the following statements is/are not violative of the principle of federalism in India?
   1. The President takes over administration of states under the emergency provisions.
   2. The Parliament has exclusive power to make any law with respect to any matter not enumerated in any of the three lists.

   Select the correct answer using the codes given below:

   (*a*) 1 only (*b*) 2 only
   (*c*) Both 1 and 2 (*d*) Neither 1 nor 2

2. Consider the following statements:
   1. Report of the First Administrative Reforms Commission of India recommended the establishment of Lokpal and Lokayukta institutions.
   2. Lokpal is conceived as the highest institution in India to investigate corruption at higher places in Government.

   Which of the statements given above is/are correct?

   (*a*) 1 only (*b*) 2 only
   (*c*) Both 1 and 2 (*d*) Neither 1 nor 2

3. The most important device of supplying power to the judiciary to invalidate a Statute in India is provided by which of the following?

   (*a*) The Directive Principles of State Policy
   (*b*) The Fundamental Rights
   (*c*) Articles 350 and 351
   (*d*) Prerogative Writs

4. Consider the following statements:
   1. Whether the expenditure is charged on the Consolidated Fund of India or it is an amount voted by the Lok Sabha, no money can be issued out of the Consolidated Fund of India unless the expenditure is authorised by an Appropriation Act.
   2. The Rajya Sabha has no power of amending or rejecting the Appropriation Bill or the Annual Finance Bill.
   3. The Rajya Sabha has no further business with the Annual Financial Statement beyond the general discussion.

   Which of the statements given above are correct?

   (*a*) 1, 2 and 3 (*b*) 1 and 2 only
   (*c*) 2 and 3 only (*d*) 1 and 3 only

5. Which among the following is not a fundamental duty as enumerated in Article 51A?
   (*a*) To develop the scientific temper, humanism and the spirit of inquiry and reform
   (*b*) To cherish and follow the noble ideals which inspired our national struggle for freedom
   (*c*) To uphold and protect the sovereignty, unity and integrity of India
   (*d*) To cherish fraternity assuring the dignity of the individual

6. Consider the following statements:
   1. The Central Vigilance Commission comprises a Central Vigilance Commissioner and three Vigilance Commissioners.
   2. The Central Vigilance Commission is a multi-member body with a statutory status.
   3. The Committee for the selection to the post of the Director in the Directorate of Enforcement, Ministry of Finance, Government of India is chaired by the Central Vigilance Commissioner.

   Which of the statements given above is/are correct?
   (*a*) 1, 2 and 3 (*b*) 2 only
   (*c*) 2 and 3 only (*d*) 1 and 3 only

7. Which one of the following fundamental rights is also available to a foreigner on Indian soil?
   (*a*) Prohibition of discrimination on grounds of religion, race, caste, sex or place of birth
   (*b*) Equality of opportunity in matters of public employment
   (*c*) Protection of life and personal liberty according to procedure established by law
   (*d*) To practise any profession or to carry on any occupation, trade or business

8. Which of the following is a feature of the Regulating Act, 1773?
   (*a*) Dyarchy
   (*b*) Federalism
   (*c*) Introduction of communal electorates
   (*d*) Creation of the office of Governor-General

9. Which one of the following Committees scrutinises and reports to the Parliament whether the power to make rules and regulations conferred by the Constitution or Statutes is being properly exercised by the delegated authority?
   (*a*) Committee on Government Assurances
   (*b*) Committee on Subordinate Legislation
   (*c*) Rules Committee
   (*d*) General Purposes Committee

10. In the post-independence period the Government appointed several committees and commissions to improve the urban local bodies. Some of them are:
    1. Rural-Urban Relationship Committee.
    2. Taxation Enquiry Commission.
    3. National Commission on Urbanisation.
    4. Local Finance Enquiry Committee.

Which one of the following is the correct chronological sequence in which the above committees and commissions were set up?

(*a*) 1, 2, 4, 3 (*b*) 4, 3, 1, 2

(*c*) 1, 3, 4, 2 (*d*) 4, 2, 1, 3

11. Consider the following statements:
    1. Lakshminarayan Sahu, a member of the Constituent Assembly, criticised the Constitution as a "slavish imitation of the west, much more – a slavish surrender to the west."
    2. Sir Ivor Jennings, a British Constitutionalist, called the Indian Constitution a "lawyer's paradise".

    Which of the statements given above is/are correct?

    (*a*) 1 only
    (*b*) 2 only
    (*c*) Both 1 and 2
    (*d*) Neither 1 nor 2

12. Which one of the following is the correct statement?

    Double Jeopardy means:

    (*a*) trying two persons jointly for the same offence.
    (*b*) trying the same person for two offences at two different times.
    (*c*) putting the same person on trial twice for the same offence.
    (*d*) trying a person for two offences committed by him in one incident.

13. Who among the following is not a member of the committee which makes recommendation to the President of India for appointment as the Chief Information Commissioner and Information Commissioners?

    (*a*) Prime Minister
    (*b*) Leader of Opposition in the Lok Sabha
    (*c*) A Union Cabinet Minister to be nominated by the Prime Minister
    (*d*) Union Law Minister

14. In case of difference of opinion amongst the Chief Election Commissioner and other Election Commissioners in the Election Commission of India:

    (*a*) the matter is to be referred to the Supreme Court of India.
    (*b*) the opinion of the Chief Election Commissioner is final.
    (*c*) the matter is to be referred to the Law Commission.
    (*d*) the matter is decided by the Election Commission by majority.

15. Which of the following statements are not correct?
    1. A Member of UPSC holds office for a term of six years or until he attains the age of 65 years.
    2. A Member of UPSC is eligible for re-appointment for the same post for a second term.
    3. A Member of UPSC can accept employment under Central or State government after retirement.
    4. A Member of UPSC can accept employment as a member of State P.S.C. after retirement.

Select the correct answer from the codes given below:

(*a*) 1 and 2 only (*b*) 1 and 4 only

(*c*) 1, 2 and 3 (*d*) 2, 3 and 4

16. An executive action taken during national emergency in violation of Article 19 of the Constitution of India:
(*a*) can only be challenged during the emergency.
(*b*) can only be challenged after the emergency is over.
(*c*) cannot be challenged at all.
(*d*) can be challenged during or after the emergency.

17. Consider the following statements:
1. The Estimates Committee comprises 20 members elected each year by the Lok Sabha from its elected members and 10 members elected each year by the Rajya Sabha from its elected members.
2. The Estimates Committee has no role in suggesting the form in which the estimates shall be presented to the Parliament as that is a function of the Comptroller and Auditor-General of India.

Which of the statements given above is/are correct?

(*a*) 1 only (*b*) 2 only

(*c*) Both 1 and 2 (*d*) Neither 1 nor 2

18. The powers of the Parliament in budgetary matters are covered in:
(*a*) Article 111 to 115
(*b*) Article 112 to 117
(*c*) Article 114 to 119
(*d*) Article 115 to 119

19. Consider the following institutions:
1. The National Human Rights Commission
2. The Supreme Court
3. The Finance Commission
4. Special Officer for Linguistic Minorities

Which of these is/are not enumerated in the Constitution of India?

(*a*) 1 and 2 only (*b*) 1 only

(*c*) 4 only (*d*) 1 and 3 only

20. Which of the following opportunities is provided by the Appropriation Bill to the legislature?
(*a*) To discuss the policy and other matters related to the expenditure of various ministries
(*b*) To change amount of demands of various ministries
(*c*) To reallocate the grants of various ministries
(*d*) To vary the amount of expenditure charged upon the Consolidated Fund of India

21. Which of the following is a grant for meeting an unexpected demand upon resources of India?
    (*a*) Vote of credit
    (*b*) Excess grant
    (*c*) Exceptional grant
    (*d*) Supplementary grant

22. Consider the following statements:
    1. The minimum prescribed age for any person to be a member of Panchayat is 25 years.
    2. A Panchayat reconstituted after premature dissolution continues only for the remainder period.
    3. The 73rd and 74th amendments to the Constitution of India do not apply to Sikkim and Arunachal Pradesh.

    Which of the statements given above is/are correct?
    (*a*) 2 only (*b*) 2 and 3 only
    (*c*) 1 and 3 only (*d*) 1, 2 and 3

23. The President of India is not empowered to proclaim:
    (*a*) emergency arising out of war, external aggression or armed rebellion.
    (*b*) emergency due to breakdown of constitutional machinery in states.
    (*c*) emergency arising out of internal disturbance.
    (*d*) emergency arising out of threat to financial stability.

24. What does the 86th Constitutional Amendment Act deal with?
    (*a*) Inclusion of Bodo, Dogri, Maithili and Santhali languages in the Eighth Schedule
    (*b*) Inclusion of service tax levied by Union and collected and appropriated by the Union and the states in the Seventh Schedule
    (*c*) Free and compulsory education for all children between the age of 6 and 14 years
    (*d*) No reservation in Panchayats need to be made in favour of Scheduled Castes in Arunachal Pradesh

25. Consider the following statements:

    The State government shall appoint a finance commission to review the financial position of the Panchayats and to make recommendations as to:
    1. the distribution between the State and Panchayats of the net proceeds of taxes, tolls and fees leviable by the states.
    2. the determination of the taxes, duties, tolls and fees which may be assigned to the Panchayats.
    3. the principles that will determine grants-in-aid to the Panchayats.

    Which of the statements given above is/are correct?
    (*a*) 1 only (*b*) 2 and 3 only
    (*c*) 1 and 3 only (*d*) 1, 2 and 3

Answers

1. (*d*)	2. (*c*)	3. (*b*)	4. (*a*)	5. (*d*)
6. (*c*)	7. (*c*)	8. (*d*)	9. (*b*)	10. (*d*)
11. (*b*)	12. (*c*)	13. (*d*)	14. (*d*)	15. (*d*)
16. (*c*)	17. (*d*)	18. (*b*)	19. (*b*)	20. (*a*)
21. (*a*)	22. (*a*)	23. (*c*)	24. (*c*)	25. (*d*)

Model Test Paper – 10

1. Consider the following statements:
   1. The Parliament and the State legislatures have concurrent power to make law prescribing punishment for untouchability.
   2. The Parliament may make law empowering any court to exercise powers of the Supreme Court to enforce the fundamental rights.

   Which of the statements given above is/are correct?

   (*a*) 1 only (*b*) 2 only
   (*c*) Both 1 and 2 (*d*) Neither 1 nor 2

2. Consider the following statements:

   On proclamation of emergency under Article 352, the Fundamental Rights guaranteed in Article 19 become automatically suspended by virtue of Article 358. Additionally, the President of India may by order under Article 359 suspend:
   1. The enforcement of all or any of the Fundamental Rights (except Articles 20 and 21) as may be specified in his order.
   2. The enforcement of all or any of the Fundamental Rights except Article 21.

   Select the correct answer using the codes given below:

   (*a*) 1 only
   (*b*) 2 only
   (*c*) Both 1 and 2
   (*d*) Neither 1 nor 2

3. Which one of the following statements is not correct about the Advocate-General of the State?
   (*a*) The Advocate-General holds office during the pleasure of the Governor.
   (*b*) The Advocate-General is appointed by the Governor.
   (*c*) The Advocate-General advises the State Government on legal matters.
   (*d*) The Advocate-General cannot take part in the proceedings in the State Legislature.

4. Which one of the following statements relating to the power of Judicial Review is correct?
   (*a*) Supreme Court can take up matters for judicial review on its own.
   (*b*) Supreme Court can be directly approached for judicial review of legislative decisions.
   (*c*) Supreme Court can review its own judgements in the light of new developments.
   (*d*) Supreme Court can ask Lower Courts to submit a case for its judicial review.

5. Which of the following fundamental rights is dealt by Article 29 of the Constitution?
   (*a*) Right to constitutional remedies
   (*b*) Protection of interests of minorities
   (*c*) Abolition of untouchability
   (*d*) Equality of opportunity in matters of public employment

6. Consider the following statements:

   The President cannot be a dictator, because:

   1. he can be impeached for violation of Constitution.
   2. the ordinances issued by him require the approval of the Parliament.
   3. the proclamation of Emergency requires Parliament's approval.
   4. he has to act on the advice of Council of Ministers.

   Which of the statements given above are correct?

   (*a*) 1 and 2 only (*b*) 2, 3 and 4
   (*c*) 3 and 4 only (*d*) 1 and 4 only

7. In the Interim Government formed in the year 1946, who of the following held the portfolio of Defence?

   (*a*) Vallabhbhai Patel (*b*) Jagjivan Ram
   (*c*) Baldev Singh (*d*) Asaf Ali

8. Consider the following statements:

   The Finance Commission is created:

   1. by the President on the advice of the Union Cabinet.
   2. under Article 280 of the Constitution of India.
   3. to suggest ways and means to augment the financial resources of the Union and the States.
   4. to make recommendations to the President defining the principles which should govern the grants-in-aid of the revenues of the States out of the Consolidated Fund of India.

   Which of the statements given above are correct?

   (*a*) 2, 3 and 4 (*b*) 1, 2 and 3
   (*c*) 1, 3 and 4 (*d*) 1, 2 and 4

9. The original jurisdiction of the Supreme Court extends to:
   (*a*) treaties and agreements signed by the Government of India.
   (*b*) disputes between the Government of India and one or more States.
   (*c*) disputes relating to implementation of the Directive Principles of State Policy.
   (*d*) a bill passed by the Parliament which is violative of the Constitution.

10. Consider the following statements:

    1. Estimates of expenditure charged upon the Consolidated Fund of India are not submitted to the vote of the Parliament and there can be no discussion on the same in either House of the Parliament.

2. Vote of credit is a grant approved by the Parliament in advance of the detailed examination of various demands presented to it.
3. Token grants do not involve additional expenditure.

Which of the statements given above is/are correct?

(*a*) 1, 2 and 3 (*b*) 3 only
(*c*) 2 only (*d*) 2 and 3 only

11. Consider the following Statements:
    1. The Committee on Panchayati Raj Elections (1965) was headed by R.K. Khanna.
    2. The Committee on Panchayati Raj Training Centres (1966) was headed by V. Ramanathan.

    Which of the Statements given above is/are correct?

    (*a*) 1 only (*b*) 2 only
    (*c*) Both 1 and 2 (*d*) Neither 1 nor 2

12. If the Prime Minister is a member of the Rajya Sabha:
    (*a*) he has to get elected to the Lok Sabha within six months.
    (*b*) he can declare the government's policies only in the Rajya Sabha.
    (*c*) he cannot take part in the voting when a vote of no-confidence is under consideration.
    (*d*) he cannot take part in the budget deliberations in the Lok Sabha.

13. Consider the following statements:

    The Comptroller and Auditor-General of India:
    1. audits all expenditures from the revenues of the Union and the States.
    2. ensures that total withdrawals by the Union Government do not exceed the amount approved by the Parliament.
    3. can comment on correctness or otherwise of financial transactions of the Union and the States.
    4. points out cases of non-compliance of rules and regulations in expenditure.

    Which of the statements given above are correct?

    (*a*) 1 and 2 only (*b*) 2, 3 and 4
    (*c*) 1, 3 and 4 (*d*) 1, 2, 3 and 4

14. The Governor of a State in his role as Administrator of an adjoining Union Territory exercises his functions, as such independently of:
    (*a*) the President of India.
    (*b*) the State Council of Ministers.
    (*c*) the Prime Minister.
    (*d*) the Union Home Minister.

15. Which one of the following statements is not correct?
    (*a*) Indian Constitution provides for unified judicial system.
    (*b*) Judiciary has power to scrutinise the acts of all branches of government.
    (*c*) Independence of judiciary is built through elaborate constitutional scheme.
    (*d*) Review of the constitutional amendments on substantive grounds is not permitted.

16. Which of the following are the common compulsory provisions of the 73rd and 74th Constitutional Amendment Acts?
    1. Five yearly elections
    2. Reservation for backward classes
    3. Reservation for women
    4. Nagar Panchayats

    Select the correct answer using the codes given below:
    (*a*) 2 and 3 only (*b*) 1 and 4 only
    (*c*) 1, 2, 3 and 4 (*d*) 1 and 3 only

17. What is a "Shadow Cabinet" in the British system?
    (*a*) A group of young members of the ruling party
    (*b*) A group of members from the opposition party who scrutinise some functions of the government and present alternative policy
    (*c*) A team of intellectuals who advise the Cabinet
    (*d*) A Cabinet Committee that functions under the guidance of the Cabinet

18. Which of the following is the name of the intermediate panchayat in the state of Gujarat?
    (*a*) Janpad Panchayat
    (*b*) Mandal Parishad
    (*c*) Mandal Panchayat
    (*d*) Taluka Panchayat

19. Which one of the following statements is not correct?
    (*a*) In the cabinet form of government prevalent in India, neither the President nor the Governor exercises the executive functions individually or personally.
    (*b*) Executive action taken in the name of the Governor is the executive action of the State.
    (*c*) The Governor cannot be held personally answerable for any portion of the address to the joint session.
    (*d*) The Governor is bound to exercise all his powers and functions on the aid and advice of his Council of Ministers.

20. The purpose of an adjournment motion is to:
    (*a*) propose a reduction in the budget.
    (*b*) seek the approval of the House on a proposal.
    (*c*) draw the attention of the House to a matter of urgent public importance.
    (*d*) seek the leave of the House to introduce a Government Bill.

21. Who among the following members of the Constituent Assembly of India called the Drafting Committee as a "Drifting Committee"?
    (*a*) P. R. Deshmukh (*b*) K. Hanumanthaiya
    (*c*) Naziruddin Ahmed (*d*) A.V. Kamath

22. Lokayukta submits his report to the:
    (*a*) Chief Minister of the State.
    (*b*) Chief Justice of the State High Court.
    (*c*) Governor of the State.
    (*d*) Speaker of State Legislative Assembly.

23. Which of the following ensure functional autonomy of the UPSC?
    1. The Chairman and Members can be removed only on the grounds given in the Constitution.
    2. The expenditure of the Commission is a charge on the Consolidated Fund of India.
    3. The Members and Chairman are allowed to accept jobs after retirement.
    4. The Chairman and Members being civil servants function in a neutral manner.

    Select the correct answer from the codes given below:
    (*a*) 1 and 2 only (*b*) 2 and 3 only
    (*c*) 1, 3 and 4 (*d*) 2, 3 and 4

24. Consider the following statements:
    1. There are 22 High Courts at present in India.
    2. Calcutta, Bombay and Madras High Courts were established in the year 1862.

    Which of the statements given above is/are correct?
    (*a*) 1 only (*b*) 2 only
    (*c*) Both 1 and 2 (*d*) Neither 1 nor 2

25. Which of the following statements is/are correct?

    Article 26 of the Constitution of India states that subject to public order, morality and health, every religious denomination or any section thereof shall have the right:
    1. to establish and maintain institutions for religious and charitable purposes.
    2. to manage its own affairs in matters of religion.
    3. to own and acquire movable and immovable property.

    Select the correct answer using the codes given below:
    (*a*) 1 only (*b*) 1 and 3 only
    (*c*) 2 and 3 only (*d*) 1, 2 and 3

Answers

1. (*b*)	2. (*a*)	3. (*d*)	4. (*b*)	5. (*b*)
6. (*d*)	7. (*c*)	8. (*d*)	9. (*b*)	10. (*b*)
11. (*d*)	12. (*c*)	13. (*d*)	14. (*b*)	15. (*d*)
16. (*d*)	17. (*b*)	18. (*d*)	19. (*d*)	20. (*c*)
21. (*c*)	22. (*c*)	23. (*a*)	24. (*b*)	25. (*d*)

